Psychotherapy for Individuals with Intellectual Disability

Edited by
Robert J. Fletcher, DSW, ACSW

Table of Contents

Foreword
Steven Reiss, Ph.D.

In the 1950s intellectual disabilities (ID) was called "mental deficiency" and was widely thought of as a biological problem. Psychology was seen as having minimal relevance beyond measuring the person's I.Q. for diagnostic purposes. Symptoms of psychiatric disorders were attributed to mental deficiency; psychotherapy was considered inappropriate because of the poor self-reflective capacity of the population. The 1953 publication of Seymour Sarason's *Psychological Problems in Mental Deficiency* stimulated interest in the psychological aspects of mental retardation.

In the 1960s, large numbers of psychologists became interested in ID. They were followers of B.F. Skinner's behaviorism, exploring the possibility of applied behavior technologies for educating people with ID. The "applied behavior analysts," as they are now called, went into large state institutions that at the time provided only custodial care. Residents were moping around day rooms with little to do. The behavior analysts, notably O.I. Lovass at UCLA and Murray Sidman at Massachusetts General Hospital, changed all of that, introducing "reinforcement therapy" and related techniques. To the surprise of many, they proved that people with ID had capabilities much greater than what was commonly thought at the time. They became the first professional group to work in institutions in significant numbers, lighting up these former human warehouses with hope, optimism, purpose, and activity.

The behavior analysts took an interest in conduct problems such as aggression, self-injurious behavior, and tantrums. They paid less attention to emotional problems such as anxiety and depression. In the 1970s three psychiatrists -- Frank Menolascino, Irving Philips, and George Tarjan -- sought to broaden clinical interests in the field of ID. They started the "dual diagnosis movement," which has had the following four important themes:

1. People with ID are vulnerable to the full range of psychiatric disorders.
2. People with a dual diagnosis (psychiatric disorder and ID) are underserved.
3. Pre-service, interdisciplinary education is needed to train professionals to work with this population.
4. Scientific research is needed to learn more about the nature, prevention, and treatment of dual diagnosis.

At first the proposition that people with ID are vulnerable to the full range of psychiatric disorders met with significant opposition. Some questioned whether or not people with ID have the cognitive capacity to worry and, thus, become anxious or depressed, while ideologically-driven behaviorists questioned whether or not anxiety and mood disorders can be studied at all since they are about inner experiences and not overt behavior. Dual diagnosis professionals responded to such criticisms. They documented that people with ID are exposed to the stressful and negative social conditions widely assumed to lead to or intensify psychiatric symptoms (Reiss, 1994). They showed that people with ID have greater exposure to negative life events as compared with the general population. They published studies of stigmatization, peer rejection, and residential transfers, all stressful events that almost anybody would find it difficult to adjust to. Since people with ID have limited capabilities to solve their problems and overcome stress, it was assumed that they are especially vulnerable to stressful conditions.

To show that people with ID are in fact vulnerable to the full range of psychiatric disorders, dual diagnosis professionals published clinical and research reports of specific disorders. Robert Sovner and Anne Hurley (1983) published an article on affective disorders. Johnny Matson (1981, 1982a, 1982b, 1983a, 1983b) published case studies of applied behavior analysis for depression and other specific disorders. Anton Dosen (1993a, 1993b; Dosen & Gielen, 1993; Dosen & Menolascino, 1990; Dosen & Petry, 1993) and Andrew Levitas (Levitas & Gilson 1987, 1989, 1990, 1994) explored psychodynamic models of affective disorders. Bryan King (1993) suggested that self-injurious behavior may be a symptom of Obsessive-Compulsive Disorder, and Johannes Rojahn and I (Reiss & Rojahn, 1993) published substantial correlations between depressed mood and aggressive behavior. Ludwik Szymanski (1980) and Andrew Reid (1972a, 1972b, 1976, 1993a, 1993b) independently published on schizophrenia and other psychotic disorders. Stephen Ruerdrich (Huang & Ruedrich, 2007) published on Attention Deficit Hyperactivity Disorder, and Ann Poindexter (1996/2000) edited a book on anxiety disorders.

Having shown that people with ID are exposed to conditions that lead to psychiatric disorders and that each of the major psychiatric disorders occurs in this population, researchers went on to document the significance of dual diagnosis. They showed that dual diagnosis usually impairs functioning and causes emotional pain and suffering as exemplified in depression or intense fear. If untreated dual diagnosis can last for years or even decades. These people may be afraid, unhappy, lonely, nervous, and rejected for long periods of time.

Evidence was collected to show that dual diagnosis is common. Large scale surveys showed that people with borderline IQs were twice as likely as those with average IQs to react to the stress of military life by developing a disorder. A study by Richard McNally (1995) at Harvard showed that symptoms of Post-Traumatic Stress Disorder lasted longer in people with borderline IQs. Psychological rating scales administered in public schools showed that students with ID have much higher scores for anxiety and sadness than non-ID students. John Jacobson (1982a, 1982b, 1988, 1990) and his colleagues surveyed New York State and California registries and reported substantial rates of behavior problems and certain psychiatric symptoms. Large data sets of the entire school population of Illinois and other states showed high rates of "multiple handicaps" for students with ID. Surveys of community programs showed high rates of dual diagnosis and/or psychiatric symptoms. Surveys of state institutions showed very high rates. I concluded that the rate of personality disorders is twice that found in the general population while the rate for mental disorders is approximately the same, for a total prevalence of about 30% (Reiss, 1994).

The next step was to demonstrate appropriate and innovative services. Frank Menolascino started an inpatient program at the University of Nebraska; George Tarjan did the same at the UCLA Neuropsychiatric Program. Robert Sovner led an innovative consultative service in Massachusetts. Michael Smull started a community-based program at Rock Creek , Maryland; I started an outpatient clinic at the University of Illinois at Chicago; and Robert Fletcher started Beacon House in upstate New York. Across the pond, Nicholas Bouras started a program in London.

By far the most influential effort to promote education was the founding of the National Association on Dual Diagnosis (NADD) by Robert Fletcher with assistance from Frank Menolascino. Since the early 1980s, Fletcher has worked tirelessly to build the NADD. He has been responsible for more training events for more people than anyone else. His NADD has given the dual diagnosis movement an organization of its own.

To make possible large scale identification of individuals who might need services, various screening tools were developed. I published a tool called the *Reiss Screen for Maladaptive Behavior*, which was the first standardized dual diagnosis instrument. It made possible inexpensive screening of large populations, identifying those who should be referred for further evaluation for possible psychiatric disorder. Johnny Matson's instrument was called the *Psychopathology Inventory of Mentally Retarded Adults* (PIMRA), and H. C. Prout and D.C. Strohmer published two personality inventories. The success of these early instruments inspired the development of additional tools, so that today professionals have choices regarding which instrument best meets their needs.

Psychotherapy for Individuals with Intellectual Disability is a collection of chapters aimed at broadening the range of therapy options for this population. Indeed, this is the most comprehensive discussion of psychotherapies with this population ever published. It expands the therapeutic options professionals can bring to bear in the treatment of dual diagnosis. Included are original chapters on the use of individual psychotherapy, group therapy, and cognitive-behavior therapy with this population.

REFERENCES

Dosen, A. (1993a). *A developmental-psychiatric approach in the diagnosis of psychiatric disorders of persons with mental retardation.* Frank J. Menolascino, M.D. Memorial Lecture at the International Congress on the Dually Diagnosed, Boston.

Dosen, A. (1993b). Diagnosis and treatment of psychiatric and behavioral disorders in mentally retarded individuals. The state of the art. *Journal of Intellectual Disability Research, 37,* 1-7.

Dosen, A. & Gielen, J. (1993). Treatment of depression in the mentally retarded. In R. Fletcher & A. Dosen (Eds.), *Mental health aspects of mental retardation – Progress in assessment and treatment.* New York: Lexington Books.

Dosen, A., & Menolascino, F.J. (Eds.). (1960). *Depression in mentally retarded children and adults.* Leiden, the Netherlands: Logon Publications.

Dosen, A., & Petry, D. (1993). Tretament of depression in the mentally retarded. In R. Fletcher & A. Dosen (Eds.), *Mental health aspects of mental retardation – Progress in assessment and treatment.* New York: Lexington Books.

Huang, H. & Ruedrich, S. (2007). Recent advances in the diagnosis and treatment of attention-deficit-hyperactivity disorder in individuals with intellectual disability. *Mental Health Aspects of Developmental Disability, 10*(4), 121-128.

Jacobson, J.W. (1982a). Problem behavior and psychiatric impairment within a developmentally disabled population. I. Behavior frequency. *Applied Research in Mental Retardation, 3,* 121-139.

Jacobson, J.W. (1982b). Problem behavior and psychiatric impairment within a developmentally disabled population. II. Behavior severity. *Applied Research in Mental Retardation, 3,* 369-3381.

Jacobson, J.W. (1988). Problem behavior and psychiatric impairment within a developmentally disabiled population. III. Psychotropic medication. *Research in Developmental Disabilities, 9,* 23-38.

Jacobson, J.W. (1990). Do some mental disorders occur less frequently among persons with mental retardation? *American Journal on Mental Retardation, 94,* 596-602.

King, Bh.H. (1993). Self-injury by people with mental retardation: A compulsive behavior hypothesis. *American Journal on Mental Retardation, 98,* 93-112.

Levitas, A., & Gilson, S. (1987). Transfereence, countertransference, and resistance. *National Association for the Dually Diagnosed Newsletter, 1,* 2-7.

Levitas, A., & Gilson, S. (1989). Psychodynamic psychotherapy with mildly and moderately retarded patients. In R. Fletcher & F.J. Menolascino (Eds.), *Mental retardation an dmental illness*: *Assessment, treatment and service for the dually diagnosed* (pp. 71-106). Lexington, MA: Lexington Books.

Levitas, A., & Gilson, S. (1990). Toward the developmental understanding of the impact of mental retardation in the assessment of psychopathology. In *Assessment of behavior problems in persons with mental retardation living in the community* (pp. 71-106). Rockville, MD: National Institute of Mental Health (DHHS Publication No. ADM 90-1652).

Levitas, A., & Gilson, S. (1994). Psychosocial development of children and adolescents with mild mental retardation. In N. Bouras (Ed.), *Mental health in mental retardation*. New York: Cambridge University Press.

Matson, J.L. (1981). Assessment and treatment of clinical fears in mentally retarded children. *Journal of Applied Behavior Analysis, 14*, 287-294.

Matson, J.L. (1982a). The treatment of behavioral characteristics of depression in the mentally retarded. *Behavior Therapy, 13*, 209-218.

Matson, J.L. (1982b). Treating obsessive-compulsive behavior in mentally retarded adults. *Behavior Modification, 6,* 551-567.

Matson, J.L. (1983a). Depression in the mentally retarded: Toward a conceptual analysis of diagnosis. In M. Hersen, R. Eisler, & P.N. Miller (Eds.), *Progress in behavior modification*, Vol. 15 (pp. 57-79). New York: Academic Press.

Matson, J.L. (1983b). The treatment of behavioral characteristics of depression in the mentally retarded. *Behavior Therapy, 13*, 209-218.

McNally, R.J., & Shin, L.M. (1994). Association of intelligence with severity of post-traumatic stress disorder symptoms in Vietnam Combat veterans. *American Journal of Psychiatry, 152*, 936-938.

Poindexter, A. (1996/2000). *Assessment and treatment of anxiety disorders in persons with mental retardation*. Kingston, NY: NADD Press.

Reid, A.H. (1972a). Psychoses in adult mental defectives. I. Manic depressive psychosis. *British Journal of Psychiatry, 120*, 205-212.

Reid, A.H. (1972b). Psychoses in adult mental defectives. II. Schizophrenic and paranoid psychoses. *British Journal of Psychiatry, 120*, 213-218.

Reid, A.H. (1976) Psychiatric disturbances in the mentally handicapped. *Proceedings of the Royal Society of Medicine, 69*, 509-512.

Reid, A.H. (1993a). Schizophrenic and paranoid syndromes in persons with mental retardation: Assessment and diagnosis. In R. Fletcher & A. Dosen (Eds.), *Mental health aspects of mental retardation – Progress in assessment and treatment* (pp. 98-110). New York: Lexington Books.

Reid, A.H. (1993b). Schizophrenic and paranoid syndromes in persons with mental retardation: Treatment and assessment. In R. Fletcher & A. Dosen (Eds.), *Mental health aspects of mental retardation*. New York: Lexington Books.

Reiss., S. (1994). *Handbook of challenging behavior*. Columbus, OH: IDS Publishing.

Reiss, S. & Rojahn, J. (1993). Joint occurrence of depression and aggression in children and adults with mental retardation. *Journal of Intellectual Disability, 37*, 287-294.

Sarason, S. B. (1953). *Psychological reasons for mental deficiency*. New York: Harper.

Sovner, R., & Hurley, A.D. (1983). Do the mentally retarded suffer from affective illness? *Archives of General Psychiatriay, 40,* 61-67.

Szymanski, L.S. (1980). Psychiatric diagnosis in retarded persons. In L.S. Szymanski & P.E. Tanguay (Eds.), *Emotional disorders of mentally retarded persons: Assessment, treatment, and consultation.* Baltimore, MD: University Park Press.

Introduction

Robert J. Fletcher DSW, ACSW

We are now in an era where there is a growing acceptance, albeit limited, with respect to the provision of psychotherapy for people who have an Intellectual Disability (ID). Historically, there have been several reasons why psychotherapy has not been used broadly for this group of people. First, maladaptive behaviors were often perceived as part of the condition of ID. Secondly, psychotherapy was not viewed by the professional community as being effective. Thirdly, there has been a bias on the part of mental health clinicians that echoes the thought that providing therapy for people with ID is not challenging or interesting. Fourthly, there has been a near absence of academic training for professionals in learning how to provide psychotherapy treatment for this group of people. Furthermore there has been a lack of professional literature on this subject matter. Traditionally, the concept of addressing people's feelings and emotions, in this population, has neither been fully addressed nor sufficiently acknowledged. The issue now, however, is not about whether people are entitled to psychotherapy or will benefit from it, but rather how psychotherapy techniques can be adapted to meet the needs of individuals who may have limitations in expressive and receptive language skills.

During the last several decades we have been moving away from a public policy of institutionalization toward community based living and supports. Also during this time period, we have recognized that some people with ID can also have significant mental health problems. People with ID are at greater risk for stress than individuals in the general population. However we have been slow to meeting the emotional and psychological needs of this group of people. Now that people who have ID are living in a community, we are beginning to understand their emotional needs, and community-based mental health providers are at an early stage of modifying therapy techniques that are appropriate for people with ID.

This book is a major contribution to the effort to make psychotherapy available to individuals who have ID. It provides the reader with insightful and useful ways to provide psychotherapy treatment for these individuals. It brings together all three modalities (individual, couple, and group), and a variety of theoretical models and techniques are discussed. The authors are respected authorities in the field of providing psychotherapy treatment for persons with ID and all have contributed to the professional literature. The hope is that this book will serve to further stimulate interest in the provision of psychotherapy treatment for individuals who have ID co-occurring with significant mental health problems.

There are four main sections to the book. The first section, Individual Therapy, offers a variety of approaches and techniques including dialectical behavioral therapy, positive psychology, mindfulness-based practice, and relaxation training. Also included in this section are chapters on specialty populations including victims of abuse, people who have Autism Spectrum Disorder, and people in mourning. The second section is a chapter on group therapy addressing trauma issues. The third section is on family and couple therapy. The fourth section covers chapters on research, ethics, and training. To give the reader information about the particular approaches, theoretical foundations, and techniques discussed in this book, the remainder of this introduction will briefly summarize each chapter.

SECTION I: INDIVIDUAL THERAPY

Dialectical Behavior Therapy (DBT) is an empirically validated, comprehensive treatment program addressing skills deficits in emotion regulation, distress tolerance, and interpersonal relationships originally developed as a treatment for individuals diagnosed with Borderline Personality Disorder. The treatment's use has been expanded to address the needs of a wide variety of clients, and Margaret Charlton, Ph.D. and Eric Dykstra, Psy.D. offer a description of Dialectical Behavior Therapy for Special Populations (DBT-SP) which was adapted specifically to address the needs of psychotherapy clients who have to develop better skills for managing their impulsivity, dealing with frustrations and interacting with others. Dr. Charlton and Dr. Dykstra provide a solid grounding in standard DBT before discussing the modifications involved in DBT-SP. The dialectical approach (a focus on the intentional bringing together of two seemingly conflicting sides) reduces rigidity, excessive judgment and blame, and ineffective fundamentalism, while at the same time broadening perspectives and allowing for a sharing of ideas. The main tasks of therapists in DBT are to expand client capabilities, to motivate the client to engage in new behaviors, to generalize the use of the new behaviors, and to establish a treatment environment that reinforces progress. There is also a commitment to maintain capable and motivated therapists. This is accomplished using a combination of individual psychotherapy, skills training groups, telephone consultations, and supervision/case consultation groups.

The adaptations involved in DSP-SP involved adjusting the presentation and language to a level that persons with IDD can more easily comprehend and that the adolescent target population would find more appealing. The language was adjusted to make concepts more accessible. Some of the concepts were paired down and/or simplified to allow better comprehension. Handouts were re-written and re-formatted to increase attention and aid in understanding. Client feedback, repetition, and rehearsals have been incorporated into the therapy structure to aid in learning, retention, and generalization.

The skills taught in DBT can serve well as a foundation for work in the areas of independent living, resolving other mental health concerns, trauma processing, and generally increasing the quality of life for each individual.

In "Dialectical Behavior Therapy for Adults who Have Intellectual Disability," Marvin Lew, Ph.D. ABPP, explains the basics of Dialectical Behavior Therapy (DBT) and discusses adaptations that are required in order to provide DBT for individuals with ID as well as some of the benefits that may be accrue and caveats to keep in mind. DBT was originally developed by Marsha Linehan in the early 1980's to treat individuals with Borderline Personality Disorder, but in the past twenty years it has proven effective when used with many different "severe and chronic multi-diagnostic difficult-to-treat patients with both Axis I and Axis II disorders." Linehan identified four "basic modes of therapy" (skills groups; individual therapy; coaching in crisis; and consultation teams), and Lew provides an overview of each mode before discussing considerations and adaptations involved in offering DBT for individuals with ID. One way that skills groups for individuals with ID differ from the typical DBT model is through the inclusion of support staff and family members in the skills groups. There is also strong reliance on concrete and experiential tasks in communicating DBT concepts to individuals with ID. Individual therapy in DBT/ID may involve modification of the length or frequency of sessions, and may require the therapist to assume greater responsibility for getting information from the client, from the skill group therapists, from the family, from the support staff, and from the school or vocational program. Individuals with ID may receive coaching in crisis from a range of providers, including individual therapists, support staff and families, and emergency personnel. Consultation teams are a core mode of DBT with the purpose of supporting the therapist, planning and trouble-shooting their treatment, monitoring their adherence to the model, ensuring clinician progress and competence, consulting with the therapist on system issues, and supporting the therapist when his/her limits are stretched.

Positive Psychology fits well with disability supports, sharing a focus on positive experiences in life and building on strengths. Daniel Baker, Ph.D. and Richard Blumberg, Ph.D. describe Positive Psychology and the contributions it offers to support for people with a dual diagnosis. Positive Psychology focuses on the experience of positive emotion and the role of healthy emotions in daily life. Data shows that therapeutic interventions based on positive emotions (rather a focus on symptoms) can produce rapid improvements in mental health. Many interventions in Positive Psychology are simple enough that they can be performed by an individual without assistance from a psychologist. Positive Psychology assumes that people can take control of their lives, make choices based on their preferences, and, with support, make decisions that lead to positive futures. The aim of Positive Psychology is to broaden the focus of clinical psychology beyond the alleviation of suffering to the development of an individual's strengths of character and a focus on positive life experiences. Four techniques for integrating the concepts of Positive Psychology into conventional forms of individual or group psychotherapy are: (1) shift the individual's focus from the negative to the positive, (2) identify a personal strength and use it each day, (3) find a balance between the negative and the positive, and (4) promote feelings of hopefulness. Interventions that are discussed include the Gratitude Visit, Three Good Things in Life, and Identifying and Using Signature Strengths.

Mindfulness-based psychotherapies may be viewed as alternative approaches to Cognitive-Behavioral Therapy (CBT) that vary in their components but generally involve behavioral practices, cognitive strategies, and practices which enhance concentration. Bronwyn Robertson, LPC reviews the ways mindfulness has been utilized in psychotherapy and examines the use of these techniques by individuals with intellectual disabilities. The main approaches to mindfulness-based psychotherapy include: Acceptance and Commitment Therapy (ACT), Minfulness-Based Stress Reduction (MBSR), Dialectical Behavior Therapy (DBT), and Mindfulness-Based Cognitive Therapy (MBCT). Mindfulness-based psychotherapy involves the use of self-regulative practices to enhance attention, awareness, acceptance, and emotion regulation. Mindfulness is an acceptance-oriented psychological process and involves relating openly, with curiosity and receptivity, to one's thoughts, sensations, and emotions, in contrast to traditional CBT which includes directly challenging an individual's "irrational thinking." Mindfulness practice involves self regulation, mind-body relaxation, and the identification and acceptance of emotions, thoughts, and sensations.

Theodosia Paclaskyj, Ph.D., BCBA offers a chapter on Behavioral Relaxation Training (BRT), a methodology that can empower individuals with ID to reduce maladaptive behaviors by decreasing the tension and anxiety surrounding those behaviors. This is accomplished through learned relaxation. BRT has treatment potential for 1) prevention of the stress response, 2) cue-controlled relaxation, and 3) as an alterantive response to a stressful situation. Typically, the client, caregivers, and therapist work together to identify the etiology of the problem and to understand the potential beneficial impact of relaxation on target behaviors or psychiatric symptoms. BRT is an outgrowth of Progressive Muscle Relaxation, and is grounded in the observation of a set of overt behaviors that co-occurred with self-reported and physiologically-measures relaxation, such as slowed breathing, no movement of the extremities, loose jaw, absence of swallowing, and closed eyes. The Behavioral Relaxation Scale is a checklist of correct and incorrect responses on 10 overt behaviors. The length of training in BRT is individualized according to the needs of the participant and may be as short as one minute although for those who are able to remain seated for a longer period of time, a 10 minute session is established as a training goal. Training is conducted using the structured teaching order of body, head, shoulders, feet, hands, throat, quiet, eyes, mouth, and breathing rate. BRT is a method of relaxation training that can be taught in a structured manner to individuals as a range of functioning levels. It is viewed as an intervention with high social acceptability and potential to improve general quality of life, especially since it can be used as a self-management tool to help an individual cope with future negative events.

As a group, people with intellectual disabilities experience more interpersonal trauma than people without disabilities. Children with ID may be 3 to 6 times more likely to suffer abuse than non-disabled children while adult women with ID may be about 5 times more likely to suffer sexual abuse than women without disabilities. In "Treating Survivors of Sexual and Interpersonal Abuse," Nancy Razza, Ph.D. and Dick Sobsey, Ed.D. first provide information about the extent and nature of sexual abuse among children and adults with intellectual disabilities and then discuss treatment approaches for abuse survivors with ID. Dr. Razza and Dr. Sobsey offer a step-by-step manner of conducting the initial assessment process that emphasizes respect for the individual and helps build a sense of safety, thus providing the foundation for a good therapy experience for trauma survivors with ID.

With some modifications and extra attention to skill-building, Cognitive Behavioral Therapy (CBT) approaches can be successfully used to address the co-morbid anxiety and mood disorders of higher functioning adults who have Autism Spectrum Disorders (ASD) as well as help them learn needed social and coping skills. In "Cognitive Behavioral Therapy for Adults with Autism Spectrum Disorder," Valerie Gaus, Ph.D. explores ASD among adults and offers the benefits of CBT for these individuals. A psychotherapist can help adults with ASD by teaching them to recognize and modify automatic maladaptive thoughts, more accurately "read" the behavior of others, and modify their own behavior in response. CBT posits that any person can develop maladaptive cognitions that cause or maintain symptoms of anxiety or depression. The primary objectives of CBT are: to identify and respond to dysfunctional automatic thoughts and cognitive distortions; to recognize and modify maladaptive intermediate beliefs; and to modify maladaptive schemas. CBT approaches teach people how to monitor their own thoughts and perceptions so that they can become aware of, and correct, interpretive errors, especially those associated with mood and anxiety problems.

When providing psychotherapy for an individual with ID who is mourning the loss of a family member, a friend, or a staff person, a key question, according to Jeffrey Kauffman, M.A., LCSW is "What does the loss mean in the experience of the person grieving." The loss may have significance as a loss of routine and predictability. The grief experience may be a continuation and exacerbation of conflicts and wounded feelings in the relationship. Focusing clinical attention on the meaning of the grief language of the client supports the client's humanity, dignity, autonomy, and self-regulative identity. Mr. Kauffman offers a therapeutic approach to mourning that respects the subjective meaningfulness of the client's experience and selfhood. The behavioral language in which grief is expressed provides the therapist the opportunity to learn the client's presenting complaint. The starting efforts of grief therapy involve learning the meaning of this complaint.

Grief may occur in reaction not only to death, but to a variety of other losses. The same behavioral distress signals occur with death and non-death losses. The therapist needs to understand grief language and mourning needs across the spectrum of loss experiences. The psychotherapist learns to recognize the functional meaning of behavioral disorders as an expressive language of grief.

Loss assessment is at the heart of this therapy approach. Assessing the meaning of a loss experience centers on reading the signs of behavior rather than gathering facts about what has happened which may affect the client's experience.

Mr. Kauffman offers four principles for supporting acute grief from a death loss. These are: (1) provide or help others to provide the facts about the loss; (2) support the person's having the maximum involving in the social environment, rituals, and informal family activities surrounding the death; (3) the death of an attachment object can damage a person's sense of security and increase the need for interpersonal connection; and (4) maximize the person's opportunities for self-expression.

SECTION II: GROUP THERAPY

Following up on the chapter by Sobsey and Razza on treating survivors of sexual and interpersonal abuse, Nancy Razza, Ph.D. and Daniel Tomasulo, Ph.D. discuss providing group psychotherapy, using the interactive-behavioral model (IBT), with trauma survivors who have intellectual disabilities. Safety and confidentiality are essential to this group work. Before beginning with the group, each member should have at least one individual intake session to establish for the individual what therapy is about and what to expect regarding how the individual will be treated. With an ongoing group, established members can teach new members the rules, but when starting a new group the facilitator must make clear what behavior is appropriate and acceptable, and the facilitator must ascertain that this information has been understood. A single sample session is described in some detail to provide the reader a sense of the process and techniques that work well for this population.

SECTION III: FAMILY AND COUPLE THERAPY

Among the broad array of techniques and theoretical perspectives for providing psychotherapy to individuals with intellectual disability, family systems theory provides a filter through which the many other models and interventions can be applied, according to Judith Hill-Weld, M.S., M.F.T. It prioritizes the reciprocal impact of the familial (or family-like) group and the individual. This perspective can enrich understanding of the problem and expand opportunities for change. Individuals with ID live in a web of relationships (families, counselors, case managers, supervisors, employers) that can restrict the ability of the individual to independently change their perceptions or behavior, but the others in that web impact the individuals' lives, their choices, and their perceptions. Ms. Hill-Weld notes that, "In family systems theory, change in individual problem behavior, while sometimes desirable, is not the primary goal." Instead, the intent is to reorganize what the problem means and the patterns that have evolved around the problem. Through reframing a problem that the family experiences as a problem that the system has accommodating the disability, it is possible to depatholigize the individual with IDD and acknowledge his or her value as a member of the system.

Although historically there has been resistance to allowing people with intellectual disabilities to become companions or couples, to live together, or to marry, over the past 40 years attitudes have been changing. There is now more support and acceptance for these individuals to form loving couple relationships, but very little literature exists regarding clinical interventions for these couples. J. Dale Munro, MSW, RSW, FAAIDD presents the "Positive Support-Couple Therapy" Model (PSCT Model) which incorporates elements of the strength-based social work perspective, positive psychology, and unconditionally constructive mediation. The model helps build effective working relationships with the couple, their extended families, and service system representatives. Therapists using the PSCT Model must determine which of four possible roles they should play: (1) a consultant role, (2) an outside mediator, (3) a more traditional couple therapist, or (4) providing individual counseling to one of the partners or making a referral to a clinical specialist. In contrast to the assessment methods utilized by most couple therapists, therapists using the PSCT model may ask the couples permission to meet with the extended family and the support agencies involved to determine the level of assistance available and support available to the couple from these sources. Munro notes a number of areas (such as family dynamics, problem-solving patterns, housing and financial stability) that the therapist should pay attention to during the assessment process.

At times supporting couples involves intervening with their extended family or service system. Mr. Munro also considers the ethical responsibilities of the therapist to both promote the self-determination of the individuals and at times to question the behavior of one or both partners if extremely unhealthy or dangerous choices are being made. Counseling couples who are involved in violent or abusive relationships is also discussed.

SECTION IV: OTHER ISSUES

H. Thompson Prout, Ph.D. and Brooke K. Reed, M.S. provide an overview of the current status of psychotherapy outcome research with persons with intellectual disabilities in their chapter on "The Effectiveness of Psychotherapy with Persons with Intellectual Disabilities." After considering general issues in psychotherapy research including a definition of psychotherapy, the meaning and distinction between effectiveness and efficacy, therapist characteristics, client characteristics, outcome measures, type of design, evidence-based empirically-supported treatments, and therapeutic alliance, they examine the research literature, beginning with four reviews of the research literature and then looking at published studies and dissertations that focused on psychotherapy with persons with intellectual disabilities in approximately the last ten years. The inclusion of dissertations among the research that is reviewed is important, as an over-reliance on published studies may yield a bias resulting in higher effect sizes and overestimations of actual treatment effectiveness because "published" studies typically are accepted for publication because they have demonstrated significant results. Using the broad definition of psychotherapy, the reviews, published reports, and dissertations support that psychotherapeutic treatments offer some degree of benefit to persons with intellectual disabilities. Far less research has been reported that concerns psychotherapy with children or adolescents who have an intellectual disability. Dr. Prout and Ms. Reed offer a number of conclusions and implications for future research.

Although a great deal has been published about ethics in psychotherapy or in counseling in general, little has been published on the ethics in counseling clients with intellectual or developmental disabilities. In "Ethical Issues in Counseling Clients with Intellectual Disabilities," Dick Sobsey, Ed.D. begins with the assumption that there are no differences in principle and only small and subtle differences in application between the ethics of counseling or carrying out psychotherapy with individuals with and without intellectual disabilities. He begins with a brief review of various approaches to counseling ethics: virtue ethics, utilitarian ethics, principle-based ethics, and relational ethics. Then he looks at several elements of codes for ethical behavior from the American Psychological Association and the National Association of Social Workers and considers how these apply and what special considerations are required when counseling individuals with intellectual or developmental disabilities. In this section he looks at concepts such as "respect for clients, "social justice," and "conflicts of interest." Finally, he considers several concepts the have emerged from the field of developmental disability that are not covered by the ethical codes of the APA or the NASW but are germane to ethical considerations for counseling individuals with intellectual disability. These concepts include "normalization," "age appropriate activities," and "dignity of risk."

In addition to the benefits of increasing the pool of clinicians trained to provide psychotherapy to individuals who have an intellectual disability, Gerald Drucker, Ph.D. suggests that training psychotherapy interns to work with people who have intellectual disabilities offers a variety of benefits to the intern. The course of therapy tends to move more slowly, which allows the intern more time to think about what the client is saying, to have more time to respond, to have more time to gauge the client's reactions, and to have more time to consult the supervisor and get input and guidance. Dr. Drucker sees the development of a working alliance as fundamental to any psychotherapy work, whether or not the client has an intellectual disability. Working with clients who do have ID, the intern must spend a large amount of at the beginning of therapy building the client's trust and feeling of security. Dr. Drucker advocates the use of a multi-theoretical approach, discussing the value of offering different theoretical "lenses" through which to observe the client's needs and abilities. Issue concerning the ending of therapy are discussed. Dr. Drucker covers building a supervisory relationship and intern selection.

SECTION I

INDIVIDUAL THERAPY

Dialectical Behavior Therapy for Special Populations: Treatment with Adolescents and Their Caregivers

Margaret Charlton, Ph.D., ABPP
Eric J. Dykstra, Psy.D.

INTRODUCTION

David's life was so miserable that he doused himself with gasoline and set himself on fire. Rachel was tired of living each day in constant fear yet could not bring herself to trust anyone enough to tell. Tara could not stand another night of panic-inducing nightmares and flashbacks so she kept cutting. Michael tried to control himself but still ended up attacking and getting restrained on a weekly basis.

All of these young people were suffering. All of them had people in their lives who wanted to help, but no one knew what to do to make things better for them.

While there is a growing awareness of the need for innovative, effective treatment approaches for individuals with intellectual disabilities (ID) and mental health concerns, much work needs be done in order to actually develop such approaches. There are a number of issues that must be addressed when providing psychotherapy to individuals with co-occurring mental health problems and ID, including but not limited to: the client's level of intellectual functioning, the presenting symptoms that led to the referral for psychotherapy, how the symptoms compare to the client's previous level of functioning, how mental health symptoms interact with behavior that is typical for the clients' DD or ID, what types of stressors the client facing, and what skills has the client used to manage similar stressors in the past. In addition, before engaging in a therapy relationship with a client who has an intellectual disability, the therapist must examine her or his own biases and views of psychotherapy, of persons with ID, and the mode of psychotherapy provided (Bütz, Bowling, & Bliss, 2000; Sue & Sue, 1999). As Hurley and colleagues (1996) noted, any effective psychotherapy must be adapted according to the needs and abilities of the client.

Dialectical Behavior Therapy for Special Populations (DBT-SP) is an adaptation of Dialectical Behavior Therapy (DBT), specifically designed to address the needs of psychotherapy clients who have to develop better skills for managing their impulsivity, dealing with frustration and interacting with others. DBT-SP helped David to learn to tolerate his distress better so that he could make more effective choices for himself and not make problems bigger. It helped Rachel to understand and regulate her emotions so they were less overwhelming and she could begin to trust others again. Tara was amazed as she participated in DBT-SP. Her nightmares and flashbacks became less intense and she learned new ways to communicate with others that didn't involve cutting. Michael still struggled to control his temper, but he is now able to express his anger verbally instead of physically. He admits that there is still a lot of work to be done, but now he can get to time out himself, instead of needing to be restrained.

Dialectical Behavior Therapy (DBT) is an empirically validated, comprehensive treatment program addressing skills deficits in emotion regulation, distress tolerance, and interpersonal relationships. This therapeutic intervention was originally developed by Marsha Linehan and is outlined in *Cognitive-Behavioral Treatment of Borderline Personality Disorder* (1993a) and the accompanying *Skills Training Manual for Treating Borderline Personality Disorder* (1993b). Though it was originally developed as a treatment for individuals diagnosed with Borderline Personality Disorder, the treatment's use has been expanded to address the needs of a wide variety of clients in a variety of settings. DBT is now best described as a treatment for clients with severe and chronic DSM-IV Axis I and II multiple diagnoses of mental disorders that are difficult to treat (Dimeff & Koerner, 2007). Of particular interest, DBT has also been adapted for use with adolescents, in a version known as DBT-A (Miller, Rathus, Linehan, Wetzler, & Leigh, 1997; Miller, Rathus, & Linehan, 2006).

Since DBT's inception as a treatment for clients with borderline personality disorder, its effectiveness has been demonstrated with a large variety of different disorders and age ranges of individuals, including suicidal adolescents (Miller, Rathus, Linehan, Wetzler, & Leigh, 1997; Katz, Cox, Gunasekara, & Miller, 2004), clients with binge eating disorders (Telch, Agras, & Linehan, 2001), clients with treatment resistant depression (Harley, Sprich, Safren, Jacobo, & Fava, 2008), community mental health center clients who chronically injure themselves and/or have experienced multiple treatment failures (Comtois, Elwood, Holdcraft, Smith, & Simpson, 2007), adolescents with bipolar disorder (Goldstein, Axelson, Birmaher, & Brent, 2007) individuals with developmental disabilities (Dykstra & Charlton, 2003; Dykstra & Charlton, 2008; Lew, Matta, Tripp-Tebo, & Watts, 2006) and group use in a residential program (Wolpow, 2000), to name a few.

Using standard DBT, therapists have five main tasks. They work to expand client capabilities, motivate the client to engage in new behaviors, generalize the use of the new behaviors, establish a treatment environment that reinforces progress, and maintain capable and motivated therapists (Linehan, 2000). These tasks are accomplished using four main components: individual psychotherapy, skills training groups, telephone consultation, and supervision/case consultation groups (Linehan, 1993a). Using these components, DBT provides strength based instruction with specific training in concrete skills, utilizing a multidimensional and multidisciplinary approach. A hierarchy of targets was also developed for DBT, with primary focus being on suicidal, para-suicidal, and other high-risk behavior. From a pragmatic perspective, effective change can only occur when a person is present, safe, and alive. Following this, the second stage focuses on therapy-interfering behaviors. The approaches used during this phase serve to fully engage the client in treatment and maintain motivation for change. Due to the all-to-common intentional and unintentional behaviors (both in-session and out-of-session) that undermine effective treatment, DBT intentionally targets this problem area. Third, treatment focuses on increasing quality of life for the client and helping him or her actually live a life worth living. This focus typically involves working on frequently-seen mental health issues, such as anxiety, depression, and trauma, in addition to further work on interpersonal skills.

More recently, an adaptation of DBT has been published for use with adolescent clients, DBT-A. DBT-A was initially developed in response to the significant need for an effective treatment approach for adolescents who exhibited characteristics of borderline personality disorder, especially suicidal/parasuicidal urges and behaviors. Retaining the focus on balancing acceptance and change, DBT-A utilizes individual and group psychotherapy, as well as parent-focused services (e.g. concurrent and integrated multi-family groups, family therapy) and other often-needed components, such as school consultation (Miller, 1999). As part of this adaptation a new module was developed to address the particular dynamics of adolescent development and parenting, called Walking the Middle Path. The comprehensive, full-length text entitled *Dialectical Behavior Therapy with Suicidal Adolescents* is an excellent resource and provides a great number of strategies and clinical teaching approaches (Miller, Rathus, & Linehan, 2006).

In the past, it was believed that psychotherapy was not effective for people with developmental/intellectual disabilities. In addition, many felt that people with DD/ID did not have the same need for psychotherapy as the general population. Today there is growing appreciation that individuals with DD/ID suffer from the same difficulties in life that the rest of the population encounters, such as feelings of anxiety and depression, grief, job stress, and so forth (Charlton, Kliethermes, Tallant, Taverne, & Tishelman, 2004; Butz, Bowling, & Bliss, 2000; Nezu & Nezu, 1994). Although there are a number of issues that must be addressed when providing psychotherapy to individuals with developmental disabilities and mental illnesses, many psychotherapeutic techniques are effective for people with developmental disabilities if they are suitably modified (Butz et al., 2000; Nezu & Nezu, 1994). Although more repetition is needed, once people with developmental disabilities make changes in therapy, the retention of the changes is similar to that displayed in the general population (Charlton et al., 2004).

To adapt psychotherapy for people with developmental disabilities, information should be provided in a variety of different modes, for example, using both auditory and visual information together (Spackman, Grigel, & MacFarlane, 1990). It is helpful to simplify language, structure the therapy session and use a more directive and active approach (Butz et al., 2000). Concrete activities such as modeling and role play are useful with clients who have language deficits, as well as setting clear limits, maintaining structure and focus to the session, and allowing flexibility for the expression of thoughts and feelings (Szymanski et al., 1994). Suggestions for change need to be specific; time should be allowed during the session to practice different ways of handling the situation; and do not assume that information will generalize from the session into other situations, unless explicit practice is done to institute this change (Charlton & Tallant, 2003).

PHILOSOPHICAL AND THEORETICAL ROOTS OF DBT

As mentioned above, DBT was originally developed by Dr. Linehan and outlined in two conjoined texts, Cognitive-Behavioral Treatment of Borderline Personality Disorder (1993a) and Skills Training Manual for Treating Borderline Personality Disorder (1993b). Because of the strong philosophical and theoretical underpinnings of DBT, it is important to understand the core philosophical assumptions. The sections below briefly summarize the philosophies and theories that give rise to the DBT model, namely dialectics and functional contextualism.

Dialectical Philosophy

While a full discourse on dialectics and the history of its inclusion and integration into the DBT model is beyond the scope of this chapter, the following should shed some light on the overarching themes and relevance. The dialectical perspective is perhaps most parsimoniously described as a focus on the intentional bringing together (synthesis) of two seemingly conflicting sides (thesis and antithesis). This philosophy is founded upon the concept of a non-absolute 'truth' model, allows for (seemingly) conflicting perspectives, and sees 'truth' as developing, evolving, and constructed over time. This is middle ground between Universalism ('ABSOLUTE TRUTH' – this is THE WAY or THE TRUTH) and complete Relativism ('NO TRUTH' – its all RELATIVE). This worldview advocates the use of words such as *'AND'* instead of *'BUT' or 'NOT'* and is intentionally inclusive in nature. From a pragmatic perspective, a dialectical approach weakens dependence on assumptions, biases, and verbal rule-governance while promoting multiple-perspective-taking and facilitating increased openness to varied experiences. In other words, it reduces rigidity, excessive judgment and blame, and ineffective fundamentalism while broadening perspectives and allowing for a sharing of ideas.

There are three core principles that underlie this Dialectical Philosophy, including Wholeness and Interrelatedness, Polarity, and Continuous Change. A clear, pragmatic example that elucidates these principles is time. When considering the concept and application of time, it is easily understood that previous moments are clearly connected to this moment … and this moment … and this moment … and so forth. Furthermore, the polarities of past versus the future are synthesized into this moment, yet this moment is only this moment for a short time as it is continuously changing as well. Said otherwise, that which is "the future" becomes "the now" which becomes "the past"; the seemingly opposing forces of past and future are part of the unrelenting and ever-changing present moment.

An appreciation for this philosophy allows us to attend to the whole person in-context, understand the push-pull experiences that clients have, and recognize how difficult the change process can be, especially if change is not fully welcomed. Practically, this philosophy undergirds the working balance between acceptance (validation) and change. This balance, tenuous and ever-changing though it may be, is foundational to effective working with individuals with significant and numerous challenges.

Functional Contextualism

Functional contextualism serves as the philosophy of science underpinning contemporary behavior analysis, a scientific approach informed by radical behaviorism and the work of B.F. Skinner (among others), within the larger field of psychology (cf. Cheisa, 1994). A variant of the worldview of contextualism, functional contextualism is best characterized by its root metaphor, the ongoing act in context (Hayes, 1993; Hayes, Blackledge, & Barnes-Holmes, 2001; Pepper, 1942). The contextualistic worldview regards the person as a psychological whole, functioning in and with an environment. Behavior is viewed as the ongoing historically situated act in context. The analytic unit entails *behavior,* its *functions,* and the *contexts* in which it occurs. The mutual interrelations comprising the unit are symmetrical, interconnected, interactive, dynamic, interpenetrative, and wholly indivisible (the web metaphor). The functional contextualistic perspective, as related to behavior analysis, holds prediction and influence of behavior with precision, scope, and depth as its analytic goals. The DBT approach is fundamentally rooted in functional contextualism and utilizes a pragmatic, functional, whole-person, behavior-analytic approach to behavior change. This philosophical foundation leads to a theory of understanding individuals and the diverse impact of various factors on each.

Bio-Psycho-Social Theory

The theory explaining why DBT successfully targeted a specific subset of individuals postulates that some people have a higher-than-typical baseline arousal level, they are highly emotionally reactive to their environments, and they have difficulty returning to a baseline arousal level. Frequently these individuals also have a history of trauma and severe emotional dysregulation, which holds both etiological and exacerbational potential. Oftentimes, these individuals also have skills deficits that inhibit effective coping with such experiences, frequently resulting in crisis-ridden lives characterized by chaotic interpersonal relationships and poor day-to-day functioning.

Said otherwise, the interplay between our biology, psychology, and interpersonal/social experiences (among other factors) is the foundation for understanding and working with individuals with numerous long-standing problems. Given the frequent occurrence of brain-based differences, increased amounts of stress in everyday life, and atypical interpersonal experiences for individuals with a range of developmental and intellectual differences, it is clear how this model applies. Furthermore, this highlights the need for individuals with DD/ID and mental health concerns to be involved with a multidisciplinary team that is well-connected and working in a consistent manner toward shared goals.

BRIEF OVERVIEW OF THE STANDARD DBT MODEL

Recognizing the ubiquity of human suffering, DBT is not aimed at reducing or getting rid of ordinary pain or discomfort, nor on ridding oneself of particular thoughts or feelings, but rather is focused on reducing *unnecessary* suffering (similar to its "relative" *Acceptance and Commitment Therapy* (ACT; Hayes, Strosahl, & Wilson, 1999) in the behavior analytic tradition). Oftentimes individuals increase their suffering by struggling against that which they cannot change, such as trying to rid themselves of their respective histories. In contrast, the focus of DBT is on reducing unnecessary suffering through skillful means, namely managing urges and emotions in the service of pursuing valued life directions despite feeling pain, experiencing negative emotions, or thinking negative thoughts. In short, the focus is on achieving a balance between changing that which one is able to change and accepting that which is unchangeable, so that the individual can behave effectively in all situations and make progress toward his or her valued life goals – living a life worth living. During the process there is a focus on reducing suffering and particular thoughts and emotions may be altered so they are more pleasant, but this is not guaranteed. The relative concreteness of these ideas makes them accessible enough for many people to understand and utilize them, including persons with DD/ID. In summary, DBT encourages clients to take responsibility for their actions, advancing the dictum that "no matter what, I choose how to act."

WORKING ASSUMPTIONS (TAKING A DBT STANCE)

These assumptions were originally published in Linehan's *Cognitive Behavioral Therapy for Borderline Personality Disorder* (1993a). They are summarized here as adapted for adolescents with dual diagnoses of intellectual disability and mental illness.

Clients are doing the best they can: This is a clearly 'person-centered' perspective. This assertion boils down to the appreciation for the fact that everyone is doing the best they can **in that moment.** This allows for variability in performance and different levels of success in various life domains. It also acknowledges that one's ability to effectively self-regulate and negotiate interpersonal relationships is fluid and affected by numerous factors in life (e.g. stress, sleep, nutrition, physical health, peer group, and so forth). Especially for those who are more vulnerable to the stressors they experience, it is important to acknowledge the effects of stress and not have rigid and unrealistic expectations. Remember that just because a client performed one way yesterday it does not mean that the client can do the same today **and at the same time** we expect that positive change will occur over time.*Clients want to improve:* The majority of people that will be involved in DBT-based treatment recognize that there are problems and they want to change. Even if the initial desire for change comes from a desire to escape from or avoid negative consequences, most often individuals do acknowledge that something should change – even if it is not themselves. This opens the door to treatment and presents an opportunity to engage in an intentional change process.

Clients need to do better, try harder: Wanting to change is not enough. Clients actually need to improve their performance. In addition, many of the clients we work with are unsuccessful in many of their attempts to help themselves. There are likely many reasons for this yet the fact remains that they are responsible for their lives. Our jobs are to encourage, build skills, maintain & increase motivation, and facilitate success. Balancing skill-based and performance-based perspectives is vital.

Clients have not caused all of their problems but they have to solve them anyway: This statement tends to hold true for most people. As so much of what happens in the world is out of one's direct control, many difficulties occur that are unavoidable. However, as human beings we are responsible and thus can choose how to respond in the multitude of situations that we face. While initially a seemingly harsh assertion, it really functions to empower clients (really all of us) to solve problems and become effective in many life situations. In addition, it allows us to maintain the stance that as professionals we cannot save people – they must work to save themselves.

Clients' lives are unbearable as they currently are: If we really listen to the life stories of the people we serve, we will realize the living hell their lives have truly been. It may be complaining about the program they are in, "the system" they are a part of, their guardian, the food that they have to eat, their roommate, or even nonspecific grumbling – all of these are indications of dissatisfaction with one's current life. This ties into the belief that people do want to change as well as needing to work on bettering themselves. While we cannot do the work for them or save them ourselves, we can work alongside to help clients change their lives.

Clients must learn new ways of being in all relevant situations: When planning for comprehensive treatment there are a couple of questions to ask to help with the generalization of skills. They are: *Success in the program is great ~ and what about real life?* and *Success with some people is great ~ what about the rest?* One of the most important measures of successful treatment is evidence that individuals have effectively generalized skills outside of the treatment environment.

Clients cannot fail in treatment: If we have a comprehensive, consistent, philosophy-to-theory-to-practice approach that doesn't work … either the treatment failed or the treaters failed. This assertion protects against a "blame the patient" tendency that is all too common and is a reminder of our fallibility as professionals. While there is no assertion, let alone a guarantee, that DBT-SP – or standard DBT for that matter – will be effective for all clients, the intentional consistency that exists from philosophy through practice provides a measure of confidence in the treatment approach. This also serves as a reminder that treatment should be customized and individualized for clients, even in an intentionally structured approach such as DBT.

Treaters (everyone on the DBT Team) *need assistance and support when working with individuals with intensive problems:* It is easy to get caught up in the crisis of the week, get burnt out, become judgmental and invalidating, lose perspective, get lost, and otherwise fail. The team is a vital resource that needs to function well in order to protect against burnout, secondary traumatic stress, caregiver fatigue, and generally ineffective working. This is not easy work and we cannot do it alone.

DBT TEAM AGREEMENTS

Because the function of the team is so critical to the success of the clients we work with, the following agreements, if valued highly and lived reasonably, should provide a good foundation for working together.

Dialectical Agreement: Because disagreements, differences of opinion, and conflict arise, we agree to search for the synthesis in these situations as opposed to "THE TRUTH." Just as there is wisdom in the actions of our clients, each of us holds a valid perspective. Our job is to work to synthesize the perspectives presented before us. We agree to consider other perspectives and work collaboratively for the best of the clients we serve.

Consultation to the Client: This agreement is centered on our role with clients. Just as we cannot "save" the individuals we work with, it is unhelpful to try and solve all of their problems for them. First, we agree to work with clients to use skills in their interactions with others. We help coach them about how to approach various treatment team members and work with them to find skillful ways of relating. Second, we agree to not intervene on their behalf nor tell other professionals how to respond to a client. It should be noted, however, that coaching, teaching, and learning as a team does not conflict with this agreement. Finally, if a team member makes a mistake, we agree to acknowledge this and help clients accept and cope with this. As team members are fallible, so are the people that the clients will interact with in everyday life. We are privileged to have the trust of our clients and we must provide them with experiences that reflect the world that they live in.

Consistency Agreement: We agree that consistency is important ... AND ... real life happens. We concurrently agree to help clients cope with failures and inconsistencies. This presents opportunities for all of us (clients and professionals alike) to practice our DBT skills. Said otherwise, we strive to be consistent and we acknowledge that this will not occur 100% of the time.

Empathic Orientation: In order to be successful in our roles we must be mindfully empathic those we work with. We agree to search for non-pejorative and non-judgmental interpretations and understandings of clients' behaviors. We also agree to approach each other in a non-judgmental way and validate each others' experiences. This is absolutely necessary, as the relationships between team members are as vital as the therapeutic ones between professionals and clients.

Fallibility Agreement: First, we agree that we are all imperfect and have permission to fail. Without this explicit statement, judgment, invalidation, and strife will poison the team. Further, as a team we agree to utilize the DBT framework to help each other remain true to the philosophy and the approach. We agree to keep each other accountable and treat each other gently and with empathy.

DEVELOPMENT OF DBT-SP

Persons with DD/ID obtain significant benefits from participation in psychotherapy to address their mental health needs, provided the psychotherapy is presented in a manner that is accessible to them (Szymanski et al., 1994). At this time, only a few types of psychotherapy have been formally adapted specifically for use with this population; much additional work is needed to provide people with DD/ID the same range of options for treatment that the non-disabled population is given. The current effort in developing DBT-SP to meet the needs of people with DD/ID is just a beginning. As more research is done in this important area, it is our hope that specific standards will be developed so that the types of modification that are most helpful in making psychotherapy accessible people with DD/ID are known. We believe, based on our current work, that psychotherapy methods that address core deficits instead of superficial symptom reduction will be needed. For example, approaches that emphasize replacing old, maladaptive behaviors with new more adaptive ones, in the manner used in DBT skill building modules, will be particularly useful for this population (Dykstra & Charlton, 2003).

Development of DBT-SP for individuals with DD/ID began with an overall assessment of the philosophy and theory, gauging its applicability to the targeted population. As mentioned previously, it seems that DBT is a "good fit" for persons with DD/ID and mental and behavioral health concerns. Given the often-seen constellation of multiple difficult-to-treat problems, vulnerability to stress, and need for intensive and long-term interventions, the DBT model provides a framework that addresses a number of the core deficit areas. The whole-person, developmentally-informed, comprehensive hierarchy of targets and skills that is found in DBT fits well for many individuals with concurrent DD/ID and mental health problems. It is also important to note that the skills taught in DBT can serve well as the foundation for further work in the areas of independent living, resolving other mental health concerns, trauma processing, and generally increasing the quality of life for each individual.

From here, adaptation moved to the areas of language and presentation. The main tenets of DBT remained unchanged, however the presentation and language were adjusted to a level that persons with DD/ID can more easily comprehend and were modified to have more appeal to our adolescent target population. Just as when working with any individual with unique needs (read: all people), one must adapt materials to meet the client's needs (Hurley et al., 1996; Pfadt, 1991). With this in mind, the curriculum was adjusted in a number of ways. First of all, the language was changed to make the concepts more accessible. Second, some of the concepts were been paired down and/or simplified to allow better comprehension and ability to apply the material. Third, the handouts were re-written and re-formatted in order to increase attention and aid in understanding. Finally, generous amounts of client feedback, repetition, and rehearsal have been incorporated into the therapy structure to aid in the learning, retention, and generalization processes.

Because the group skills training material was the most formalized and structured in standard DBT, the early phases of adaptation was focused here. In modifying the handouts suggested for use in the DBT group skills modules (Linehan, 1993b) we worked to use language that was accessible to and easily understood by our clients. For example, rather than talking about reducing emotional vulnerability, we focused on understanding how emotions affect us and on making good decisions when experiencing an emotion (Figure 1, Emotional Regulation Handout 1). We also used a visual presentation style that makes it easier for clients with DD/ID to absorb the information. This type of adaptation is illustrated in Emotion Regulation Handouts 3a and 3b (Figures 2 and 3), where we reduced the number of interactions we attempted to teach, used more prominent arrows, illustrated the components with different types of shapes to help make them easier to remember, and simplified the language. As "choice" was a main concept we wished to teach in this module, we also added it to this handout to provide an additional repetition.

Figure 1. Emotion Regulation Handout 1

GOALS OF EMOTION REGULATION

Understanding Your Emotions

1. Look at your emotions
2. Identify your emotions
3. Understand what emotions do

Control Your Behavior

1. Understand how emotions effect you
2. Make good decisions
3. Don't let emotions control you

Stop Feeling Bad All The Time

1. Accept and let go of painful emotions
2. Good choices = Good rewards

Figure 2. Emotion Regulation Handout 3a

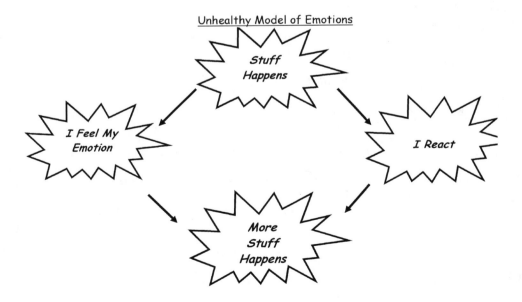

Figure 3. Emotion Regulation Handout 3b

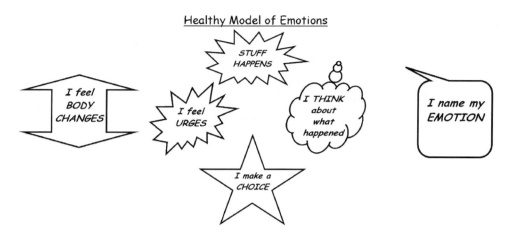

Another example of the type of adaptation is made with regard to the topic of emotional vulnerability. Linehan (1993b) uses the acronym "PLEASE MASTER" in her handout addressing how to reduce vulnerability to negative emotions. We modified this to "SEEDS GROW" and discussed controlling emotions instead of reducing vulnerability (see Emotion Regulation Handout 10, Figure 4). This modification allowed us to use simpler language that was already in our clients' vocabulary, provided another opportunity to emphasize that we control our emotions—they do not control us, and simplified the visual presentation of the material.

Figure 4. Emotion Regulation Handout 10

Keeping Control of Your Emotions	
A good way to remember these skills is "SEEDS GROW"	
Sickness needs to be treated.	You need to take care of yourself and your body. See your doctor and take your medicine.
Eat right.	You need to eat good food. Don't eat too much or too little.
Exercise every day.	Do some exercise every day. Stay in shape.
Drugs are bad.	Stay away from drugs and alcohol. They make you out of control.
Sleep well.	Get enough sleep at night so you are not tired during the day.
GROW every day.	Do something you are good at every day try doing something new every day.

In addition to the handouts and other materials, the structure of the group skills-training sessions and various environmental considerations are open to adaptation. While many of the standard DBT group skills training sessions are scheduled for 90 minutes or more, we have found that using 30-60 minute sessions at a higher frequency (e.g. twice per week) allows clients to fully attend and participate for the entire session, tends to avoid overloading them with new material, and allows greater opportunity for review, practice, and integration of skills into everyday life. Moreover, the more frequent sessions provide more frequent contact with group leaders, other clients, and involvement in the treatment setting, all of which can aid in accountability (for homework completion, attendance, etc.), generalization of skills, and prompting greater stability in life.

Another adaptation to the skills training is to consider including other caregivers in the group. In the primary pilot site, an educational and therapeutic day-treatment program serving adolescents with developmental and mental health challenges, we have successfully included skills training groups as a part of our classroom curriculum, so that the teacher and paraprofessionals in the classroom learn the skills at the same time as the students. As incidents occur within the school setting they are able coach the students on skill use and facilitate their practice and use of skills in the moment. When the model is used with outpatient clients, we generally have the clients develop a note for their parents/caregivers at the end of the group. Writing a note about what they learned in group provides a good review of the information presented. It also often provides the therapist with insight regarding how much of the material has been retained by the clients and how accurately. Then the note goes home to the caregivers, so that they can help with practice during the week.

As the skills training manual adaptations were progressing it was clear that adaptations for individual therapy approaches needed to be considered. One of the main changes was to make review of the daily diary cards part of individual therapy instead of group. In the traditional version of DBT the group discusses the cards together, but our clients had trouble maintaining attention when the discussion focused on other client's challenges. We now address problems with self care, such as not getting enough sleep or skipping medication as part of the individual sessions. Then therapist can discuss the impact on thoughts and behavior during the day, for example, if you don't get much sleep, you are likely to be more irritable and to have more trouble dealing with negative thoughts and feelings. When your resistance is down, you are also more likely to act on negative thoughts and feelings. In other ways, the individual therapy component of DBT remained the same. Individual therapy still targets the same hierarchy of issues as traditional DBT. It also provides a venue for individualized skills coaching and skills training, processing of critical incidents, and working on family-related problems.

Family involvement (including family therapy) was also an important component to consider, especially given the high frequency of problems that were related to and/or affected family life, issues relating to foster care placements, and so forth. In addition, environmental consistency is vital to the generalization of language, skills, and general change process. Furthermore, including the family in some way when working with adolescents with intensive problems should be a foregone conclusion. While family therapy is strongly encouraged as part of DBT-SP, to date it has not been made a prerequisite to participation. From a pragmatic perspective, the family component is quite flexible and can be achieved in a number of ways. While ideally the parents/caregivers would participate in family therapy as well as a concurrent skills training group, this is not always logistically possible. Instead, options like saving some time at the end of each group to meet with parents and briefly review that week's lesson and the associated homework, using time during individual or family sessions to also review the group skills training material and homework, or coordinating via the telephone are all viable, though clearly with their respective drawbacks. We are also flexible in using a wider range of caregivers than are typically considered for participation in "family therapy" since we find that this flexibility better meets the needs of our clients who are involved in different types of treatment settings. For example, some of our clients are in foster care and have both biological and foster parents involved in their care. In such situations we often involved both biological and foster parents in the family therapy sessions. For some clients who have been moved around a lot, their department of human services case managers have an important long term perspective on the client's behaviors over time and the struggles they have encountered. We often try to include the case managers in regular team meetings where we talk about the progress in therapy and the skills that are being developed. At times when the client is in a group home setting with shift staff who transition quickly, the client may prefer to work closely with a teacher or paraprofessional who they spend more consistent time with. We find that including such caregivers also works well.

Crisis Access: As with traditional DBT, it is important in DBT-SP for the client to have access to coaching when attempting to implement new skills or when feeling overwhelmed. We try to provide this support in a number of ways. First of all, the students have immediate access to the classroom staff, who have all been thoroughly trained in the model and serve as front-line coaches and teachers. Further, clients are given direct dial numbers for their therapists and whenever possible, the therapists take the calls as they come in. If the therapist is with another client, the call can be redirected to the office manager; this individual also has basic training in DBT-SP skills and can often help the client to manage until the therapist is free. The office manager can also connect the client to one of the other therapists in the program to provide immediate help. For after-hours emergencies, we have an emergency services department with therapists on call to provide problem solving and coaching.

Supervision/Consultation: As this aspect of the model has not needed adaptation, only a brief summary will be provided here. Interested readers are encouraged to consult Dr. Linehan's landmark text, *Cognitive-Behavioral Therapy for Treating*

Borderline Personality Disorder (1993a). In a nutshell, the supervision/consultation is designed to maintain fidelity to the model, encourage and sustain motivation for doing difficult and taxing work, and provide ongoing training and mentoring. DBT teams are asked to commit to the work in the same way that clients are and work intentionally to keep each other accountable in all areas of the work, from the overarching philosophy to the day-to-day practice and application.

INTRODUCTION TO SKILLS TRAINING AND SKILLS GROUP FORMAT

In the DBT model, group skills training is designed as one of three treatment-focused components. In addition to skills training groups, the model calls for all clients to participate in individual psychotherapy and for therapists to participate in a consultation group through which they can receive support in maintaining fidelity to the model (as noted above). In the original model, four different skills groups were presented: Mindfulness, Interpersonal Effectiveness, Emotion Regulation, and Distress Tolerance. However, we found that when Mindfulness was taught only as a separate module, many of the concepts presented were too abstract and difficult for our clients to comprehend. In order to continue to present key concepts of mindfulness in a more accessible fashion, we chose not to make Mindfulness a separate module that stands alone, but to integrate elements of mindfulness into each of the other three skill-building sections. Also, in DBT-SP skills training, Interpersonal Effectiveness is referred to as Relationship Effectiveness, as this language was more easily accessible to our target population. Throughout this section, examples from the DBT-SP skills manual are used, for more detailed information and all of the adapted materials, please refer to the full manual (Dykstra & Charlton, 2003; Dykstra & Charlton, 2008)In providing adapted psychotherapy groups to adolescents with DD/ID, it can be helpful to maintain a consistent structure for each session. In our work with this adapted model, we have used the following session structure. It is presented here as a suggestion for how to integrate all of the necessary components of the skills training in an accessible manner.

When introducing each of the modules, begin by giving the name and explaining the general focus of the group. Define the goals of the group and use specific and concrete terms when discussing how and why the skills taught in the group are likely to be important to the group members. Encourage the group members to talk about the types of problems they have encountered in the particular skill area. Group leaders should be prepared to offer suggestions and examples of the type of problems that will be addressed, including situations from their lives and other clinical situations, in case group members need a little help in getting started with the discussion.

Since many adolescents with DD/ID may have limited experience with psychotherapy and because they may have some difficulty in learning social rules, we suggest that after the introduction the group work together to develop group rules and a group contract. Especially if many of your members have not been in a group before, it is important to talk about what to expect in group. It can be helpful to write down all of the rules that are developed as a group and for the first few sessions review the group rules at the beginning of the session. This review is continued until it appears that the group members remember and understand the rules as demonstrated by their behavior during the group. This process is not only helpful in guiding behavior, it can facilitate the joining of group members and the development of group cohesion.

The group members should be encouraged to talk about the rules they feel the group should follow. However, group leaders should also be prepared to introduce some basic rules if the members do not bring them up. All groups should include a discussion of informed consent and confidentiality in language that is accessible at the functioning level of the group members. For example, it is important to be sure members understand that it is not OK to "gossip" about what happens in group with friends. It would not be appropriate for members to share problems that other clients talk about; however, it may be appropriate for them to talk about some of the skills they are learning or the problems they are experiencing with parents, foster parents, host home families, and so forth. These boundaries should be clarified when the rules are developed and should be reviewed until the members clearly retain the key concepts.

Respect for group leaders and other group members is another concept that is often included in the group rules. As group members are talking about rules, the concept of respect is often first expressed through rules against disrespectful behaviors, like interrupting, cursing, hitting and name calling. It is helpful for the group leader to clarify that all of these specific "do not's" are part of a general concept of showing respect for others during the group process. Many group members conceptualize this respect in terms of treating others in the way that they would like to be treated.

Another element of successful groups is setting clear limits on respect for oneself. Many of the clients we work with struggle with interpersonal boundaries. They need assistance in knowing whether it is appropriate to give personal information about sexual abuse history, specific living situations such as foster care and termination of parental rights, in addition to a large variety of other topics. In a process-oriented psychotherapy group, sharing a great deal of personal information might be desirable. In a more psychoeducational group, like skills training, it may be appropriate to share fewer intimate details. It is helpful for the group leader to think about what level of sharing will be appropriate for the current group and then to be sure that guidelines about sharing are incorporated into the group rules. These guidelines should also address the amount of contact that group members may have with each other during the course of the group. Think about whether it is OK with you (the group leader) for members to exchange phone numbers, to become friends with, or to date other members during the group. Group leaders should also be aware that these standards can change over time. It is not uncommon for group members to share very little personal information at the beginning of skills training, though over time the familiarity and comfort level increases, such that more personal sharing and interpersonal processing occurs in an appropriate manner.

In setting up the group it is also helpful to develop a contract between the therapist and group members. This contracting may begin with a discussion of the benefits the leader thinks members will receive from participating in the group. In some cases, the leader may do a test at the end to demonstrate retention of material or to identify need for further work in certain areas. If any type of evaluation is anticipated, it should be explained to group members at the onset of the group. Group members also need to know if there will be any type of celebration or graduation ceremony at the completion of the group. Further, a portion of the contract should be dedicated to establishing attendance policies, exclusion from group, and other pertinent information. All of these details serve to develop a clear contract between the group leader and the group members so that everyone knows what to expect in the course of the group.

Once the basic structure of the group has been decided on, we suggest following a consistent format for each group session. As described previously, for the first few sessions the group format would include a review of the group rules. In addition, we suggest the following components:

Check-in: At the beginning of each group it is helpful to get some basic information regarding how group members are feeling. There are a variety of methods that can be used to check in, including a verbal report, a check-in sheet (Check-In Sheet, Figure 5), or some other means to obtain this information. A typically important aspect of checking in is to have group members share what emotion(s) they are feeling and to talk about what is contributing to that experience (i.e. prompting events). This routine helps to get members focused on group activity and encourages the beginning of discussion and sharing, as well as promoting group cohesion. It also is a way of practicing a variety of skills, including mindfulness to current emotions, understanding how emotions work, increasing emotion-based vocabulary, and so forth.

Figure 5. Check-In Sheet

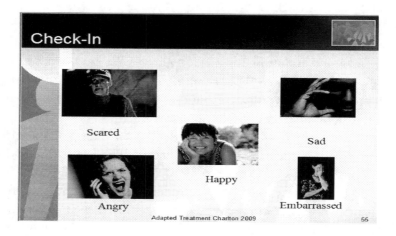

29

Mindfulness Activity: The leader should choose a mindfulness exercise that will complement the work that is going to be done in the session. If the group members had trouble participating in the previous session, an interactive exercise might be used. If group members struggled more with staying on task in the previous session, the leader might want to select a mindfulness exercise that improves focus such as a quiet, meditative activity.

Discussion of Mindfulness Skills: After the mindfulness exercise, the leader should facilitate a discussion about the skills that are presented in the exercise. This presents a good time to review the basic concepts of mindfulness. Depending on the skills training material to be presented later in the session, the leader might focus on the concept of wise mind; the "What's" of mindfulness—observing, describing and participating; or the "How's" of mindfulness—accepting, doing one thing at a time and working effectively.

Review of Homework Assignments: It seems very basic, but surprisingly, many therapists give homework assignments and then neglect to follow up and talk about these assignments at the next session. It is very important that homework be given, because many adolescents with DD/ID have difficulty in generalizing skills from one setting into another. The use of homework assignments is one method of facilitating this generalization. Another way is to be sure that clients have samples of the information they learned during the group to take home to review with their caregivers. Reviewing homework assignments during group helps in a variety of ways. First of all it makes a clear statement that the group leader thinks the assignments are important. Second, homework review reinforces the clients who remember to do the assignments and helps those who forgot to realize how important the assignments are. It also gives the group leader a chance to talk about strategies for remembering the homework assignments after the end of the group session—another technique to facilitate use of the skills in other situations.

Presentation of Skill Training Material: The group leader should spend part of each group presenting new information on the skill that is being developed in the particular module. The DBT-SP Skills Manual provides a full series of handouts for each module (Dykstra & Charlton, 2008). In addition, specific suggestions for the use of these handouts are made in the chapters on Mindfulness; Distress Tolerance; Emotion Regulation; and Relationship Effectiveness. We find it helpful to give out the handouts on a weekly basis so that group members can put them into a notebook. The notebook helps them to review information with key caregivers and gives them a reference manual to look at after completing the group.

Review: Because repetition of material is essential for our clients to effectively absorb and retain information, each session should end with a discussion of what has been learned in the session. This is an opportunity for members to demonstrate what they have learned. It is also an opportunity for the group leader to assess clients' progress and what material needs further review. Group leaders may also find it effective to review and highlight the vital material from the previous group prior to introducing that week's topic.

CASE EXAMPLES

Pilot Study: We have completed a pilot study in an effort to determine the effectiveness of DBT-SP. The study was conducted with adolescent clients in the day treatment program at Intercept Center, a specialized program of Aurora Mental Health Center, providing education and treatment for children and adolescents with significant developmental and behavioral health needs. In the study, we utilized all three components of DBT, in addition to our normal milieu management techniques, so that clients received DBT-SP focused individual therapy, skills training groups using the DBT-SP skills training manual, and all of our treatment team staff members participated in a DBT-SP supervision/consultation group. We collected observations of client behavior by staff, client outcome when leaving the program, and daily diary card information. We used an adapted daily diary card, shown in Figure 6.

Figure 6. DBT-SP Daily Diary Card

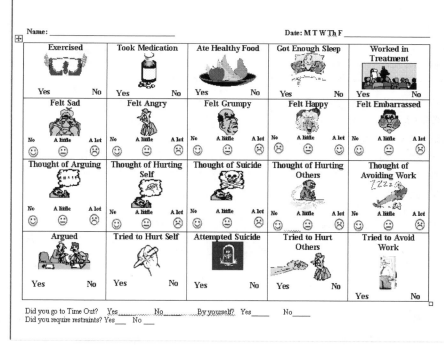

As with most pilot studies, there are many limitations to our data. While each client serves as his/her own control we do not have a random control group of any sort (e.g. TAU, wait-list, etc.), as all of the youth participating in the day treatment program receive DBT-SP. Further, DBT-SP is being used in conjunction with other techniques and we lack the ability to control many factors in the students' environment that influence their behavior. In addition, clients enter and leave the program at different times, so that the data we gather can be hard to interpret. Thus far the data we have collected is suggestive, but not in any way conclusive regarding the effectiveness of DBT-SP.

Our observational results indicate that clients are spontaneously using "DBT-SP Language." They are displaying the skills they have been learning, both spontaneously and when cued by staff members. In addition, over time in treatment, our clients are becoming more insightful into situations, emotions, thoughts, and actions that are maladaptive, as evidenced by the greater ease they show in processing such incidents.

Table 1 illustrates the outcome when leaving the program for the students who participated in DBT-SP thus far. Of 19 students who have completed 2 or more DBP-SP skills training modules, three students were lost to follow-up; three moved to more restrictive environments; three remain stable in a day treatment environment; and ten have moved to less restrictive environments.

Table 1. Results: Outcome When Leaving Program

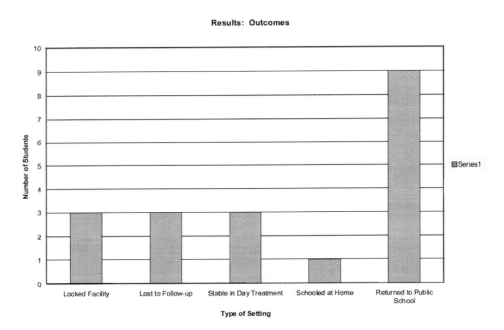

Information from the daily diary cards is shown in tables 2 (action items), 3 (thoughts), and 4 (feelings items). The action items (argued, tried to hurt self, attempted suicide, tried to hurt others and tried to avoid work) produced a correlation of mean composite of actions with month of -0.27, which is statistically significant at the 0.001 level (two tailed). That is, as the number of months in the program increased, the average number of combined negative actions decreased. A similar trend was noted for negative thoughts (-0.22, significant at the 0.001 level, two tailed) and feelings (-0.25, significant at the 0.001 level, two tailed).

Table 2. Results: Daily Diary Cards Action Items

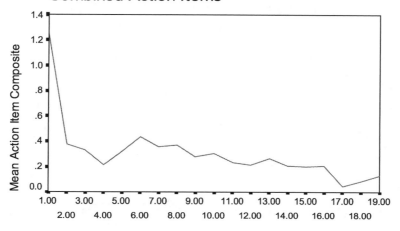

Mean Number of Events by Month in Program

Combined Action Items

Table 3. Results Daily Diary Cards Thoughts

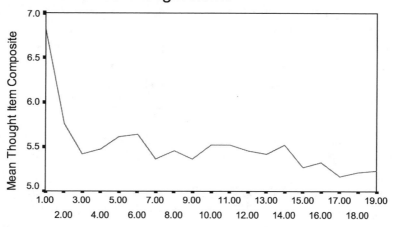

Mean Number of Events by Month in Program

Combined Thought Items

Table 4. Results Daily Diary Card Feelings Items

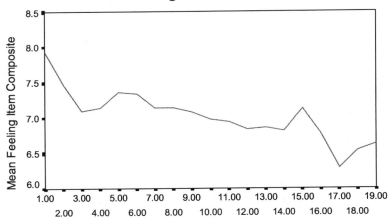

Mean Number of Events by Month in Program

Combined Feeling Items

CONCLUSION

There is much more work to be done before we will be sure that DBT-SP is as effective as traditional DBT. However, so far the trends observed with our pilot study are positive. There is a great need for the development of more effective treatment techniques to meet the needs of people with developmental disabilities. We know that people with developmental disabilities and mental health issues benefit from participation in psychotherapy, provided the psychotherapy is presented in a manner that is accessible to them (Szymanski et al., 1994). Much additional effort is needed to provide people with developmental disabilities the same range of options for treatment that the general population has access to. The DBT-SP model is just a beginning.

REFERENCES

Bütz, M. R., Bowling, J. B., & Bliss, C. A. (2000). Psychotherapy with the mentally retarded: A review of the literature and the implications. *Professional Psychology: Research and Practice, 31*, 42-47.

Charlton, M., Kliethermes, M., Tallant, B., Taverne, A., & Tishelman, A. (2004). Facts on traumatic stress and children with developmental disabilities. In National Child Traumatic Stress Network: Adapted Trauma Treatment Subgroup on Developmental Disabilities (Ed.). (Available from National Child Traumatic Stress Network, www.NCTSNet.org).

Charlton, M., & Tallant, B. (2003). Trauma treatment with clients who have dual diagnoses: Developmental disabilities and mental illness. *National Association for the Dually Diagnosed Annual Conference* (Vol. 20; pp. 29-32). Kingston, NY: NADD Press.

Chiesa, M. (1994). *Radical behaviorism: The philosophy and the science.* Boston: Authors Cooperative, Inc.

Comtois, K., Elwood, L., Holdcraft, L. C., Smith, W. R., & Simpson, T. L. (2007). Effectiveness of dialectical behavior therapy in a community mental health center. *Cognitive and Behavioral Practice, 14*(4), 406-414.

Dimeff, L. & Koerner, K. (Eds.). (2007). *Dialectical behavior therapy in clinical practice: Applications across disorders and settings.* New York: The Guilford Press.

Dykstra, E., & Charlton, M. (2003). Dialectical behavior therapy: A new direction in psychotherapy. *Proceedings of the National Association for the Dually Diagnosed Annual Conference* (Vol. 20, pp. 33-37). Kingston, NY: NADD Press.

Dykstra, E., & Charlton, M. (2008). *Dialectical behavior therapy skills training: Adapted for special population.* Unpublished manuscript, Aurora Mental Health Center, Intercept Center 16905 E 2nd Avenue Aurora, CO 80011, contact Dr_Charlton@yahoo.com for copies.

Goldstein, T. R., Axelson, D. A., Birmaher, B., & Brent, D. A., (2007). Dialectical behavior therapy for adolescents with bipolar disorder: A 1-years open trial. *Journal of the American Academy of Child & Adolescent Psychiatry, 46*(7), 820-830.

Hayes, S. C. (1993). Analytic goals and the varieties of scientific contextualism. In S. C. Hayes, L. J. Hayes, H. W. Reese, & T. R. Sarbin (Eds.), *Varieties of scientific contextualism* (pp. 11-27). Reno, NV: Context Press.

Hayes, S. C., Blackledge, J. T., & Barnes-Holmes, D. (2001). Language and cognition: Constructing an alternative approach within the behavioral tradition. In S. C. Hayes, D. Barnes-Holmes, & B. Roche (Eds.), *Relational frame theory: A post-Skinnerian account of human language and cognition* (pp. 3-20). New York: Kluwer Academic/Plenum Publishers.

Harley, R., Sprich, S., Safren, S., Jacobo, M., Fava, M. (2008). Adaptation of dialectical behavior therapy skills training group for treatment-resistant depression. *Journal of Nervous and Mental Disease, 196*(2), 136-143.

Hayes, S. C., Strosahl, K. D., & Wilson, K. G. (1999). *Acceptance and commitment therapy.* New York: The Guilford Press.

Hurley, A. D., Pfadt, A., Tomasulo, D., & Gardner, W. I. (1996). Counseling and psychotherapy. In J. W. Jacobson & J. A. Mulick (Eds.), *Manual of diagnosis and professional practice in mental retardation* (pp. 371-380). Washington, DC: American Psychological Association.

Katz, L., Cox, B., Gunasekara, S., & Miller, A. (2004). Feasibility of dialectical behavior therapy for suicidal adolescent inpatients. *Journal of the American Academy of Child and Adolescent Psychiatry, 43*, 276-283.

Lew, M., Matta, C., Tripp-Tebo, C., & Watts, D., (2006). Dialectical behavior therapy (DBT) for individuals with intellectual disabilities: A program description. *Mental Health Aspects of Developmental Disabilities, 9*(1), 1-12.

Linehan, M. M. (1993a). *Cognitive-behavioral treatment of borderline personality disorder.* New York: The Guilford Press.

Linehan, M. M. (1993b). *Skills training manual for treating borderline personality disorder.* New York: The Guilford Press.

Linehan, M. (2000). Commentary on innovations in dialectical behavior therapy. *Cognitive and Behavioral Practice, 7*, 478-481.

Miller, A. (1999). Dialectical behavior therapy: A new treatment approach for suicidal adolescents. *American Journal of Psychotherapy, 53,* 413-417.

Miller, A., Rathus, J., Linehan, M., Wetzler, S., & Leigh, E. (1997). Dialectical behavior therapy adapted for suicidal adolescents. *Journal of Practical Psychiatry and Behavioral Health, 3,* 78-86.

Miller, A.L., Rathus, J.H., & Linehan, M.M. (2006). *Dialectical behavior therapy with suicidal adolescents.* New York: The Guilford Press.

Nezu, C., & Nezu, A. (1994). Outpatient psychotherapy for adults with mental retardation and concomitant psychopathology: Reasearch and clinical imperatives. *Journal of Consulting and Clinical Psychology, 62,* 34-43.

Pepper, S. C. (1942). *World hypotheses: A study in evidence.* Berkeley, CA: University of California Press.

Pfadt, A. (1991). Group psychotherapy with mentally retarded adults: Issues related to design, implementation, and evaluation. *Research in Developmental Disabilities, 12,* 261-285.

Spackman, R., Grigel, M., & MacFarlane, C. (1990). Individual counseling and therapy for the mentally handicapped. *Alberta Psychology, 19*(5), 14-18.

Sue, D. W. & Sue, D. (1999). *Counseling the culturally different: Theory and practice* (3rd Ed.). New York: John Wiley & Sons.

Szymanski, L., King, B., Feinstein, C., Weisblatt, S., Stark, J., & Ryan, R. (1994). *American Psychiatric Association committee draft practice guidelines for mental health care for persons with developmental disabilities.* Washington, DC: American Psychiatric Association.

Telch, C., Agras, W., & Linehan, M. (2001). Dialectical behavior therapy for binge eating disorder. *Journal of Consulting and Clinical Psychology, 69,* 1061-1065.

Wolpow, S. (2000). Adapting a dialectical behavior therapy (DBT) group for use in a residential program. *Psychiatric Rehabilitation Journal, 24,* 135-141.

CHAPTER 2

Dialectical Behavior Therapy for Adults Who Have Intellectual Disability

Marvin Lew, Ph.D., ABPP

INTRODUCTION

For even the most seasoned psychotherapist working with individuals who have an intellectual disability (ID), there are some clients who present with serious difficulties with emotion regulation. These are clients who require an inordinate amount of time, energy, supervision, and patience. These are also the clients who exact an emotional toll from their therapists, support staff, and family members. At times, we as therapists may be so stressed from such individuals that we hope for missed appointments or perhaps premature termination.

It is in these situations that we as clinicians can benefit from the application of Marsha Linehan's Dialectical Behavior Therapy (DBT) work to our population. Linehan's work was developed in the early 1980's as an outpatient application of an integrative psychotherapy for normal IQ women with Borderline Personality Disorder (BPD). Her patients exhibited less suicidal behaviors, less self-injurious behaviors, less inpatient hospitalization days, as well as fewer drop-outs from treatment. There have since been more than a dozen clinical trials across multiple populations and settings which indicate that the therapy can be adopted in its manualized format and adapted to a number of variants from the original population and setting with encouraging results (Dimeff & Koerner, 2007). Though not a clinical trial, one such program previously described for adults with ID (Lew, Matta, Tripp-Tebo & Watts, 2006) demonstrated less risky behaviors. Another, discussed Charlton and Dykstra in this volume, has also had encouraging results with the adolescent population. A third implementation has been reported by Verhoeven (in press) with offenders who have ID.

This chapter will examine the rationale for using DBT with individuals who have ID, some of the adjustments that are necessary, some of the benefits that may be derived, and some of the caveats as well.

LITERATURE REVIEW

DBT is one of a number of "third wave behavioral therapies" (Ost, 2008) that each integrate aspects of cognitive behavioral therapies along with Eastern mindfulness meditation approaches. Others include Acceptance and Commitment Therapy (Hayes, Strosahl, & Wilson, 1999), Mindfulness Based Cognitive Therapy (Williams, Teasdale, Segal, & Kabat-Zinn, 2007), and Mindfulness Based Stress Reduction (Kabat-Zinn, 1982).

According to Behavioral Tech, Marsha Linehan's international dissemination group, which has trained thousands of clinicians, "DBT is designed for severe and chronic multi-diagnostic difficult-to-treat patients with both Axis I and Axis II disorders." The data from nearly twenty years of studies indicates that not only do individuals with Borderline Personality Disorder (BPD) benefit from treatment (e.g., Linehan, 1993a), but so do individuals with Eating Disorders (Wisniewski, Safer & Chen, 2007), forensic involvement (McCann, Ivanoff, Schmidt, & Beach, 2007), substance abuse and dependence (Linehan, Schmidt & Dimeff, 1999), as well as comorbid Depression (Lynch & Cheavens, 2007).

The range of settings that DBT has operated within has also varied from the original Linehan study. In addition to outpatient settings (e.g., Comtois, Koons, Kim, Manning, Bellows et al., 2007), DBT has demonstrated success in inpatient units (Swenson, Witterholt, & Bohus, 2007), residential programs (McCann et al., 2007), and with assertive community treatment teams (Reynolds, Wolbert, Abney-Cunningham, & Patterson, 2007). Moreover, there is a wealth of studies with families (Miller, Rathus, DuBose, Dexter-Mazza, & Goldklang, 2007) and couples (Fruzetti, Santisteban, & Hoffman, 2007) that indicate that the use of DBT within these clinical formats can benefit identified clients with various types of problems. In each of these adaptations of DBT, adjustments were tailored to different environments (e.g., having more frequent groups during relatively short hospital stays) while at the same time adhering to the basic principles and procedures in DBT. Generally, the data from twelve clinical trials and dozens of other experimental studies (Koerner & Dimeff, 2007) suggests that DBT may provide benefit to a wide range of populations where emotion regulation is a core problem.

THEORETICAL FOUNDATION

DBT is grounded in biosocial theory. From this perspective BPD is a disorder of pervasive emotional dysregulation. This emotional dysregulation is a result of the transactional process between one's biological vulnerability with an invalidating environment. This model is similar to other diathesis-stress models (e.g., Barlow & Durand, 2009), but looks at the particular nuances of emotional vulnerability for someone with BPD that stem from 1) high sensitivity to stimuli resulting in a low threshold for emotional responsiveness and immediate reactions, 2) high reactivity to people and events leading to extreme highs or extreme lows, and 3) a slow return to baseline once one does respond resulting in long lasting reactions.

From this perspective people with emotion regulation problems who have suicidal, self-injurious and otherwise self-destructive behaviors have them as a result of maladaptive attempts to manage extreme emotions. People are inclined to develop problems with emotion regulation when problems occur with their biological vulnerability in response to an invalidating environment. This same transactional model may help us to understand some of the challenges with emotion regulation in the ID population as well.

Biological Vulnerability in Individuals Who Have ID

An extensive range of psychosocial conditions associated with ID may contribute to an individual's fragility. People can no longer be served at home or may endure loss of multiple out-of-home placements often-times not because of their ID, but because of a combination of disabilities including cognitive, behavioral, physical, medical, and so on. Such components of biological vulnerability associated with ID may result in sickness or extra attention due to early or repeated hospitalizations. Conditions associated with physical disabilities that may result in immobility or facial or body anomalies may exact additional emotional tolls from clients who are kept at a social distance from others as well. Those who live in the community, and thus are not kept at some social distance, may endure ridicule or teasing, thus resulting in further emotional strains.

The Invalidating Environment for Individuals Who Have ID

The characteristics of an invalidating environment according to DBT are three-fold. First, there is an indiscriminate rejection of the communication of private experience. Second, there is punishment of emotional displays and the intermittent reinforcement of emotional escalation. Third, there is an oversimplification of the ease of problem solving and the consequent meeting of goals. In this manner, individuals are not only unable to communicate their emotions, but any attempts they make are rejected and escalations are reinforced. Such individuals have great trouble at expressing their emotions in an effective manner and consequently do not learn to trust their own emotions, thus affecting their ability to solve everyday problems.

As pointed out in Lew, Matta, Tripp-Tebo, & Watts (2006) people with Intellectual Disabilities are at high risk for these components, though in somewhat different configurations than individuals with BPD. On many occasions we have observed caregivers making decisions despite their charges' complaints and protest. We have also seen low levels of protest neglected and invalidated until the client has created enough of a firestorm, sometimes in public, to make it impossible for caretakers to avoid. We have also seen caretakers wonder how seemingly capable clients are unable to solve a problem that they "should be able to solve." Client goals are left unmet, and the relationship with their caretaker suffers as the caretaker may determine they are doing something "for attention" or for some other simplistic reason.

As one might surmise, an invalidating environment can exist in many places. It can be in a family, a school, or perhaps a residence with particular stresses associated with each of those domains. False assumptions may occur when clients try to portray themselves as more capable than they are, something depicted in DBT as "apparent competence." This in turn may result in unreasonable expectations on the part of the caregiver who may unintentionally create a milieu that is invalidating. Invalidation can be observed in very loving but uninformed environments. One may notice invalidation in a number of different ways. First, people may use pejorative or judgmental language such as "she's manipulative" or "she just does it to get her way." Secondly, people may convey a dismissive or disregarding attitude that demeans the individual's independent decision, by perhaps not giving them important choices. Third, people may actually directly critique or punish a person's sharing of emotions as in saying "You don't really hate your sister because she is having a baby." Fourth, they may pathologize normative responses such as wanting a social life or to be more independent from one's loved ones. Under these conditions clinicians should not be surprised to find clients who do not have a great deal of confidence in their experiencing or sharing of their emotions.

Integrated Model

DBT is a therapeutic approach that, at its core, integrates three separate models. First is behavior therapy. DBT integrates the basic tenets and universal principles associated with behaviorism. Extrapolated from this model is the notion that we explicitly "target" problems with our clients and teach skills to our clients. There is attention to the management of environmental contingencies that influence a client and also with regard to the therapist's relationship with the client. In this manner there is a good deal of confluence of DBT with the "Functional Analytic" perspective of Kohlenberg & Tsai (1991). DBT also incorporates standard Cognitive Behavioral Therapy (CBT) approaches. Linehan's original text (Linehan, 1993a) explicates the role of cognitions, feelings, and action urges which lead to behaviors. There is a good deal of attention in DBT to generalization of skills to individual's natural supports. Ultimately the goal of the therapist is to provide "consultation to the patient" (Linehan, 1993a) so clients can eventually solve their own problems and manage their own natural supports. This makes it particularly compatible with many contemporary therapeutic approaches for individuals with ID.

A second "core" model for DBT is Zen practice. Zen is meant to balance the empirical valence of behaviorism. The "mindfulness" (e.g., Thich Nhat Hanh, 1975, Kabat-Zinn, 1990) module taught in DBT groups is one important aspect of this, but so are the attitudes and cognitions taught to therapeutic providers. "Clients are doing the best that they can" is a mantra that helps the therapist to not "blame the victim" and assists him/her in maintaining motivation for another day. In both teaching mindfulness as a skill and taking on the therapeutic role in DBT, the intention of "suspending judgment" looms large. Becoming mindfully aware of our own judgments as therapists ultimately helps us to become better therapists. Teaching our clients to become mindfully aware of their own judgments about others and often-times themselves enhances the quality of any behavior therapy they may receive. The mindfulness bell or "singing bowl" is a nice discriminative stimulus for paying attention to the moment and helps client and staff attendees to be fully aware that "mindfulness" is always present.

The third "core" model integrated in DBT is that of Dialectics. This represents an awareness of contradictions and an attempt to create a synthesis from opposing elements or forces. An example is the central dialectic of "acceptance and change." Behaviorism is full of "change" strategies that assist a client in addressing his/her problems; however, a client may not improve much if a change agent (therapist, parent, staff member) does not really "get" a client. In fact, many clients may "resist treatment" or even drop out if they do not feel accepted and validated by the change agent. Thus, to work on change, you must also work on acceptance. Dialectics in DBT guides its assumptions about the genesis/etiology of problems as in the interface of biological vulnerability and the invalidating environment, and it informs us about our goals and treatment strategies as well. Sometimes this leads us to question what is "missing" from our assessment of a situation. Additionally, it occasions us to look at and teach our clients to look at the "grays" rather than the black vs. white. With a client with ID this may lead us to looking for the "kernel of truth" in their complaint about their new roommate or to acknowledge that there may be more than one truth when a parent and an individual with ID play out a conflictual interchange during therapy.

A central dialectic that is present, for individuals with ID, is that of "Consultation to the Patient" vs. "Structuring the Environment." Consultation to the patient refers to the concept raised by Linehan that in DBT we are always trying to teach the client to fight his/her own battles, solve his/her own problems, and otherwise navigate skillfully within their own environments. Yet, she recognizes that in some populations clients may be unable to solve their problems independently or the outcome of the problem may be so important that one may not have an opportunity to exercise patience. Thus, there may be times when clinicians need to facilitate "Structuring of the Environment" in order to best serve their DBT/ID clients. An example of this was when one of my clients was on the verge of losing her apartment as a result of loud dysregulated behaviors and invitations to her home offered to "seedy" community members. The ideal would have been to allow her to negotiate directly with her landlord while using interpersonally effective strategies. My clinical knowledge of this client dictated that this would have been a poor idea that would have failed and resulted in her homelessness. Thus, I elected to participate in helping her to negotiate (by preparing her and attending the meeting with her), developing a clearer communication system from the landlord to her case manager, and developing a positive reinforcement based behavioral contract for following the rules negotiated at the meeting and practicing selective Interpersonal Effectiveness (primarily "GIVE") skills taught in DBT. The long term aim would be that in time, with increased skills as well as improved relationships, this client could eventually solve her problems more independently and with less input from support staff.

The Benefits of Providing DBT for Individuals with ID

There are a number of benefits of using the DBT model with individuals who have ID. These have previously been summarized in Lew et al. (2006). First, DBT represents a skills-based model that is consistent with psycho-educational and habilitative practice. For those of us who have worked within the ID field, this is familiar to us in that we often seek to teach replacement behaviors rather than simply remove, terminate, or otherwise punish behavior problems. Second, a focus of the Interpersonal Effectiveness skill module is to teach assertiveness and empowerment skills. These skills, along with a commitment to the "consultation to patient," help foster independence. Third, DBT is a fundamentally positive psychotherapy. There is an active attempt to teach our clients to suspend their judgments of themselves and others. Likewise, therapists using DBT are taught to "suspend their judgments" of their clients and families. In DBT there is also a value on not casting blame or speaking pejoratively. This is consistent with the anti-victimization and anti-stigmatization efforts that many members of the ID community are familiar with. Finally, emotionally dysregulated clients with ID present with a good deal of community risk and experience many complications in treatment. This highlights the question, "Why should individuals with ID be denied an effective treatment?" Whether someone has a genuine BPD diagnosis or is a multi-diagnostic difficult-to-treat client with ID and emotion regulation issues, that person is a significant challenge to his or her clinicians and team. Without available tools, we are left serving people who are often treatment resistant, can burn-out our provider network, and in some cases cause fractures in teams such that they can be split and ineffective. In summary, there can be a great incentive for us as providers to seek a treatment that is both compatible with our field and a considerable source of clinical optimism.

MODES OF THERAPY

Since the specific tenets, principles and procedures of DBT are presented in detail in Linehan's text (1993a) and work-book (1993b) this chapter will only offer a brief summary of its general approach along with more specific adjustments that clinicians might make for individuals with ID. DBT, according to Linehan (1993a), identifies four basic modes of therapy. These are: 1) Skills Groups, 2) Individual Therapy, 3) Coaching in Crisis, and 4) Consultation Team. As of this writing the data indicate that all of these modes are necessary in order to get the clinical improvements associated with DBT (Linehan, Heard & Armstrong, 1993) although there are some current studies which seek to differentiate the active agents in DBT. Thus, just doing skills groups is not considered enough to do DBT, nor is it considered DBT to conduct all the aspects of therapy without participation in a consultation team.

Skills Groups in DBT Overview

Change, that is behavior change, in DBT draws from the Zen concept of learning skillful means. Teaching skills within a group therapy context so that individuals can learn the skills they have never acquired or have not successfully practiced follows from this concept. Linehan (1993a) developed a manual which articulated the structure of the skills groups and the skill sets to be presented. A full description of the way the group is conceptualized can be obtained from the manual itself, but a brief summary of the general features is included here. First, there are both a skill presentation and a homework component. New skills are presented during skills presentation, whereas, the homework component is both a review and a check of client adherence to his/her practice of the skill outside of group. Second, a round of group sessions covers or does its best to cover all the sub-skills presented in the manual. This can be done in approximately 6 months or about 25 group sessionss at one per week. Standard DBT has people participate in two rounds of group sessions. Third, there are a number of group rules that are designed to help the therapist(s) stay on track while managing a difficult-to-serve population. The rules relate to dropping out after four missed appointments, staying in individual therapy while in group, not attending while under the influence, no sharing of war-stories, when asking or calling for help accepting the help offered, keeping information and names confidential, calling if late or not attending, no forming of private relationships, and no sexual partners in the group.

The DBT framework explicitly teaches skillful behaviors to replace problem behaviors for the BPD population. In effect cognitive dysregulation problems such as being overwhelmed or feeling empty are addressed through teaching Mindfulness skills. Interpersonal dysregulation deficits related to feelings of abandonment, loneliness, and interpersonal chaos are addressed with teaching interpersonal effectiveness skills. Emotional dysregulation problems associated with labile affect and excessive anger are addressed by teaching emotion regulation skills. Finally, behavioral dysregulation issues such as impulsive behavior, suicide threats, and self-injury are addressed through distress tolerance skills.

Groups are highly structured with an agenda based upon the skill is being taught that session. Group leaders are given some modest degree of discretion with regards to the teaching of the skill but the general framework typically includes a rationale for the skill, a presentation and elicitation of examples, a practice, role-play, and/or discussion within the group, and a homework assignment. Key targets for skills training are skill acquisition, skill strengthening, and skill generalization.

Skills Groups in DBT/ID

Providing therapeutic services within the ID community requires a good deal of attention to administrative pragmatics. Educating referral agents about who to refer is important as many may assume that only individuals with a diagnosis of BPD should be referred. Beginning with clients who may benefit from training in emotion regulation often is a good starting point. Additionally, it is of benefit if clients are willing to commit to the year of treatment. In the ID community, this may require a commitment beyond the client. Many individuals referred for services need rides. Many are dependent on support staff or families and thus dependent on the supporters' schedules. These parameters may be discussed during an orientation that may occur individually or in a group. Having an orientation session allows for there to be a provision of "informed consent" so that the client understands the program parameters, and any support personnel, for whom treatment is often dependent, can agree with them as well. This should allow for some discussion with clients and supporters about expectations and the rules when participating in DBT. It also allows for an opportunity to sign a commitment contract to stay in individual therapy, attend groups, and work on reducing risky behaviors for at least a one year period. Upon signing, group members receive personalized binders that hold their training materials and homework assignments that are distributed on a weekly basis.

One important way that our groups departed from the typical DBT model was through the inclusion of support staff and family members (i.e., supporters) in skills groups. Certainly there are reasons why this may not have been ideal. In particular we ran the risk of infantilizing our clients and not providing the "consultation to patient" approach defined by Linehan; however, on balance (see Table 1) this approach provided enough pragmatic advantages for the population that this was an adaptation we chose to make. Given that many clients in our population were poor informants and required multiple trials in order to learn conceptual and practical information, it was determined that a departure from traditional DBT groups was both necessary and advantageous. Probably the most important advantages incurred from this adaptation had to do with 1) the training of supporters who received a much better understanding of what their charges were learning and 2) the facilitation of generalization as supporters could help to prompt skills in the natural environment and improve adherence to homework and data collection routines. One might say that "supporters" participated in the group itself on an "as needed" basis. Usually, while members sat on the inside of the group supporters would sit on the outside and help to individualize group exercises when requested by group leaders.

Table 1. A Comparison of Skills Groups with and without Supporters in Attendance

Skills Group Comparison	With Supporters	Without Supporters
Confidentiality Concerns	Requires extra consents to account for families and staff in attendance	Only a consideration among the clients themselves
Administrative	Direct communication to families and staff facilitated by group attendance	May allow clients to be empowered and be the source of direct communication
Training	Attendees get a better understanding of philosophy and techniques in DBT	Separate trainings are needed to educate "supporters" about DBT
Terminology	Learning DBT expressions and terminology is facilitated and generalized by repetition and "supporter" participation	Use of DBT expressions less likely to be reinforced
Client Anxiety	Clients may be intimidated to speak in front of support staff or loved ones	Clients may give inaccurate information which can derail clinical work
Learning of Skills	May sustain dependence upon others as it may diminish from "consultation to patient"	Encourages more (initial) independence
Real World Generalization	May be facilitated to include better real life issues	Relies largely on clients who often can be inaccurate informants
Group Observation	Interactions among "supporters" and clients adds to clinical information	Interactions observed are only those with peers and group leaders
Homework	More reliably completed on a week by week basis	Often not completed without communication/reminders outside of group
Trouble-shooting	Misinterpretations of group content or process caught sooner	Client frustrations may arise from misinterpretations

Groups met once a week for 26 sessions. Each session lasted approximately 2-2.5 hours with homework review (30-45 minutes) preceding the skills presentation (60-75 minutes) with a (15-30 minute) finger food meal eaten in between. Since many individuals had jobs or were in vocational programs, the group was arranged for after-work hours. In questioning clients and "supporters," it was determined that once a week was more viable than trying to get clients to come twice a week.

Groups are ideally run with a leader and co-leader. The leader may be considered the agenda manager and is responsible for conveying the content to the group members for that week. The leader treats the group as a class, keeps a singular focus on the agenda, encourages everyone to take turns, uses concrete examples and exercises for instruction, and is responsible for presenting the next homework assignment. The co-leader may be considered more of the group process and behavior manager and seeks to be mindful of emotions on display, but tries to ignore therapy interference where possible, notices member improvements in the course of the group, role-models appropriate use of skills, sits near disruptive clients, helps redirect if necessary, plans in advance by speaking to clients between or before groups, and shares difficult problems for follow-up with the individual therapist. Given the often specialized funding, clinical considerations, and administrative systems for individuals with ID, it may be more likely that group therapists also do some individual DBT for clients in their groups. Though the traditional DBT model has different people in these roles, there can also be obvious advantages when they are the same person.

The sequence of groups with the number of groups for each module included in parenthesis were Introduction/Orientation (1) Mindfulness (2), Distress Tolerance (6), Mindfulness (2), Emotion Regulation (6), Mindfulness (2), Interpersonal Effectiveness (6), and Celebration (1) for a total of 26 groups. Although members initially signed up for a commitment of a year, most actually participated in three group repetitions over a year and a half. All groups begin with a mindfulness exercise, whether or not that is the skill on the agenda. For this purpose a simple, consistent, and repetitively taught exercise such as "Breathe-in, Breathe-out" for 1-3 minutes (see Table 2) is ideal. The format for the exercises follows that taught by Linehan and Behavioral Tech during their intensives and is used as a way of teaching colleagues and peers different mindfulness exercises. It may also be used as a template for teaching clients.

Table 2. "Breathe in – Breathe out"

Comments that would not be addressed to clients are printed in italics.
1. Goal – Today we are going to practice the skill of observing. We are going to focus on bringing our awareness to our breathing. The breath is always with you and is central to many therapies used in medical clinics. (*See for example Kabat-Zinn, 1990.*)
Learning to focus on your breath can help to anchor you in the present moment. Focusing on breathing usually has a calming effect.
2. Link to Personal Experience – In my training as a Psychologist, I was well versed in the use of "relaxation" therapies for anxiety disorders and the like and always thought of breathing techniques as synonymous with relaxation. From my study of DBT, I have learned that it is more far-reaching than that and use it not just for my clients but for myself as well.
3. Here's the Mindfulness-This mindfulness exercise works particularly well if practiced in group and also for homework in both non-stressed and stressed times.

continued next page

4. Give one thing to Practice – You will begin the exercise by just tuning in to the feeling of the breath coming in and out of your body. Just focus on your breathing and knowing your breathing. Today's exercise is an exercise we call "Breathe in- Breathe out."

• Get settled in a comfortable position

• Focus your attention on your breath

• Close your eyes if you are comfortable doing so (or focus on the floor)

• Say "in" to yourself as you inhale

• Say "out" to yourself as you exhale

• If you get distracted, gently bring yourself back to your breath and say "in" on the inhale and "out" on the exhale

5. Troubleshoot – The first few times you do breathing exercises you may feel silly or awkward. You may feel funny or silly while sitting in the group while breathing. That is all very normal. If you do feel silly or awkward, I want you to just notice that feeling and let it pass like a cloud passes in the sky. If you feel fidgety and uncomfortable and have the urge to talk or move around, that also is normal. Try and let those urges pass as well. Gently bring your attention back to your breath saying "in" on the inhale and "out" on the exhale.

6. Orient to the Bell – I will ring the mindfulness bell to begin the exercise. You will have about 3 minutes to focus on your breath. I will ring the bell, again, to signal the end of the exercise. So get settled in your chairs, close your eyes or find another place on the floor to focus, and take a moment to get centered on your breathing.

7. Ring the Bell

8. Process

Mindfulness is referred to as "Core Mindfulness" by Linehan as it is central to learning the other skills. It should be noted that other clinicians have had success with other mindfulness exercises with individuals who have ID (Singh, Wahler, Adkins & Myers, 2003). Mindfulness is taught first, interspersed in the training, and, especially for individuals with ID, integrated in other skill activities. For example, one might practice mindful breathing prior to doing an Interpersonal Effectiveness role-play. A more advanced mindfulness exercise that would be used in a second round of groups for clients with ID is included here as Table 3, "The Wise Mind Mentor." This mindfulness exercise works particularly well if each group member has a concrete description of his or her mentor expedited by a drawing exercise done in the previous group session. This exercise also links nicely with distress tolerance as it can be at the core of teaching someone how to wait when he or she is lonely.

Table 3. The "Wise-Mind Mentor"

Comments that would not be addressed to clients are printed in italics.
1. Goal- The goal of this mindfulness exercise is to help us focus on wise-mind. In this exercise we will get back to wise-mind by recalling a person in our life who represented wise-mind to us. Wise-mind could be represented by our grandparent who was always there to support us. It could be our parent. It could be a priest or rabbi or teacher. Undoubtedly, we all have someone.
2. Link to Personal Experience- This is an adaptation of a mindfulness exercise conducted by Dr. Ronald Alexander. He is a Buddhist psychologist who has arrived at the use of mindfulness after many years of study from a very spiritual orientation. On top of that we will hear a familiar song that you may find carries a different meaning than when you originally heard it.
3. Here's the Mindfulness- The first step is to identify someone from your life who represents wise-mind and write down his or her name. *[With our clients who have ID it is helpful to have them draw a picture or at least have a discussion with a supporter as to who a "Wise Mind Mentor" may be for them.]* Next, we are going to think of a dilemma that you have to make a decision in. It could be an interpersonal problem with your spouse, or your roommate, or your child. Or, it could be a problem in decision making, something like whether you should quit your job, move to another part of the country, etc… Pick your problem and write that down.
4. Give one thing to Practice- Start with your mindful (breathe-in breathe-out) diaphragmatic breathing. Let us do that for a couple of minutes. Get into your mindful place… Now, let's, visualize you with your "wise-mind mentor." Picture yourself being supported. Bring yourself to a place where you are sitting and get a clear picture of his or her face. Try to imagine your mentor with you. You and your mentor are in synch. In your minds you communicate. Let the mentor help you solve your problems. Try to envision how they would solve it, what he or she would say to you about your problem, and what he or she would communicate to support you. Imagine how your mentor looks, what he or she would say, what you would say. Now we are ready for the next phase of this mindfulness exercise. Breathe into your thoughts and feelings while you get this advice. In a moment I will be putting on a song (The Beatles, "Let it Be") that will be familiar to

continued next page

nearly all of you. Try to use this background music to help you expand on your visualization of your wise-mind mentor.
Now let's thank our wise-mind mentor and say "good-bye". We'll count backwards from 5... 4...3...2...1 and open your eyes (ring mindfulness bell).
5. Troubleshoot- If you are distracted, bring yourself back. Use your breath and the music to bring yourself back to the goal of this mindfulness exercise, which is to help you find your wise-mind mentor and allow you to solve your problem.
6. Orient to the Bell- We will ring the mindfulness bell to start the exercise and ring the bell to end the exercise.
7. Ring the Bell
8. Process

DBT for ID groups require increased attention to concrete, hands-on, and sensory- oriented activities. Groups began with the Linehan (1993b) workbook but would typically evolve into a combination of discussion, role-play, and 1:1 activities that clients actively participate in and relate to. It is essential for group members to provide examples from their everyday life pertaining to the agenda of the day. "Breaking out" into one-to-one sessions with the client's support may facilitate this, since some individuals may be less inclined to initiate in the large group. Fun engaging activities where there are concrete referents generally work well. In this clip, from the movie "Star Trek: The Wrath of Khan", three of the main characters display a wide range of emotional responses. Group members need to "observe" and "describe" the various crew members' emotions (See Table 4).

Table 4. The Use of Videos in Noticing Mindfulness

Comments that would not be addressed to clients are printed in italics.
1. Goal- The goal of this mindfulness exercise is to help us focus on the differences among Wise-Mind, Emotion-Mind and Reasonable-Mind. In this exercise we will watch a five-minute video from the movie Star Trek: The Wrath of Khan. Our objective is to watch the different characters and notice the different types of "mind states" that the characters demonstrate.
2. Link to Personal Experience- *Lots of our clients enjoy movies, and they often are familiar with ones that we may show in our groups. It is usually pretty easy to get discussion going, and video allows you to stop action and examine the nuances of people's emotions such as facial expression.*

continued next page

3. Here's the Mindfulness- Each of you should take a sheet of paper and write down three headings: *Wise-Mind, Emotion-Mind, and Reasonable-Mind.* You will recall that Reasonable-Mind is logical, full of thinking, and practically without emotion. Emotion-Mind is when your emotions take the lead with anger, anxiety, sadness or some other prominent emotion. It is full of intensity. Wise-Mind takes the best of both worlds by integrating thinking as well as emotion in helping people to manage their emotions and attend to their goals. As we watch this video note that each of the three primary characters (The Doctor, Kirk and Spock) represents one of these although at times they may show elements of more than one.

4. Give one thing to Practice-Jot down any examples of Wise-Mind, Emotion-Mind and Reasonable-Mind. Be sure to include *verbal and non-verbal behaviors.* The clip is about five minutes long and after the clip we will discuss the examples you observe and how you feel this might work for you.

5. Troubleshoot- If you are distracted, bring yourself back to the task. Use your breath and your paper assignment to help you get back to the mindfulness exercise at hand.

6. Orient to the Bell- We will ring the mindfulness bell to start the exercise and ring the bell to end the exercise.

7. Ring the Bell

8. Process

As one can see, there is a strong reliance on concrete and experiential tasks in communicating DBT concepts to individuals with ID. Adhering to the DBT model meant explaining each of the work-book exercises using pictures, role-plays, one-to one discussions, and other concrete learning experiences. There were occasions when there was insufficient time to cover all the material. This resulted in a clinical decision to, at times, continue with that skill the following week and spend less time on another or in some cases counting on clients having further opportunity to practice that skill in the second or third round of the groups.

We stressed fun because many people came to the groups with negative learning histories from school and other similar experiences. Yet others enjoyed the idea of calling it a "class." A good deal of attention was spent listening to the words and expressions that people used. When one of our clients preferred the use of "quiet mind" to "wise mind" that was fine. Though it was our intention to teach all of our clients all of the skills, it was more important to us if a client found a few selective skills that they could accept and use in their everyday lives and that truly had functional value for them.

The homework component of the group is done at the beginning of each session. It too begins with a brief mindfulness activity, generally only one minute of "Breathe-in

Breathe-out." The homework component is designed to reinforce the practice of the prior week's skill(s). Homework components provide an opportunity for the skills leaders to scan the client data sheets, which are called "Diary Cards." These are personalized, simplified, and pictorially enhanced versions of Linehans' self-monitoring system. Diary Cards (see Lew et al, 2006; Charlton & Dykstra, this volume) reflect data on a client's practice of skills initially and later include sample data on target behaviors identified for each client by the individual DBT therapist. Practice of skills learned in the group is shaped in a behavioral manner: practice is socially reinforced; practicing despite obstacles is reinforced; and independent practice is reinforced. If someone has not made an effort at their homework the following questions are then raised: "If you didn't practice then why not? What got in the way? And what will you do to practice this week?"

Individual Therapy in DBT Overview

The individual therapist in DBT is the person responsible for individually tailoring the DBT skills and a treatment plan based upon those skills to the client. Although sessions are commonly once a week for an hour, they may be more frequent at the initiation of treatment or with the need to address crises in a client's life. Linehan (1993a) refers to Stage 1 targets which are the primary targets involving behavioral control discussed in this chapter. The individual therapist maintains a focus on treatment priorities overall and session by session based on these targets. Behaviors of concern include (1) suicidal and life threatening behaviors (suicide and life-threatening crisis behaviors, self-injurious acts, changes in suicidal ideation and communications, suicide-related expectancies, and suicide-related affects), (2) therapy interfering behaviors (non-attending, non-collaborative, or non-adherence), and (3) quality of life interference (high risk or unprotected sex, extreme financial difficulties, criminal behaviors that may lead to jail, employment or school-related dysfunctionality, illness-related dysfunctional behaviors, and housing-related dysfunctional behaviors). Positive behaviors that are fostered include Mindfulness, Distress Tolerance, Emotion Regulation, and Interpersonal Effectiveness.

When multi-problem clients come to therapy they have often seen a multitude of previous therapists, most of whom do not practice DBT. They may come to unload and vent to their therapist and thereby guide their own session agendas. This is decidedly not DBT. Part of a therapist's role is to help orient the individual to DBT and how this differs from their previous therapy. This includes teaching the individual about biosocial theory and partnering with the individual to "get a life worth living."

Linehan refers to the flow of individual therapy in DBT as "jazz" in that it is an ongoing interaction between the dialectic of acceptance and change. The therapist is constantly assessing the need to validate individuals in the service of getting them to change or accept change strategies such as those used in behavior therapy or cognitive behavior therapy. At its core, validation can only be beneficial if the client views it as validating from their vantage point. Consequently, the therapist has a responsibility to validate at relevant and meaningful times. Linehan stresses always exercising a non-judgmental stance by listening for the "kernel of truth" in clients' words and behaviors as this orientation allows us to sustain a more validating perspective. For the validating therapist this may include: 1) staying awake by providing unbiased listening and observing, 2) accurately reflecting, 3) articulating the un-verbalized emotions, thoughts, and behavior patterns, 4) validating in terms of past learning or biology, 5) validating in terms of present context or norm, and 6) demonstrating radical genuineness.

The DBT therapist needs to be well schooled in standard behavior therapy and cognitive behavior therapy as there is an unrelenting focus on the hierarchy of targets. Therapists utilize their knowledge of learning principles (see e.g., Pryor, 2002) in order to provide psycho-education for their clients and are aware of systemic behavioral influences such as the therapist him/herself, the family, support staff, or hospital units. The individual therapist is continually in assessment mode, thinking through prompting events (antecedents), thoughts, emotions, action urges, and behaviors and the short term and long term consequences to those behaviors. These are graphically displayed in behavioral chain analyses which are done when clients perform behaviors of particular concern.

Additionally, the DBT therapist never assumes that, just because a client has committed to the treatment initially, the client's commitment is unwavering. In essence, there is always a recommitment process which identifies sources of motivation for staying in the treatment by committing to "a life worth living", all the required modes of treatment (group, individual, and coaching), and particular aspects of an individual plan as clinically indicated.

Also of great importance is the fact that there is recognition that a DBT therapist is at high risk of burn-out. Therapists working with multi-diagnostic/multi-problem clients can have great struggles with their own therapy-interfering behaviors that result in excesses in therapeutic acceptance or change orientation, excesses in flexibility or rigidity, excesses in nurturing or withholding behavior, or judgmental and invalidating behavior. To this end, therapists in DBT are required to participate in a consultation team that supports therapists in maintaining the DBT framework and an overall nonjudgmental stance. This will be further discussed in a separate section.

Individual Therapy in DBT/ID

Generally DBT/ID clients are seen once a week for an hour, but some flexibility may be indicated for people who can best benefit from shorter, more frequent sessions. One may conceptualize the DBT/ID therapist in a number of key roles: 1) Team Leader, 2) Clinical Individualizer, 3) Skills Coach, and 4) Cheerleader.

The individual therapist has to assume responsibility for clinically knowing the client. The therapist needs to take the lead in getting information from the client, from the skill group therapists, from the family, from the support staff, from the school or vocational program, and from any other augmentative service such as hospital or psychiatry. While staying within the DBT frame, all attempts should be made to maintain the "consultation to patient" and make the client the center of communication; however, the therapist should pay attention to the need for reasonably accurate communication among providers. Holding team members accountable while still maintaining a non-judgmental stance that "they are each doing the best that they can" is often beneficial. The therapist may also identify training needs. For example trainings in "biosocial theory" or "validation" may be especially beneficial to families and support staff. Individualized trainings on a particular client's DBT treatment plan may be especially well received by emergency services staff or hospital staff.

The therapist makes it a priority to clinically individualize the treatment for a client. The therapist should be well aware of the client's values, wishes and goals and help the client to see how his or her dysregulated emotions are getting in the way of these goals. The therapist should be aware of and in many cases writes or participates in the writing of treatment plan goals for the client. Table 5 is a sample Individual DBT Treatment Plan that can serve as a template. The client depicted in the Individual DBT Treatment Plan is a compilation of a number of "real" clients who have gone through DBT/ID. She is a 30 year old emotionally dysregulated woman who lives with five adult relatives including her mother, two sisters, and a mentally ill brother with Bipolar Disorder. The woman has a long history of hospitalization leading to periods of disappearance after running away from her home following incidents of interpersonal conflict. She has half-hour tantrums that can anger her family and her neighbors. She sometimes hoards and subsequently overdoses on prescribed psychotropic medication although her last incident of this was last year. The therapist also uses the client's self-monitoring Diary Card to assess both the skill implementation and the behavioral target frequency and intensity. In this client's case, she frequently loses her card so two copies are kept, one by her sister. This client has frequently been talked into giving money away to a family member. It has been identified that she needs to learn and use both Mindfulness skills ("Wise –Mind" and "Effectively") and Interpersonal Effectiveness skills. Practice of these skills has specifically been put on her Diary Card as has the negative target of "gave money away." In this case the client was first exposed to these skills in group, and then the individual therapist did repetition of role plays in which they each played the family member and the client. The group skills trainers present general information and may even provide some 1:1 opportunities and instruction, but the individual therapist negotiates, instructs, and role-plays with the client so he or she may practically use DBT skills in his/her everyday life.

Table 5. Individual DBT Treatment Plan

ASSESSMENT	
Target Behaviors:	
Life Threatening Behaviors	Runs away from home in "panic" state. (Missing for hours at a time.) ODs on prescribed medicines.
Therapy Interfering Behaviors	Cheeks and hoards medicine. Overcalls sister when client is alone thereby angering a primary caretaker.
Quality of Life Interfering Behaviors	Gives money away to family members. Tantrums (1x per week) for a ½ hour period.
Commitment: What is the person's current commitment to decrease the target behavior? What is the commitment to using DBT strategies? What is the commitment to their current treatment plan?	
Committed to a life worth living. Wants to improve relationships with family. Attends individual therapy reliably and group 75% of the time.	
Contingencies: What influences, maintains, strengthens, or reinforces the problem behaviors? And what weakens or decreases the problem behavior?	
Running away, ODs, tantrums are escape behaviors from interpersonal conflict. Giving money away is arguably also escape in that the relative leaves (temporarily).	
Antecedents: What sets off the problem behavior? What precipitates or triggers the problem behavior.	
Day-to-day conflict with her sister lead to thoughts of "vengeance" by hoarding meds ("I'll get her back"). Inability to say 'no' to family member asking for money directly leads to tantrums and sometimes runaway behavior.	

continued next page

Treatment Plan	
Skills:	
Mindfulness	Identify description of a "Wise Mind Mentor" for use during panic.
Emotion Regulation	Identify a thermometer of emotions (0-100)
Distress Tolerance	Identify pros and cons of hoarding meds. Use Distress Tolerance – self soothing box at 70+ on thermometer of emotions or when feeling lonely.
Interpersonal Effectiveness	Use "DearMan" to effectively say 'no' to family member who asks for money.
DBT Treatment Strategies: What additional DBT treatment strategies will be utilized, in order to decrease target behaviors and address specific antecedents?	
Commitment	Check in to reiterate commitment to each new strategy. Brings in Diary Card to therapy routinely.
Contingencies: reinforcers, shaping, exposure	Have client practice "DearMan" with sister before using it on other family member.
Chain Analysis	Review options client can do at 50/70/90 on thermometer.
Validation Strategies: What communicates that the person's responses are understandable in a particular situation?	Provide training to sister on validation (in group or 1:1).

continued next page

Structuring the Treatment Plan	
Individual Therapy	DBT-trained
Psychiatry	Seen for psychopharmacology 1 time per month. Stable. Let MD know about client's involvement in DBT.
In-patient	One time in last two years. Follow-up if individual has repeat hospitalizations.
Emergency/Crisis Management	Crisis team may benefit from invitation to case conference, sharing of treatment plan and possible training.
Case Management	May benefit from invitation to case conference and sharing of treatment plan.
Day Treatment/Programming	Client is stable at part-time job.
Other (Sister)	Attends family counseling one time per month along with client. Benefits from invitation to group, case conference, and training in validation.
DBT Coaching in Crisis Plan	

Sister will first prompt client to use Distress Tolerance self-soothing box. If client hasn't calmed, client will call individual therapist. Individual therapist will coach client for up to fifteen minutes in mindfulness (the "Wise Mind Mentor"). If individual therapist is unavailable or if still not calm after fifteen minutes, the client will call the crisis team. The crisis team will prompt the client to use her "Wise Mind Mentor" to regulate her emotions. The crisis team will monitor the client and have her screened in person if she is not in control.

The individual therapist considers review of a client's diary card an important source of data. The individual therapist tries to get clients to take responsibility for the diary card, but the therapist needs to be pragmatic about whether it will be repeatedly lost or left alone without being filled out. Initially the diary card may include skills practiced within the group such as using breathing mindfulness or using "gentle" speech in the "Give" Interpersonal Effectiveness skill. Then selective negative DBT targets that correspond with life-threats, therapy interference, or quality of life interference are added. These might include things like threats to hurt others who live in the group home, taking medications reliably, and interpersonal (over)reactions with other members of the community. Diary cards are updated regularly (perhaps every 3-6 months) but it's important to make sure the cards or their data collection doesn't get too complicated as this may lower adherence to its use. Having 3-5 positive and negative behaviors gives the clinician lots of information and an opportunity to match a replacement DBT skill for the client's repertoire. Sometimes the clinician waits until a client learns a skill such as "Self Soothing" through the senses in group. Sometimes clinicians teach and facilitate practice of a skill even if the group is not getting to it for months. This depends of the clinician's assessment of what the client may need at that point in time.

A very important tool is that of the behavioral chain analysis (See Figure 1). This is a grid of antecedents, behaviors, and consequences that is used to illustrate what triggers thoughts, emotions, action urges, or behaviors and in turn what results from them. Figure 1 represents a graphic tool that may be used along with the Individual DBT Treatment Plan to formulate, update, communicate, and evaluate clinical outcomes. During therapy sessions mini-chains are done for the most egregious behaviors. For example, a clinician may discuss a client's overdosing on prescription medicine with them, look at the prompting events involving family pressure feelings of invalidation, anxiety, and frustration using a thermometer of emotions which at "70" is indicative of where this client sees herself moving from "wise mind" into "emotion mind." The clinician also "chains" the consequences of a particular behavior(s) such as going into a hospital unit which may at the same time have both positive (escape) and negative (shame, loss of independence, and family disapproval) outcomes. Clients respond to simple displays, often with pictures included to facilitate receptive communication. If clients have sufficient insight to see it may not be in their interest to continue the same behaviors, they can be prompted to examine choices of DBT skills they have to disrupt the chain.

Figure 1. Behavioral Chain Analysis

Vulnerability Factors Precipitating Events Prompting Events	Problem Behavior(s)	Consequences Aftereffects
Hx: invalidation: • "People don't listen to me anyways" • ("Some people get away with taking advantage of me by taking my money") Lives with large family all with their own agenda Not competent at getting point across verbally Identify when at 70 on the DBT emotion thermometer	Overcalls sister when alone Gives money away to mentally ill family member Tantrums (1/2 hour x 1 week) Running away behavior (1 x month) Cheeks and hoards meds (1 x year) OD's on prescribed meds (1x year)	Sister gets angrier and is perceived as even more invalidating. Feels demoralized…Stops him from, badgering her Behaviors place client at risk in community when she disappears (leading family to limit independence)

Emotional Dysregulation

DBT Skills	**DBT Skills**	**DBT Skills**
Role-play sessions with sister practicing "Dear Man." Do validation training for sister. Teach "Wise mind mentor."	Use "Distress Tolerance Self-Soothing 'box' at 70 on Emotion thermometer. Focus on tolerating loneliness.	Clarify coaching in crisis plan with family and crisis team. Contact the hospital (if necessary) to encourage skillful means.

Coaching in Crisis in DBT Overview

Coaching in Crisis is another mode of therapy in DBT. Clients who are referred for DBT services have frequent and intense escalations and as a result may present as in crisis, unsafe, or even in need of a higher level of care. The coaching in crisis mode allows clients to be coached after phoning or otherwise requesting help at the time of need. In Linehan's (1993a) model the typical coach is the individual DBT therapist who helps the client focus on "affect tolerance" by managing the individual's negative mood or anxiety state through the use of skillful means. Such practice allows for the generalization of skills outside of the therapeutic group or individual session and therefore provides a very practical learning opportunity for the client. Linehan stresses that the client needs to make the crisis request or phone-call in response to a negative emotion or action urge, but prior to the display of any risky behavioral act. Coaching in crisis requires a set of guidelines or rules that clients adhere to that encourage the use of skills but do not serve to burn out the therapist. Included in such rules are teaching that venting is not the purpose of coaching, that people who ask for help need to follow through with therapist suggestions, and that crisis sessions only last a predetermined period of time such as ten or fifteen minutes. Should clients engage in risky behaviors then normal channels such as police or ER will be used. Therapists also engage in a "24-hour no-contact" rule if a client does not follow through with these guidelines. It is important that the therapist observes his/her own personal limits about such calls or visits such as only taking calls between 3-5:00 pm, so as not to be overwhelmed by excessive coaching requests.

Coaching in Crisis in DBT/ID

For practical purposes there are a range of providers within the ID system who may be involved in coaching clients at times of need. A grid which looks at the various coaching providers as well as strategies and caveats germane to their roles is included in Table 6.

Table 6. Strategies and Caveats for Providers using Coaching in Crisis for DBT/ID

Provider	Strategies	Caveats
Individual Therapist	Collaborate with other therapists (e.g., group) to share pager or crisis hours while observing personal limits using scheduled as well as pre-emptive calls. Help include and make other team members aware of DBT coaching in crisis plan.	Observe limits as a therapist so as not to "burn out."
Supporters (support staff and families)	Receive specialized training on validation and client's DBT coaching plan. Encourage and plan for "user friendly" options such as a "Self Soothing Distress Tolerance" box in the home. Participate in development of and receive a copy of DBT coaching plan.	Be aware that many supporters are already "burned-out" and may find it hard to be validating. Become aware of the invalidating nature of statements like "just use your skills."

— *continued next page* —

Emergency Personnel (ER, crisis-line, crisis-team)	Receive specialized training on client's DBT coaching plan as well as a summarized copy of the plan. Alert them to "consultation to patient" needs.	Be aware that emergency personnel roles may not always allow them to practice DBT (e.g., to sit with emotion in a time of crisis).

The individual therapist him/herself may be part of a team that runs skills groups or otherwise provides services. In such cases the coaching load may be shared. In our system (Lew et al., 2006) 3-4 clinicians shared a pager that they held for a week at a time for anywhere from 8-16 clients. On average, a crisis phone-call was fielded every 1-2 days. For individuals who called frequently, plans were developed to call clients proactively and to schedule pre-determined times to speak. In extreme cases, when clients called as many as a dozen times, they were briefly put on "vacation" by their therapist who clarified this behavioral contingency. This occurred with one individual who only wanted to speak to "her" therapist and not whoever was on-call. After a brief "vacation" she learned that the rules were to accept help from whoever answered. She both learned to practice her requisite skill (in her case "mindfully breathing") and reduce her crisis calling as a result.

In many cases individuals with ID live with family members or in staff-supported settings. Such "supporters" may be the first line of defense in crisis coaching. It was found to be very helpful to include these individuals in the development of a DBT crisis plan as part of their behavior planning process. In so doing, extra attention should be paid to training such "supporters" in validation skills so as to limit the potential of a "just use your skills" response that clients may perceive as dismissive and demeaning. We had particularly good luck preparing "self-soothing distress tolerance boxes" which were personally chosen to include stimulating and sensory items that clients may elect to use at times of stress and crisis. These could sometimes serve as a mindful option for clients when they are particularly stressed and need such options to prevent further crisis. It is also beneficial for the supporters and the various crisis team members to be aware of this option as well. This sometimes serves as a successful alternative behavior and interrupts further escalation. Sample items selected for these boxes are included in Table 7.

Table 7. Sample items helpful for creating "Self-soothing Distress Tolerance" boxes for Individuals with ID

Sense	Items for use
Taste	gum, hard candy, chewy candy, tic tacs, breath strips, mints, spicy tea
Touch	soft stuffed animal, rabbit foot, rubber bands, lotion, koosh ball, stress ball, bubble wrap, putty, modeling clay, smooth rocks
Smell	potpourri, scented candles, essences
Vision	coloring sheets, peaceful pictures and photos, animal photos, slinkees, lava-lamps, reading books or magazines, video-games, movies
Hearing	calming music, dance CD's, mindfulness (CD) exercises
Other Activity	word finds, crosswords, sudokus, journals, phone numbers (of supports)

There are times that supporters need to observe their own limits in managing a crisis and either alert the on-call therapist themselves or encourage the client to contact them directly.

Finally, in many systems crisis personnel including emergency rooms, hotlines, and crisis teams are involved. Such individuals welcome specialized training and discussion with regard to this population though it helps to do this at their site. They are invariably interested in what works for a particular client and appreciate a brief summary of a coaching strategy (e.g., Table 5) in advance. By speaking with crisis personnel and alerting them to the plan, clients are encouraged to deal directly with emergency workers. Gradually, a number of individuals can be coached to "effectively" converse with ER personnel and to inform them of the skills the individual could use rather than enter another level of care.

Consultation Team in DBT Overview

The Consultation Team is a core mode of DBT because it serves to keep clinicians on track with their use of DBT. As difficult as the clientele is, clinicians are challenged to stay within the therapeutic stance. The team is present to support the therapist, plan and trouble-shoot their treatment, monitor their adherence to the model, ensure clinician progress and competence, consult with the therapist on system issues, and support the therapist when his/her limits are stretched.

A typical consultation team meets weekly and includes clinicians or personnel who are using DBT. Meetings commonly begin with a rotating mindfulness practice and have an agenda that includes addressing life-threatening behaviors and serious treatment interference or burn-out issues as well as a specific DBT topic. Other agenda items may relate to a review of programmatic concerns, successes or challenges in skills group progress, specific case consultation with the clinician, and training or systems implementation issues.

Participating in the consultation team implies a commitment to improving one's DBT skills as well as an acknowledgement of the vulnerability that we as clinicians experience in servicing particularly stressful clients. The consultation team agreements are: 1)to accept Dialectical philosophy, that there is no absolute truth, 2)to consult with the client on how to interact with other therapists and not to tell other therapists how to interact with the client, 3)to accept that consistency of therapists with one another (even with the same client) is not necessarily expected, 4)that all therapists are to observe their own limits, 5)to search for non-pejorative, phenomenologically empathic interpretation's of client's behavior, and 6)to agree that all therapists are fallible.

Consultation Team in DBT/ID

Depending on administrative structures, a consultation team in ID may include clinicians, residential supports, administrators, case managers, emergency workers, hospital representatives, or other service providers. Cross agency clinical networking can be very beneficial for "complicated-to-serve" clients. Various system roles may be included to enhance the knowledge of DBT in general and client needs in particular. This may depend on the configuration of professionals who address the needs of the DBT/ID clinical community. The author has been part of various consultation teams in ID, one which included only clinicians, another which crossed clinical and residential teams with all attendees dealing with the ID population, another which met more intermittently but included interagency clinicians all of whom had some DBT/ID clients and system involvement, and another of DBT/ID professionals conducted through video-conferencing with 4-5 teams of people connected through the Internet. Each of these models serves a purpose in supporting the clinicians and the practice of DBT/ID in the community.

It is particularly important that the consultation team be a warm, welcoming, and non-judgmental meeting. Participants need a nurturing environment in order to share their concerns about their clients and their worries as clinicians.

DISCUSSION

Though it was originally developed for a non-ID population with Borderline Personality Disorder, DBT is also a useful therapy for multi-diagnostic, emotionally dysregulated, and complicated-to-serve individuals who have ID. DBT offers clinicians working with this population an adoptable clinical model for teaching clients how to regulate their emotions and behavior. Various adaptations such as the inclusion of "supporters" in group skill training, an Individualized DBT Treatment Plan, and systems planning considerations may be indicated for serving individuals with ID, but these adaptations can readily occur while adhering to the principles of DBT.

Being able to stay in the DBT frame is always a challenge for clinicians. These are clients who require extraordinary effort and clinical resources and as a result clinicians are consistently threatened with burnout. Clinicians benefit from the rich support offered within the consultation team. The "Zen" concepts help each clinician to "stay in the moment" while managing his/her own reactions and transference issues.

There are several applications of DBT for individuals with ID that are being studied currently, all of which point to promising results with the population. Undoubtedly more data with these adapted curricula and techniques will clarify its usage.

REFERENCES

Barlow, D. & Durand, M. (2009). *Abnormal psychology; An integrative approach.* Belmont, CA: Wadsworth-Cengage.

Comtois, K., Koons, C., Kim, S., Manning, S., Bellows, E., & Dimeff, L. (2007). Implementing standard outpatient dialectical behavior therapy in an outpatient setting. In L. Dimeff & K. Koerner (Eds.), *Dialectical behavior therapy in clinical practice* (pp. 37-68).New York: The Guilford Press.

Dimeff, L., & Koerner, K. (Eds.). (2007). *Dialectical behavior therapy in clinical practice.* New York: The Guilford Press.

Eaton, L. & Menolascino, F. (1982) Psychiatric disorders in the mentally retarded: Types, problems, and challenges. *American Journal of Psychiatry, 139,* 1297-1303.

Fruzetti, A., Santisteban, D., & Hoffman, P. (2007). Dialectical behavior therapy with families. In L. Dimeff & K. Koerner (Eds.), *Dialectical Behavior Therapy in clinical practice* (pp. 222-244).New York: The Guilford Press.

Hanh, Thich Nhat (1975). *The miracle of mindfulness: A manual on meditation.* Boston: Beacon Press.

Hayes, S., Strosahl, K., & Wilson, K. (1999). *Acceptance and commitment therapy.* New York: The Guilford Press.

Jacobson, J. (1993) The prevalence of mental illness in the mentally retarded. In *Proceedings of the International Congress on the Dually Diagnosed.* Boston.

Kabat-Zinn, J. (1990). *Full catastrophe living: Using the wisdom of your body and mind to face stress, pain and illness.* New York: Delta.

Kohlenberg, R. & Tsai, M. (1991). *Functional analytic psychotherapy.* New York: Plenum Press.

Levitas, A. (1993) Toward the connections between the unique genetic mechanism of the Fragile-X syndrome and its psychiatric phenotype. In *Proceedings of the International Congress on the Dually Diagnosed*. Boston.

Lew, M., Matta, C., Tripp-Tebo, C., & Watts D. (2006). Dialectical behavior therapy (DBT) for individuals with intellectual disabilities: A program description. *Mental Health Aspects of Developmental Disabilities, 9(1),* 1-12.

Linehan, M. (1993a). *Cognitive behavioral treatment of borderline personality disorder.* New York: The Guilford Press.

Linehan, M. (1993b) *Skills Training manual for treating borderline personality disorder.* New York: The Guilford Press.

Linehan, M., Heard, H., & Armstrong, H., (1993). Naturalistic follow-up of behavioral treatment for chronically para-suicidal borderline patients. *Archives of General Psychiatry, 50,* 971-974.

Linehan, M., Schmidt, H., & Dimeff, L. (1999). Dialectical behavior therapy for patients with borderline personality and drug dependence. *American Journal of Addiction, 8,* 279-292.

Lynch, T. & Cheavens, J. (2007). Dialectical Behavior therapy for depression and co-morbid personality disorder (pp.264-297). In L Dimeff & K. Koerner (Eds.), *Dialectical Behavior Therapy in Clinical Practice* New York: The Guilford Press.

McCann, R, Ivanoff, A., Schmidt, H., & Beach, B. (2007). Implementing dialectical behavior therapy in residential forensic settings with adults and juveniles. In L Dimeff & K. Koerner (Eds.), *Dialectical behavior in clinical practice* (pp. 112-144). New York: The Guilford Press.

Miller, A., Rathus, J., DuBose, A., Dexter-Mazza, E. & Golgklang, A. (2007). Dialectical behavior therapy for adolescents. In L. Dimeff & K. Koerner (Eds.), *Dialectical behavior therapy in clinical practice*(pp. 245-263). New York: The Guilford Press.

Ost, L. (2008). Efficacy of the third wave of behavioral therapies: A systematic review and meta-analysis. *Behavior Research and Therapy, 46(3),* 296-321.

Pary, R., Loschen, E., & Tomkowiak, S. (1996). Mood disorders and Down syndrome. *Seminars in Clinical Neuropsychiatry, 1(2),* 148-153.

Pryor, K. (2002). *Don't shoot the dog: The new art of teaching and training.* Glouchestershire: Ringpress.

Reynolds, S., Wolbert, R., Abney-Cunningham, G., & Patterson, K. (2007) Dialectical behavior therapy for assertive community treatment teams (pp. 298-325). In L. Dimeff & K. Koerner (Eds.), *Dialectical Behavior Therapy in Clinical Practice.* New York: The Guilford Press.

Singh, N., Wahler, R., Adkins, A., & Myers, R.E. (2003). Soles of the feet: A mindfulness based intervention for aggression by an individual with mild mental retardation and mental illness. *Research in Developmental Disabilities, 24,* 158-169.

Swenson, C., Witterholt, S., & Bohus, M. (2007). Dialectical behavior therapy on in-patient units (pp. 69-111). In L. Dimeff & K. Koerner (Eds.), *Dialectical behavior therapy in clinical practice*. New York: The Guilford Press.

Verhoeven, M. (in press). Journeying to wise mind: Dialectical behavior therapy and offenders with an intellectual disability. In L.A. Craig, K.D.Browne & W.R.Lindsay (Eds.), *Assessment and treatment of sexual offenders with intellectual disabilities: A handbook*. New York: Wiley & Son.

Williams M., Teasdale J., Segal Z., & Kabat-Zinn J. (2007). *The mindful way through depression*. New York: The Guilford Press.

Chapter 3

Positive Psychology for Persons with Intellectual or Developmental Disabilities

Daniel J. Baker, Ph.D.
E. Richard Blumberg, Ph.D.

INTRODUCTION

In this chapter, we will describe Positive Psychology and note the contributions that Positive Psychology offers to support for people with the dual diagnoses of an Intellectual or Developmental Disability and a Mental Illness. We will consider the many parallels between dual diagnosis supports and Positive Psychology and will present illustrative case studies. In considering these points, we will illustrate some historical factors in disability support that make Positive Psychology uniquely well-suited to applications for persons with Intellectual or Developmental Disability and Mental Illness.

LITERATURE REVIEW

Positive Psychology is a branch of psychological inquiry that focuses on the experience of positive emotion and the role of healthy emotions in daily life (Seligmann, Steen, Park, & Peterson, 2005). Psychology as a whole has been criticized as a field in which illness is studied rather than wellness. Negative emotions typically have been the unit of analysis rather than positive emotions. Positive Psychology researchers have amassed data to show that therapeutic interventions based on positive emotion can produce rapid improvements in mental health (Seligmann et al.).

While consideration of positive emotion has been a feature of psychology for quite some time (Rogers, 1951), Positive Psychology has gained increasing attention in recent years. Due to the accumulation of empirical data, the appeal of the philosophy, and the simplicity of interventions, significant public attention has been given to Positive Psychology, culminating in a 2005 cover story in *Time Magazine* about Positive Psychology entitled, "The Science of Happiness" (Wallis, 2005). While *Time*

Magazine may not be known for its focus on empirical science, it is a measure of the appeal and effectiveness of Positive Psychology. Positive Psychology offers many proven interventions and provides significant resources for the study of positive emotion (Linley & Joseph, 2004). *Character Strengths and Virtues: A Handbook and Classification* (Peterson & Seligman, 2004) provides a categorization of the traits that are seen as contributing to happiness. Interestingly, the traits have been shown to be replicated across cultures, suggesting that there is a commonality in human experience. This echoes the cross-cultural research that led to the Wellness Scale entitled "What is right with your life?" (Cannon, 1997). Critically, this research directs us to empirically validated interventions that improve positive emotion and reduce negative symptomatology (Seligmann et al., 2005). For example, one proven intervention is an exercise in which research participants were asked to write down three things that went well and the causes for those things every night for one consecutive week. The focus on strengths in Positive Psychology mirrors a similar movement in the study of supports for persons with disabilities, which will be detailed briefly in the next section of this chapter.

THEORETICAL FOUNDATION OF DISABILITY SUPPORTS

The philosophy and theoretical underpinnings of supports for persons with Intellectual or Developmental Disabilities (IDD) have changed dramatically in recent years. Prior to the 20th Century, there were few services for persons with developmental disabilities, but there were few specialized services for any person. As civilizations and cultures began to include specialized professions and areas of learning, resources for persons with a disability began to emerge. Some examples include the Oral School for the Deaf established by Samuel Heinicke in 1755; the Massachusetts Asylum for the Blind (later renamed the Perkins School for the Blind) opened in 1832 by Samuel Gridley Howe, who in 1984 established the first residential instructional and training program for "idiotic" children; and the establishment of special education classes by the State of New Jersey in 1911. Each of these "places" in which persons with disabilities lived or were educated was created based on the perspective that the individual had a deficit of some sort, and a "place" was created where that person could have that deficit addressed or somehow ameliorated. In a similar vein, institutions and therapies were developed to ameliorate psychological problems.

The growth in services and supports for persons with disabilities created an impetus for the creation of a class of professionals working in this burgeoning industry. A science of habilitation and rehabilitation was established. The National Committee for Mental Hygiene was founded in 1909. Additionally, the rehabilitation of injured veterans drove systemic improvements. In 1918, the Smith-Sear Veterans Vocational Rehabilitation Act authorized the Federal Board for Vocational Education for World War I veterans who had acquired disabilities during combat or other military service, putting significant federal funds behind rehabilitation and thus creating rehabilitation professionals and governmental systems. Once again, the rehabilitation practices and sciences were developed in order to address a deficit within the person, occurring congenitally or occurring during a person's lifetime.

A theme throughout all of these systemic improvements has been the identification of some type of deficit, labeled a disability, and then the creation of services to address or ameliorate that disability. This philosophy of support necessitated the creation of different groups of professional, best practices, and skill areas (Benjamin, 1989). Different institutions were established for people with different types of disabilities, and different training programs were created in which professionals could learn the technologies for each. Professional journals were established, such as *Journal of Psycho-asthenics* (1912) with its lead article, "A revision of the Simon-Binet system for measuring the intelligence of children" (Kuhlmann, 1912), and the book *Mental Defectives: Their history, treatment, and training* published in 1904 (Barr, 1904).

In more recent times, however, the philosophy of support has shifted away from the identification of a deficit and the subsequent design of interventions to address that weakness. An essential concept in the development of the support paradigm is the principle of normalization. First articulated by Bengt Nirje of Sweden, the idea was brought to the United States in the 1960's by Wolf Wolfensberger. Nirje (1985) proposed that normalization meant making available to all persons with disabilities, regardless of the severity of their disability, patterns of life and conditions as similar to, or the same as, those experienced by non-disabled individuals.

In the mid 1980's, the broad realization emerged that with appropriate supports, even people with significant disabilities can live and be fully included in the activities of their community (Lakin & Bruininks, 1985; O'Brien, 1989). This concept was informed by the Independent Living movement (DeJong, 1979; NCIL, 2009) and reinforced by the enactment in 1990 of the landmark Americans with Disabilities Act which mandated that accommodations be made by community entities such as schools, businesses, and public transportation to ensure people with disabilities enjoy their full rights as citizens.

Supports for persons with IDD have switched to an approach in which a person's strengths are identified, and the strengths and interests become the focus of support for the person, rather than focusing on the deficits, which are often difficult to change in persons with IDD. Consider as an example employment supports for persons with IDD. Previously, if a person was identified as having IDD, often, the individual spent a significant part of his or her work life in a place where other persons with IDD went to work. The person was deemed unemployable in the general community and went to a sheltered workshop (Close, Sowers, Halpern, & Bourbeau, 1985). In supported employment, the focus instead is on finding what the person is good at and what the person wants to do, and then locating an employment position in the community where the person's work abilities will contribute to an employer's business (Nisbet & Hagner, 1988). While the concept of supported employment has not changed work life for all persons with IDD, a sizable number of persons with IDD are employed in community (Larson, Lakin, & Huang, 2003). With recreation for persons with IDD, rather than noting that a person has IDD and then enrolling the person in a specialized recreation program, the question would be what types of recreation does the person enjoy, and how can the person access those kind of activities in the community.

In no way does this approach to disability supports ignore the presence of a disability, but the starting question changes. It is no longer, "what is wrong with you and where do we send you to get you fixed." The question is "what do you want to do, what are you good at, and how do we figure out how to access it." Accessing the community site becomes an issue of teaching the individual with IDD requisite skills and creating proper, necessary accommodations. Note the tremendous degree of overlap with positive psychology, which asks the same kinds of questions.

There are many methods of asking the initial questions about what a person is good at and what a person wants to do. The strategies for accomplishing this are often referred to as methods for "Person-centered Planning." O'Brien and O'Brien (1998) provide an excellent overview of different methods of person-centered planning. Some key themes of all the different strategies include: (a) a focus on identifying the skills and interests that the person has, (b) identifying resources that the person can use, (c) working with individual to identify specific support needs, and (d) arranging support to address those needs.

The supports that a person uses often are arranged to increase a person's sense of wellness and improve the individual's quality of life (Brown, 1988; Sheppard-Jones, Prout, & Kleinert, 2005). Supporting a healthy lifestyle and culturally typical levels of activity are often the desired outcomes of supports for persons with IDD. This includes the strategies used in addressing problem behaviors among persons with IDD. Recent approaches to addressing problem behavior also start with identification of strengths and interests rather than simply focusing on the problem behavior (Horner, et al., 1990). Intervention targets strength based planning, support identification, teaching and wellness approaches, rather than simply reducing frequencies of problem behavior.

Positive Behavioral Support

Perhaps the most compelling example of the intersection of disability supports and positive psychology is the set of values and practices referred to as Positive Behavioral Support (PBS). In recognition of the complex, ever changing influences upon human behavior, PBS emerged from the field of Applied Behavioral Analysis in the 1970's and has generated a rich and varied literature of research and methodology. PBS incorporates person centered values and a concern for individual dignity, in an effort to create environments and supports that promote a person's capabilities, expand opportunities, and enhance lifestyles (Koegel, Koegel & Dunlap, 2001). PBS utilizes multiple methods of assessment to create a useful understanding of a person's wellness: the quality of the current environment and routines; individual learning style and functional skills; and existing relationships and supports. Functional assessment information results in a holistic profile of the individual for the purpose of creating supports and environments that enable a person to develop needed skills to achieve personally meaningful goals (Janney & Snell, 2000). PBS recognizes the important role of mental health and includes consideration of mental illness in the theoretical constructs of behavior (Baker & Blumberg, 2002)

In contrast to the problem-focused nature of traditional psychotherapy, from the perspective of Positive Psychology the overall goal of psychotherapy is to help people lead fulfilling lives (Park & Peterson, 2008). The focus of therapy in Positive Psychology is not fixing people or problems; nor is it helping people with disabilities to endure, but to thrive. To do this, the therapist assists individuals and families to fully recognize their strengths, to use these to meet the challenges of everyday living, and, through the therapeutic process, to build more satisfying futures. The goals of therapy are to help individuals with disabilities (and their families) to build additional strengths, resources, and abilities (Naidoo, 2005).

Positive Psychology merges with the concept of Self Determination in that it assumes that people with and without disabilities can take control of their lives, make choices based on their preferences, and, with support, make decisions that lead to positive futures (Wehmeyer & Mithaug, 2006). The clinical practice of Positive Psychology does not ignore the real challenges that individuals with disabilities experience as they attempt to live fulfilling lives, but seeks to balance the traditional focus of psychotherapy on pathology and disability with a focus on positive emotions and building individual strengths (Park & Peterson, 2008).

Kaufman (2006) identifies four techniques for integrating concepts of Positive Psychology into conventional forms of individual or group psychotherapy:

- *Shift the individual's focus from the negative to the positive.* Since most individuals seek therapy to obtain relief from the problems they are experiencing, they tend to focus their attention on negative events, and the process of traditional therapy may encourage this. To change this pattern, individuals can be instructed to keep a daily record of positive events or interactions. They can record lists of accomplishments, instead of the number of times they performed "problem behaviors."

- *Identify a personal strength and use it each day.* Just as we exercise our bodies to become stronger, using personal strengths regularly can improve our life functioning. In this technique, the therapist, family members, or care-providers can serve as coaches, to remind, encourage, and reinforce the use of personal strengths.

- *Find a balance between the negative and positive.* In this case, it is important for the people who interact with the individual to actively recognize the person's strengths, while providing constructive feedback regarding problems the person experiences. All too often, it is the reactions of others that keep the focus on problems and ignore the many ways the individual attempts to improve him/herself.

- *Promote feelings of hopefulness.* Feelings of hopefulness may increase the ability of individuals and family members to deal with problems they encounter. Individuals seeking therapy may have come to feel overwhelmed by the duration, scope, or intensity of problems. In this case the therapist works to make the problem more manageable, by creating incremental, achievable goals. One way this can be done is by breaking the problem into smaller parts and addressing each part sequentially.

Positive Psychology aims to broaden the focus of clinical psychology beyond the alleviation of suffering to the development of an individual's strengths of character and a focus on positive life experiences. Positive Psychotherapy (PPT) interventions are designed to increase an individual's experience of positive emotions, engagement with life, and discovery of meaning in life. Emerging research suggests that through the experience of positive emotions, engagement, and meaning individuals may obtain relief from psychological disorders such as anxiety and depression (Duckworth, Steen & Seligman, 2005; Frederikson, 2000).

Seligman, Rashid & Parks (2006) describe PPT interventions designed to counteract the tendency of individuals with depression to recall negative memories, attend to negative events, and harbor negative expectations of the future. These interventions are designed to refocus attention, memory, and expectations from the negative toward the positive. An example of this is the "three good things" exercise that directs a person at bedtime to write down three things that went well during the day and why they went well. This exercise counteracts the tendency of people with depression to ruminate about their problems and enables the person to bias recall toward positive events. A related activity, the "gratitude visit" directs a person to write a letter to someone expressing gratitude for something they have done for you. Then the person visits the subject of the letter and reads it to them. The purpose of the gratitude visit is to shift a person's memories from the negative events of the past toward a recall of the acts of kindness and support they have experienced in their lives. A more thorough list of empirically-validated PPT interventions appears later in this chapter.

POSITIVE PSYCHOTHERAPY WITH INDIVIDUALS WITH IDD

Thus far, research in Positive Psychology has not included the development and/or evaluation of clinical interventions for individuals with IDD. Yet, the focus of Positive Psychology on recognizing and building upon peoples strengths, abilities, and virtues is reflected in recent developments in the conceptualization of IDD and the support paradigm. There are intriguing and meaningful convergences in the emerging practices of Positive Psychology and what we understand about best practice in the treatment of individuals with IDD.

Bellini (2006) has explored the problem of social anxiety in individuals with Autism Spectrum Disorders. He observes that social anxiety is the most prevalent comorbid condition in individuals with Autism Spectrum Disorders. In a recent study, he found clinically significant levels of anxiety in 49 percent of a group of randomly selected youth with ASDs (Bellini, 2006). Problems with social functioning have been well documented in the literature concerning ASDs, suggesting that social skills deficits commonly displayed by individuals with ASDs, may contribute to the development of social anxiety.

The development of social anxiety appears to be the result of multiple factors determined by individual predispositions, quality of social interactions, and development of self protective behaviors (Vasey & Dadds, 2001). One conceptualization of the developmental pathways to social anxiety begins with an individual's social withdrawal which impairs the development of age appropriate social skills. These social skills deficits lead to negative peer interactions, which result in increased social anxiety, leading to increased social withdrawal. Social withdrawal provides negative reinforcement by removing or lessening social anxiety (Rubin & Burgess, 2001).

The social withdrawal and social anxiety of individuals with ASDs results in restricted social relationships and impoverished social networks. This social isolation prevents individuals from developing the interpersonal skills that are necessary for success in education, employment, and civic engagement. Individuals with such severe isolation are vulnerable to a variety of co-occurring mental health disorders including depression (Tantam, 2000).

Within the field of Positive Psychology, conceptual frameworks have emerged that have relevance for the treatment and support of individuals with IDD. Fredrickson (2002) has suggested that negative emotions such as anxiety narrow a person's responses to an event (thought-action repertoires), making it more likely that the person will engage in limited, self protective behaviors. Conversely, positive emotions broaden a person's responses, creating opportunities for personal growth and increasing repertoires of positive, adaptive emotion, cognition, and behavior. This "broaden and build" theory of positive emotions suggests that positive affective experiences contribute to personal well-being, growth, and development.

There is growing clinical evidence that positive mood states help individuals develop a variety of adaptive behaviors including greater persistence, flexibility, and resourcefulness in problem solving. Relationships have been suggested between positive mood states and improvements in learning and the development of effective responses to stressful situations. The experience of positive emotions has been linked to increased creativity, productivity, and longevity (Carr, 2004).

Negative emotions have adaptive functions, such as preparing us to defend ourselves against possible threats. To do his, they necessarily narrow our attention to the perceived source of the threat. Positive emotions broaden the focus of our attention, making it possible for us to consider alternative explanations for events and more creative solutions to the challenges of living. Positive emotions provide opportunities to create new and better relationships and expand our activities and networks.

Traditionally, the field of Developmental Disabilities has focused on the remediation of skills deficits as way of helping individuals improve the quality of their lives. In the preceding reference to social withdrawal and anxiety, social skills deficits were posited to be a contributing factor in the development of these problems. There is strong support for the relationship between social functioning and social anxiety in youth with Autism (Ginsburg, La Greca, & Silerman, 1998). The research validated intervention in this case would be to provide social skills instruction.

The emerging literature of Positive Psychology suggests that a comprehensive intervention also would include attention to the affective experiences of the individual in the context of social interaction. Instruction in discrete skills is indeed important (Kauffman, 2006), but the Positive Psychology literature suggests that individuals are more likely to learn and use social skills when they experience positive emotions and feelings of well-being. In the context of positive emotional experiences, individuals are more likely to perceive opportunities for successful interaction, move toward increasing social activity, and demonstrate increased creativity in their approach to novel or challenging situations.

Individuals with IDD have been found to experience depression at higher rates than individuals without IDD (Day, 1990; Tsiouris, 2001). The reasons for this are varied and complex. One contributing variable appears to be social isolation and the lack of social support. For many individuals with IDD, social relationship and support is provided by paid caregivers. One way that many individuals with IDD attempt to engage the attention of caregivers is to seek assistance with "problems." Often caregivers encourage this behavior by the quality and content of their communication. If a caregiver asks, "How are you feeling today," individuals with IDD soon learn that answering "I'm feeling great" is likely to yield less sustained attention than the expression of "problems."

Another salient variable in the development of depression in people with IDD is external locus of control. This may be the result of the tendency of individuals with IDD to be dependent upon others for important life activities and/or access to desirable items or activities. Individuals with IDD report a high frequency of physical, emotional, and sexual abuse (Sobsey, Sharmaine, Wells, Pyper, & Reimer-Heck, 1992). These incidences of abuse may reinforce feelings of lack of control combined with lack of worth.

Often the dominant narratives in the lives of people with IDD are complaints about the quality of care-giving that they receive or lack of access to desired items or activities. When asked to remember important life events, they may often speak of disappointments or abuse. This tendency among many persons with IDD and depression to focus on negative life events is often unintentionally reinforced by caregivers and helping professionals.

The PPT interventions such as "three good things" or the "gratitude visit" may be adapted and supported by others to refocus a person's attention and recall, and to increase positive emotions. Simple accommodations such as having someone else write down the positive events as a person speaks them, or using a tape recorder to keep a log of them, can help the person achieve the benefits of this exercise. If an individual has difficulty recalling three good things, then a reasonable adaptation might be to just record a single event. The gratitude visits can be similarly adapted and accommodated. The important thing is that the person spend some reasonable and regular time focusing his or her attention and recall on positive events in his/her lives and the good things that others have done to display affection and support to him or her. Adaptation of mental health supports to fit persons with IDD have been well-documented in the literature base. Morasky (2007) and Munro (2007) have both published excellent clinical articles that have addressed strategies for accommodating persons whose intellectual abilities render typical psychological support strategies ineffective. Morasky noted that the dimensions for adaptation include speed, number, abstraction, and complexity. Table 1 describes 10 Positive Therapy Techniques and suggests methods for adapting them for use with individuals with IDD.

Table 1. PPT techniques and potential adaptations.

Intervention	Citation	Description	Suggested Accommodation	Example
Gratitude visit	Seligman et al., 2005	Participants were given one week to write and then deliver a letter of gratitude in person to someone who had been especially kind to them but had never been properly thanked.	Abstraction Complexity	Assisting via choice menus Assist with visit Write out expression of gratitude Scripting Provide examples Conduct role play Picture schedule or social story Direct instruction
Three good things in life	Seligman et al., 2005	Participants were asked to write down three things that went well each day every night for one week. In addition, they were asked to provide a causal explanation for each good thing.	Number Abstraction Complexity	Assisting via choice menus Assist with visit Write out expression of gratitude Scripting Provide examples Conduct role play Picture schedule or social story Direct instruction Give camera to allow person to identify good things via pictures Use insight oriented examples Interview caregivers to get examples Keep ongoing log Why 3? Use a smaller number of good things Direct instruction

continued next page

You at your best	Seligman et al., 2005	Participants were asked to write about a time when they were at their best and then to reflect on the personal strengths displayed in the story. They were told to review their story once every day for a week and to reflect on the strengths they had identified.	Abstraction Complexity	Repeat Give camera to allow person to identify good things via pictures Use insight oriented examples Forced choice Interview caregivers to get examples Keep ongoing log Point out when person is at his or her best Direct instruction
Using signature strengths in a new way	Seligman et al., 2005 Peterson et al., 2005a	Participants were asked to take an inventory of character strengths online at www.authentichappiness.org and to receive individualized feedback about their top five ("signature") strengths. They were then asked to use one of these top strengths in a new and different way every day for one week.	Abstraction Complexity	Social story Direct instruction Examples from popular media or current events Role play Rehearsal Examples of past uses of signature strengths
Identifying signature strengths	Seligman et al., 2005	Same as previous item without the instruction to use signature strengths in new ways. Participants were asked to take the survey, to note their five highest strengths, and to use them more often during the next week.	Number Abstraction Complexity	Caregivers and others complete the assessment Use of non-reading response
Detailed instruction on increasing happiness via socialization and activity	Fordyce, 1977	Students in community college classes were given detailed instruction on strategies for increasing happiness, with a focus on activities seen as producing happiness.	Speed Number Abstraction Complexity	Mentoring Peer buddies Adapt instruction for learned with differing ability Wellness supports so the person actually is socializing and having activities

— *continued next page* —

77

Writing about positive experience	Burton & King, 2004	Participants were assigned to write about experiences that made them happy for 20-minute intervals on three consecutive days	Number Abstraction Complexity	Use something other than writing (e.g., tape, video, picture Use graphic organizer Provide samples Have person respond to sample
Gratitude journals	Emmons & McCullough, 2003	Participants wrote weekly about five things for which they were thankful for 10 weeks	Number Abstraction Complexity	Use something other than writing (e.g., tape, video, picture) Provide samples Use graphic organizer Have person respond to sample Caregiver support
Count Your Blessings & Acts of Kindess	Lyubomirsky et al., 2005	(1) Participants were asked to either count their blessings once per week or three times per week (2) Some participants were asked to perform five acts of kindness all in one day and another group of participants were asked to perform five acts of kindness spread out over one week	Number Abstraction Complexity	Volunteering Support participation in family and community rituals and events such as holiday observations and teach and support (e g teach about sending birthday cards) Develop happiness books (create album or scrapbook of thing that make you happy) Funny do-list Caregivers create opportunities Service learning projects Increase wellness Develop social networks Teach collateral skills such as hobbies Count your blessing same Social stories Examples from popular media

continued next page

| Reading & instruction on improving your life | Grant et al., 1995 | Participants were assigned to read about strategies for increasing their satisfaction in various domains of life (e.g., health, self-esteem, goals, values, money, work, play, learning, creativity, love, helping, friends, children, relatives, home, neighborhood, and community) and then met weekly for 15 weeks to discuss the assigned readings | Number Abstraction Complexity | Introduce humor

Teach collateral skills such as hobbies

Use something other than writing and adapt instruction

Use assistive technology programs to "read"

Use graphic organizer |

APPLICATION OF THE TECHNIQUES

The existing research in Positive Psychology has largely been conducted with persons of average measured intelligence, many of these college students. Although persons with IDD have not featured prominently in current studies, references to Positive Psychology and persons with IDD have begun to appear. Naidoo (2006) describes the case of "Hannah" a five year old girl with Cerebral Palsy. She describes the constraints upon Hannah's functioning due to her disability and describes the existing strengths that could be built upon, from the perspective of Positive Psychology. These strengths include Hannah's curious nature, strong will, and capacity for perseverance. Hannah is also confident, sociable, kind, and gentle. She is able to walk independently, and shows independence in self care, appropriate to her developmental level. Hannah also has a strong social support system that includes her parents, extended family, and neighbors. The author does not suggest methods of building upon Hannah's strengths or other possible PPT interventions.

In her discussion of a meaningful life for individuals with IDD, Dykens (2006) cites several examples of persons with IDD caring for others, engaging in volunteer activities, and other forms of community service. Examples cited include individuals with Down Syndrome caring for severely disabled peers in a large institution, a 45 year old man with ID volunteering to coach a bowling league in a nursing home, a 25 year old woman with ID volunteering for Meals on Wheels, and a group of musicians with Williams Syndrome playing at a benefit to raise funds for family support programs. The author cites studies that have included measurements of happiness within intervention studies involving persons with IDD.

CASE EXAMPLES

The following case studies are intended to provide examples of specific PPT interventions used in psychotherapy with youth and adults with IDD. The examples are taken from the private psychotherapy practice of the second author. No attempt is made to systematically evaluate the effectiveness of the interventions using statistical or other indices of change.

Nathan

At the time Nathan presented for therapy he was 17 years old, completing his Junior year in high school. He was accompanied by his father who participated in the initial evaluation session. Nathan's father expressed concerns that Nathan seemed depressed, and was socially isolated. He reported that Nathan appeared to have problems with stress and sometimes had angry emotional outbursts. He reported that Nathan had previously been in therapy but had terminated treatment because he didn't like his therapist. The former therapist had diagnosed Nathan with Asperger's Syndrome and Generalized Anxiety Disorder.

Nathan reported that he did not like school because of problems with peers and found much of his coursework to be boring and irrelevant. He reported that his activities included reading, mostly science and philosophy, and listening to music. He agreed with is father that he felt depressed at times, experiencing low energy, negative thoughts about himself and others, and difficulty sleeping. Nathan displayed flat affect, spoke in a monotone, and made infrequent eye contact with the therapist.

Further evaluation included a discussion of Nathan's strengths. Nathan had difficulty identifying things he did well, other than excelling at some academic subjects such as science and math. He said that he had no close friends and did not have regular activities outside of home and school. He had no employment or volunteer experience and had not participated in clubs or civic organizations. To continue the assessment, Nathan was asked to complete the VIA Signature Strengths Assessment on-line (www.authentichappiness.org) and to begin to keep a journal recording three good things that had happened to him each day, as well as thoughts and questions that emerged for him throughout the week between sessions. He was also asked to read two first person accounts of people with Asperger's Syndrome and to record any reactions or questions he had about the readings.

Nathan completed the VIA Signature Strengths Assessment and shared the results with the therapist. His top five strengths included self control; bravery and valor; industry and diligence; caution, prudence, and discretion; and fairness, equity, and justice. Nathan expressed that he thought the assessment was inaccurate because his top strength was self control, and he felt he had little self control. The therapist and Nathan discussed the many ways that he displayed self-control through discipline and perseverance. Nathan seemed to appreciate these strengths within himself, but he expressed concern about the times he displayed angry outbursts. After further discussion, Nathan and the therapist agreed to develop a goal of improving Nathan's ability to better manage his anger by finding ways to calm himself when upset and to use his journal to record and better express angry thoughts and feelings. He was instructed to keep a daily mood rating scale, and his parents were asked to also rate his moods on a scale of 1-5 with one representing very depressed and 5 representing a very positive mood. Initially Nathan and his parents were rating his mood as 2 or mildly depressed.

Nathan complained of difficulties with verbal communication and social interaction. He stated that it was sometimes difficult to ascertain the meaning of other people's behavior, and he had difficulty initiating and maintaining conversations. These problems made him feel anxious in social situations, and as a result he had become isolated with no relationships outside of family. Nathan agreed to participate in social skills instruction and to practice self-relaxation exercises. He also agreed to join a local gym and begin to work with a personal trainer to develop an appropriate exercise program to reduce his feelings of stress.

Further review of Nathan's signature strengths suggested that his bravery and valor, industry and diligence, and concerns with fairness, equity and justice might be productively directed toward some form of community service or service learning. This could also provide a structured setting for the development of social skills and social relationships. Nathan agreed to conduct some research to identify possible service learning opportunities at school or in his local community. Nathan's older sister assisted him in this activity.

Nathan expressed an interest in the presidential campaign of a particular candidate and began volunteering at a local campaign headquarters doing computer data entry. He eventually joined the local Habitat for Humanity group and participated in meetings and fund raising activities. He regularly attended his neighborhood gym and began having regular conversations with a number of other gym members.

Nathan did not initially find the "three good things" exercise easy to do. He required extensive coaching and support to identify even one good thing that he could recall in the previous week. Slowly as his social network became larger, and his social activities increased, he began to record daily positive events and soon was recording at least two good things each day. His mood ratings had improved to an average of 3-3.5, indicating no feelings of depression.

One of the most painful experiences that continually presented during therapy was Nathan's experience of rejection by peers and some harassment by peers. These experiences continued through his Senior year in high school, despite his increased social activities and growth in social skills. Nathan graduated from high school and was accepted into two local colleges. In the beginning of his freshman year at college, he continued to talk about the pain of social rejection during high school. Nathan recalled that his high school guidance counselor and a biology teacher had been sources of social support and had helped him through difficult emotional periods. He expressed appreciation for their support and reluctantly agreed to write each of them a letter expressing his gratitude. His therapist and his father helped him write the letters. He did not want to personally present them, but mailed them. He received responses from both and seemed surprised by the many positive things his mentors had to say about him in their replies.

Nathan is now a successful college student. He continues to struggle with social relationships but no longer experiences significant depression. He has friendships and has had some girlfriends. He plans to attend graduate school. PPT interventions appeared to help Nathan identify and build upon his personal strengths. Focusing on positive daily events appeared to support improvements in mood as he increased social activities and developed social skills. Finally, Nathan's expressions of gratitude may have helped him begin to think about his high school experience as something more than social rejection and harassment by peers. Following the gratitude letters and the responses he received, he no longer spoke about high school, but focused his attention on the present and his future goals.

Robert

At the time Robert was referred for therapy, he was twenty-eight years old and living in a small group home. His referral listed a diagnosis of Mild ID and cited problems with anger and aggression as reasons for referral. He was attending a sheltered workshop/day program and had recently begun to refuse to go the program, and, on days he did attend, he often refused to work and frequently argued with co-workers.

Robert was accompanied to his first appointment by a staff member from the group home. Robert stated that the reason for coming to therapy was because he didn't like his job, the place he lived, or his housemates. He reported that he didn't have any activities outside of his day program and that his group home staff wouldn't take him anywhere. He appeared to be unhappy and frustrated. He made numerous complaints about staff at his day program and group home. He made numerous complaints about his housemates. Robert appeared to be a young man who experienced few positive emotions and was not engaged in his life. For him, the meaning in life seemed to be restricted to an ongoing litany of complaints about services and staff. He appeared to want to talk about little else.

Robert's support provider reported that Robert had become increasingly difficult to support over the last year or so. He stated that Robert made unreasonable demands on staff and typically refused to participate in scheduled activities. He argued frequently with housemates. He was difficult to get up in the morning and often refused to go to work. Behavioral programs, such as contingent reinforcement, did not seem to work. Staff were frustrated with Robert and felt helpless to improve the situation.

In response to questions about things he liked to do, Robert responded that he liked to spend his own money, but quickly responded that staff wouldn't let him. He liked to visit his parents but added that he often fought with his brother. He liked to visit his girlfriend but again often fought with her. He reported that he was good at house and office cleaning and that he enjoyed the feeling of accomplishment when he was able to make things look "nice." He was not able to identify other personal strengths. Provided with some examples of strengths his therapist had observed during the session, Robert agreed that he was a tireless self advocate, that relationships were important to him, that he liked orderly and clean environments, and that he had high standards of quality when it came to his work. Robert was instructed to meet with his residential support staff each evening before bedtime and to think of three good things that had happened that day. The staff member would help him reflect on positive events and record these for him. We would discuss these at our next weekly session.

Robert's parents and support provider were invited to the next session. It began with setting an agenda, with input from Robert, his parents, and support provider. The agenda began with a discussion of the good things that happened during the past week, a discussion of Robert's strengths, his relationships with support staff and his roommate, visits to his parent's home, and goal setting. Robert's support provider read the list of positive events and experiences, and Robert commented on these. The good things included eating foods that he liked, watching favorite television shows, shopping, and, interestingly, several incidents when Robert had helped or been kind to someone else. The group reviewed Robert's strengths from the previous session and added that he was good at recognizing other people's needs and providing help; he was very good at conversation and had a big vocabulary; he excelled at managing his money; and he had an excellent memory, being able to remember details of conversations, birthdays, and other personal information about people in his life. The information about positive events and signature strengths was summarized and recorded.

Robert's parents shared their concerns that he appeared to be unhappy with his home and work situation. They stated that they found it difficult to listen to his many complaints and wished he could build a more satisfying life. Robert's support provider agreed with the parent's observations and commented that Robert could be kind and helpful but also often was disrespectful and verbally abusive to others.

The next topic was goal setting, and the therapist suggested that the group could consider building on Robert's strengths and the events he had experienced that provided him with positive emotion. The group considered ways in which Robert could use his signature strengths in different ways throughout the week. A brainstorming list was created that included volunteer opportunities; finding a new job in home or office maintenance; sending birthday and holiday cards to friends and family; creating a "happiness book" of pictures of friends, family, vacations and trips; and creating a picture menu of favorite foods to use when shopping for groceries. Robert agreed to continue his journal of good things that happened each day and that at least once a week he and his support provider would call his parents to share these with them.

In subsequent sessions, Robert, his parents, and support provider continued to review the positive events in his life. Robert continued to complain about various people and events, but his complaints steadily decreased. He began volunteering at a nursing home in the afternoons by assisting the nursing home staff, delivering mail, and talking with residents about current events, sports, or other topics. At home, he became responsible for taking inventory of food and household supplies, and using pictures and labels, developed the bi-weekly shopping menu. His happiness book evolved into a "happiness wall" in his bedroom. He took up "power walking" with one of his housemates, and began to lose excess weight.

Robert's story is typical of many people with IDD who become dissatisfied with the lack of pleasure and meaning in their lives. Robert's attempts at self advocacy had become a problem for others and eventually for him, keeping him locked in an emotional state of frustration and anger. PPT interventions shifted the focus of Robert's attention and the attention of those around him from negative events and emotion to positive feelings and activities. Robert's support providers reported that his change of behavior and emotion influenced positive changes in his housemates and made the home a more enjoyable place to work. Robert's parents reported more pleasurable phone calls and home visits.

The Social Skills Group

PPT interventions can provide a useful context for the development of social skills. The social skills group consisted of four adolescent males with disability labels of Autism and Intellectual Disability. These teens had been referred for social skills training because of failure to develop age-appropriate social relationships and the communication skills and related behaviors necessary for social functioning in school and community settings. These young men had become socially isolated, and two displayed symptoms of mild depression.

Each of the young men attending the group had completed a social skills assessment that identified specific skills deficits to be targeted for training. Most of the group members had the following skills deficits: difficulty initiating and maintaining a conversation; speaking for too long about an obsessive interest; shifting topics and not allowing others to speak; questioning others; using appropriate voice volume or tone; making eye contact or not staring; and maintaining appropriate posture and physical distance when speaking. The lists of skills deficits for each of the young men were extensive, and most of these deficits were displayed during the first group session.

Seligman et al. (2006) provide an "idealized session by session" model of positive psychotherapy describing a developmental approach to the use of PPT techniques (pp.782-783). This model was adapted for use with adolescents with IDD to provide a therapeutic context for skill development and a meaningful structure for social interaction and dialogue among group members.

The purpose of the initial group session is: (a) to introduce group members to each other; (b) to introduce the basic concepts of social skills instruction and the objectives of the group; (c) to develop group norms or rules for group process; and (d) to model these norms through an initial warm-up exercise. The initial exercise is usually not very challenging to allow members to focus on learning expected group behaviors. The therapist provides feedback to group member performance and invites group members to provide feedback to each other. The session ends with a summary of the session and a "homework" assignment. For this session, the assignment was to bring an object that signifies a goal the member worked hard to achieve and be prepared to tell the group about it. Each group member was given a homework journal to record the assignment in and asked to share the assignment with his parent(s).

The following week, each group member brought an item, and members took turns presenting their items, talking about their goals and the process they underwent to achieve their goals. Each member was directed to think of one question to ask each presenter and to think of words to describe the experience of goal attainment. The first young man to speak brought the certificate he received upon completion of his Bar Mitzvah. He told of how difficult it was to learn the prayers in Hebrew and to recite them during the ceremony. With modeling and prompting from the therapist, each group member asked him a question about the experience, and he answered these with support from the therapist. Then each member was asked to think of words that described the presenter in the context of what he had accomplished. These words were then recorded on a white board. The therapist gave feedback to the presenter and to other group members, providing examples of appropriate social skills and inviting members to provide their feedback. This process was repeated for each member of the group.

The Goal Attainment exercise was intended as an introduction to the concept of signature strengths. In response to the Bar Mitzvah presentation, group members said of the presenter, "he works real hard," "he has a good memory," and "he speaks Hebrew." Each member recorded the feedback he received in his homework journal and then was asked to share this feedback with family and friends. The activity engaged the attention of group members, encouraged members to think in positive ways about themselves and others to experience positive emotions, and provided a meaningful structure for the practice of social skills.

The homework assignment for the following week was to complete the on-line VIA Strength Survey for Children with the support of a parent or caregiver. The Strengths Survey is a 240 item questionnaire, which might be too lengthy, and asks respondents to reflect on social qualities and behaviors, which might be difficult for youth with ASD to comprehend. For this reason, it was suggested to let a parent or adult caregiver complete items that were unclear or portions of the assessment the child was unable or unwilling to complete.

At the third session, all group members had completed the survey and shared their results. They compared the survey feedback with the statements from the initial

"Goals" exercise and discussed how they were similar or different. The Signature Strengths activity engaged the attention of group members, encouraged them to think in novel, positive ways about themselves and others, and provided opportunities for modeling and practicing social skills.

The social skills group continued to combine development of specific social skills with PPT interventions. The social skills group participated in the following PPT exercises in subsequent sessions.

- *Using signature strengths.* Group members were asked to use one of their identified strengths each day and to journal about how using that strength helped them to develop a social skill and/or social relationship. For example, a member who was very good at math skills helped another student complete a difficult problem in class.
- *Three good things.* Group members were directed to keep a record of three good things that had happened each day in the process of practicing social skills. For example, group members recorded positive social interactions including: eating lunch with peers at school and enjoying a conversation about Anime; talking with a waitress in a restaurant about the weather before having a favorite meal; and getting a "high five" from a peer after making a spoken presentation in class.
- *Expressions of Gratitude.* In this exercise, members were asked to think of a person who had been helpful or supportive in a significant way and to write a brief letter to that person expressing gratitude. Then, the member was directed to read the letter to the person face to face. Examples included an elementary school teacher who was kind and helped a member when he was being teased by peers, a veterinarian who cared for a member's pet, and an uncle who had taught a member to fish.
- *Engagement and Flow.* This exercise involved using activities that were engaging and generated positive emotion as a context for sustained social interaction. Each member was asked to identify an activity and to engage in the activity with at least one other person for gradually increasing intervals of time. Examples included reading with younger family members (siblings and cousins) at family gatherings and playing Uno with peers in the school cafeteria at lunchtime.

In youth with Autism and ID, the development of social skills often involves creating a meaningful structure for social interaction and overcoming social anxiety and perceptions of low self efficacy. Including PPT exercises within the social skills training program appeared to increase the engagement of group members in the process of developing social skills. The experience of positive emotion through a focus on strengths and positive events appeared to help members experience increased motivation and persistence. The use of journaling to record each member's progress, along with parental report and tools like video monitoring, assisted members to fully appreciate their progress in skill development. Members who had previously displayed symptoms of mild depression reported decreased experience of symptoms and an increase of positive emotion and feelings of hope for the future.

THE INTERSECTION OF POSITIVE PSYCHOLOGY AND DUAL DIAGNOSIS SUPPORTS

A review of the philosophy of Positive Psychology shows that there is considerable overlap between Positive Psychology and best practices in supports for people with the dual diagnoses of IDD and MI. For example, both often focus on the strengths of the individual. Additionally, both look to identify factors that lead to success. Both have the philosophy that proper treatment needs to be provided but that the best success comes from enhancing a person's strengths. Supported employment has an axiom that nobody ever gets a job because of what they can't do; they get jobs because of what they can do.

As noted previously, one of the reasons for the rapid growth in Positive Psychology is the fact that the interventions are simple, as well as being effective. Seligmann et al. (2005) describe the results of a large empirically-controlled study in which they evaluated the effectiveness of Positive Psychology interventions. Many PPT techniques are simple interventions that do not require an office visit and might be enjoyable. Furthermore, the exercises can be easily adapted for persons with IDD and MI using strategies described by Morasky (2007) and Munro (2007). We conclude this chapter with a recommendation for use of PPT interventions in support of persons with IDD and MI. Of particular note is the fact that many of these interventions can be performed by an individual without assistance from a psychologist, unlike many more traditional therapies. Care providers, educators, or family members might be able to provide the support. Positive Psychology is a good fit with disability supports, and they share a focus on positive experiences in life and building upon strengths.

REFERENCES

Baker, D.J., Blumberg, R., & Freeman, R. (2002). Considerations for functional assessment of problem behavior among persons with developmental disabilities and mental illness. In J. Jacobson, J. Mulick, & S. Holburn (Eds.), *Programs and services for people with dual developmental and psychiatric disabilities* (pp. 51-66). Kingston, NY: NADD.

Barr, M.W. (1904). *Mental defectives: Their history, treatment, and training.* Philadelphia, PA: P. Blakiston's Son & Co.

Bellini, S. (2006). The development of social anxiety in high-functioning adolescents with Autism Spectrum Disorders. *Focus on Autism and other Developmental Disabilities, 21(3),* 138-145

Benjamin, S. (1989). An ideascape for education: What futurists recommend. *Educational Leadership, 47,* 8-14.

Brown, R.I. (Ed.). (1988). *Quality of life for handicapped people.* New York: Croom Helm.

Cannon, J. (1997). *What is right with your life?* Monterrey, CA.: Inward Bound Ventures.

Day, K.A. (1990). Depression in mildly and moderately retarded adults. In A. Dosen & F.J. Menolascino (Eds.) *Depression in mentally retarded children and adults.* Leiden, Netherlands: Logon.

DeJong, G. (1979). Independent living: From social movement to analytic paradigm. *Archives of Physical Medicine and Rehabilitation, 60,* 435-446.

Duckworth, A., Steen, T. & Seligan, M. (2005) Positive psychology in clinical practice. *Annual Review of Clinical Psychology, 1,* 629-651.

Dykens, E.M. (2006) Toward a positive psychology of mental retardation. *American Journal of Orthopsychiatry,76(2),* 185-193.

Fredrickson, B.L. (2000) Cultivating positive emotions to optimize health and well-being. *Prevention and Treatment, 3,* Article 1.

Fredrickson, B.L. & Joiner, T. (2002) Positive emotions trigger upward spirals toward emotional well-being. *Psychological Science, 13,* 172-175.

Ginsburg, G., La Greca, A.M., & Silerman, W.S. (1998) Social anxiety in children with anxiety disorders: Relation with social and emotional functioning. *Journal of Abnormal Psychology, 26,* 175-185.

Horner, R. H., Dunlap, G., Koegel, R. L., Carr, E. G., Sailor, W., Anderson, J., et al. (1990). Toward a technology of "nonaversive" behavioral support. *Journal of the Association for Persons with Severe Handicaps, 15,* 125-132.

Janney, R. & Snell, M. *Behavioral support.* Baltimore: Paul H. Brookes.

Kauffman, C. (2006) Positive psychology: The science at the heart of coaching. In D.R. Stober & A.M Grant (Eds.), *Evidenced based coaching handbook: Putting best practices to work for your clients* (pp. 219-253). Hoboken, NJ: John Wiley.

Koegel, L., Koegel, R., & Dunlap, G. (1996) *Positive behavioral support.* Baltimore: Paul H. Brookes.

Kuhlmann, F. (1912). A revision of the Simon-Binet system for measuring the intelligence of children, *Journal of Psycho-asthenics, 1*(1), 3-41.

Larson, S., Lakin, C., & Huang, J. (2003). Service use by and needs of adults with functional limitations or ID/DD in the NHIS-D: Difference by age, gender, and disability. *DD Data Brief.* Minneapolis, MN: University of Minnesota, Research and Training Center on Community Living.

Linley, P. A., & Joseph, S. (Eds.). (2004). *Positive psychology in practice.* Hoboken, NJ: Wiley.

Morasky, R. (2007). Making counseling/therapy intellectually attainable. *The NADD Bulletin, 10,* 58-61.

Munro, D. (2007). Couple therapy and support: A positive model for people with intellectual disabilities. *The NADD Bulletin, 10,* 58-61.

Naidoo, P (2006) Potential contributions to disability theorizing and research from positive psychology. *Disability and Rehabilitation, 28*(9), 595-602.

National Center for Independent Living. (2009). *The disability rights and independent living movements.* Retrieved June, 2009 from www.ncil.org.

Nirje, B. (1985) The basis and logic of the normalization principle. *Australia and New Zealand Journal of Developmental Disabilities, 11,* 65-68.

O'Brien, J. (1989) *What's worth working for? Leadership for better quality human services.* Lithonia, GA: Responsive Systems Assoc.

O'Brien, J., & Lyle O'Brien, C. (1998). *A Little Book About Person Centered Planning.* Toronto, ONT: Inclusion Press.

Morasky, R. (2007). Making counseling/therapy intellectually attainable. *The NADD Bulletin, 10*(3), 58-62.

Munro, D. (2007). Couple therapy and support. *The NADD Bulletin, 10,* 102-109.

Nisbet, J., & Hagner, D. (1988). Natural supports in the workplace: A reexamination of supported employment. *Journal of the Association for Persons with Severe Handicaps, 13,* 260-267.

Park, N. (2008). Positive psychology and character strengths: Application to strengths-based school counseling. *Professional School Counseling,* 12 (2), 85-92.

Park, N. & Peterson, C. (2008). The cultivation of character strengths. In M. Ferrari & G. Potworowski (Eds.), *Teaching for wisdom* (pp. 57-75). Mahwah, NJ: Erlbaum.

Peterson, C., & Seligman, M. E. P. (2004). *Character strengths and virtues: A handbook and classification.* Washington, DC: American Psychological Association.

Rogers, C. R. (1951). *Client-centered therapy: Its current practice, implications, and theory.* Boston: Houghton Mifflin.

Rubin, K.H. & Burgess, K. (2001). Social withdrawal. In M.W. Vasey & M.R. Dadds (Eds.), *The developmental psychopathology of anxiety* (pp. 407-434). Oxford, UK: Oxford University Press.

Shogren, K.A., Wehmeyer, M.L., Buchanan, C.L. & Lopez, S.J. (2006). The application of positive psychology and self-determination to research in Intellectual Disability: A content analysis of 30 years of literature. *Research & Practice for Persons with Severe Disabilities, 31*(4), 338-345.

Seligman, M., Rashid, T. & Parks, A. (2006) Positive psychotherapy. *American Psychologist, 61*(8), 774-788.

Seligman, M, Steen, T., Park, N., & Peterson, C. (2005). Positive psychology progress: Empirical validation of interventions. *American Psychologist, 60,* 410–421.

Sheppard-Jones, K., Prout, H.T., & Kleinert, H. (2005). Quality of life dimensions for adults with developmental disabilities: A comparative study. *Mental Retardation, 43*(4), 281–291.

Sobsey, D., Sharmaine, G., Wells, D., Pyper, D., & Reimer-Heck, B. (1992). *Disability, sexuality, and abuse: An annotated bibliography.* Baltimore: Paul H Brookes.

Tantam, D.(2000) Adolescence and adulthood of individuals with Asperger syndrome. In A. Klin, F. Volkmar & S. Sparrow, (Eds.), *Asperger syndrome* (pp. 367-402). New York: The Guilford Press.

Tsiouris, J.A. (2001). The diagnosis of depression in people with severe/profound intellectual disability. *Journal of Intellectual Disability Research, 47,* 14-21.

Wallis, C. (2005, January 17). The new science of happiness. *Time.*

CHAPTER 4

The Adaptation and Application of Mindfulness-Based Psychotherapeutic Practices for Individuals with Intellectual Disabilities

Bronwyn L. Robertson, M.S.Ed., LPC

INTRODUCTION

Mindfulness-based psychotherapy utilizes self-regulative practices to enhance attention, awareness, acceptance, and emotion regulation. Research indicates these practices are effective in the management of many mental health challenges, notably anxiety, depression, anger, and stress, and are associated with beneficial neurophysiological and physiological changes including alterations in cortical and subcortical brain regions, decreased cortisol levels, and reduced blood pressure, heart, and respiration rate (Dusek, Out, Wohlhueter, Bhasin, & Zerbini, 2008; Stein, Ives-Deliperi, & Thomas, 2008). In the past two decades, mindfulness-based practices have become increasingly more integrated within mainstream psychotherapy and have been effectively adapted and applied to varying populations, ranging from inmates at correctional facilities to the elderly (Kenny & Williams, 2007; Samuelson, Carmody, Kabat-Zinn, & Bratt, 2007). In comparison, very little has been published on the adaptation and application of mindfulness-based psychotherapeutic practices for individuals with intellectual disabilities (ID), the population most at risk for developing anxiety and mood disorders and most likely to experience difficulty with self regulation, anger, and stress management.

According to the National Association for Dual Diagnosis (Fletcher, Stavakaki, Loschen, & First, 2006), 30 to 35% of individuals with ID have mental health disorders, nearly three times that of the general population (American Psychiatric Association, 2000). Likewise, the prevalence of anxiety and mood disorders within the ID population is more than double that of the general population, and at least 15% of individuals with ID engage in maladaptive behavior such as physical and/or verbal aggression, property damage, and self injury (American Psychiatric Association, 2000; Fletcher et al., 2006; Holden & Gitlesen, 2006). Given the mental health and behavioral challenges faced by this population, there is a great need for individuals with ID to have effective and practical treatment such as mindfulness-based psychotherapy.

This chapter will explore the main mindfulness-based psychotherapies and ways in which mindfulness-based psychotherapeutic practices have been adapted and applied for ID. This writer will provide examples of how mindfulness psychotherapy can be adapted and applied for individual and group therapy treatment of anxiety, depression, aggression and self-injury for individuals with ID.

THE PRACTICE OF MINDFULNESS

Mindfulness practice involves self regulation, mind-body relaxation, and the identification and acceptance of emotions, thoughts, and sensations. It is the "intentional self regulation of attention" and involves "paying attention in a particular way, on purpose, in the present moment, and nonjudgmentally" (Kabat-Zinn, 1982, 1994). As noted by Teasdale, Segal and Williams (2003), the main skills involved in mindfulness practice include:

1) Skills in sustained attention – identification and sustained awareness of emotional states, thoughts, and sensations
2) Self regulation of attention - flexibility of attention and ability to shift focus from one object or experience to another

Research supports that the practice of mindfulness skills, such as the identification and labeling of one's emotional states and sensations, produces significant alterations in brain electrical activity measurable via brain imaging. These alterations include greater activation of the prefrontal cortex, associated with enhanced self regulation, and deactivation of the amygdale, resulting in decreased emotional reactivity (Johnstone, van Reekum, Urry, Kalin & Davidson, 2007; Milad, 2002; Ochsner & Gross, 2005; Stein, 2007; 2008). As noted by Dusek et al.

(2008):

Emotional regulation appears to be accompanied by increased activation in prefrontal cortex (PFC) and/or decreased activation in regions such as amygdale and insula. Failure of emotional regulation may play a key role in anxiety and in depression. The dorsolateral PFC may be important in conscious reframing and control of external behavioral processes, while ventrolateral PFC and orbitiofrontal cortex may be particularly important in emotion evaluation and control of internal states. (p. 753)

Mindfulness-based, mind-body relaxation practices, such as meditation, yoga, breathing exercises, progressive muscle relaxation, guided imagery, and Qigong, induce a relaxation response (RR) which counteracts the physiological effects of stress (Benson, 1982). The RR is characterized by reductions in blood pressure, heart rate, respiration rate, oxygen consumption and cortisol levels, reduced psychological distress, and alterations in cortical and subcortical brain regions (Astin, Shapiro, Eisenberg, Forys, 2003; Benson, Beary, & Carol, 1974; Dusek et al., 2008; Jacobs, Benson, Friendman, 1996; Lazar, Bush, Gollub, Fricchione, Khalsa, 2000). Studies show that the beneficial effects of these practices can be achieved quickly and are long lasting. As noted by Zeidan, Gordon, Merchant and Goolkasian (2009), participants in their study on meditation showed reduced anxiety and enhanced ability to focus within three days of startingpractice. In another study on mindfulness meditation, 8 weeks of training resulted in enhanced emotion regulation and increased left sided anterior activation of the brain, an area which is associated with positive affect (Davidson, et al., 2003).

The mental training involved in the practice of mindfulness meditation can "significantly affect attention and brain function" including improvement in sustained attention, attentional processing, entrainment to sensory input, and enhanced ability to control the content of attention, according to Lutz, Slagter, Rawlings, Greischar, and Davidson (2009). Research indicates that mindfulness meditation is particularly effective when combined with other mind-body relaxation practices. Results from a 45 year follow-up study of Qigong and meditation practitioners, comparing their EEG readings from 1962 to the present, suggest that combined practice may alter both the EEG pattern and its underlying neurophysiology (Qin, Jin, Lin, & Hermanowicz, 2009). The practice of yoga combined with meditation has been associated with improved memory, attention, and concentration, as seen in elevated scores on the Wechsler memory scale, and decreases in both state and trait anxiety, as measured by Spielberger's State-Trait Anxiety Inventory (Subramanya & Telles, 2009).

Studies also support that the practice of yoga is effective in the management of anxiety disorders such as post-traumatic stress disorders (PTSD), obsessive compulsive disorder (OCD), and specific phobias (Kirkwood & Rampes, 2005). For example, yoga is being used extensively in the treatment of trauma related disorders in many different populations, including inner city children, survivors of natural disasters, and active duty military (Berger, Silver & Stein, 2009; Descilo, et al., 2009; Harvard Mental Health Letter, 2009). The Walter Reed Army Medical Center in Washington, DC is using the yogic practice of deep relaxation and meditation, known as yoga nidra, in the treatment of PTSD for active duty military returning from combat in Afghanistan and Iraq (Harvard Mental Health Letter, 2009).

MINDFULNESS-BASED PSYCHOTHERAPY

More than two decades of research support that the integration of mindfulness-based practices within psychotherapy is clinically effective, cost effective, and practical (Kabat-Zinn, 1982; Singh, Lancioni, Wahler, Winton, & Singh, 2008). Studies suggest that individuals who engage in mindfulness-based therapeutic treatment programs are highly likely to complete treatment and use the mindfulness-based skills acquired during therapy long after treatment has ended. Baer (2003), for example, found 83% treatment compliance among clients participating in mindfulness-based psychotherapy. Teasdale et al. (2003) noted that the "widespread" beneficial effects of mindfulness therapy "target processes across a range of disorders" via the training of "generically useful skills" that enhance the individual's ability to "switch out" of automatic patterns of reaction into "more intentional, considered choice of response:"

> The apparently simple procedure of teaching people to pay attention 'in a particular way' has benefits across a wide range of disorders; benefits can be obtained when patients are seen in large groups, with mixed diagnoses, and in situations in which it may appear that the training is not tailored to specific formulations of particular conditions but, rather, is offered in much the same way to all. In such situations, a generic form of mindfulness training apparently yields clinically useful effects. From such evidence it might seem that mindfulness training offers a cheap, general-purpose, therapeutic technology. (p.157)

Mindfulness skills have much in common with those that are utilized in more traditional psychotherapies. As noted by Dimidjian and Linehan (2003), the key components of mindfulness-based psychotherapy, such as observing, noticing, describing, labeling, and participating, are similar to those used in cognitive-behavioral therapy (CBT). Borkovec and Roemer (1994) compare the monitoring techniques utilized in CBT to that of "mindfulness exercise." Singh, Lancioni, Wahler, et al. (2008) view mindfulness-based psychotherapies as essentially newer, alternative approaches to CBT that may vary in their components but generally involve behavioral practices, cognitive strategies, and practices which enhance concentration. These main approaches to mindfulness-based psychotherapy include:

- Acceptance and Commitment Therapy (ACT)
- Mindfulness-Based Stress Reduction (MBSR)
- Dialectical Behavior Therapy (DBT)
- Mindfulness-Based Cognitive Therapy (MBCT)

Steven Hayes, the founder of ACT, likens the adaptation and application of mindfulness-based practices within psychotherapy to a "third wave of cognitive-behavior therapy" that has adopted "more experiential and indirect change strategies" with "a considerably broaden[ed] focus of change" (Hayes, Follette, & Linehan, 2004). Similarly, Jon Kabat-Zinn (1990), the pioneer of MBSR, notes comparisons between mindfulness training and cognitive behaviorial treatment procedures such as self-directed attention, sustained exposure to sensations, thoughts, and emotions, desensitization of conditioned responses, and reduction of avoidance behavior. Marsha Linehan (1993), the developer of DBT, suggests that the mindfulness practice of sustained attention, as in prolonged observation of thoughts, emotions, and sensations, is a form of exposure and can result in the extinction of avoidance and fear responses. Teasdale, et al. (2003), the developers of MBCT, share a similar view:

> The practice of mindfulness skills may improve patients' ability to tolerate negative emotional states and ability to cope with them….Mindfulness-based interventions appear to be conceptually consistent with many other empirically supported treatment approaches and may provide a technology of acceptance to complement the technology of change exemplified by most cognitive-behavioral procedures (p.139)

ACCEPTANCE AND SELF REGULATION

Mindfulness is an acceptance-oriented psychological process of relating openly, with curiosity and receptivity, to one's thoughts, sensations, and emotions (Eifert, Forsyth & Hayes, 2005). Studies indicate that the practice of acceptance skills, which counter the suppression of unwanted thoughts, feelings, and sessions, leads to the alleviation of short-term distress and enhanced emotion regulation (Masicampo & Baumeister, 2007).

Acceptance involves the noticing, observation, and "letting go" of unpleasant experiences. In this respect, mindfulness-based psychotherapy differs from traditional cognitive behavioral therapy in that its focus is on the awareness and acceptance of experience rather than in challenging and reframing it. As noted by Singh, Lancioni, Wahler, et al. (2008):

> One of the basic foundations of traditional cognitive behavior therapy (CBT) has been to directly challenge an individual's irrational thinking (i.e. erroneous cognitions) that leads to maladaptive behavior. Some of the newer approaches in CBT, however, are focused less on challenging an individual's irrational or negative thinking and more on changing the individual's relationship to thoughts and feelings through acceptance and mindfulness. (p.660).

Eifert et al. (2005) note that acceptance-based ideas have only recently been integrated into cognitive-behavioral therapies through manualization, systematic conceptualization, and operationalization as exemplified in the limited-time, semi-structured group treatment model of MBSR, structured treatment team format of DBT, and the flexible individual and group treatment approach of ACT. Current research suggests that, compared with more traditional applications of CBT, mindfulness-based approaches may offer more applicable and effective interventions. For example, multivariate analyses from a recent study comparing MBSR with cognitive-behavioral stress reduction (CBSR) on subjects' perceived stress, depression, psychological well-being, neuroticism, binge eating, energy, pain, and mindfulness, indicated that MBSR was most effective across all measures (Smith, et al., 2008). MBSR participants showed improvement in all eight outcomes while those participating in CBSR improved in 6. Results also suggested that MBSR was particularly effective on outcomes related to participants' perceived stress, depression, energy, pain and binge eating.

THE ADAPTATION AND APPLICATION OF MINDFULNESS-BASED PSYCHOTHERAPEUTIC PRACTICES FOR ID

MBSR is provided in an eight week, semi-structured group format using meditation, gentle yoga, and relaxation exercises. Its originator, Jon Kabat-Zinn, established the Center for Mindfulness, the world's oldest and largest medical center-based stress reduction program, within the Department of Medicine at the University of Massachusetts Medical School in 1995. According to the Center, there are presently no published studies on the adaptation and application of MBSR specifically for individuals for ID (M. Blacker, personal communication, October 14, 2009). MBSR has, however, been adapted for parents and caregivers of individuals with ID via a 2008 pilot study conductedin association with the Westside Regional Center in Culver City, California:

> Stress among parents and caregivers of children with developmental disabilities is pervasive and linked to lower quality of life, unhealthy family functioning, and negative psychological consequences. Our goal was to develop, implement, and evaluate the feasibility of an MBSR program designed for caregivers in a community-based participatory setting. A community-based MBSR program can be an effective intervention to reduce stress and improve psychological well-being for caregivers (Alicia Bazzano, personal communication, October 13, 2009).

This eight week program consisted of group training in meditation practice, group discussion of stressors affecting parents/caregivers, and gentle stretching. Results via pre- and post-scores on the Mindfulness Attention Awareness Scale (MAAS), Self-Compassion Scale (SCS), Scale of Psychological Well-Being (PWB), Perceived Stress Scale-10 Items (PSS10), and Parental Stress Scale (PSS) showed participants experienced significantly less stress and increased mindfulness, self-compassion, and well-being after completing the training.

DBT is a comprehensive, manualized treatment program consisting of weekly individual therapy, group skills training, and team consultation. Treatment can vary from three weeks to one year and provides strengths-based training in concrete, core mindfulness skills. DBT was originally developed by Lineham (1993) to treat individuals with borderline personality disorder and parasuicidal behavior but has been adapted for treatment of varying disorders and populations.

DBT has been successfully adapted for both children and adults with ID (Charlton, 2006; Dykstra & Charlton, 2004). As noted by Charlton (2006), the adaptation of DBT for the ID population required simplified language, multimodal presentation of information, the use of concrete activities, modeling, more structured and longer therapy sessions, and a more directive and active approach. The greatest challenge in adapting DBT for ID, however, is in the modification of training materials (Charlton, 2006).

For emotion regulation handout 1, rather than talking about reducing emotional vulnerability, as in Dr. Linehan's handout, we worked on understanding how emotions affect us and on making good decisions when experiencing an emotion. We also used a visual presentation style that would make it easier for clients with developmental disabilities to absorb the information…This modification allowed us to use simpler language that was already in our clients' vocabulary. It also provided another opportunity to emphasize that we control our emotions; they do not control us (pgs. 91-92).

ACT provides comprehensive, manualized, individualized, and flexible treatment, has broad applicability, can be delivered in both individual and group formats, and relies heavily on experiential exercises, stories, and metaphor (Hayes, Masuda, Bissett, Luoma, & Guerroro, 2004). The length of treatment varies, can range from 4 sessions over 3 weeks to 48 sessions over 26 weeks, depending upon the needs of the individual. For example, Hayes and Blackledge (2006) successfully adapted ACT for parents of children with Autism in a two day, 14 hour workshop setting utilizing the same material presented in individual therapy.

ACT's emphasis is on "the development of new responses in the presence of the previously avoided event that diminish its behavior regulatory power" (Pankey & Hayes, 2003, pg. 324). It involves metaphorical and experiential exercises that promote reflection upon and acceptance of experience such as the "river of thought metaphor" in which participants imagine themselves on a boat riding in a river without attempting to steer or stop the boat. This imagery reinforces the observation, noticing, and "letting go" of thoughts, feelings and sensations.

In adapting ACT for individuals with severe learning disabilities and OCD, Brown and Hooper (2009) found that its emphasis on experiential exercises and activities offers "a more accessible intervention model for learning disabled people than traditional CBT models based on verbal reasoning skills." ACT's developer, Steven Hayes, notes that are "new studies coming" involving the adaptation for the ID population (personal communication, September 23, 2009). Hayes' colleague, Julieann Pankey, a pioneer in the adaptation of ACT for ID, is preparing a publication for press on a recent study of ACT and ID (Personal communication, October 19, 2009). She also co-authored a 2003 study with Hayes on the adaptation of ACT for an individual with

ID and schizophrenia (Pankey & Hayes 2003):

> One of the more promising aspects of this early psychosis work is that it indicates that ACT may be useful even with patients experiencing significant cognitive disabilities…[I]ts heavy reliance on stories and exercises actually seem to recommend it for persons with cognitive problems or developmental delays (p.323).

Pankey and Hayes' 2003 study examined the effect of a short, four session psychosis treatment protocol with follow-up for a 22-year-old female with mild intellectual disability, a full scale IQ of 58, undifferentiated schizophrenia, and a history of abuse, neglect, and multiple foster home placements. This individual, who was residing in a 24-hour intensive supportive living situation, presented with command auditory hallucinations that told her to kill herself and delusions related to giving birth, staff members being family members, and health problems such as heart failure, seizures, and leg weakness. The study focused on four key outcome measures: compliance with medication; eating; ceasing taking apart her appliances in her apartment; and sleeping. Pankey and Hayes found improvement in all outcome measures as assessed by staff and client report:

> Believability, distress, frequency of symptoms were measured weekly by a 10 point Likert scale. Level of distress showed the most change through the ACT intervention. Level of distress related to her auditory hallucinations went from 8 in session 1 to 2 at the month follow up. By session 2, her thoughts that staff were her family members reach zero believability (p. 324)

Although published studies on the adaptation of mindfulness-based psychotherapy for ID are limited and relatively recent, mindfulness-based, mind-body relaxation practices have been used effectively with this population for decades. Uma, Nagarathna, Vaidehi, and Seethalakshmi (1989) pioneered the use of yoga as a therapeutic tool for children with ID. They found that sustained yoga practice by their participants resulted in decreased anxiety along with increases in IQ and overall adaptive functioning.

Beauchemin, Hutchins and Patterson (2008) conducted a pilot study using mindfulness meditation with 34 adolescents. Results of this study showed decreased state and trait anxiety, enhanced social skills, and improved focus of attention and academic performance in subjects.

Recent studies have explored the adaptation and application of a specific mindfulness-based meditation practice, known as "Meditations on the Soles of the Feet," for the management of physical aggression exhibited by adult offenders with mild ID and individuals with moderate ID at risk of losing their community placements (Singh, Lanciono, Winton, et al. 2008; Singh, Lancioni, Winton, Adkins, Singh, & Singh, 2007). In both studies, participants were taught to redirect, or shift, their focus from the object of their anger to a neutral spot on the soles of their feet. As noted by Singh et al. (2007), this training encourages participants to "stop and think before acting" by redirecting their attention from their anger to a neutral emotion and to focus on a neutral part of their body so that they can calm down before reacting. Results showed a substantial decrease in physical aggression exhibited by adult offenders with ID immediately after completion of treatment and as seen in a 12 month follow up (Singh, Lancioni, Winton, et al., 2008). Benefit-cost analysis showed a 95.7% reduction in costs related to medical leave and medical treatment for injuries sustained by staff working with individuals at risk of losing community placement (Singh et al., 2007). These participants were able to manage their physical aggression and maintain their community placements for at least 2 years post treatment (Singh et al., 2007). As noted by Singh et al. (2007), "individuals, even with moderate mental retardation, can successfully learn to control aggressive behaviors using the mindfulness procedure" (pg. 810).

Paclawskyj and Yoo (2006) adapted Behavioral Relaxation Training (BRT) for individuals with severe to mild ID and co-morbid mood and/or anxiety disorders. Of the 18 participants in their study, 5 were receiving inpatient treatment and 13 were being treated in outpatient settings. The participants received training in relaxation skills, or postures, which "disrupt" previously reinforced maladaptive behaviors associated with avoidance, such as aggression and self-injury. Relaxation skills were taught in 10 minute sessions via 10 postures (Paclawskyj & Yoo, 2006):

1. Head – motionless, supported by pillow

2. Eyes – lightly closed

3. Mouth – lips parted slightly

4. Throat – absence of motion

5. Shoulders rounded, symmetric

6. Body – torso is still with hips and legs symmetric to midline

7. Hands – fingers gently curved and resting on chair

8. Feet – still toes pointed away from each other to form a V

9. Absence of vocalization

10. Breathing – rate slower than baseline

Progress in BRT is typically measured via self assessment and, as noted by Paclawskyj and Yoo, the primary challenge in adapting it for the ID population is in development of a method that does not rely on subjective reports of internal states. Individuals with ID, depending upon the level of disability, may experience difficulty assessing and communicating such experiences. Through the modeling of both relaxed and non-relaxed postures for participants, and through assessment by trained observers, they found that 17 out of 18 participants were able to acquire relaxation skills in an average of two hours of training. Seventy five percent of their participants showed a significant decrease in maladaptive behaviors once training was completed.

Individualized, strengths-based treatment is the key to effective mindfulness-based psychotherapy. Clients can guide their own treatment based on their preferences, interests, strengths, and needs. While one client may respond well to guided imagery, another may benefit more from meditative exercises or yoga, and yet another may prefer to work with expressive arts such as mandalas. Training of staff, caregivers, and family members in the same practices as the client is also helpful in creating therapeutic, supportive environments for clients both within and outside of therapy sessions.

In preparation for mindfulness-based treatments, clients benefit from training in the vocabulary and basic skills needed in the identification and rating of emotional states and sensations. Materials, such as emotion identification and mood charts, have been modified for ID and are very helpful (Benson, 1992, 1994). Alternatively, clinicians can develop their own materials and tailor them to the specific application, format, or client, as does this writer.

CASE EXAMPLES

For more than a decade, this writer has utilized mindfulness-based practices in the treatment of anxiety, depression, physical aggression and self injury for individuals with ID in community agency and private practice settings, and as a consultant. By combining elements of ACT, expressive therapy, mind-body relaxation, and meditative exercises based on everyday activities such as breathing, exercising, and playing, this author has adapted and applied mindfulness-based psychotherapeutic practices for individuals functioning in the lower moderate to mild range of ID, in both individual and group therapy formats, and in the integration of individuals with ID into mainstream mental health psychotherapy groups.

The case examples presented are based on a flexible, strengths-based, individualized treatment approach with longer and more frequent therapy sessions, telephone consultation with the client in the initial stages of therapy, and ongoing consultation with staff, employers, caregivers, and family members. Length of treatment in each case varied depending on the client's specific needs, strengths, and goals.

Through modeling and experiential exercises, simple, highly effective, mindfulness-based relaxation practices can be taught to clients with lower moderate ID. For example, a 35-year-old, nonverbal, male, with a full scale IQ of 48, was able to learn and apply simple breathing and self soothing techniques to manage his physical aggression and self injury. At risk of losing his day support services due to periodic, explosive physical aggression, self-injury, and property damage, this client utilized a deep breathing technique, similar to silent "whistling", humming, and simple yoga poses to self soothe, calm, and redirect himself. Staff were trained to cue the client to use these techniques periodically throughout the day and during times when the he was exhibiting signs of distress or agitation. Within 6 months, weekly sessions were tapered to twice monthly, incidents of serious aggression and self injury decreased from twice weekly to less than once monthly, and the client was able to maintain day support services.

Mindfulness practices are useful in helping clients with PTSD create a sense of safety and empowerment within themselves as in the case of a 24-year-old female with mild ID, full scale IQ 69, an early childhood history of severe sexual/physical abuse by her biological parents, and physical abuse by multiple foster care providers. She was referred for therapy as she was at risk of losing her community supportive living placement and employment due to her severe, explosive physical aggression which often resulted in injury to staff and was causing high staff turnover. Episodes of aggression were periodic but intense and were increasing in frequency at the time of referral, occurring at least once every two weeks. Subjected to extreme physical and sexual abuse, beginning in early childhood and continuing until age 18, the client reported experiencing nightmares and flashbacks on a daily basis, suffered severe insomnia, was isolative, had no friends, and was experiencing frequent, passive suicidal ideation. She participated in individual therapy sessions for 11 months, beginning with twice weekly sessions for the first two months.

During the first two months of therapy, the focus was on creating rapport, trust, and a safe, therapeutic environment. During this time, the client was also introduced to deep breathing techniques, guided imagery and expressive arts exercises such as mandalas and "creating a safe place" drawings and journaling. Deep breathing was introduced via modeling and use of woodwind instruments, pinwheels, and blowing bubbles. Guided imagery, presented by the author, involved metaphors and images associated with safety, security, calmness and peace. Through guided imagery and expressive art exercises, the client was guided in finding her own images, sensations, places, colors, and textures associated with safety and peace. The client's identified safe, calming colors, aromas, textures and objects were used during relaxation exercises while in session and were placed throughout her apartment and at her work station.

After completion of the first two months of therapy, the client began work in earnest on identifying her triggers, observing, noticing and "letting go" of intense, unpleasant thoughts, feelings and sensations, and redirecting her attention to "safe, calm" images, thoughts, experiences, and emotions. The client was given daily mindfulness practice homework, which she eagerly completed.

Incidents of aggression increased to twice weekly during the first few weeks of treatment but with less intensity, and tapered over the course of treatment. No staff sustained injuries during this time. By the sixth month of treatment, there were no reported incidents of aggression in the client's work environment, and incidents at her residence decreased to less than once monthly. And, she was no longer reporting suicidal ideation and indicated her nightmares had decreased from nightly occurrences to an average twice weekly. Two year follow up showed the client had maintained both her employment and supported living services.

Individuals with ID can make much progress in a mindfulness-based group therapy format, provided they can be screened and placed appropriately. This writer developed a mindfulness-based trauma therapy group for three males, all of whom were diagnosed with mild ID and PTSD, had histories of childhood sexual trauma, and were in their early to late 20s. All three were experiencing difficulty with frequent nightmares, hyper-reactivity, pervasive anxiety, and flashbacks. As these three men shared an interest in superhero movies, books, and games, group exercises and homework focused on the mindful "superhero" within each member. In example, Qigong exercises, which clients regarded as "martial arts," were used to enhance relaxation, self regulation, and self empowerment. After two months of weekly group treatment, members reported decreased nightmares and a greater sense of "power."

This author utilizes the same mindfulness-based practices in therapy for individuals with and without ID, in both individual and group treatment. The experiential, skills-based practices of mindfulness psychotherapy make it very adaptable and applicable to many different populations and mental health challenges, and are useful in integrating clients with ID into mixed psychotherapy groups, with individuals of varying IQs and functioning levels. After 2 years of monthly ACT oriented individual therapy, a client with mild ID transferred into a mainstream weekly anxiety management group also facilitated by this writer. The client, a 28-year-old male with full scale IQ of 69, panic disorder with agoraphobia and major depressive disorder, found yogic breathing exercises, mandalas, simple yoga postures, and journaling were most useful in managing his anxiety. Regular use of these practices enabled him to overcome agoraphobia and better manage his panic attacks and depressive episodes which significantly decreased in frequency and severity since he began therapy. He was able to successfully integrate into the mainstream group as the only member diagnosed with ID due in part to his familiarity with the practices utilized in group and through sharing a common mindfulness "language" with other group members. He actively participated in group and was able to learn and effectively practice meditative exercises involving the identification of thoughts, feelings, and sensations, imagery exercises which conceptualize thoughts, emotions, and sensations as passing waves, and several yogic deep breathing exercises.

DISCUSSION

Mindfulness-based psychotherapeutic practices hold most promise for the treatment of mental health and behavioral challenges for individuals with ID. Thus far, these practices have been shown to be clinically effective, highly applicable and adaptable for use with this population. Presently, published studies are few and there are no specific assessment tools designed specifically to measure mindfulness-based progress for individuals with ID. Further study, practice and the development of ID specific mindfulness assessment tools are greatly needed.

REFERENCES

American Psychiatric Association. (2000). *Diagnostic and statistical manual of mental ealth (4th edition, text revision)*. Washington, DC: Authors.

Astin, J.A., Shapiro, S.L., Eisenberg, D.M., & Forys, K.L. (2003). Mind-body medicine: State of the science, implications for practice. *Journal of American Board Family Practice, 16*, 131-147.

Baer, R. (2003). Mindfulness training as a clinical intervention: A conceptual and empirical review. *Clinical Psychology: Science and Practice, 10(2)*, 125-143.

Beauchemin, J., Hutchins, T., & Paterson, F. (2008). Mindfulness meditation may lessen anxiety, promote social skills, and improve academic performance among adolescents with learning disabilities. *Complementary Health Practice Review, 13(1)*, 34-45.

Benson, B.A. (1992). *Teaching anger management training to persons with mental retardation*. Worthington, OH: International Diagnostic Systems.

Benson B.A. (1994). Anger management training: A self-control program for people with mild mental retardation. In N.Bouras (Ed.), *Mental health in mental retardation* (pp. 224-232). Cambridge, United Kingdom: Cambridge University Press.

Benson, H. (1982). The relaxation response: History, physiological basis and clinical usefulness. *Acta Med Scand Supplmentum, 660*, 231-237.

Benson, H., Beary, J.F., Carol, M.P. (1974). The relaxation response. *Psychiatry, 37*, 37-46.

Berger, D, Silver, E, & Stein, R. (2009). Effects of yoga on inner-city children's well-being: a pilot study. *Alternative Therapy Health Medicine, 15(5)*, 36-42.

Borkovec, T.D., & Roemer, L. (1994). Generalized anxiety disorder. In R.T. Ammerman & M. Hersen (eds.), *Handbook of prescriptive treatments for adults* (pp. 261-281). New York: Plenum.

Brown, F. & Hooper, S. (2009). Acceptance and Commitment Therapy (ACT) with a learning disabled young person experiencing anxious and obsessive thoughts. *Journal of Intellectual Disability, 13(3)*, 195-201.

Charlton, M. (2006). Dialectical behavior therapy for children with developmental disabilities. *NADD Bulletin, 9(5)*, 90-94.

Davidson, R., Kabat-Zinn, J., Schumacher, J., Rosenkranz, M., Muller, D., Santorelli, S., et al. (2003). Alterations in brain and immune function produced by mindfulness meditation. *Psychosomatic Medicine, 65*, 564-570. Available at http://www.urmc. rochester.edu/smd/Psych/research/documents/00006842-200307000-00014.pdf.

Desciolo, T., Vedamurtachar, A., Gerberg, P.L., Nagaraja, D., Gangadhar, B.N., Damodaran, B., et al. (2009). Effects of yoga breath intervention alone and in combination with an exposure therapy for post-traumatic stress disorder and depression in survivors of the 2004 South-East Asia tsunami. *Acta Psychiatric Scandanavia, 121(4)* 289-300.

Dimidjian, S., & Linehan, M. (2003). Defining an agenda for future research on the clinical application of mindfulness practice. *Clinical Psychology: Science and Practice, 10(2),* 166-171.

Dusek, J.A., Out, H.H., Wohlhueter, A.L., Bhasin, M., & Zerbini. (2008). Genonmic counter-stress changes induced by the relaxation response. *PLoS one 3(7),* e2576.

Dykstra E., & Charlton M. (2004). *Dialectical behavior therapy skills training: Adapted for special populations.* University of Denver, Colorado: Aurora Mental Health.

Eifert, G., Forsyth, J., & Hayes, S. (2005). *Acceptance and commitment therapy for anxiety disorders.* Oakland, CA: New Harbinger Publications, Inc.

Fletcher, R., Stavakaki, C., Loschen, E, & First, M, (2006). *DSM-IV-ID.* Symposium conducted at the meeting of the International Congress of the National Association on Dual Diagnosis, Boston, MA.

Harvard Mental Health Letter. (2009, April). Yoga for anxiety and depression. 1-4.

Hayes, S, & Blackledge, J. (2006). Using acceptance and commitment training in the support of parents of children diagnosed with autism. *Child and Family Behavior Therapy, 28(1),* 1-18.

Hayes, S.C., Follette, V.M., & Linehan, M.M. (2004). *Mindfulness and acceptance: Expanding the cognitive-behavioral tradition.* New York: Guilford Press.

Hayes, S., Masuda, A., Bissett, R., Luoma, J., & Guerrero, L. (2004). DBT, FAP, and ACT: How empirically oriented are the new behavior therapy technologies. *Behavior Therapy, 35*, 35-39.

Holden, B., & Gitlesen, J.P. (2006). A total population study of challenging behavior in the county of Hedmark, Norway: Prevalence and risk markers. *Research in Developmental Disabilities, 27*, 456-465.

Jacobs, G.D., Benson, H., & Friendman, R. (1996). Topographic EEG mapping of the relaxation response. *Biofeedback Self Regulation, 21*, 121-129.

Johnstone, T., van Reekum, C., Urry, H., Kalin, N., & Davidson, R. (2007). Failure to regulate: Counterproductive recruitment of top-down prefrontal-subcortical circuitry in major depression. *Journal of Neuroscience, 27*, 887-8884.

Kabat-Zinn, J. (1982). An outpatient program in behavioral medicine: Theoretical considerations and preliminary results. *General Hospital Psychiatry, 4*, 33-47.

Kabat-Zinn, J. (1990). *Full catastrophe living: Using the wisdom of your mind to face stress, pain and illness.* New York: Dell Publishing.

Kabat-Zinn, J. (1994). *Whenever you go there you are.* New York: Hyperion.

Kenny, M. A., & Williams, J. M. G. (2007). Treatment-resistant depressed patients show a good response to mindfulness-based cognitive therapy. *Behaviour Research and Therapy, 45(3)*, 617-625.

Kirkwood, G, Rampes, H. (2005). Yoga for Anxiety: Systematic review of the research evidence. *British Journal of Sports Medicine, 39*, 12, 884-891.

Lazar, S.W., Bush, G., Gollub, R.L., Fricchione, G.L., & Khalsa, G. (2000). Functional brain mapping of the relaxation response and meditation. *Neuroreport, 11*, 1581-1585.

Linehan, M. (1993). *Cognitive-behavioral treatment of borderline personality disorder.* New York: The Guilford Press.

Lutz, A., Slagter, H., Rawlings, N., Greischar, L., & Davidson, R. (2009). Mental training enhances attentional stability: neural and behavioral evidence. *Journal of Neuroscience, 29(42)*, 13418-13427.

Masicampo, E. & Baumeister, R. (2007). Relating mindfulness and self-regulatory processes. *Journal of Psychological Inquiry, 18*, 255-258.

Milad, M. & Quirk, G. (2002). Neurons in prefrontal cortex signal memory for fear extinction. *Nature, 420*, 70-74.

Ochsner, K. & Gross, J. (2005). The cognitive control of emotion. *Trends in Cognitive Science, 9*, 242-249.

Paclawskyj, T. R., & Yoo, J. H. (2006). Behavioral Relaxation Training (BRT): Facilitating acquisition in individuals with developmental disabilities. *The NADD Bulletin, 9*, 13-18.

Pankey, J. & Hayes, S. (2003). Acceptance and Commitment Therapy for Psychosis. *International Journal of Psychology and Psychological Therapy, 3(2)*, 311-328.

Qin, Z, Jin,Y., Lin, S., & Hermanowicz, N. (2009). A forty-five year follow-up EEG of Qigong practice. *International Journal of Neuroscience, 119(4)*, 538-552.

Roemer, L., & Orsillio, S. (2002). Expanding our conception of and treatment for generalized anxiety disorder: Integrating Mindfulness/Acceptance-Based Approaches with existing cognitive-behavioral models. *Clinical Psychology: Science and Practice, 9(1)*, 54-68.

Samuelson, M., Carmody, J., Kabat-Zinn, J., & Bratt, M. A. (2007). Mindfulness-based stress reduction in Massachusetts correctional facilities. *The Prison Journal, 87(2)*, 254-268.

Singh, N. N., Lancioni, G. E., Wahler, R. G., Winton, A. S. W., & Singh, J. (2008). Mindfulness approaches in cognitive behavior therapy. *Behavioural and Cognitive Psychotherapy, 36,* 659–666.

Singh, N.N., Lancioni, G., Winton, A., Adkins, A., Singh, J., & Singh, A. (2007). Mindfulness Training Assists Individuals with Moderate Mental Retardation to Maintain Their Community Placements. *Behavior Modification, 31 (6)*, 800-814.

Singh, N.N., Lancioni, G., Winton, Singh, A., A., Adkins, & A., Singh, J. (2008). Clinical and benefit-cost outcome of teaching a mindfulness-based procedure to adult offenders w/ID. *Behavior Modification, 32(5)*, 622-637.

Smith, B., Shelly, B., Dalen, J., Wiggins, k., Tooley, E., & Bernard, J. (2008). A pilot study comparing the effects of mindfulness-based and cognitive-behavioral stress reduction. *Journal of Complementary Alternative Medicine, 14(3)*, 251-258.

Stein, D. (2007). What is self? A psychobiological perspective. *CNS Spectrums, 12*, 333-336.

Stein, D. (2008). Emotional regulation: Implications for the psychobiology of psychotherapy. *CNS Spectrums, 13*, 195-198.

Stein, D., Ives-Deliperi, V., & Thomas, K. (2008). Psychobiology of Mindfulness. *The International Journal of Neuropsychiatric Medicine, 13(9)*, 752-756.

Subramanya, P. & Telles, S. (2009). Effects of two yoga-based relaxation techniques on memory scores and state anxiety. *Biopsychosocial Medicine, 13*, 3-8.

Teasdale, J.D, Segal, Z., & Williams, J.M.G. (2003). Mindfulness training and problem formulation. *Clinical Psychology, 10(2)*, 157-160.

Uma, K. Nagarathna, R., Nagendra, H. R., Vaidehi. S. & Seethalakshmi. R. (1989). The integrated approach of Yoga: A therapeutic tool for mentally retarded children: A one-year controlled study. *Journal of Mental Deficiency Research, 33*, 415-421.

Zeidan, F., Gordon, N.S., Merchant, J, & Goolkasian, P. (2009). The effects of brief mindfulness meditation training on experiementally induced pain. *Journal of Pain, 11(3)*, 199-209.

CHAPTER 5

Behavioral Relaxation Training (BRT) for Persons Who Have Intellectual Disability

Theodosia R. Paclawskyj, Ph.D., BCBA

INTRODUCTION

While it is well-established that persons with intellectual disabilities (ID) have higher rates of psychiatric disorders than the typical population (AACAP, 1999; IAS-SID, 2001; Fletcher, Loschen, Stavrakaki, & First, 2007), the availability of psychological treatments for individuals with ID does not match the breadth of interventions available for typically functioning persons. Adaptations of the cognitive-behavioral procedures for general psychiatric disorders have been slow to develop and may not always be realistically modified for individuals with ID who are nonverbal.

The one domain of psychology in which psychological treatment has been consistently demonstrated to be effective for persons with ID is Applied Behavior Analysis. The Expert Consensus Guidelines on the Treatment of Psychiatric and Behavioral Problems in Mental Retardation published in the *American Journal on Mental Retardation* (Rush & Frances, 2000) recommend the use of Applied Behavior Analysis (ABA) as a psychosocial intervention for every major psychiatric disorder and symptom. Such interventions include reinforcement-based strategies; behavior interruption and prevention; caregiver training; and training in replacement behaviors such as communication and social skills for specific problem behaviors as well as anxiety, hyperactivity, impulsivity, excessive dependence, social withdrawal, and noncompliance. However, the greatest volume of research in ABA has focused specifically on remediation of maladaptive behaviors such as self-injury, aggression, property destruction, pica, and others (Arndorfer & Miltenberger, 1993; Association for Behavior Analysis, Task Force on the Right to Effective Behavioral Treatment, 1988; National Institutes of Health, Consensus Development Panel on Destructive Behaviors in Persons with Developmental Disabilities, 1989; Sprague & Horner, 1995). .

The current standard of care in Applied Behavior Analytic treatment of maladaptive behavior involves manipulation of reinforcement contingencies to maximize the probability of the occurrence of specific adaptive responses and minimize the likelihood of maladaptive behaviors. It also involves antecedent interventions such as those designed to alter the physical structure of the environment, emphasize a structured schedule, modify curricula, and modify social groupings. However, behavioral interventions are not successful in all cases. Didden, Duker, and Korzilius (1997) conducted a meta-analysis of 482 studies from 1968-1994 and found that only 57.8% were fairly or highly effective (defined as percentage of nonoverlapping points between baseline and treatment data graphs).

Yet in the most recent decade, antecedent interventions have been increasingly explored (Cooper, Heron, & Heward, 2007; Horner, Carr, Strain, Todd, & Reed, 2002). Antecedent interventions can minimize risk to the individual and their caregivers as they are implemented prior to the occurrence of maladaptive behaviors (Cooper et al.). One such group of interventions involves manipulating motivating operations; that is, external events that have the effect of altering the potency of reinforcement contingencies. Such external events can include physiological states such as fatigue or illness as well as level of emotional arousal. Horner, Day, and Day (1997) demonstrated the effectiveness of manipulation of motivating operations when examining the impact of calming activities on maladaptive behavior occurring several hours later in participants for whom specific circumstances produced agitation. Further research in this area would be highly beneficial, for investigators have long called for the extension of procedures used for managing respondent behavior (such as emotional arousal) in the general population to persons with ID (e.g., Harvey, 1979).

Formal relaxation training is a logical technique to investigate when considering calming activities. Relaxation has long been used as means to reduce anxiety and to cope with stress-eliciting situations in the typically-functioning population (Poppen, 1998). In addition, a significant contributor to the development of psychiatric disorders in persons with ID is a lack of coping skills (Eaton & Menolascino, 1982; Lindsay & Olley, 1998). Rates of anxiety disorders in this population range from 0.7%-4% (Crews, Bonaventura, & Rowe, 1994; Glick & Zigler, 1995; Harden & Sahl, 1997; Rojahn, Borthwick-Duffy, & Jacobson, 1993), and symptoms of anxiety are one of the most common reasons for psychiatric referral (King, DeAntonio, McCracken, Forness, & Ackerland, 1994). However, an additional potential benefit of relaxation training is the opportunity for the individual to acquire a coping skill that could become self-directed; that is, used at any time without depending on a caregiver to implement the intervention (Zipkin, 1985).

Finding appropriate methods of relaxation training in persons with ID is not without its challenges (Luiselli, 1980). Investigations conducted over the past three decades employed varying techniques, target behaviors, and methods of evaluation; unfortunately, the majority lack sufficient experimental rigor to provide definitive conclusions. In addition, existing group studies have rarely used both observational and physiological methods of data collection to measure the emotional arousal that occurs with anxiety or agitation.

Of the various existing methods of relaxation training (e.g., Progressive Muscle Relaxation, EMG biofeedback, autogenic training), the most promising method to date is a procedure within Applied Behavior Analysis known as Behavioral Relaxation Training (BRT; Poppen, 1998; Schilling & Poppen, 1983). Existing research on BRT (e.g., Lindsay & Baty, 1989; Lindsay, Baty, Michie, & Richardson, 1989) has demonstrated that this procedure can be acquired rapidly and effectively. Of note is that BRT does not require any verbal report of internal states, therefore making it amenable even for persons who are nonverbal. BRT can teach the ability to tolerate the range of distressing emotions that can result from the onset or consequence of unpleasant events.

In a typical intervention that includes BRT, the client, caregivers and therapist work collaboratively to identify the etiology of the problem through functional assessment. With mutual understanding of the potential beneficial impact of relaxation on target behaviors or psychiatric symptoms, BRT is taught in a structured format in a clinic setting. Following successful acquisition of the procedure, relaxation is generalized and practiced through caregiver cues or self-regulation in the client's daily environment.

THEORETICAL FOUNDATION

Relaxation training is a proactive intervention aimed at decreasing the occurrence of tension and anxiety via inhibition of the beta sympathetic nervous system and reduction of peripheral muscle activity (Freedman, Sabharwal, Lanni, Desai, Wenig, et al., 1988; Luiselli, 1980). The relaxation response that is produced via relaxation training counters the stress response within the body, which consists of physiological arousal such as increased heart rate and blood pressure, slowed digestive functioning, decreased blood flow to the extremities, increased release of hormones such as cortisol and adrenalin, and other processes that prepare the body for "fight or flight." Methods to evoke the relaxation response generally target one or more of the following domains: cognitive, physiological, and behavioral. BRT focuses on the latter and incorporates systematic observation and data collection, a hallmark of Applied Behavior Analysis (Poppen, 1998).

BRT was developed by Schilling and Poppen (1983), who noted that patients who completed Progressive Muscle Relaxation (PR) displayed a set of overt behaviors that co-occurred with self-reported and physiologically-measured relaxation. Such behaviors included slowed breathing, no movement of the extremities, loose jaw, absence of swallowing, and closed eyes. These authors chose to systematically investigate the possibility that specific instruction in these observable behaviors might induce the relaxation response. They identified ten target behaviors in various parts of the body for specific training (see Table 1). These overt behaviors could be measured objectively and did not rely on self-report. Using a participant group of 32 typically functioning adults, Schilling and Poppen (1983) demonstrated in their initial study of BRT that the physiological relaxation response was elicited during the procedure. Validity measures included frontalis EMG recording (a measure of muscle activity, which is lower during relaxation), finger temperature (which is higher during relaxation), skin conductance level (a measure of electrical resistance of the skin, which is higher during relaxation), the Behavioral Relaxation Scale (BRS; a checklist of correct and incorrect responses on the 10 overt behaviors) and self-report. Participants trained in BRT reported improvements on the self-report scale and also demonstrated decreased EMG and improvement in BRS scores. In contrast, those trained in PR demonstrated improvements only in self-report and BRS scores. Those trained in EMG biofeedback demonstrated similar improvements to those in the BRT group, although gains were not maintained at 4 to 6 weeks follow-up; and those in the control group of listening to music showed no improvement except on the self-report scale. Temperature and skin conduction proved to be unrelated to any of the procedures. Therefore, BRT proved to be a viable method of eliciting the relaxation response and a simple procedure to teach individuals that did not require subjective understanding of relaxed states.

Table 1. The ten target behaviors within BRT

Target Behavior	
Head	The head is motionless and supported by the chair/cushion with the nose in the midline of the body. Parts of the nostrils and the underside of the chin are visible.
Eyes	The eyelids are lightly closed with a smooth appearance and no motion of eyes beneath the eyelids.
Mouth	The lips are parted at the center of the mouth from ¼ inch to 1 inch with the front teeth also parted.
Throat	There is an absence of motion.
Shoulders	Both shoulders appear rounded and transect the same horizontal plane. They rest against the chair with no motion other than respiration.
Body	The torso, hips, and legs are symmetrical around midline, resting against the chair, with no movement.
Hands	Both hands are resting on the armrest of the chair or on the lap with palms down and the fingers curled in a claw-like fashion. The fingers are sufficiently curled if a pencil can pass freely beneath the highest point of the arc other than the thumb.

— continued next page —

Feet	The feet are pointed away from each other at an angle between 60° and 90° from a horizontal plane.
Quiet	There are no vocalizations or loud respiratory sounds.
Breathing	Scored as correct if the breath frequency is less than that observed during baseline with no breathing interruptions. One breath equals one complete inhale-exhale cycle. A breath is counted if any part of the inhale occurs on the cue starting the observation interval and any part of the exhale occurs on the cue ending the observation interval.

LITERATURE REVIEW

As previously stated, in the population of typically functioning individuals, relaxation training has been used to reduce anxiety, agitation, pain, and stress (Bernstein & Borkovec, 1973; Craske, Rapee, & Barlow, 1992; Jacobson, 1938; Turk, Rudy, & Sorkin, 1992). However, these techniques so readily available to the general population have not been sufficiently investigated or employed to any comparable degree in persons with ID. The existing body of research on the effectiveness of relaxation training focuses primarily on adults with ID who display stress-related symptoms (e.g., Morrissey, Franzin, & Karen, 1992; Reese, Sherman, & Sheldon, 1984; Schloss, Smith, Santori, & Bryant, 1989; Wells, Turner, Bellack, & Hersen, 1978). Yet many of these studies are either case reports or lack experimental control, and not all relaxation procedures have been demonstrated to be effective. In addition, clinical use of relaxation procedures has been so variable that some clinicians choose not to pursue their use due to treatment failures that result from inadequate knowledge of the procedures for training (Lindsay & Olley, 1998).

Biofeedback

Use of biofeedback; that is, relaxation training that relies on physiological measurement to signal the individual when they are in a relaxed and nonrelaxed state, has rarely been studied in individuals with ID and generally has been incorporated with other procedures (Lindsay & Olley, 1998). Although the study was confounded by the use of reinforcement and EMG biofeedback simultaneously, Schroeder, Peterson, Solomon, and Artley (1977) demonstrated reductions in self-injury for two individuals with severe ID. Calamari, Geist, & Shahbazian (1987) included biofeedback into a multi-component relaxation training intervention with reinforcement, modeling, and adapted Progressive Muscle Relaxation (PR; see below) but the relative contribution of each intervention was not assessed.

Progressive Muscle Relaxation

The relaxation procedure most researched with individuals with developmental disabilities is an abbreviated form of Progressive Muscle Relaxation (PR; Lindsay & Baty, 1989; Luiselli, 1980). With PR it is assumed that through a series of tense-release muscle exercises, an individual will become aware of the difference in sensation between tensed and relaxed states, resulting in an overall decrease in muscle activity and subsequent decreased autonomic arousal (Bernstein & Borkovec, 1973). Some experimentally controlled studies have demonstrated that PR can reduce maladaptive behaviors in adults with ID (e.g., McPhail & Chamove, 1989). However, a limitation of this procedure is that it requires the person to subjectively identify tension and relaxation and to correctly imitate muscle tensing and releasing, which may be difficult for some individuals who are more cognitively impaired (Lindsay, Baty, Michie, & Richardon, 1989; Michulka, Poppen, & Blanchard, 1988; Poppen, 1998). In addition, some studies found that practice in tensing muscles may make individuals more agitated or excited (Lindsay & Baty, 1986, 1989). Finally, several controlled studies failed to demonstrate abbreviated PR as more effective than other procedures (see Luiselli, 1980 for a review).

Behavioral Relaxation Training

Since the initial study by Schilling and Poppen (1983) BRT has been evaluated for a diverse range of disorders and conditions. These include hyperactivity (Brandon, Eason, & Smith, 1986; Donney & Poppen, 1989; Eason, Brandon, Smith, & Serpas, 1986; Raymer & Poppen, 1985), essential and Parkinsonian tremor (Chung, Poppen, & Lundervold, 1995; Lundervold, Belwood, Craney, & Poppen, 1999), student anxiety (Rasid & Parish, 1998; Tatum, Lundervold, & Ament, 2006), tension headaches (Blanchard et al., 1991), stress management for caregivers at risk for child abuse and neglect (Lutzker, Wesch, & Rice, 1984), non-insulin-dependent diabetes (Aikens, Kiolbasa, & Sobel, 1997), traumatic brain injury (Eastridge & Mozzoni, 2008; Guercio, Ferguson, & McMorrow, 2001), Huntington's Disease (Fecteau & Boyne, 1987), and tension headaches (Eufemia & Wesolowski, 1983) among others.

To date, fifteen studies and case reports have been conducted to evaluate both the feasibility and efficacy of utilizing BRT with individuals with ID. However, not all demonstrated experimental control of treatment effects (see Table 2). Those utilizing controlled methodology included two studies that assessed the impact of BRT on anxiety and concentration (Lindsay, Baty, Michie, & Richardson, 1989; Lindsay, Fee, Michie, & Heap, 1994). Lindsay et al. (1989) assess anxiety via pulse rate and the Behavioural Anxiety Rating Scale (BAR), a modification of the BRS in which the 10 BRT behaviors were rated on a five-point Likert scale of "completely relaxed" to "very anxious." Participants were adults with moderate to severe ID and were divided into five groups: group BRT instruction, group PR instruction, individual BRT instruction, individual PR instruction, and control (no instruction in relaxation). While the control group showed no change in scores, the individual BRT training group demonstrated an over 80-point improvement on the BAR; the group BRT training group showed the second greatest change, followed by the individual PR group and the group PR group. In terms of pulse rate, no significant changes were found in any group.

Lindsay et al. (1994) further evaluated the clinical potential of BRT by assessing whether or not cue control words alone could be used to induce the relaxation response following training in BRT. Five participants diagnosed with severe ID were included in the study. Each participant displayed a variety of anxious and agitated symptoms including pacing, perseverative speech, shouting or screaming, avoidance of others, and overactivity. Four conditions were compared via single-case methodology for each participant: baseline (sitting in a chair), cue control-only (the therapist stating the words "quiet and still"), training in BRT with the addition of the same cue control words at the sixth training session, followed by cue control-only. In each condition, the participant was asked to complete simple tasks and was videotaped during and after the activity. The BAR again was used to rate degree of anxiety and relaxation; additionally, the amount of time spent on task was calculated. For each participant, the amount of time spent on task increased significantly during BRT and was maintained during the subsequent cue control phase, whereas time on task did not change from baseline to the first cue control-only phase that occurred prior to BRT acquisition. The results on BAR scores were identical in that anxiety ratings decreased only after BRT training and the subsequent cue control-only sessions that followed training.

Two additional studies evaluated the impact of BRT on more specific cognitive performance (Lindsay & Morrison, 1996; Morrison & Lindsay, 1997). In the former, the authors determined that further assessment of BRT beyond impact on activity level and agitation was needed. Two groups of 10 adults diagnosed with moderate to severe ID were divided into group BRT sessions or a control group of quiet reading. Each group was assessed with measures of short-term memory (digit span), long term memory (general information), and attention (incidental learning task) pre-and post-training. Each measure was developed by the authors for the purpose of this study. The BRT group demonstrated improvements in short-term memory and attention but not long-term memory, which is consistent with what has been documented regarding the effects of anxiety on memory and attention (Eysenck, 1982)

In the latter study, Morrison and Lindsay (1997) replicated and extended upon these findings with a group of 30 adults diagnosed with moderate ID who were as-signed to either an experimental group receiving BRT training or a placebo con-trol. The results indicated that, again, short-term memory and incidental learning improved following BRT, and long-term memory did not change. Additionally, par-ticipants in the BRT group reported decreased scores on the modified Zung Anxiety Inventory.

A single-case investigation of the effects of BRT on the disruptive behavior of an adolescent with Asperger syndrome demonstrated a 55% reduction in the occurrence of disruptive behavior per week when compared to no intervention in a multi-element design (Concors & Ciasca, 2003). The participant was a student who practiced BRT on a noncontingent schedule at school, and weeks with BRT sessions alternated with baseline contingencies to provide experimental control over treatment effects. The percent of intervals in which he displayed disruptive behaviors dropped from an average of 44% to 20% during the BRT phase.

The final study with experimental control was an investigation of BRT training with positive reinforcement and prompt fading on seizure frequency and hyperventilation in a 6-year-old child diagnosed with epilepsy and profound intellectual disability (Kiesel, Lutzger, & Campbell, 1989). Hyperventilation typically was followed by seizure incidents prior to treatment. Treatment effectiveness was assessed using a multiple baseline design across settings (home and school). Following training in BRT, the frequency of episodes of hyperventilation and subsequent seizures both decreased by greater than 50%. Six-month follow-up data demonstrated maintained treatment gains.

The remaining studies, although lacking experimental control, nonetheless suggested positive outcomes. Several examined the feasibility of BRT as a relaxation procedure and in comparison to abbreviated progressive relaxation (e.g., Lindsay & Baty, 1989; Lindsay, Richardson, & Michie, 1989; Lundervold, 1986); however, what was missing from these investigations was the use of a control condition to account for other variables in relaxation training such as sitting still, receiving 1:1 attention, etc. Another study consisted of three descriptive case reports on the rate of acquisition, which was less than 3 hours for each patient, and the benefit of BRT on reducing the frequency of self-injury and aggression (Paclawskyj, 2002). These cases led to a subsequent investigation of potential predictors of success with BRT acquisition (see below). Another study assessed concentration and positive affect in participants diagnosed with profound ID and compared relaxation with access to a Snoezelen room. While both procedures were rated as enjoyable by outside raters and yielded improved concentration, access to the Snoezelen room resulted in greater relaxation (Lindsay, Pitcaithly, Geelen, Buntin, Broxholme, & Ashby, 1997). The remaining studies demonstrated that BRT appeared to be an effective treatment component for phobias (Lindsay, Michie, Baty, & McKenzie, 1988), ritualistic behavior and aggression (Lindsay, Overand, Allan, & Williams, 1998), and chronic headaches (Michultka, Poppen, & Blanchard, 1988). These were conducted as case studies and are the remaining examples of BRT used in a treatment context for anxiety-related behaviors.

In our outpatient and inpatient programs at the Kennedy Krieger Institute Neurobehavioral Unit, we have conducted training in BRT to 29 patients in the past 7 years referred either for clinic-based services, inpatient treatment, or outpatient

Table 2. Summary of BRT research in persons with ID

Authors	Design	n	Target(s)	Age	Level of ID	Measures	Results	Follow-up
Linsday & Baty, 1986	case study	3	anxiety, agitation	41–55	moderate, severe	BAR (Behavioural Anxiety Scale, pulse rate	BAR scores decreased, pulse rate decreased for 2/3 of sample	none
Lundervold, 1986	single-case AB	1	agitation	32	mild	# relaxed postures, # correct self-instructions, mean frontalis EMG readings	% relaxed behaviors increased, # correct instructions increased, no significant change on EMG	none
Lindsay, Michie, Baty, & McKenzie, 1988	single-case AB	2	dog phobia	26–42	mild, moderate	frequency of both positive and negative approach and requests to remove dog	combined approach reduced phobia	none
Michultka, Poppen, & Blanchard, 1988	single-case AB	1	headaches	29	severe	frequency of headache complaints and analgesic consumption, BRS	headache decreased by half, consumption of analgesics decreased by half, BRT proficiency achieved	2 mo.
Kiesel, Lutzker, & Campbell, 1989 CONTROLLED STUDY	**single-case multiple baseline**	1	**seizures, hyperventilation**	**6**	**profound**	**frequency of seizures and hyperventilation**	**modified BRT decreased both seizures and hyperventilation**	**6 mo.**
Lindsay & Baty, 1989	group w/two treatments	20	restlessness, comparison of BRT versus PR	30–69	moderate, severe	BAR, pulse rate	significant change w/both groups, BRT more effective than PR, no change in pulse rate	none
Lindsay, Baty, Michie, & Richardson, 1989 CONTROLLED STUDY	**group w/ control**	**50**	**anxiety, group versus individual treatment, BRT versus PR**	**25–51**	**moderate, severe**	**BAR, pulse rate**	**BRT more effective than PR, no change in pulse rates in any group**	**none**
Lindsay, Richardson, & Michie, 1989	group w/two treatments	20	anxiety, restlessness, BRT versus PR	25–51	moderate, severe	4-point Likert scales on speech, anxious movement, anxiety	BRT showed rapid improvements across measures but scores were similar at follow-up	2 wks

— continued next page

115

Study	Design	N	Target	Age	Severity	Measures	Results	
Lindsay, Fee, Michie, & Heap, 1994 CONTROLLED STUDY	single-case w/ component analysis	5	anxiety, agitation, concentration, efficacy of cue control	29-48	severe	BAR, on-task behavior	relaxation ratings, digit span and on-task improved for BRT and BRT with cue-control	none
Lindsay & Morrison, 1996 CONTROLLED STUDY	group w/ placebo control	20	short and long-term memory	adult	moderate, severe	BAR, digit span, incidental learning, general knowledge test	improved on digit span, incidental learning, no change in general knowledge	none
Lindsay, Pitcaithly, Geelen, Buntin, Broxholme, & Ashby, 1997	group w/ crossover	8	concentration, observable enjoyment of procedure	23-62	profound	on-task movements, Likert rating scale on responsiveness	BRT had lesser effect than Snoezelen, both rated as therapeutic and enjoyable	none
Morrison & Lindsay, 1997 CONTROLLED STUDY	group w/ matched placebo control	30	anxiety, cognitive performance	28-53	moderate	Zung Anxiety Inventory, digit span, peg and board test, general knowledge test	significant decline on Zung Anxiety Inventory scores, improvement on digit span and peg board task, no effect on general knowledge	none
Lindsay, Black, Broxholme, Pitcaithly, & Hornsby, 2001	group w/four treatments	8	positive and negative communication	23-62	profound	5 positive, 5 negative variables scored on a Likert scale	Snoezelen and BRT increase positive communication, less effect on negative communication	none
Paclawskyj, 2002	single-case AB	3	BRT acquisition, self-injury, aggression	6-14	mild, moderate	frequency of problem behaviors	acquisition <3 hours, >80% decrease in self-injury and aggression	none
Paclawskyj & Yoo, 2006	group w/2 teaching formats	19	BRT acquisition	6-32	mild, moderate, severe	acquisition to 80% criterion in BRS	structured teaching order resulted in greater generalization across untrained behavior, no changes in training time for either group	none

consultation for agitated or anxious behaviors co-occurring with self-injury, aggression, or other disruptive behaviors. Patients who received training were referred from three primary sources: (1) the current clinician who made a clinical judgment that training was appropriate, (2) the screening process for admission into the Neurobehavioral Unit inpatient or outpatient programs, or (3) from institute psychiatrists.

Anecdotal observation within the first two years of use of BRT in our programs indicated that training the 10 behaviors specified in the BRT procedure appeared more difficult when taught in an unspecified order, especially when behaviors involving fine motor skills (e.g., keeping eyes lightly closed) were interspersed with gross motor behaviors (e.g., keeping torso in contact with the back of a cushioned chair). Consequently, clinicians were instructed to train the 10 behaviors in a structured order of large-to-small muscle groups: *body, head, shoulders, feet, hands, throat, mouth, eyes,* and finally *breathing* and *quiet.*

Our data demonstrated significant improvements in skill acquisition when the structured training sequence was utilized (Paclawskyj & Yoo, 2006). Ten patients were taught using the structured order and nine using a random order. Of those taught in a random order, two did not master BRT. The largest proportion of our sample (47%) consisted of individuals diagnosed with moderate intellectual disability; the remaining patients were diagnosed with either mild (37%), severe (11%), or unspecified intellectual (5%). Patients were taught to engage in BRT for 2-10 minutes (m=7) and required 12-520 minutes (m=124 minutes) to achieve mastery, defined as three consecutive sessions with at least 80% of behavioral criteria met. Those patients trained using the structured sequence displayed more generalization across untrained behaviors (m=4) than those trained in a random order (m=1). That is, training in the structured order on average required teaching only 6/10 responses. Total time to mastery, however, was unaffected and may reflect the variability in age and functioning levels of the different participants (Paclawskyj & Yoo, 2006).

Since that time an additional eght patients have received training. Although the groups were small and not of equal size, there were some variables for which there was at least a two-fold difference between the Successful and Unsuccessful groups. Large differences were found in patient diagnoses. A total of 78% of patients in the Unsuccessful group were high-functioning (mild or no intellectual disability), whereas only 25% of patients in the Successful group functioned in this range. Additionally, considerably more patients in the Unsuccessful group were diagnosed with ADHD (78% versus 35%) and Bipolar Disorder (56% versus 5%); yet 50% of the patients in the Successful group had no psychiatric diagnosis as opposed to 11% of the Unsuccessful group. Taken together, these data allow preliminary hypotheses as to the predictors of successful acquisition: patients who receive a comprehensive course of treatment, who are diagnosed at the mild-moderate range of intellectual disability or lower, and who do not present with clinically significant levels of overactivity and/or mood instability are most likely to acquire BRT (Paclawskyj, in preparation).

In addition to a lack of experimental control, many of the existing studies on BRT have other limitations. Specifically, only three report follow-up data, several employ a small sample size that does not allow for evaluation of effects across participants, several lack blind raters of relaxation and other target behaviors, only three of the group studies include a placebo control group, and only one provides physiological data to substantiate the relaxation response. Such variables remain an important consideration for research on BRT to progress to a level where the clinical implications can be definitively validated.

DESCRIPTION OF THERAPY TECHNIQUE

BRT Training

The length of training in BRT is individualized according to the needs of the participant. For those who are able to remain seated for a longer period of time, the typical 10-minute session length is established as a training goal. However, if a person finds a longer time period difficult to tolerate, the session length can be shortened to as little as one minute in length. The following descriptions specify the structured manner of teaching conducted in the Neurobehavioral Unit programs; alternative teaching approaches can be found in Poppen (1998).

Behavioral Rating Scale (BRS) Scoring

The BRS is a partial interval recording system developed by Schilling and Poppen (1983) and available in Poppen (1998) in which the presence or absence of each relaxed behavior is scored within a 1-minute interval for a total of 10 minutes. For the first 30 seconds of the interval, the observer records breath frequency. For the next 15 seconds, the observer scans the patient from head to feet. For the final 15 seconds, the observer records the presence or absence of all 10 relaxed behaviors. The percent relaxed responding for each of the 10 behaviors is calculated by dividing the number of intervals scored as correct by the total number of intervals. Percent relaxed responding is calculated for each of the 10 behaviors as well as averaged across the results for all 10 to obtain a total percent relaxed score. Data are graphed using a multiple baseline design (see Kazdin, 1982 for a description) across all 10 behaviors; the total percent relaxed score also can be charted to measure general progress.

Pre-teaching Baseline

The therapist tells the patient to sit in the chair that will be used for teaching. The therapist then tells patient to relax and gives no other instructions or feedback. The session starts after the prompt to relax and ends when the patient stands up from the chair or after 10 minutes elapse. The length of time in-seat and the presence of relaxed/unrelaxed behaviors as specified on the BRS are both recorded. Baseline sessions are conducted until there is stability or a downward trend in responding for three sessions across each behavior. Mean length of time in-seat is used to calculate the length of time for the BRT training sessions. The starting goal is the longer of the following: baseline time in-seat rounded up to the nearest whole minute or 10 minutes. As the person acquires the skills, the total time in-seat can be gradually increased until a minimum of 5 minutes have passed.

Training

If during baseline sessions the participant already displayed the correct form of a particular behavior, formal training of that behavior is not conducted. However, the therapist praises the participant for continued correct responding during training of the remaining behaviors. Generally, two or three behaviors are trained at a time until 80% correct responding is achieved in each behavior; more or fewer behaviors can be trained if appropriate for the individual's typical rate of skill acquisition. More sets of behaviors are trained until correct responding averages 80% across all 10 behaviors. Training is conducted using the structured teaching order of body, head, shoulders, feet, hands, throat, quiet, eyes, mouth, and breathing rate.

Training typically is conducted using a therapist/confederate model and a least-to-most prompt hierarchy. The confederate therapist serves as both a model for the participant and as a stimulus to lessen the demand aspects of the session; that is, for individuals who have a history of maladaptive behaviors associated with the presentation of demands, seeing another person being taught the behavior lessens the resemblance of the situation to a required demand activity.

First, the therapist asks the confederate to model the correct response. Then, using a sequence of verbal, gestural, and physical prompts, the therapist guides the participant to achieve the correct position. As most individuals do not understand the ultimate goal of relaxation training, using extrinsic reinforcers becomes necessary in the early stages of acquisition of the skills. A highly preferred item identified from a reinforcer assessment is given to the participant following all sessions during which the participant displayed at least 80% relaxed behaviors across the set being trained. Training is complete when the participant displays at least 80% total relaxed responding across three consecutive sessions. Finally, generalization sessions are conducted in which the participant is taken to different locations and asked to engage in BRT to ensure that the skills are feasible to do across settings. Training is considered complete when caregivers also are trained in prompting the individual to engage in BRT at the appropriate times.

APPLICATION OF THE TECHNIQUE

As with other methods of relaxation training (Luiselli, 1980), BRT has treatment potential across three situations: 1) prevention of the stress response, 2) cue-controlled relaxation, and 3) as an alternative response to a stressful situation. In terms of prevention, BRT can be conducted either on a noncontingent schedule (e.g., every 3-4 hours) or just prior to the onset of a stressful activity (e.g., dentist visit). With cue control, a particular word or phrase such as "It's time to relax" is paired with the relaxed state such that over time, the phrase alone can elicit the relaxation response. This can be effective either when the individual repeats the phrase or if caregivers cue the individual to engage in relaxation. Finally, BRT can be utilized contingently upon the occurrence of anxious or agitated symptoms that arise either in response to a known stimulus or an unclear antecedent.

Given the demonstrated effectiveness of BRT in producing an observable relaxed response in persons with intellectual disability, there appears to be potential to extend its use to managing the agitation that can accompany behavior problems such as aggression and self-injury (Luiselli, 1980; Schroeder, Peterson, Solomon, & Artley, 1977). Although other aspects of behavioral intervention may target the consequences that are typically involved in the maintenance of problem behavior, they may not address the agitation and arousal that sometimes accompany problem behaviors and could make the individual less sensitive to ongoing intervention. Physiological arousal results in the individual seeking more optimal levels of stimulation (Baldwin & Baldwin, 1986). When applied to maladaptive behavior, this tendency can result in the individual becoming more likely to attempt to avoid stimulation from unpleasant events. For example, escape from nonpreferred tasks can become more reinforcing when an individual is agitated and is seeking less stimulation. Therefore, the likelihood of maladaptive behaviors can significantly increase with such internal states. Strategies that can combine operant techniques with respondent procedures can assist an individual in modulating their internal state, which has considerable potential to enhance the effectiveness of behavioral interventions for individuals who do not respond to standard of care strategies.

CASE EXAMPLES

The following case examples present demonstrations of the effectiveness of BRT in the treatment of three patients who received either inpatient or outpatient assessment and treatment of severe behavior problems and psychiatric disorders in the Neurobehavioral Unit at the Kennedy Krieger Institute. The first patient, a teenager with mild intellectual disability and a tic disorder showed initial reduction in the frequency with BRT that was followed by greater reduction when a behavioral procedure was added. In the second case, BRT was added following an unsuccessful behavioral intervention for the maladaptive behavior of a teenager with moderate intellectual disability and autism; the combined treatment resulted in successful reduction of problem behavior. For the final patient, who was diagnosed with severe intellectual disability and autism, BRT added to a comprehensive behavioral intervention led to greater reduction in the frequency of self-injury, aggression, and destructive behavior than before treatment and with the behavioral intervention alone when the three were compared simultaneously.

Each case is described in greater detail below.

Figure 1. Mean rates of problem behaviors pre- and post-treatment

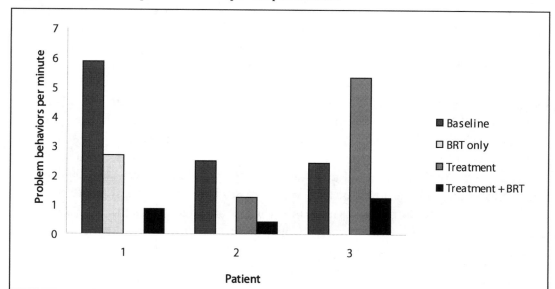

Patient #1 (M.)

M. was a 15-year-old male previously diagnosed with Mild Intellectual Disability, Tic Disorder, and Obsessive-Compulsive Disorder. M. presented with high frequency motor tics that significantly disrupted his social interaction and participation in daily activities.

Baseline: M. was observed via one-way mirror in a session room with a therapist present and preferred materials available for 10-minute session periods. On a 30-second schedule, the therapist provided brief verbal attention if not already engaged with M. in conversation.

BRT: M. was instructed to engage in BRT for the duration of the 10-minute session. If he moved he was prompted to return to the relaxed position.

BRT + Treatment: M. engaged in BRT for the duration of the session but earned tokens to exchange for time with preferred videos for each 30-second interval with no tics. The combined intervention resulted in an 84% reduction in rate of tics during the session period (see Figure 1).

Patient #2 (A.)

A. was a 15-year-old female diagnosed with Moderate Intellectual Disability, Autistic Disorder, Stereotypic Movement Disorder with Self-Injurious Behavior, and Disruptive Behavior Disorder NOS. A. presented with self-injury, aggression, and disruptive behavior (throwing items, knocking over furniture). Parent report indicated a high frequency of maladaptive behaviors and tantrums when A.'s mother engaged in household chores.

Baseline: In this condition, her mother and A. were in a room together and her mother engaged in various chores such as cleaning and organizing the materials present in the room. A. was instructed to play with toys. If A. engaged in a maladaptive behavior, her mother provided her with 5-10 seconds of attention (e.g., "don't do that"). Sessions were 5 minutes in length and A. and her mother were observed via one-way mirror by two therapists collecting data via laptop computer. This baseline assessment with chores was conducted as a part of the functional analysis for A.'s maladaptive behavior and was the condition in which the highest rates of maladaptive behaviors were seen.

Treatment: As the functional analysis indicated that her behavior resulted in her mother stopping her cleaning routine, a replacement behavior of appropriate communication (Functional Communication training) was selected as the primary behavioral intervention. A. was trained to ask, "Stop, please" to request the cessation of chores and "Talk to me, please" to request attention. The sessions started with her mother engaging in chores. If A. said "Stop, please" her mother would stop working for 30 seconds; if she said "Talk to me, please" her mother would provide her with attention but would not cease working. Her mother ignored any maladaptive behavior that occurred. Sessions continued to be 5 minutes in length. This phase was terminated after two sessions during which A.'s maladaptive behaviors increased in frequency and intensity.

Treatment plus BRT: Prior to this phase, A. was taught to engage in BRT for 10 minutes at a time. A. met criteria for proficiency after thirty six 10-minute training sessions. When this treatment phase was introduced, the sessions were identical to the initial treatment except that a 10-minute BRT session was conducted prior to each 5-minute treatment session. A.'s maladaptive behaviors decreased by 83% with the combined treatment (see Figure 1).

Patient #3 (F.)

F. was a 9-year-old male previously diagnosed with Severe Intellectual Disability, Autism, Stereotypic Movement Disorder with Self-Injurious Behavior, and Disruptive Behavior Disorder NOS. F. presented with self-injury, aggression, and destructive behavior with tantrums. An extensive functional analysis on the NBU inpatient program identified multiple functions for his problem behaviors, including escape from academic tasks and access to tangible items.

Baseline: During this condition, therapists working with F. between the hours of 9:00-4:00 provided standard pre-treatment contingencies for his maladaptive behaviors. Such contingencies included providing verbal attention for maladaptive behavior, permitting escape from tasks upon display of maladaptive behavior, and allowing access to preferred items contingent on maladaptive behavior following denied requests. These contingencies are intended to reinforce the maladaptive responses so that the precipitants and consequences for the behaviors can be readily identified.

Treatment: A comprehensive treatment was developed to address F.'s communication deficits and to structure his environment to allow him to understand when preferred vs. nonpreferred activities would occur. The specific components included Functional Communication Training (teaching F. to request desired items), use of a schedule book, scheduled access to preferred items, and blocking and ignoring of maladaptive behaviors.

Treatment with BRT: In addition to the treatment components mentioned, F. was prompted to engage in 5 minutes of BRT contingent on the display of agitated behaviors (e.g., crying, screaming, covering ears). F. exhibited fewer maladaptive behaviors in the treatment with BRT condition (m=1.25 per hour) than in baseline (m=2.43 per hour) or during treatment without BRT (m=5.43). Upon discharge to home, F. was initially prompted to engage in BRT contingent on agitated behaviors; however, within a 2-month period he began to self-initiate relaxation and behavioral gains continued.

DISCUSSION

Summary

Behavioral Relaxation Training has much potential as an intervention for a range of issues and concerns in persons with ID. It is a method of relaxation training that can be taught in a structured manner to individuals at a range of functioning levels using objective data to measure success. BRT can be implemented to improve psychiatric symptoms such as anxiety and poor concentration, to minimize the likelihood of maladaptive behaviors that may be exacerbated by negative internal states, to aid in the management of specific medical symptoms, or to maintain a calmer state during exposure to specific stressors. It is one of the few behavioral interventions that can be used as a self-management tool to help an individual cope with future negative events. Consequently, it is viewed as an intervention with high social acceptability and potential to improve general quality of life.

Recommendations

Research on BRT for individuals with ID has significant potential for expansion as well as improvement in methodology. First, case report data pose interesting clinical questions, but validation of treatment effects via single-case design will better establish the range of clinical concerns and target behaviors that could potentially be further addressed and validated via controlled group methodology. Any study using group design should include a placebo control that would address confounding variables such as therapist attention, resting in a chair, and time away from regularly scheduled activities. If other activities have potential for inducing the relaxation response (e.g., a Snoezelen room), relative costs versus treatment efficacy and time in treatment need to be explored (Luiselli, 1980). Additionally, generalization and follow-up data would allow for a more definitive determination of the value of BRT across settings, with non-trained caregivers, and over time.

One specific factor to investigate given the existing efficacy data on BRT is the identification of variables that predict successful acquisition and implementation of the technique. Though some pilot data exist (Paclawskyj, in preparation), substantiation of potential factors would be of clinical utility in that clinicians would be able to avoid spending unnecessary time with an intervention unlikely to be successful. In addition, standardization of training procedures, including supportive strategies such as the presence or absence of music, ambient lighting, etc., would result in more effective outcomes across clinicians.

Research into the assessment and treatment of problem behaviors such as aggression and self-injury also has potential expansion when interventions targeting respondent behavior are included. That is, high levels of agitation that co-occur with maladaptive behaviors could be addressed via inclusion of BRT into the treatment; whereas maladaptive behaviors without co-occurring agitation might continue to be responsive to operant techniques alone. Such investigations also could examine possible differential impact of implementing BRT on a contingent or noncontingent schedule in relation to the problem behaviors and precursors of such behaviors.

Finally, the field of telemetrics, in which technology can be used to remotely monitor variables such as vital signs, has much to offer to the general body of research into relaxation training. Monitors can be embedded into clothing to provide non-intrusive continuous measurement of vital signs (Goodwin, Velicer, & Intille, 2008). Use of technology such as the LifeShirt (Vivometrics, Inc.) has already been demonstrated to be effective in the evaluation of stress responses in children with autism (Goodwin et al., 2006). With continued advances in this field, the possibility of validation of the effectiveness of interventions such as BRT is of great benefit to individuals both with and without ID.

REFERENCES

Aikens, J. E., Kiolbasa, T. A., & Sobel, R. (1997). Psychological predictors of glycemic change with relaxation training in non-insulin-dependent diabetes mellitus. *Psychotherapy and Psychosomatics, 66,* 302-306.

American Academy of Child and Adolescent Psychiatry. (AACAP; 1999). Practice parameters for the assessment and treatment of children, adolescents, and adults with mental retardation and comorbid mental disorders. *Journal of the American Academy of Child and Adolescent Psychiatry, 38,* 5S-31S.

Arndorfer, R. E., & Miltenberger, R. G. (1993). Functional assessment and treatment of challenging behavior: A review with implications for early childhood. *Topics in Early Childhood Special Education, 13,* 82-105.

Association for Behavior Analysis, Task Force on the Right to Effective Behavioral Treatment. (1988). The right to effective behavioral treatment. *Journal of Applied Behavior Analysis, 21,* 381-384.

Baldwin, J. D., & Baldwin, J. I. (1986). *Behavior principles in everyday life.* Englewood Cliffs, NJ: Prentice-Hall.

Bernstein, D. A., & Borkovec, T. D. (1973). *Progressive relaxation training.* Champaign, IL: Research Press.

Blanchard, E. B., Nicholson, N. L., Taylor, A. E., Steffek, B. D., Radnitz, C. L., & Appelbaum, K. A. (1991). The role of regular home practice in the relaxation treatment of tension headache. *Journal of Consulting and Clinical Psychology, 59,* 467-470.

Brandon, J. E., Eason, R. L., & Smith, T. L. (1986). Behavioral relaxation training and motor performance of learning disabled children with hyperactive behaviors. *Adapted Physical Activity Quarterly, 3,* 67-79.

Calamari, J. E., Geist, G. O., & Shahbazian, M. J. (1987). Evaluation of multiple component relaxation training with developmentally disabled persons. *Research in Developmental Disabilities, 8,* 55-70.

Chung, W., Poppen, R., & Lundervold, D. A. (1995). Behavioral relaxation training for tremor disorders in older adults. *Biofeedback and Self-Regulation, 20,* 123-135.

Concors, P.L., & Ciasca, K. M. (2003, May). Behavioral and physiological assessment of Behavioral Relaxation Training (BRT) for a learner with Asperger's Disorder. Poster presented at the annual conference of the Association for Behavior Analysis, San Francisco, CA.

Cooper, J. O., Heron, T. E., & Heward, W. L. (2007). *Applied Behavior Analysis, 2nd ed.* Upper Saddle River, NJ: Pearson Merrill Prentice Hall.

Craske, M. G., Rapee, R. M., & Barlow, D. H. (1992). Cognitive-behavioral treatment of panic disorder, agoraphobia, and generalized anxiety disorder. In S. M. Turner, K. S. Calhoun, & H. E. Adams (Eds.). *Handbook of clinical behavior therapy, 2nd ed.,* (pp. 39-66). New York: John Wiley & Sons, Inc.

Crews, W. D., Bonaventura, S., & Rowe, F. (1994). Dual diagnosis: Prevalence of psychiatric disorders in a large state residential facility for individuals with mental retardation. *American Journal on Mental Retardation, 98,* 724-731.

Didden, R., Duker, P. C., & Korzilius, H. (1997). Meta-analytic study on treatment effectiveness for problem behaviors with individuals who have mental retardation. *American Journal on Mental Retardation, 101,* 387-399.

Donney, V. K., & Poppen, R. (1989). Teaching parents to conduct behavioral relaxation training with their hyperactive children. *Journal of Behavior Therapy and Experimental Psychiatry, 20,* 319-325.

Eason, R. L., Brandon, J. E., Smith, T. L., & Serpas, D. C. (1986). Relaxation training effects on reaction/response time, frontalis EMG, and behavioral measures of relaxation with hyperactive males. *Adapted Physical Activity Quarterly, 3,* 329-341.

Eastridge, D., & Mozzoni, M. (2008). Efficacy of behavioral relaxation training for individuals with traumatic brain injury. *Journal of Head Trauma Rehabilitation, 23,* 354.

Eaton, L. F., & Menolascino, F. J. (1982). Psychiatric disorders in the mentally retarded: Types, problems, and challenges. *American Journal of Psychiatry, 139,* 1297-1303.

Eufemia, R. L., & Wesolowski, M. D. (1983). The use of a new relaxation method in a case of tension headache. *Journal of Behavior Therapy and Experimental Psychiatry, 14,* 355-358.

Fecteau, G. W., & Boyne, J. (1987). Behavioural relaxation training with Huntington's Disease patients: A pilot study. *Psychological Reports, 61,* 151-157.

Fletcher, R., Loschen, E., Stavrakaki, C., & First, M. (2007). *Diagnostic manual-intellectual disability: A textbook of diagnosis of mental disorders in persons with intellectual disability.* Kingston, NY: NADD Press.

Freedman, R. L., Sabharwal, S.C., Ianni, P., Desai, N., Wenig, P., & Mayes, M. (1988). Nonneural beta-adrenergic vasodilating mechanism in temperature biofeedback. *Psychosomatic Medicine, 50,* 394-401.

Glick, M., & Zigler, E. (1995). Developmental differences in the symptomatology of psychiatric inpatients with and without mild mental retardation. *American Journal on Mental Retardation, 99,* 407-417.

Goodwin, M. S., Groden, J., Velicer, W. F., Lipsitt, L. P., Baron, M. G., Hofmann, S. G., et al. (2006). Cardiovascular arousal in individuals with autism. *Focus on Autism and Other Developmental Disabilities, 21,* 100-123.

Goodwin, M. S., Velicer, W. F., & Intille, S. S. (2008). Telemetric monitoring in the behavior sciences. *Behavior Research Methods, 40,* 328-241.

Guercio, J. M., Ferguson, K. E., & McMorrow, M. J. (2001). Increasing functional communication through relaxation training and neuromuscular feedback. *Brain Injury, 15,* 1073-1082.

Harden, A., & Sahl, R. (1997). Psychopathology in children and adolescents with developmental disorders. *Research in Developmental Disabilities, 18,* 369-382.

Harvey, J. R. (1979). The potential of relaxation training for the mentally retarded. *Mental Retardation, 17,* 71-76.

Horner, R. H., Carr, E. G., Strain, P. S., Todd, A. W., & Reed, H. K. (2002). Problem behavior interventions for young children with autism: A research synthesis. *Journal of Autism and Developmental Disorders, 32,* 423-446.

Horner, R. H., Day, H. M., & Day, J. R. (1997). Using neutralizing routines to reduce problem behaviors. *Journal of Applied Behavior Analysis, 30,* 601-614.

International Association for the Scientific Study of Intellectual Disabilities (IASSID; 2001). *Mental health and intellectual disabilities: Addressing the mental health needs of people with intellectual disabilities,* Report to the World Health Organization.

Jacobson, E. (1938). *Progressive relaxation.* Chicago: University of Chicago Press.

Kazdin, A. E. Single-case research design: *Methods for clinical and applied settings.* Oxford: Oxford University Press.

Kiesel, K. B., Lutzker, J. R., & Campbell, R. V. (1989). Behavioral relaxation training to reduce hyperventilation and seizures in a profoundly retarded epileptic child. *Journal of the Multihandicapped Person, 2,* 179-190.

King, B. H., DeAntonio, C., McCracken, J. T., Forness, S. R., & Ackerland, V. (1994). Psychiatric consultation in severe and profound mental retardation. *American Journal of Psychiatry, 151,* 1802-1808.

Lindsay, W. R., & Baty, F. J. (1986). Behavioural relaxation training: Exploration with adults who are mentally handicapped. *Mental Handicap, 14,* 160-162.

Lindsay, W. R., & Baty, F. J. (1989). Group relaxation training with adults who are mentally handicapped. *Behavioural Psychotherapy, 17,* 43-51.

Lindsay, W. R., Baty, F. J., Michie, A. M., & Richardson, I. (1989). A comparison of anxiety treatments with adults who have moderate and severe retardation. *Research in Developmental Disabilities, 10,* 129-140.

Lindsay, W. R., Fee, M., Michie, A., & Heap, I. (1994). The effects of cue control relaxation on adults with severe mental retardation. *Research in Developmental Disabilities, 15,* 425-437.

Lindsay, W. R., Michie, A. M., Baty, F. J., & McKenzie, K. (1988). Dog phobia in people with mental handicaps: Anxiety management and exposure treatments. *Mental Handicap Research, 1,* 39-48.

Lindsay, W. R., & Morrison, F. M. (1996). The effects of behavioural relaxation on cognitive performance in adults with severe intellectual disabilities. *Journal of Intellectual Disability Research, 40,* 285-290.

Lindsay, W. R., & Olley, C. M. (1998). Psychological treatment for anxiety and depression for people with learning disabilities. In N. Fraser, D. Sines, & M. Kerr (Eds.). *Hallas' The care of people with intellectual disabilities,* 9th ed., (pp. 235-252). Oxford: Butterworth Heinemann.

Lindsay, W. R., Richardson, I., & Michie, A. M. (1989). Short-term generalised effects of relaxation training on adults with moderate and severe mental handicaps. *Mental Handicap Research, 2,* 197-206.

Luiselli, J. K. (1980). Relaxation training with the developmentally disabled: A reappraisal. *Behavior Research of Severe Developmental Disabilities, 1,* 191-213.

Lundervold, D. (1986). The effects of behavioral relaxation and self-instruction training: A case study. *Rehabilitation Counseling Bulletin, 30,* 124-128.

Lundervold, D. A., Belwood, M. F., Craney, J. L., & Poppen, R. (1999). Reduction of tremor severity and disability following behavioral relaxation training. *Journal of Behavior Therapy and Experimental Psychiatry, 30,* 119-135.

Lutzker, J. R., Wesch, D., & Rice, J. M. (1984). A review of 'Project 12-Ways': An ecobehavioral approach to the treatment and prevention of child abuse and neglect. *Advances in Behavior Research and Therapy, 6,* 63-73.

McPhail, C., & Chamove, A. (1989). Relaxation reduces disruption in mentally handicapped adults. *Journal of Mental Deficiency Research, 33,* 399-406.

Michulka, D. M., Poppen, R. L., & Blanchard, E. B. (1988). Relaxation training as a treatment for chronic headaches in an individual having severe developmental disabilities. *Biofeedback and Self Regulation, 13,* 257-266.

Morrissey, P. A., Franzini, L. R., & Karen, R. L. (1992). The salutary effects of light calisthenics and relaxation training on self-stimulation in the developmentally disabled. *Behavioral Residential Treatment, 7,* 373-389.

Morrison, F. J., & Lindsay, W. R. (1997). Reductions in self-assessed anxiety and concurrent improvement in cognitive performance in adults who have moderate intellectual disabilities. *Journal of Applied Research in Intellectual Disabilities, 10,* 33-40.

National Institutes of Health, Consensus Development Panel on Destructive Behaviors in Persons with Developmental Disabilities. (1989). *Treatment of destructive behaviors in persons with developmental disabilities* (NIH Publication No. 91-2410). Bethesda, MD: U.S. Department of Health and Human Services.

Paclawskyj, T. R. (2002). Behavioral Relaxation Training (BRT) with children with dual diagnoses. *The NADD Bulletin, 5,* 81-82.

Paclawskyj, T. R., & Yoo, J. H. (2006). Behavioral Relaxation Training (BRT): Facilitating acquisition in individuals with developmental disabilities. *The NADD Bulletin, 9,* 13-18.

Poppen, R. (1998). *Behavioral relaxation training and assessment, 2nd ed.* Thousand Oaks, CA: SAGE Publications.

Rasid, Z. M., & Parish, T. S. (1998). The effects of two types of relaxation training on students' levels of anxiety. *Adolescence, 33,* 99-101.

Raymer, R., & Poppen, R. (1985). Behavioral relaxation training with hyperactive children. *Journal of Behavioral Therapy and Experimental Psychiatry, 16,* 309-316.

Reese, R. M., Sherman, J. A., & Sheldon, J. (1984). Reducing agitated disruptive behavior of mentally retarded residents of community group homes: The role of self-recording and peer-prompted self-recording. *Analysis and Intervention in Developmental Disabilities, 4,* 91-107.

Rojahn, J., Borthwick-Duffy, S. A., & Jacobson, J. W. (1993). The association between psychiatric diagnoses and severe behavior problems in mental retardation. *Annals of Clinical Psychiatry, 5,* 163-170.

Rush, A. J., & Frances, A. (Eds.) (2000). Expert consensus guideline series: Treatment of psychiatric and behavioral problems in mental retardation. *American Journal on Mental Retardation, 105,* 159-228.

Schilling, D., & Poppen, R. (1983). Behavioral relaxation training and assessment. *Journal of Behavior Therapy and Experimental Psychiatry, 14,* 99-107.

Schloss, P. J., Smith, M., Santora, C., & Bryant, R. (1989). A respondent conditioning approach to reducing anger responses of a dually diagnosed man with mild mental retardation. *Behavior Therapy, 20,* 459-464.

Schroeder, S. R., Peterson, C. R., Solomon, L. J., & Artley, J. J. (1977). EMG feedback and the contingent restraint of self-injurious behavior among the severely retarded: Two case illustrations. *Behavior Therapy, 8,* 738-741.

Sprague, J. R., & Horner, R. H. (1995). Functional assessment and intervention in community settings. *Mental Retardation and Developmental Disabilities Research Reviews, 1,* 89-93.

Tatum, T., Lundervold, D. A., & Ament, P. (2006). Abbreviated upright behavioral relaxation training for test anxiety among college students: Initial results. *International Journal of Behavioral Consultation and Therapy, 2,* 475-480.

Turk, D. C., Rudy, T. E., & Sorkin, B. A. (1992). Chronic pain: Behavioral conceptualizations and interventions. In S. M. Turner, K. S. Calhoun, & H. E. Adams (Eds.). *Handbook of clinical behavior therapy, 2nd ed.,* (pp. 373-396). New York: John Wiley & Sons, Inc.

Wells, K. C., Turner, S. M., Bellack, A. S., & Hersen, M. (1978). Effects of cue-controlled relaxation on psychomotor seizures: An experimental analysis. *Behaviour Research and Therapy, 16,* 51-53.

CHAPTER 6

Treating Survivors of Sexual and Interpersonal Abuse (in Psychotherapy for People with Intellectual Disabilities)

Nancy J. Razza, Ph.D.
Dick Sobsey, Ed.D.

ABSTRACT

This chapter begins by describing nature and extent of sexual abuse issues among children and adults with intellectual disabilities. It then describes approaches to therapy and considers issues in treating victims of abuse.

INTERPERSONAL TRAUMA

The vast majority of, if not all, human beings experience some psychological trauma at some time during their lives. Trauma may be the result of a severe illness or injury or the loss of a loved one. It can also result from intentional physical, sexual, or emotional violence inflicted by another person.

Some people experience trauma that is more severe, more frequent, or more chronic than others experience. In addition, even when trauma experiences appear similar to an outside observer, some individuals are more severely affected by trauma than others, and some individuals require more help to address the effects of their trauma.

As a group, people with intellectual disabilities experience more interpersonal trauma than people without disabilities. While their responses to interpersonal trauma appear to be much like the responses of others, they often require more support and assistance to successfully manage the results of trauma.

Child Maltreatment and Disability

There have been many studies linking child maltreatment to intellectual disabilities. Most have been relatively small-scale studies and have had significant design limitations that made it difficult to depend on any individual study for precise interpretations (Sobsey, 2005). Nevertheless, the fact that almost all of these studies reached a similar conclusion, that children with intellectual disabilities were more frequently abused than children without disabilities, lends confidence to this general finding.

Two large-scale, well-designed studies of child abuse and disability have been conducted that clarify this relationship. Although these studies were conducted in two different countries and used slightly different methods, the results are very consistent and together they provide powerful evidence of a strong link between child maltreatment and intellectual disability.

Sullivan and Knutson (2000) studied a cohort of about 40,000 children who attended school programs in Omaha, Nebraska. By matching school records that included information on disability status with child welfare, police, and foster care review records that included information on reported maltreatment, they were able to compute rates of maltreatment for children without disabilities and for children identified with various categories of disability. Children diagnosed with intellectual disabilities were 3.7 times as likely to be neglected, 3.8 times as likely to be emotionally abused, 3.8 times as likely to physically abused, and 4.0 times as likely to be sexually abused. Overall, children with intellectual disabilities were 4.0 times as likely to experience at least one type of maltreatment as other children. Children with many other categories of disability were also at increased risk, but compared to all other categories combined, children with intellectual disabilities appeared to have a somewhat increased risk (odds ratio 4.0 compared to 3.2). It should be noted, however, that children diagnosed with behavior disorders had the highest rate of maltreatment.

Spencer and colleagues (2005) studied a cohort of more than 119,000 children born between 1983 and 2001 in West Sussex in the United Kingdom. They compared data on disability status with data from the child protection registry in order to compute the odds ratio or relative risk of a child with a disability being on the child protection registry. They found that children with moderate to severe intellectual disabilities were 2.9 times as likely to be emotionally abused, 3.4 times as likely to be physically abused, 5.3 times as likely to be neglected, and 6.4 times as likely to be sexually abused. Overall, children with moderate to severe intellectual disabilities were 6.5 times as likely to be on the child abuse register for at least one category of maltreatment, but this odds ratio dropped to 4.7 times when it was adjusted for socioeconomic status.

Taken together, these two studies suggest that children with disabilities are 4 or more times as likely as children without disabilities to experience maltreatment. While there can be little question about the association, it is important to distinguish between association and cause. Does maltreatment cause or aggravate disability? Does the presence of a disability in the child increase risk vulnerability to or risk for maltreatment? In spite of the commendable adjustment for socioeconomic status, could some additional factor increase risk for both disability and violence? It appears likely that all three of these pathways contribute to the association, but it is difficult to determine how much each pathway contributes to the relationship (Sobsey, 2005).

From the therapist's perspective, the nature of the pathway may be important in some individual cases, but the more general question of which of these mechanisms operates in most cases is not so important. What matters is that this is a frequent problem for many people with intellectual disabilities, and it needs to be addressed.

It is also important to recognize that these studies provide information on the relative frequency of abuse being reported or substantiated and not on the actual occurrence of abuse. Child abuse often goes unreported. While research reports (e.g., Sullivan & Knutson, 2000) that about 30% of children with intellectual disabilities have a *known* history of abuse, an unknown number of additional cases go unreported. Children with disabilities are less likely to self-disclose abuse than children without disabilities (Hershkowitz, Lamb, &. Horowitz, 2007), which is likely to result in greater underreporting among children with disabilities, and therefore their relative risk for abuse may be even higher than the odds ratios determined on the basis of reported abuse.

In addition, there is some evidence that children with intellectual disabilities experience more chronic, intrusive, and severe abuse than that experienced by children without disabilities (e.g., Hershkowitz et al., 2007). This finding could be the result of underreporting. For example, the finding that bodily injuries are more common among children with disabilities than children without disabilities may actually reflect the fact that physical abuse of children with disabilities is unlikely to be reported if it is not severe enough to result in physical injuries.

Violence Against Adults with Intellectual Disabilities

There has been much less systematic study of violence against adults with disabilities, particularly against adults with intellectual disabilities. Nevertheless, the research that is available suggests a pattern of increased risk similar to the pattern found among children. Here are a few studies that suggest the probable nature and extent of the problem.

A study of more than 5000 women in North Carolina found that women with cognitive impairments were 2.6 times as likely as women without disabilities to be sexually assaulted in the past year. When the analysis was controlled for demographic variables, however, their relative risk was estimated at 5.2 times that of women without disabilities (Martin et al., 2006).

A Canadian study of more than 7,000 women married or living in a common law relationship with a male partner reported that women with any kind of disability were 1.4 times as likely to experience intimate partner violence in the last 5 years (Brownridge, 2006). Women with disabilities were particularly more likely to experience some of the more severe forms of violence. Women with disabilities were twice as likely to be beaten, kicked, or bitten and three times as likely to be forced into sexual activity than women without disabilities.

Congregate residential care and program settings also can contribute to risk for violence. In a survey of 122 staff providing care to people with intellectual disabilities in group homes and day programs, 14% of staff admitted to acts of violence against their clients in the past year, and 35% said they had witnessed violence against clients in the past year (Strand, Benzein, & Saveman, 2004). Most of the staff who acknowledged witnessing or perpetrating violence indicated that they saw violent acts a few times per month to a few times per week. The researchers conclude, "violence seems to be a daily matter in the care of adult persons with intellectual disabilities" (p. 513).

People with intellectual and developmental disabilities are also over-represented in jail, prison, youth detention, and community-based detention populations. These environments are often permeated by physical, sexual, and emotional violence. In 2003, the United States Congress passed the National Prison Rape Elimination Act, which established a Commission to study sexual assault in American prisons. Their report released in June of 2009 estimates that more than 60,000 men and women in American prisons are raped one or more times in the span of one year, and that inmates with intellectual and developmental disabilities are among the most frequently victimized by other inmates and by staff. For example, the report recounts the rape of a 15-year-old boy with a tested IQ of 32 by a 17-year-old sex offender who was assigned to change the younger inmate's diaper by staff at a Florida youth detention facility. The same report describes the case of woman with a developmental disability who became pregnant as a result of rape by an officer in a Delaware Correctional facility. In spite of her emotional distress and request for counseling, the facility refused to provide her with any supports other than antidepressant medication.

The traumatic effects of these intentional acts of violence interact with the individual's other life experiences and personal disposition. Many people with intellectual disabilities have experienced other traumatic events. For many, current instances of traumatic abuse bring back memories of previous episodes of victimization at earlier stages in their lives. In addition to these blatant offenses against people with intellectual disabilities, some people with developmental disabilities have been traumatized by aversive procedures used to alter their behavior. Individuals who do not understand the reason for procedures, such as pelvic or rectal examinations and suturing lacerations, may experience trauma when these procedures are performed on them. Many have experienced the loss of a parent or caregiver. Some have been repeatedly moved though series of placements with little opportunity to form or maintain enduring human attachments.

Based on the available information, violence and the trauma that it inflicts are extremely common in the lives of individuals with intellectual disabilities. Ideally, we would prevent the violence and abuse that inflicts this harm, but until that ideal can be achieved, we can still reduce the degree of harm inflicted through support and therapy for survivors of violence with intellectual disabilities.

TREATMENT APPROACHES

In giving thought to the psychological treatment of abuse survivors with ID, it is important to acknowledge that survivor treatment in general is relatively young. It was not until the late 1970s that the prevalence of sexual abuse, incest, and domestic violence against women and girls began to be documented in the literature (Herman, 1992). From this followed a growth in understanding of the psychological sequelae of abuse and initial treatment efforts.

The even younger discipline of mental health treatment for people with ID and psychological disorders is, as a result, drawing on a body of knowledge that is itself still evolving. That being said, a good deal has been learned about the ways in which traumatic experiences affect developing individuals. Understanding these effects has led to more informed and sensitive treatment approaches for survivors, both children and adults, and importantly, has shed light on the role of developmental level in the experience of trauma.

Preeminent researcher Bessel van der Kolk has concluded that the effect of trauma is intimately tied to developmental level, with younger organisms, both human and animal, suffering psychological as well as biological consequences (van der Kolk, van der Hart, & Burbridge, 2002). Van der Kolk et al. (2002) note that childhood abuse has ". . . far-reaching biological effects, including lasting biological changes which affect the capacity to modulate emotions, difficulty in learning new coping skills, alterations in immune competency, and impairment in the capacity to engage in meaningful social affiliation" (p. 31). With this understanding in mind, we must consider that people whose development is already comprised might, in fact, be even more adversely affected. Indeed, a developmental lag often exists between chronological age and intellectual and emotional level in people with ID, suggesting increased vulnerability to the effects of trauma.

Treatment Implications: What Can We Learn from the Literature?

Interpersonal trauma, i.e., trauma that is delivered at the hands of a fellow human being, carries profound implications for the treatment process.

When trauma is the result of a natural disaster, the victim may have grave distress and significant symptoms, yet may be able to relate in a reasonably comfortable way to a therapist. When trauma is the result of an experience with another person or persons, especially with persons one should have been able to trust, such as parents or caregivers, the ability to relate to others is affected. The victim has already learned that people can be harmful. For some survivors of interpersonal trauma, this effect is dramatic; for others, it is less pronounced. Some survivors have had some good and trustworthy people in their lives, as well as harmful ones; some have had only hurtful experiences. In any case, establishing the safety of the relationship is considered the first order of business in survivor treatment generally (Ford, Courtois, Steele, van der Hart, & Nijenhuis, 2005; van der Kolk, van der Hart, & Burbridge, 2002), as well as in treatment for survivors with ID (Razza & Tomasulo, 2005; Sinason, 2002). A recent study with survivors who have ID (Mitchell, Clegg, and Furniss, 2006) led the authors to the same conclusion. Six trauma survivors with ID were interviewed and evaluated with respect to their symptoms and ensuing beliefs. From these interviews the authors established, as their primary conclusion, that "Clinicians need to create safe environments where trust can develop and individuals have opportunities to talk about traumatic experiences" (p. 140).

In this chapter we will look at a number of critical treatment implications, but anything else we do, any treatment techniques we use, will ultimately fail if those techniques do not rest on a foundation of safety. So let's go through the treatment process from the ground up. The most beautifully constructed house won't last one winter if it sits on the sand.

The Treatment Foundation

Safety First

The following discussion presents a manner of conducting the initial assessment process that is crucial to the foundation of a good therapy experience for the trauma survivor with ID. Broadly defined, these can be thought of a set of techniques though, perhaps more accurately, they describe a process for establishing what should be a unique relationship in the patient's life. The techniques do not reflect any one theoretical orientation; they are a common denominator in any good therapy. For our purposes, the steps are elaborated in order to ensure that patients with serious cognitive problems and with known interpersonal trauma have a maximal opportunity to benefit.

The initial meeting with the patient is of key importance. From the first moment of contact, it is essential that the clinician prioritize the patient's sense of safety. The number one goal of the first session is *not* the gathering of information; it is the demonstration to the patient that this relationship is one in which their safety and well-being is of foremost concern. How do we demonstrate this? We show unfailing respect. It is through respect for the patient that we convey the safety of the therapeutic relationship and lay the foundation for a working alliance.

Conducting ourselves respectfully may seem like it goes without saying, yet it is easy to be rushed and pressured in the settings in which many of us work. Such pressure may be conveyed to the patient and make them feel less than valued.

Individual and Collateral Interviews, Consent to Treatment, and Guardianship

A majority of people with ID do not present themselves independently for a psychotherapy evaluation. Many people with ID are referred by family members or caregiving staff. Typically an involved caregiver accompanies the individual to the initial intake.

In some cases, the patient has been informed about the evaluation and the prospect of therapy; in other cases, she has not. It is essential to clarify the nature of the meeting to the patient and make sure that she or he fully understands what it is about. (Of course, whether or not the accompanying caregiver has explained the visit to the patient will give you some insight into the nature of their relationship and may have a bearing on your work.) At any rate, as the clinician you convey respect to the patient when you begin your discussion by making certain that the patient understands who you are and why she is meeting with you. Explain, in language the person can understand, what psychotherapy is. Ask the patient to repeat back to you her sense of what you have said. Be affirming of her efforts in this regard and work with her until her understanding is clarified. If the caregiver should attempt to circumvent the process, firmly and respectfully maintain control of the session. Inform the caregiver that this explanation is part of your clinical responsibility to the patient and ask to be allowed some time to learn how to communicate with the patient.

Once the patient is clear about why she is there, the next topic to address is consent to treatment. If we have conveyed to the patient a good sense of what therapy is, we can then ask if she is agreeable to trying it out.

In some cases, the patient may have a legal guardian. That person must consent in writing to the patient's treatment before therapy can proceed. However, even when the patient has a legal guardian, it is essential to the therapeutic relationship that the patient's consent be ascertained as well. The clinician needs to explain the voluntary nature of treatment to the patient and explain that even if the patient's guardian signs the form --or if she herself signs-- it does not mean the patient is compelled to come to therapy. She can change her mind, and she can stop treatment at any point if she decides to.

When the patient has been referred by and brought into the session by a third party, whether it is a staff person or a family member, we have the opportunity to explore three valuable sources of information regarding the patient: the patient's self-report; the caregiver's report; and the relationship dynamics between the caregiver and the patient. Because each facet can contribute to our assessment of the case, it is important to do all three. Again, however, we need to weigh the merits of information gathering against the need to establish safety for the patient. Some patients may be accompanied by a caregiver whom they trust. They may feel safer when that person is present. For others, the situation may be just the reverse. After many years of experience, the following strategy for the interview process seems to yield the best outcome.

Step one: Begin by inviting the patient and the caregiver to meet with you jointly. Avoid doing the individual meeting first. The problem with doing the individual patient interview first is that often the patient begins to feel safe with the clinician, and then feels that sense of safety betrayed when the caregiver is brought in. This is a considerable risk when the relationship with the caregiver is antagonistic, or when the caregiver relates a number of concerns, which may be legitimate symptoms ("She acts out every time she gets back from a family visit!") in a tone that portrays the patient as a "bad child" who is "non-compliant." Conversely, for the patient who is accompanied by a caregiver she trusts, having the caregiver with her during her initial time with you will help her to feel at ease with you. Note that the accompanying caregiver may or may not be the legal guardian. If there is a legal guardian who is not present, remember that the consent for treatment still needs to be signed by that person if it hasn't been completed already.

Inform the patient and the caregiver that you would like to meet with both of them briefly. You can begin the process of explaining to the patient what the meeting is about, as discussed above. After clarifying the nature of the meeting and the prospect of therapy, I generally tell the patient that, while her caregiver is present, I would like to ask the caregiver to give his thoughts about what things therapy might help with and what concerns he has regarding the patient.

Take note of the caregiver's presentation of his concerns and the patient's reaction to them. Does the patient understand and agree? Does the patient become upset, angry, embarrassed, or defensive? Does the patient simply tune out and stop listening? Many patients with severe ID simply wait, without listening, while the caregiver speaks to the clinician, as though the content does not concern them.

Next, ask the caregiver to explain directly to the patient what his chief concern is, helping the two of them to work together to achieve the patient's understanding. Encourage the patient to repeat back what her understanding is and have the caregiver clarify it if necessary. Give the patient (and the caregiver) your verbal support for working with this process and make a point of supporting the patient strongly if she is able to understand the caregiver's concern yet does not agree with it. Model for them both an attitude that conveys acceptance of differences and stresses the value of each person's perspective.

It is sometimes the case that the caregiver is reluctant to describe the patient's problem in front of her; he may express this reluctance and ask to speak to you privately. It is best to be upfront with the caregiver and explain to him that therapy generally proceeds more efficiently if the patient understands the concerns that those around her see. Offer your support to the caregiver to help him relate his concern to the patient in terms that are clear as well as non-offensive.

Assessing the Individual

Throughout the collateral interview you will, of course, be getting a sense of the patient's interpersonal style and level of intellectual and adaptive functioning. In addition, you will have at least some tentative formulation of the key problem or problems as a result of the collateral discussion.

When you complete the collateral interview, thank the caregiver for his input and ask that he wait in a designated waiting area while you conduct the individual interview. Begin the interview by thanking the patient for her efforts thus far and ask her how she is feeling at this point. Let her know that you understand that it can be difficult to meet a new person and immediately start talking about problems. Inform her that you would like to get to know her and will be asking her some questions. Then ask if she is agreeable to continuing with this plan. This is another opportunity to help the patient feel respected.

Get the Patient's Take on the Problem

It can be helpful to begin with some neutral, non-threatening questions regarding the patient's living situation and work or day program activities. Make a point of letting the patient know that the better you understand her, the better able you will be to offer help. Once the patient has responded to the questions regarding work and home –which may or may not have touched on the problem – ask her what she feels the problem is. For people at higher cognitive levels, the question may be as simple as this. For more impaired adults, or for children, you might ask about what makes them unhappy. However, rather than saying, "Is there anything that makes you unhappy," which is vague and unstructured, try a more concrete and directive approach. For example, you can say, "Tell me one thing that makes you happy (or that makes you feel good) and one thing that makes you not happy (or makes you feel bad)." This makes the question both clearer and less threatening to the patient and allows you the opportunity to show your interest in different aspects of her life. Clarify your understanding of the patient's answer with her.

Assess Coping and Defense Mechanisms

A simple question such as, "What do you do when you start to feel bad," can begin your inquiry into this area. Many patients cannot identify anything in particular, though as you walk them through it, patients often end up describing what they do. You can then feed this back to them for their clarification. For example, one woman with whom we worked had been abandoned and left homeless by her mother. The woman had fetal alcohol syndrome, mild to moderate ID, and was grossly overweight for her short stature. She was able to say she "felt bad" about what happened with her mother. When asked, "What do you do when you start to feel bad," the patient replied, "Nothing. I stop thinking about it."

This can then be repeated back to the patient to increase her own awareness of her process ("So, when you think back on when your mother threw you out, you start to feel bad. And when you feel bad, you stop thinking about it. So, trying not to think about what happened is something you do to help yourself feel better, is that right?") In this case, the patient is describing simple suppression; we might speculate that she also does other things, of which she is less aware. These can be further investigated if the patient is able to respond, but it does not all have to be done in the first session. It is also likely that the patient may *show* us how she copes, even when she cannot tell us. For example, the patient who abruptly changes topic to tell you something she is clearly happy about, or who becomes withdrawn or agitated, may be demonstrating what she does outside of session as well. In the case of the patient in this example, over the course of her therapy, she went on to describe more of her coping, although she did not initially understand herself well enough to describe her behavior as coping. She described being very invested in helping her boyfriend, the man who took her in when she was left homeless. She also found two stray kittens and took them in. She described great pleasure in caring for them. Also, she and the boyfriend would often take in other people who were in need of housing. Sometimes these people would become detrimental to them, yet the patient would not consider asking them to leave (until much later in her treatment). At any rate, a good deal of therapeutic work was accomplished through helping the patient to become aware of the many activities she had come up with to defend against some of her abandonment pain.

Of course, we want to note the degree to which the patient is using adaptive responses, which we call coping, versus the degree to which her responding is maladaptive. It is important to clarify both adaptive and maladaptive responses back to the patient. Further, the patient's adaptive responses provide us with a sense of direction for the therapy.

Investigate Symptoms

Throughout the interview, we are continually looking for symptoms of affective distress and thought disorder. Additionally, questions regarding sleep and appetite change, which are often addressed during the collateral interview, can be revisited here. It may be necessary to try using a number of different words to help the patient clarify her feelings. "Jumpy" or "scared" might describe anxiety for some individuals.

A further complication when evaluating children or more severely impaired adults is that they may not know that distressing emotional reactions are *normal* and to be expected following certain traumatic experiences. Many people with ID have a learned fear of expressing problems, thinking it means something is wrong with them or that they might get in trouble. If the patient cannot describe any symptoms, even with help, yet you can see distress (and perhaps it was reported by the caregiver), it can help to say something such as, "Very often, when people go through something like you did, they have some bad feelings. Sometimes they feel sad, sometimes they feel mad; sometime they feel very confused; and sometimes they are afraid that something else really bad is going to happen. Do you sometimes feel things like that?"

Assess Self-Concept

There is considerable evidence that victimizing experiences contribute to a lowered sense of self-esteem as well as a sense of powerlessness among people in the general population (Frazier, 2003; van der Kolk, 1996). People with ID frequently have a lowered sense of self-esteem and personal power (often called self-efficacy) because of the experience of growing up with a significant disability. For these individuals, the experience of victimization can further diminish an already compromised sense of self. Careful attention to the patient's self-concept during assessment and treatment is crucial to the healing process.

One way in which self-concept is often damaged in abuse survivors is through the survivor's belief that the abuse was in some way her own fault. Self-blame is extremely common, even among non-disabled survivors who were abused as very young children (Filipas & Ullman, 2006). Filipas and Ullman (2006) surveyed 577 female college students. 28.7% had experienced some form of sexual abuse as children, ranging from fondling to penetration. More than half of these women reported blaming themselves at the time of the abuse; moreover, more than one-third still blamed themselves currently.

Self-blame, in addition to the subjective distress it causes, has been found to predict additional consequences, such as difficulty adjusting to interpersonal situations, increased PTSD symptoms, and greater physical health consequences (Koss, Figueredo, & Prince (2002).

Some patients will describe the abuse in a way that lets you know they blame themselves. For example, one woman with whom we worked suffered from cerebral palsy that left her unable to walk as well as having mild ID. Because of extreme poverty in the country of birth, she was without the benefit of a wheelchair. She would fairly regularly be left alone with an older male cousin who would sexually abuse her. She believed it was entirely her fault because she was unable to get away. She would cry painfully about this for a long time early in treatment and clearly suffered with feeling fundamentally inadequate. (After a long therapy, she could acknowledge her disabilities but hold her cousin responsible for the abuse.)

For some people, determining their sense of culpability or fallibility is not so easy. If standard questioning does shed much light, a helpful inquiry can be, "If you were all in court, what do you think the judge should do with (the perpetrator)?" There is a world of difference between the person who says the judge should lock him up forever, and the one who shrugs her shoulders and says, "I don't know; I guess he should put him in jail."

Formulate a Treatment Plan

Growing efficacy research on abuse and trauma treatment suggests that patients can benefit from various modalities. There is now considerable support for the utility of group psychotherapy for adult, child, and adolescent survivors of trauma (Foy, Eriksson, & Trice, 2001); importantly, these authors investigated group models across three different theoretical orientations, supportive, psychodynamic, and cognitive-behavioral, and found enough support for each to warrant continuing treatment and research applications. Foy et al. note that while these models differ in their understanding of how symptoms develop and how best to intervene, ". . .they share a set of key features that build a therapeutic, safe, and respectful environment" (p. 4). Similarly, research is beginning to mount in support of group psychotherapy models designed for survivors with ID (Barber, Jenkins, & Jones, 2000; Peckham, Howlett, & Corbett, 2007; Razza & Tomasulo, 2005).

In an extensive review of published outcome research from 1989 to 2003, Putnam (2003) looked at the efficacy of treating child victims of sexual abuse, and determined that the treatment with the greatest efficacy to date is cognitive-behaviorally based therapy for the abused child along with a non-offending parent. Experts in working with adults who experienced severe abuse as children and suffer with complex post-traumatic symptoms outline a multi-phase treatment plan that incorporates a range of techniques (Ford, Courtois, Steele, van der Hart, & Nijenhuis, 2005). While cognitive-behavioral research has made perhaps the greatest contribution to efficacy research generally, psychodynamic work has been found to have demonstrable efficacy as well (Price, Hilsenroth, Callahan, Petretic-Jackson, & Bonge, 2004) with adult survivors of sexual abuse from the general population. Sinason (2002) and Berry (2003) describe the use of psychodynamic psychotherapy with patients who have ID.

Considering the needs of the patient before you, and extensive literature in the area of survivor treatment, how should you proceed? We begin with the establishment of respect and safety, and then consider that we have a number of reasonable treatment options. If you have access to a therapy group for survivors, and the patient being assessed is a good fit for the group, this may be the best option. Note that it is critical that the patient not be an outlier in any way. A patient whose intellectual level or symptom level is radically different from that of the rest of the group members will not have a good experience in the group. If group is not a viable option, individual models can be used. Most importantly, as a clinician, use a model you yourself are comfortable with and well-versed in. The next most important consideration is to be sure to have good supervision when doing work with abuse survivors. Abuse treatment is demanding for the clinician as it is for the patient, and support for the clinician is crucial to the treatment outcome.

Chapter 8 describes a model of group psychotherapy for abuse survivors with ID, and provides guidance for clinicians endeavoring to conduct treatment for these deserving individuals.

REFERENCES

Barber, M., Jenkins, R. & Jones, C. (2000). A survivors group for women who have a learning disability. *The British Journal of Developmental Disabilities, 46*, 31-41.

Berry, P. (2003). Psychodynamic therapy and intellectual disabilities: Dealing with challenging behavior. *International Journal of Disability, Development, and Education 50*(1), 39-51.

Bouras, N. & Holt, G. (2007). *Psychiatric and behavioural disorders in intellectual and developmental disabilities.* Cambridge, UK: Cambridge University Press.

Brownridge, D. A. (2006). Partner violence against women with disabilities: prevalence, risk, and explanations. *Violence Against Women, 12(*9), 805-822.

Butz, M., Bowling, J., & Bliss, C. (2000). Psychotherapy with the mentally retarded: A review of the literature and the implications. *Professional Psychology: Research and Practice, 31*, 42-47.

Filipas, H.H. & Ullman, S.E. (2006). Child sexual abuse, coping responses, self-blame, posttraumatic stress disorder, and adult sexual revictimization. *Journal of Interpersonal Violence, 21*(5), 652-672.

Ford, J. D., Courtois, C.A., Steele, K., van der Hart, O., & Nijenhuis, E.R.S. (2005). Treatment of complex posttraumatic self-dysregulation. *Journal of Traumatic Stress, 18*(5), 437-447.

Foy, D.W., Eriksson, C.B., & Trice, G.A. (2001). Introduction to group interventions for trauma survivors. *Group Dynamics: Theory, Research and Practice, 5,* 246-251.

Frazier, P.A. (2003). Perceived control and distress following sexual assault: A longitudinal test of a new model. *Journal of Personality and Social Psychology, 84*(6), 1257-1269.

Herman, J.L. (1992). *Trauma and recovery.* New York: Basic Books.

Hershkowitz, I., Lamb, M. E., &. Horowitz, D. (2007). Victimization of children with disabilities. *American Journal of Orthopsychiatry, 77(*4),629-35.

Hollins, S. & Sinason, V. (2000). Psychotherapy, learning disabilities and trauma: New perspectives. *British Journal of Psychiatry, 176*, 32-36.

Koss, Figueredo, & prince (2002). Cognitive mediation of rape's mental, physical, and social health impact; Tests of four models in cross-sectional data. *Journal of Consulting and Clinical Psychology, 70*(4),926-941.

Martin, S. L., Ray, N., Sotres-Alvarez, D., Kupper, L. L., Moracco, K. E., Dickens, P. A., et al. (2006). Physical and sexual assault of women with disabilities. *Violence Against Women, 12*(9), 823-837.

Mitchell, A., Clegg, J., & Furniss, F. (2006). Exploring the meaning of trauma with adults with intellectual disabilities. *Journal of Applied Research in Intellectual Disabilities, 19*, 131-142.

National Prison Rape Elimination Commission. (2009, June). *National Prison Rape Elimination Commission report.* Washington, DC: National Prison Rape Elimination Commission.

Peckham, N.G., Howlett, S., & Corbett, A. (2007). Evaluating a survivors group pilot for women with significant intellectual disabilities who have been sexually abused. *Journal of Applied Research in Intellectual Disabilities, 20,* 308-322.

Price, J.L., Hilsenroth, M.J., Callahan, K.L., Petretic-Jackson, P.A., & Bonge, D. (2004). A pilot study of psychodynamic psychotherapy for adult survivors of childhood sexual abuse. *Clinical Psychology and Psychotherapy, 11*(6), 378-391.

Razza, N. & Tomasulo, D. (2005). *Healing trauma: The power of group treatment for people with intellectual disabilities.* Washington, DC: American Psychological Association.

Sinason, V. (2002). Treating people with learning disabilities after physical or sexual abuse. *Advances in Psychiatric Treatment, 8*(6): 424-431.

Sobsey, D. (2005). Violence & disability. In W. M. Nehring (Ed.). *Health promotion for persons with intellectual/developmental disabilities: The state of scientific evidence.* Washington, DC: American Association on Mental Retardation.

Spencer, N., Devereux, E., Wallace, A., Sundrum, R., Shenoy, M., Bacchus, C. & Logan, S. (2005, September). Disabling conditions and registration for child abuse and neglect: A population-based study. *Pediatrics, 116(3),* 609-614.

Strand, M., Benzein, E., & Saveman, B. I. (2004). Violence in the care of adult persons with intellectual disabilities. *Journal of Clinical Nursing, 13*(4), 506-514.

Sullivan, P. M., & Knutson, J. F. (2000). Maltreatment and disabilities: a population-based epidemiological study. *Child Abuse & Neglect, 24*(10), 1257-1273

van der Kolk, B.A. (1996.). The complexity of adaptation to trauma: Self-regulation, stimulus discrimination, and characterological development. In B.A. van der Kolk, A.C. McFarlane, L. Weisaeth (Eds.), *Traumatic stress: The effects of overwhelming experience on mind, body, and society* (pp. 182-213). New York: Guilford Press.

van der Kolk, B.A., van der Hart, O., & Burbridge, J. (2002). Approaches to the treatment of PTSD. In M.B. Williams & J.F. Sommer (Eds.), *Simple and complex post-traumatic stress disorder: Strategies for comprehensive treatment in clinical practice.*

Chapter 7

Cognitive Behavioral Therapy for Adults with Autism Spectrum Disorder

Valerie L. Gaus, Ph.D.

INTRODUCTION

This chapter will focus on psychotherapy approaches that can be useful for persons with autism spectrum disorders (ASD). Because they are defined as developmental disorders, ASD's have traditionally been thought of as childhood problems. However, increasing numbers of adults are being identified with this syndrome, and they are seeking out treatment. This chapter will first describe ASD's as they are currently defined in the *DSM-IV-TR* (American Psychiatric Association, 2000). The fact that a larger and more heterogeneous group of patients are meeting criteria for an ASD than in past decades will be discussed along with the implications for mental health practitioners who are serving them. A description of adult ASD will follow with a proposal that older teens and adults on the higher-functioning end of the autism spectrum are the people most likely to seek out psychotherapy services. Common presenting problems will be outlined with assessment strategies, along with a proposed framework for conceptualizing the mental health issues facing adults with ASD's. This will lead to a rationale for the use of Cognitive Behavioral Therapy (CBT) with these patients. Finally, a case example will be provided to illustrate the concepts described throughout the chapter.

In contrast to other chapters in this book, the present subject focuses on patients who may have little to no intellectual disability as defined by standard IQ tests. In fact, some people with ASD have above-average to superior intelligence, but demonstrate significant impairments in the social and communication domains of functioning. The collection of syndromes usually referred to in the scientific and clinical literature under the term ASD are also called "Pervasive Developmental Disorders" (PDD) in the current version of the *Diagnostic and Statistical Manual of Mental Disorders* (DSM-IV-TR; American Psychiatric Association, 2000). There are five disorders listed under the PDD category in that volume, and they are Autistic Disorder, Rett's Disorder, Childhood Disintegrative Disorder, Asperger's Disorder, and Pervasive Developmental Disorder - Not Otherwise Specified. While there are clear distinctions between these five syndromes, all are marked by impairment in social interaction/communication skills as well as a restricted range of interests and activities and/or stereotyped behavior.

There was a dramatic shift in how the PDD's were defined in North America with the publication of *DSM-IV* in 1994 (American Psychiatric Association, 1994), which widened the range of functioning levels demonstrated by people who meet criteria for ASD. With the addition of Asperger's Disorder, which had not appeared in previous versions of *DSM*, the clinical community saw a new group of individuals being included under the umbrella of PDD who would not have met criteria for a PDD in earlier years. Asperger's Disorder (also called Asperger Syndrome in much of the literature) has been described in a very similar way to autism in that individuals who meet criteria for the diagnosis demonstrate "impairment in social interaction" and "restricted repetitive patterns of behavior, interests and activities". But in contrast to Autistic Disorder, the diagnosis is ruled out if an individual has clinically significant delays in language, cognitive development, self-help skill development, adaptive behavior, or curiosity about the environment. By definition, all people with Asperger's Disorder are verbal and none have co-morbid intellectual disability. That is not to say that all individuals who meet criteria for Autistic Disorder are non-verbal and have intellectual disability. On the contrary, there has been growing recognition in the clinical and scientific community that Autistic Disorder can appear in individuals who are "high functioning" with normal or above cognitive ability and potential for independent living. The case of Austen, presented at the end of this chapter, is one such example.

There are several criticisms of current classification systems for autism spectrum disorders, and we may see changes in future versions of *DSM* and *ICD* (see Volkmar & Klin, 2005). One ongoing debate surrounds the question of whether Asperger's Disorder is qualitatively different from Autistic Disorder, warranting its own separate diagnostic category. Some researchers have suggested that it is simply "high-IQ autism", while others claim that "high-functioning autism" (HFA) is distinguishable from Asperger's Disorder (see Ozonoff & Griffith, 2000, for a review of evidence on both sides of this debate). That discussion is outside the scope of this chapter so, for practical purposes, a psychotherapy model will be presented that can be applied to any patient with ASD who has enough verbal ability and interest to engage in regular sessions with a psychotherapist, regardless of specific ASD diagnosis. This includes patients with Asperger's Disorder (which will be referred to as Asperger Syndrome or AS for the remainder of this chapter), "high functioning" Autism (HFA), and Pervasive Developmental Disorder not otherwise specified (PDD-NOS). Patients with Rett's Disorder and Childhood Disintegrative Disorder almost always have severe to profound intellectual disability, and would be less likely to possess the verbal ability to benefit from the therapeutic strategies described here.

THE PHENOMENON OF ADULT ASD

The prevalence of ASD has not been studied closely in adult populations. A recent study conducted in Great Britain produced an estimate of 1 in 100 adults living with an ASD (Burgha et al. 2009). Most other epidemiological studies have focused on children, but we can infer from them about the population of adults with ASD. In 2007, the Centers for Disease Control estimated that the prevalence of all PDD's in the American population is 1 in 150 children, which is based on a range of findings from 3.3-9.9 per 1000 children across two multi-site studies (Centers for Disease Control and Prevention, 2007a, 2007b). In the same series of studies, the PDD's were observed more in boys than girls at a ratio of 2.8-6.5:1 (Centers for Disease Control, 2007a, 2007b). In a more recent report, the United States population estimate was 1 in 100, with the male to female ratio being 4:1 (Kogan et al., 2009). If we consider all of these data, and note the lack of evidence that individuals "grow out" of autism, we can assume that there is a sizable population of adults living with a PDD and that there are three to four men for every woman meeting criteria for a diagnosis.

It is fitting that research and practice has focused on children in the field of ASD. After all, ASD's are classified in *DSM-IV-TR* with problems "usually first diagnosed in infancy, childhood or adolescence", and it is imperative to increase our understanding of early developmental processes and to intervene in a proactive way early in life. However, given the epidemiological information described above, it stands to reason that there would be a significant enough number of adults with ASD seeking help to warrant an understanding in the mental health community about their needs, as well as the availability of evidence-based interventions. Anecdotally speaking, this author has observed in her own practice and those of her colleagues two major cohorts of adults meeting criteria for ASD who present for psychotherapy. The first includes the people born before the mid-seventies who were already adults before the syndrome was made known to the American mental health community in 1994. When these individuals were children (in the 1940's, 1950's and 1960's), they presented very differently than their counterparts with "classic autism," the latter being mostly nonverbal, unresponsive to other people, and having intellectual disability. At the time they would not have been considered autistic, as many had normal to superior intelligence and advanced verbal skills, demonstrated varied academic success, and some ability to relate to people, even if they did connect more easily to adults than peers. In cases where these children were identified by parents and/or teachers as needing help because of their struggles relating to other children and/or being obsessively involved with a special interest (e.g., insects, trains, astronomy), they were often classified in the education system as "emotionally disturbed," but not identified as having any sort of developmental or learning disorder. In fact, their profiles did not clearly fit any diagnostic category during the forty-year span between the 1950's and 1990's in the American classification system. They have, therefore, lived most of their lives with an array of undiagnosed or misdiagnosed problems. In clinical practice, this author has observed that many such individuals have achieved college or graduate degrees, but are grossly under-employed because of problems managing the social aspects of the workplace. These individuals report loneliness because they tend to struggle with making or keeping friends and/or romantic partners.

The second cohort of adults this author has seen frequently presenting for psychotherapy are those who were born after the mid-seventies. These young people are more likely to have been properly diagnosed in childhood or adolescence (although not always). Even under the best circumstances, when given appropriate support and intervention, these individuals need help with the overwhelming transition into adulthood as they "age out" of the education system (Gerhardt & Holmes, 2005). A common clinical observation of this author is that some adolescents with ASD who thrive and succeed in highly structured environments may give the false impression that they can handle more than they really can once they leave school. When they enter "the real world" of college or work, the decrease in structure is often too abrupt and their functioning level regresses. The case of Austen, presented later, illustrates this. These individuals frequently seek help from a psychotherapist because they no longer have access to the supports provided by their school systems. Since autism spectrum disorders are being diagnosed in children at a higher rate than ever before (CDC, 2007a, 2007b; Kogan, et al, 2009), this group of young adults is going to continue to get bigger.

PRESENTING PROBLEMS FOR PSYCHOTHERAPY

Historically, psychotherapy was not considered a viable treatment option for people with developmental disabilities, including autism spectrum disorders. With the growing recognition that people with developmental disabilities can suffer from co-morbid mental health problems, has come the need to offer patients evidence-based approaches to treat these conditions, which includes protocols that are delivered in a psychotherapy context. The onset of this trend is fairly recent for all developmental and intellectual disabilities (e.g., Kroese, Dagnan & Loumidis, 1997; Nezu & Nezu, 1994; Strohmer & Prout, 1994) and even more recent for people with ASD specifically (e.g., Attwood, 2006b; Gaus, 2000, 2007, in press; Jacobsen, 2003). Psychotherapists may receive referrals from a variety of sources, including a diagnostician who has established ASD in a patient, a patient who suspects ASD after reading about it, a family member who suspects ASD in a loved one after reading about it, an inpatient psychiatry team that suspects or establishes ASD for a patient and refers to outpatient treatment upon discharge or, alternatively, a psychotherapist already treating an individual for another reason who may realize that ASD may be present.

Adults with ASD are prone to a poorer quality of life than same-age peers (Jennes-Coussens, Magill-Evans, & Koning, 2006) for any number of reasons. Based on this author's clinical cases, complaints that patients with ASD report during intake involve several domains of functioning. The most common issues appear below, with the first list outlining typical struggles as described by the patients themselves and the second list outlining these struggles as reported by their family members who may see the problems from a different perspective.

Self-Reported Problems

Loneliness. Some patients report a sense of isolation or at least some dissatisfaction with the number or quality of the relationships they have in their lives. Contrary to popular belief about people on the autism spectrum, these individuals are usually quite motivated to have friends and romantic partners.

Social anxiety. Many patients report that they feel highly anxious in some or all types of social situations.

Depression. Most patients report some level of sadness, "feeling down", and feelings of helplessness and/or hopelessness. Some also report suicidal ideation, presently and/or by history. Interestingly, less social impairment and higher cognitive ability were associated with *more* self-reported depressive symptoms in one sample of adults diagnosed with autism spectrum disorders (Sterling, Dawson, Estes & Greenson, 2008).

Interpersonal conflicts and anger control problems. Some patients complain about not being able to "get along" with others; they have repeated conflicts with others (whether openly dealt with or not), at times resulting in overt fights and/or various negative consequences to the patient (e.g., loss of job, legal action).

Employment dissatisfaction. The majority of adults with ASD report employment problems of one kind or another. Despite the high level of talent and education seen in this population, a large portion of them are unemployed or are working at jobs that do not relate to their talents, education, or interests. Those who are employed face workplace problems including difficulty understanding the social domains of the job (e.g., interfacing with co-workers, bosses, customers) or managing the tasks of the job (e.g., time management, organization).

Frustration with living situation. Many patients complain at intake about not being able to achieve independence. They may be dependent on their families or housing programs (e.g., group home, supportive apartment). Their living arrangements sometimes lead to infringements on their rights to privacy and choice-making. This can be a powerful stressor contributing to the helplessness and hopelessness mentioned earlier.

Problems with dating and sexuality. Individuals on the autism spectrum are vulnerable to sexual problems because they do not have the educational or social experiences in adolescence through which typical people develop a healthy sexual self (Aston, 2003; Attwood, 2006b; Hénault, 2005; Koller, 2000). Some patients and their families are inhibited about discussing these issues and the problems may not be mentioned until the patient builds trust with the therapist. Examples include lack of sexual information, anxiety about dating, confusion about sexual identity/orientation, aversion to touch, sexual side-effects from psychotropic medication, preoccupation with sexual media (pornographic magazines, movies, websites) or less commonly, paraphilias.

Family-Reported Problems

Anger outbursts. A common complaint coming from family members, when involved in the intake, surrounds the patient's expression of anger. These patients are often described as having "meltdowns" which include explosive, unpredictable, or violent displays of rage. These entail screaming, cursing, threatening others, stomping feet, destroying property (throwing and breaking items, punching holes in walls), self-injury (slapping or hitting self, banging head on hard surface), and, less frequently, physical aggression toward others (shoving, kicking, punching or choking).

Obsessions/ intense and narrow interests. There is often concern about the patient being "obsessed" with a particular topic or activity (e.g., astronomy, sports, transit systems, aviation, cinema, meteorology). While the activity itself may or may not be maladaptive, there can be a problem with the inordinate amount of time and/ or money that the individual spends on it, to the exclusion of other potentially more adaptive activities.

Compulsive behavior. A topic of interest, as discussed above, may lead to repetitive, maladaptive behaviors that family members see as problematic or even self-destructive. Individuals with ASD may make errors based on poor judgment about health, safety, or money because they are so immersed in their interest without the inherent awareness of the impact of their behavior on self or others.

Withdrawal/depression. Involved family members may report concern about the individual's isolation and depressed mood. Sometimes a dramatic change in mood state is what triggers a family member to refer a patient to therapy, as it is usually accompanied by a change from the person's usual way of functioning (e.g., regression in self-care skills, less social engagement than usual).

Lack of motivation/ procrastination. One of the most frustrating issues for parents of adult children is what appears to them to be a lack of motivation to take responsibility for life decisions. The high level of intellectual functioning leads parents to say, for example, "he should know better" or "she should be more interested in her budget."

Poor ADL skills/ self-care and organization. Another common source of aggravation for family members is inconsistency in taking care of basic grooming and housekeeping responsibilities. The discrepancy between intellectual and adaptive functioning is puzzling to family members; it seems as though self-care should come more naturally.

Odd behavior in the community/ legal problems. Some referrals to treatment are triggered by incidents where a patient gets "in trouble" with members of the community and/or the legal system. Odd behaviors and poor social judgment lead others to misconstrue the intentions of a person with ASD. For example, a man with ASD who does not understand some social norms may not recognize the need to be subtle when looking at an attractive woman in the community. If he stares too long at her, he may be viewed as being predatory or having ill intentions, when in reality he simply does not know the "unwritten rules" about when to look away.

ASSESSMENT CONSIDERATIONS

When a therapist first meets an adult with ASD who is presenting with any combination of the above-listed problems, it can be difficult to get a clear view of the symptom picture. Challenges to the therapist can be found in the patient's response to the clinical interview, differential diagnosis issues, and the presence of co-morbid disorders.

Interviewing Considerations

In many ways a patient with higher-functioning ASD can be interviewed using the same approach a therapist would use with any patient. After all, these individuals are verbal, are often very articulate and function intellectually in the average or above range. Nevertheless, there are some modifications or adaptations that must be considered in order to successfully build rapport and obtain accurate information from the patient. These individuals, by definition, have difficulty navigating social situations and the clinical interview is no exception. In the absence of clinical research in this area, the following recommendations are based on the writings of clinicians working in the autism field (Gaus, 2007; Jacobsen, 2003) as well those working with patients with schizophrenia (Kingdon & Turkington, 2005) because of similar challenges in communication.

Pace. The therapist may need to devote extra time to the assessment process than normally required for other non-ASD patients. People with ASD may take longer than others to describe their problems to the therapist for a number of reasons. Some are highly anxious during initial sessions and are easily overwhelmed by the questioning process. Others talk incessantly and do not respond to cues or prompts to shift direction, which can slow down the interview.

Language use. As mentioned, people with ASD are verbal and often have superior command of the language. However, they may use language in unusual ways and tend to interpret what others say in a very literal fashion. The therapist must be mindful of the words he or she uses and should phrase questions and provide explanations to the patient using more detail and concrete terms than might be used with a patient who does not have an autism spectrum disorder.

Communication of boundaries and respect. People with ASD have difficulty inferring the expectations of others, and they often miss the nonverbal aspects of communication. For most patients this has contributed to a lifelong pattern of making social mistakes and receiving unfavorable feedback from others. This will be detailed more in the next session but is worth mentioning here as it relates to the therapy relationship. The therapist is challenged to set clear boundaries in the relationship using terms that are more explicit than might be used with other patients, but the therapist must be careful not to convey a judgmental tone while doing so. During the early sessions, this can be accomplished by giving the patient a clear set of "office rules" which may be things a typical population could just infer (e.g., what door to use, where to sit while waiting, when to knock or not, how to sign in, etc.) in order to reduce the likelihood of an error the therapist would need to correct. In addition, the therapist should avoid confronting the patient about odd social behavior (that is harmless) displayed in the initial sessions, as they may be serving a self-regulating functioning within a situation that is highly anxiety-provoking to the individual (e.g., avoiding eye contact, facial grimaces, whole body movements, unusual hand gestures). These behaviors can be discussed once rapport has been established and treatment is more underway.

Differential Diagnosis

The features of ASD can often mimic other DSM-defined disorders, so differential diagnosis is an important goal during the assessment process. Space limitations do not allow for a full set of guidelines on differentiating ASD from other disorders (see Gaus, 2007; Ghazuiddin, 2005; Tsai, 2006). For the present purposes, therapists working with this population should be aware that some symptoms of ASD can also appear in patients who have psychotic disorders, attention-deficit/hyperactivity disorder, anxiety disorders (particularly obsessive-compulsive disorder and social phobia), mood disorders, and some personality disorders. Only a careful assessment, including a thorough developmental history, can allow a therapist to make the differentiation.

Assessing for Comorbid Disorders

Despite the differential diagnosis concerns raised above, there are many instances when a patient will meet criteria for ASD, *plus* meet the criteria for a co-existing mental health problem. There have not been any thorough investigations of the incidence of mental health problems in the adult ASD population, but the model that will be presented in the next section hypothesizes the reasons an adult with ASD is at risk for the development of mental health problems. A preliminary study indicated that 32% of a sample of adults with AS reported having a co-morbid mental health problem, and that 15% had planned or attempted suicide (Barnard, Harvey, Potter & Prior, 2001). There have been no systematic investigations of the prevalence of co-morbid disorders within the adult Asperger's syndrome population, but studies have shown higher rates of anxiety and depression in children with Asperger's syndrome (e.g., Bolton, Pickles, Murphy & Rutter, 1998; Kim, Szatmari, Bryson, Streiner & Wilson, 2000; Piven & Palmer, 1999). These findings are consistent with this author's anecdotal experience as well as the clinical accounts of other authors; a therapist treating adult patients with ASD is likely to observe anxiety and mood disorders as co-morbid conditions more often than any other disorders (see Attwood, 2006b, Gaus, 2007; Ghazuiddin, 2005; Tsai, 2006).

ASPERGER SYNDROME AS A DISORDER OF INFORMATION PROCESSING

This author has argued elsewhere that many of the problems presented by adults with ASD stem from a basic *information processing disorder* (Gaus, 2007). People with ASD have an idiosyncratic way of processing both social and non-social information that has been present since birth or early childhood. Their unique perception has adversely affected their development and social experiences, resulting in negative consequences. Their perception causes them to exhibit behavior that is unappealing to others and contributes to the recurrent rejection and ridicule they encounter. It also leads to impairment in non-social areas of functioning, such as organization and self-direction, which increases the level of stress in daily living. Klin and his colleagues (Klin, Jones, Schultz, Volkmar & Cohen, 2002a) propose that, although ASD is a complex syndrome including an array of communication, learning and behavioral symptoms, all of the problems can be traced to a "core social disorder." These authors describe how individuals with ASD each have a dysfunctional "enactive mind" (Klin, Jones, Shultz, & Volkmar, 2005). This involves a continuous interaction between idiosyncratic attention to social cues, erroneous interpretation of social information, and maladaptive behavioral responses, all of which affect childhood development as well as current adult functioning. This author finds this process-oriented model useful when conceptualizing an individual adult psychotherapy case, when considering the role of the core factors, or dysfunctional "enactive mind," in the development and maintenance of the presenting problems for which the patient is seeking help. Each patient presents very differently and no two have the same profile of these deficits. Nevertheless, practitioners need to be familiar with all of these possible areas of dysfunction in order to do a comprehensive conceptualization and treatment plan.

Figure 1 presents the author's conceptualization of the problems commonly reported by adults with ASD. Based on evidence about cognitive dysfunction in ASD which has been reviewed elsewhere (Gaus, 2007), this model is meant to provide a framework to guide clinicians in considering a wide range of factors during the assessment and treatment planning process for adult ASD patients.

Figure 1. Core problems in Asperger syndrome and pathways to mental health problems. From *Cognitive-Behavioral Therapy for Adult Asperger Syndrome* (p. 41), by V. L. Gaus. Reprinted with permission.

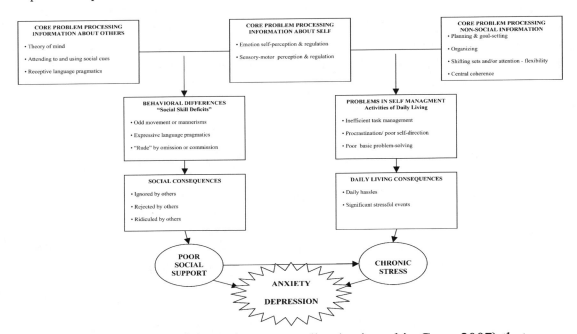

It has been established through many studies (reviewed in Gaus, 2007) that people with ASD process information in an idiosyncratic fashion. The types of information that people with ASD process erroneously can be classified into three major categories, which appear at the top of Figure 1: information about others, information about self, and non-social information. Processing information about others, or social cognition, is dysfunctional in that people with ASD demonstrate impairments in the ability to formulate ideas about what other people are thinking or feeling ("theory of mind"), to use non-verbal cues to understand social interactions, and to make adaptive use of social language ("pragmatics"). Processing information about themselves is dysfunctional in terms of the internal feedback loops involved in self-perception and self-regulation. People with ASD appear to have difficulty perceiving and regulating their own emotional experiences and have atypical sensation and motor experiences (hyper or hypo reactivity to stimulation of any of the sensory systems). Processing of non-social information is dysfunctional in individuals with ASD who have problems managing input that is not necessarily related to other people. These include deficits in planning, organization, goal-setting, and cognitive flexibility ("executive functions") as well as difficulty processing incoming pieces of information within a context ("gist" or "central coherence" as per Frith, 1989), or "seeing the big picture"

Assigning these information processing problems into three separate categories is somewhat arbitrary, as these phenomena probably occur in a dimensional way and interact with each other in a multi-directional fashion. Figure 2 represents the overlap that exists between the categories. While researchers are still years away from establishing these connections or evidence for the direction of causality, a clinician can find these concepts helpful in understanding the history and development of an individual patient's presenting problems.

Figure 2. Interrelationship between core problems in AS.
From *Cognitive-Behavioral Therapy for Adult Asperger Syndrome* (p. 42), by V. L. Gaus. Reprinted with permission.

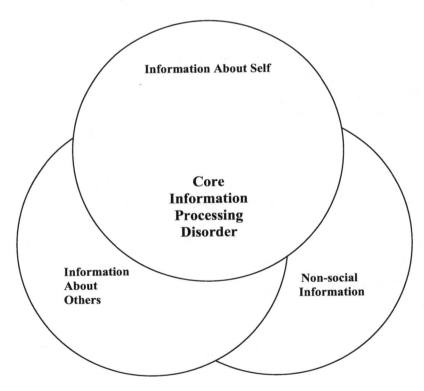

Going back to Figure 1, the diagram illustrates how the core problems combine and lead to difficulties when these individuals interact with their environments. The "social skill deficits," represented by the mid-left box, which are part of the diagnostic criteria for ASD (e.g., DSM-IV-TR), are hypothesized to be the behavioral outcome of a combination of erroneous social inference, self-perception problems, and lack of typical social learning during critical periods of development. Because individuals with ASD are misperceiving many social situations, they do not know how to respond to others or what others expect from them. Their odd mannerisms, poor language pragmatics, and "rude" behavior lead others to become frustrated or angry with them, resulting in negative social consequences. They experience being ignored, rejected, and ridiculed, without knowing why. Those people in their lives who are more compassionate may try to tell them that their behavior is "inappropriate," but they may not always understand or explain why.

Difficulties in the non-social domains appear as problems in self-management and activities of daily living, represented by the box on the mid-right side of the diagram. These are the behavioral outcomes of a combination of problems with executive function and self-perception. They appear as inefficient task management, procrastination, poor self-direction, and poor basic problem-solving. It is common, but often surprising, to see a huge discrepancy between IQ and formal measures of adaptive behavior, such as the Vineland Adaptive Behavior Scales (e.g., Green, Gilchrist, Burton & Cox, 2000). The folk stereotype of "the absent-minded professor" is fitting in that the person may be brilliant but can barely take care of the things necessary to live independently. This leads to the daily living consequences of daily hassles as well as a preponderance of significant stressful events.

The model ends at the bottom of the figure with the hypothesized outcomes of the repeated failures in the domains described above. The negative consequences of dysfunctional information processing and the resultant maladaptive behavior lead to the emotional distress reported by adult patients seeking psychotherapy; the social consequences of ASD lead to poor social support, and the daily living consequences of ASD lead to chronic stress. Poor social support and chronic stress are known risk factors for mental illness in the typical population (e.g., Cohen & Wills, 1985; Sarason & Sarason, 1985) and, therefore, are hypothesized to increase the vulnerability in adults with ASD to develop co-morbid conditions.

COGNITIVE-BEHAVIORAL THERAPY: DESCRIPTION AND RATIONALE FOR ITS USE WITH ASD

Some professionals may argue that early intervention is the only way the problems associated with ASD can be ameliorated. It is true that treatment can have a dramatic impact when it comes early in life, but many of today's adults with ASD were not identified as being on the autism spectrum when they were very young, so they did not have that opportunity. Considering a lifespan developmental perspective, however, it is widely accepted that learning and change does not stop at age 18 or 21 for typical people, so there is no reason to believe it would for people with ASD. A new skill learned at any age can affect life in a positive way from that point on. A psychotherapist can help these adults by teaching them to recognize and modify automatic maladaptive thoughts, more accurately "read" the behavior of others to better understand social interactions, and modify their own behavior in response. This new learning helps the individual with ASD improve social functioning, increase coping/ stress management skills, and prevent or reduce symptoms of anxiety and depression.

There is no evidence-based protocol yet established for treating adult ASD. There are, however, numerous such strategies available for the treatment of the co-morbid disorders often bringing these patients into treatment. Cognitive-Behavioral Therapy (CBT) refers to a set of strategies for addressing mental health problems that has existed for over 40 years and has very large empirical literature supporting its validity. Butler, Chapman, Forman, and Beck (2006) provide a recent review of meta-analytic studies supporting its efficacy for treating unipolar depression, generalized anxiety disorder, panic disorder, agoraphobia, social phobia and post-traumatic stress disorder. Although adults with ASD were not mentioned in any of the studies cited, the mental health problems treated successfully by these protocols have been reported in clinical descriptions of adult ASD (Attwood, 1998, 2006b; Gaus, 2007; Ghaziuddin, 2005). CBT approaches are designed to teach people how to monitor their own thoughts and perceptions in order to become more aware of interpretive errors and to target those that are associated with mood and anxiety problems.

Several authors have recommended the use of CBT for children and adolescents with ASD (Attwood, 1998, 2004, 2006b; Chalfant, Rapee, Carroll, 2007; Klinger & Williams, 2009; Reaven, Blakely-Smith, Nichols, Dasari, Flinigan & Hepburn 2009; Sofronoff, Attwood & Hinton, 2005; Sofronoff, Attwood, Hinton & Lewis, 2007; Sze & Wood, 2007; Wood, Drahota, Sze, Har, Chiu & Langer, 2009) as well as adult ASD (Attwood, 1998, 2004, 2006b; Cardaciotto & Herbert, 2004; Gaus, 2000, 2007, in press; Hare & Paine, 1997; Tsai, 2006), but there are only a handful of published studies supporting its use in this population. Of the six known case examples, only two were adult cases (Cardaciotto & Herbert, 2004; Hare, 1997). Of the others, three were descriptions of child cases (Reaven & Hepburn, 2003; Sze & Wood, 2007, 2008) and one an adolescent (Beebe & Risi, 2003).

To date there have been 5 published controlled investigations of CBT for children with ASD. Sofronoff, Attwood & Hinton (2005) applied a CBT-based group treatment protocol to subjects aged 10-12 years diagnosed with AS in order to reduce anxiety symptoms across six two-hour sessions. Compared to wait-list controls, the participants showed significant improvement in ability to generate coping responses to a hypothetical scenario, as well as a reduction in parent-reported measures of anxiety symptoms. In a similar study aimed to reduce anger symptoms, Sofronoff, Attwood, Hinton & Lewis (2007) applied the same CBT protocol to a group of 10-14 year old subjects diagnosed with AS. Compared to wait-list controls, these children showed a significant decrease in the frequency of parent-reported anger episodes and improvement in their ability to generate coping responses in a hypothetical scenario. Chalfant, Rapee & Carroll (2007) implemented a 12-week group CBT protocol for children who met criteria for both HFA and a comorbid anxiety disorder. Compared to wait-list controls, the treatment groups demonstrated significant reduction in anxiety symptoms as measured by self-report, parent report and teacher report; 71% of the children who received treatment no longer met criteria for an anxiety disorder post-treatment. In a similar study (Reaven et al., 2009), investigators aimed to reduce the severity of anxiety symptoms in a sample of children with ASD. After completing a CBT group protocol that included parents, the children demonstrated significant reductions in the severity of anxiety symptoms compared to wait-list controls. Wood et al. (2009) adapted a standard evidence-based protocol for childhood anxiety disorders and augmented it with additional components which addressed social and adaptive skill deficits that are observed in children with ASD. In a randomized controlled trial, they delivered the intervention to children 7-11 years old who met criteria for ASD and comorbid anxiety disorders. As a departure from the group therapy interventions outlined above, this intervention was delivered in individual/family sessions. The treatment group showed significant improvements as measured by anxiety symptoms checklists compared to wait-list controls.

If we combine the research results supporting CBT to treat co-morbid disorders in typical populations, with the promising preliminary data on the success of CBT for children with higher-functioning ASD, there is enough evidence to suggest practicing clinicians can turn to CBT to address the presenting problems of adult patients with higher-functioning ASD.

The Cognitive Model and Asperger Syndrome

The foundation for CBT, the cognitive model, was born in the early 1960's, with different versions being described by Ellis (1962) and Beck (1963). Because Beck's model has served as the basis for many empirically validated adult psychotherapy protocols (Butler, Chapman, Forman & Beck, 2006), it has been used as a foundation for conceptualizing adult ASD cases in CBT (Gaus, 2007, in press). Beck's (1976) model for emotional disturbance proposed that people process information according to schemas, which are cognitive structures guiding and organizing the perception of events and experiences. They involve core beliefs that are learned, beginning early in life, through experiences interacting with the environment and the groups of people to which they belong (e.g., family, peers, culture, religious community). They influence the way a person thinks, feels, and behaves in response to the environment. An event will activate a related schema that triggers a cycle of cognitions influencing emotion/mood which influences behavior which influences cognitions and so forth. This feedback cycle then loops back and further influences the schema, by reinforcing it or causing it to be modified. At times schema can lead a person to habitually distort events and can become maladaptive. Beck (1976) proposed that mental health problems are driven by an excess of such distortions. Throughout life, schemas are continuously changing and evolving as new information is taken in, necessitating rules and beliefs to be modified. This process can also be maladaptive if a person fails to take in new information and hangs onto a previously functional schema that no longer fits with current life circumstances. Another problem can arise if there is a disproportionate amount of negative over positive beliefs about the self, others, the world, or the future. A negative schema may lead a person to selectively focus only on information that fits with that belief system and ignore information that could possibly refute it.

Schemas and ASD

Considering the cognitive deficits that have been found in people with ASD, these individuals are at risk for developing a whole host of maladaptive schemas. The cognitive model assumes that other people are an important source of teaching, modeling, and reinforcing the beliefs that make up schemas. However, social cognition deficits make it much harder for a person with ASD to infer and make use of information that comes from other people in a social context. They are, therefore, missing out on a rich source of input for developing and evolving healthy schemas over time. Their cognitive inflexibility is also a risk factor in that they may hold on too strongly to a schema that is non-functional. Their frequent experiences of negative life events, such as social rejection and repeated employment failures, are likely to reinforce negative beliefs about self, others, the world, and the future.

Figure 3 is a duplicate of the core problems conceptual model shown earlier, with the added schema symbols, illustrating the points at which negative beliefs may develop or be reinforced. The struggles with social skills and self management could easily give rise to negative schema about the self. The social consequences of being ignored, rejected, or ridiculed can foster the development of negative schema about others and the self. The daily living consequences of increased daily hassles and stressful events may contribute to negative beliefs about the world and the self, and ultimately all of the above can lead to negative ideas about what is to come or negative schema about the future.

Figure 3. The vulnerability to maladaptive schema development in Asperger syndrome.
From *Cognitive-Behavioral Therapy for Adult Asperger Syndrome* (p. 64), by V. L. Gaus. Reprinted with permission.

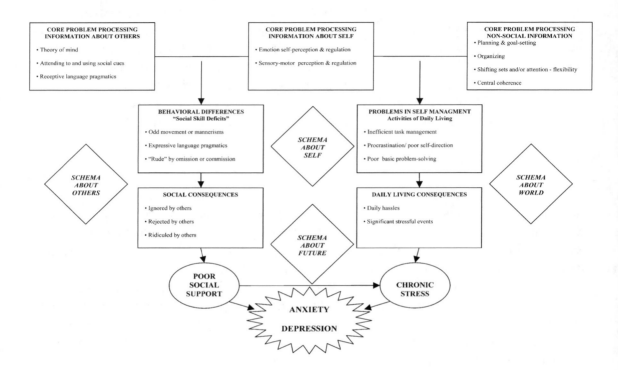

APPLICATION OF CBT

Each set of factors in the model outlined in Figure 3 represents a possible point of intervention for a therapist. When a person with ASD presents with an anxiety or mood disorder, it is an outcome of many variables that have interacted with each other throughout his or her history up to the point of intake. The idea that the mental health problem has resulted from this process is illustrated by placing anxiety and depression at the bottom, or end, of the diagram. Through the assessment and case conceptualization phases of treatment, the therapist must hypothesize about the developmental processes that led up to the current issues and identify targets for change. Using this approach, there are general categories of therapy goals for adults with ASD. There can be goals to increase competencies and skills in order to improve relationship and occupational functioning, which have previously been impaired by the symptoms of ASD. These are related to the issues listed in the top to middle region of the Figure 3. Then there are goals that aim to decrease symptoms of co-morbid Axis I problems, such as anxiety and mood disorders, related to the issues listed in the middle to bottom region of the diagram.

In-depth instructions on CBT for depression or anxiety are beyond the scope of this chapter; the literature is so vast that a brief review is not even possible. Gaus (2007) provides a comprehensive overview of techniques that are applicable to this population. Several of those key strategies appropriate for increasing skills and reducing symptoms of anxiety and depression will be outlined here and then illustrated through a case example.

Increasing Skills

There are two broad categories of skill development needed in this population. They are *social skills* and *coping skills*. Referring back to Figure 3, these intervention categories are meant to address the problems listed in the middle boxes.

Social Skills. Teaching social skills will address the behavioral differences with their social consequences. Social skill development must be multifaceted, including strategies to teach not only superficial polite behavior (e.g., greeting people, smiling, taking turns, looking the other people's eyes) but also increase fund of social knowledge and ability to "read" another person during a dynamic interaction. For this the therapist must be able to do the following.

1) *Provide information about the "unwritten rules" of social conduct.* Many social norms and codes of conduct are assumed by members of a culture but are not actually documented or taught in a formal way (e.g., how far away to stand from someone while chatting at a cocktail party, what one should or shouldn't say to a grocery store cashier, how or whether to interact with a stranger sitting next to you on an airplane, etc.). Most people without an ASD develop this knowledge base by making inferences during observations of others and by accurately reading the nonverbal feedback they get from others as they grow and mature through life. Since people with ASD have difficulty learning through those means (as addressed below), they need a therapist to help them catch up to their same-age peers by giving them a crash course in the rules they have not learned yet. Myles, Trautman & Shelvan (2004) serves as a resource for this purpose as well as Gray (1995, 1998) who offers an approach using social narratives.

2) *Teach strategies to improve social cognition.* To be socially effective, one must be able to assess the social context of a situation, observe the verbal and nonverbal behavior of other people, infer the others' mental states, understand what is expected by others, and then carry out what is expected. This complex set of skills is referred to as "social cognition" because it involves thinking about other people and what *they* are thinking. People with ASD have great difficulty carrying out these operations, which come naturally to those without ASD. There a several means by which a therapist can provide opportunities to learn these skills, which include:

- Presentation of commercially available materials and tools (e.g., Winner, 2000, 2002)
- Retrospective discussions about encounters the patient reports
- Behavioral rehearsal of planned encounters
- Incidental feedback on the behavior displayed during interactions with the therapist

Coping Skills. As illustrated in Figure 3, people with ASD have self-management difficulties that lead to daily consequences that can accumulate to create chronic stress. Coping skills that can alleviate this include but are not limited to:

- Time management skills
- Problem-solving skills
- Relaxation skills
- Assertiveness skills

Decreasing Symptoms of Co-morbid Disorders

When co-morbid mental health problems are present, patients with ASD should be offered the same CBT interventions that would be offered to any adult who is struggling with anxiety, depression, or chronic stress. The only difference for people with ASD is that there may be extra skill-building components as outlined above. (For an introduction to the fundamentals of Cognitive-Behavioral Therapy as per Beck's cognitive theory, see J. Beck, 1995, and Persons, Davidson & Tompkins, 2000, both excellent and easy to understand descriptions for the newcomer). CBT is based on the assumption that any person can develop maladaptive cognitions that cause or maintain symptoms of anxiety or depression. Because people with ASD have idiosyncratic ways of processing information, it makes them vulnerable to the types of maladaptive thoughts, beliefs, and schemas that are involved with anxiety and depression. For example, people with ASD may demonstrate a rigid adherence to non-functional rules or may be prone to dichotomous or "black and white" thinking.

The primary objectives of CBT follow, with examples of techniques that are particulary useful for patients with ASD.

1) Identify and respond to dysfunctional automatic thoughts and cognitive distortions (Self-talk in a very specific situation, e.g., "This new assignment at work is too hard for me – I can never learn things like this."). Techniques and tools that can help the patient who has ASD are

- Self-assessment of cognitive distortions (e.g., Gaus, 2007)
- Dysfunctional thought record (e.g., Beck, 1995; Persons et al., 2000)

2) Recognize and modify maladaptive intermediate beliefs (the rules that are used to assess and appraise a wide variety of similar situations, e.g., "If I don't learn something on the first try it means I will never learn it"). Useful techniques for patients with ASD described in Gaus (2007) include:

- Activity log
- Dysfunctional beliefs worksheet

3) Modify maladaptive schemas (core beliefs about self, others, world and future that are pervasive e.g., "I am stupid."). For ASD, these strategies can be useful:

- Continuum techniques (e.g, Beck, 1995; Gaus, 2000; Padesky, 1994; Persons et al., 2000)
- Core beliefs worksheet (e.g., Beck, 1995).

CASE EXAMPLE

Austen

Austen is a 19-year old single man who attends a community college on a part-time basis and lives with his mother, father, and one brother. Austen's parents referred him to therapy because they were concerned he might be depressed. Austen agreed to meet the therapist because he was "tired" of living with his parents.

Austen was at the beginning of his second year of college at the time of intake. He had recently become more withdrawn from his family, was sleeping more than usual, and was having difficulty concentrating on his school work. His freshman year had been "a nightmare" as described by his mother. He had gone straight into college from high school and signed up for a full-time course load. He fell behind on his work very early on but did not tell anyone and did not seek help. He got 2 F's, 2 D's and a C. In the second semester of that year, he reduced his course load to 3 classes, but the same pattern repeated; he fell behind and did not seek help. His grades were slightly better, but not acceptable to him or his parents (2 C's and a D) and have been the source of many arguments. In the current semester, he was taking three courses again, but was already behind at the time of intake. His parents were becoming increasingly frustrated with him.

Austen's parents reported that he had had significant "autistic signs" since he was a toddler, including a significant language delay, social difficulties, tantrums, distress with changes, and hyperactivity. He was diagnosed with Autistic Disorder when he was 3 ½. His parents were told at that time that Austen was very bright. He was enrolled in early intervention and responded well. His language skills improved significantly and his tantrums decreased. He was able to enroll in public school for kindergarten. Throughout his school years he was mainstreamed but received speech therapy in elementary and middle school and resource room throughout high school. His parents reported that they were very satisfied with the school he attended, and they are grateful for the support the school gave to him. They also provided him with extra support by hiring private tutors to help him with his difficult subject areas. Austen did not like having tutors and was sometimes uncooperative with them. Austen excelled in math and science, but he struggled with English and social studies.

He often grasped new material very easily, but had difficulty organizing himself and getting his homework done; his parents described him as a procrastinator. He had always been "obsessed" with sports and could recite all kinds of statistics ever since he was very young. He did not have any close friends, but his love of sports did connect him to peers for some events (e.g., he would sometimes go to a game with a peer). He graduated from high school with a regular diploma and an A average. College seemed like a natural next step for Austen.

The initial assessment was conducted across three sessions. One interview included his parents, and the other two were with him alone. He was also administered the Beck Depression Inventory, which yielded a score of 27 (in the range of moderate depression). His school records and most recent psychological testing report were also reviewed. The following diagnosis and case formulation was generated:

DSM-TR Diagnosis

Axis I	Autistic Disorder
	Major Depressive Disorder, Moderate
Axis II	No diagnosis
Axis III	No diagnosis
Axis IV	Poor adjustment to college, family conflict
Axis V	GAD: 50

Case Formulation

Austen's depressive symptoms and impaired school functioning were being maintained by a combination of core ASD symptoms, learning history factors, and cognitive factors.

Core ASD Symptoms: Despite his intellectual strengths, Austen showed signs of executive function problems. He had difficulty organizing, goal setting, and planning ahead to get tasks done. He had been more reliant on the supports he received from resource room and his private tutors than he or his parents had realized. His intelligence and excellent grades made everyone, including him, think that college would be manageable for him. Only after he entered college and was required to function with less structure did he begin to struggle.

Learning History: Austen had historically dealt with stressful situations by avoiding them. His escape-motivated behaviors were reinforced because they often worked to get him out of tasks that were aversive to him (e.g., being uncooperative with a tutor sometimes led to the session ending early). When he began to encounter difficulties in college, he dealt with his dilemmas by avoiding them. He hid his struggles from his parents because he did not want them to hire tutors for him as they had done in high school.

Cognitive Factors: Austen had several schemas that were maladaptive, including "I am a failure" and "I am defective". He believed that he was failing at school because he had a disability and therefore was not meant to be in college. He discredited himself for his success in high school because he attributed his grades to his resource room and tutors. The longer his college struggles continued, the more he believed he was not capable of succeeding. He also believed that if he sought help, it would just prove his incompetence, which is why he avoided reporting his struggles to his parents or to anyone else who might help him. He was prone to black and white thinking, which contributed to his tendency to think he must do all of his work with no help or else he was a total failure. This was interfering with the practice of healthy coping skills (e.g., seeking help).

Treatment Plan

Based on the formulation, the following treatment strategies were implemented.
1) Time management skills were taught. Using an activity log worksheet, he tracked his time use for one week for baseline data. That was used to identify key areas where he was either trying to do too many things at once or not making best use of some time that was free. Because he enjoyed electronic equipment, he was taught how to set up a schedule and alarm system in his cell phone. Self-reliance on these tools would decrease his need to avoid tasks.
2) Psycho-education was provided regarding autism. He had previously had only a vague idea of what it was. Providing accurate information to him about his symptoms and implications would help to re-evaluate the schema, "I am defective," and to re-frame it as "I have autism, which means I have these strengths… and these needs…"
3) He was encouraged to find on-campus resources for help so that he would have the option of getting support without involving his parents. This would serve to challenge his belief that he was incompetent.
4) The dysfunctional thought record was used to keep track of thoughts and beliefs that were triggered by situations on campus and at home throughout each week.
5) A continuum technique was used to help him rate his success each week in 3 domains using a scale that ranged from 1 (totally failed) to 10 (achieved total success). The domains were:
   a) followed my schedule
   b) completed all of my week's assignments
   c) accessed help on campus

This exercise was meant to decrease his dichotomous thinking and also served to frame "accessing help" as a success, rather than a symbol of failure.

Outcome

Sessions occurred weekly across seven months. After 25 sessions, Austen no longer met criteria for Major Depressive Disorder. His BDI score was 14, which reflected very few mild symptoms. He had finished the fall semester (where therapy had begun halfway through) with 2 B's and a C. In the spring, he signed up for 4 classes and finished with 3 B's and an A. The therapist and he agreed to meet every other week through the summer and increase to every week again when school started.

CONCLUDING COMMENTS

There is a growing population of adults meeting criteria for AS or HFA who will be seeking help from psychotherapists in the years to come. At the time of this writing, researchers are only beginning to look at the adult ASD population, particularly in terms of intervention and services. In the meantime, practitioners need evidence-based approaches that can be realistically used with the individuals that they are working with every day. The data we do have tell us that people with ASD process information in an idiosyncratic way, and their differences are likely at play in the social problems they report. In addition, these adult patients often have co-morbid anxiety and mood disorders for which we do have evidence-based protocols found in the literature on CBT. With some modifications and extra attention to skill-building, these approaches can be successful with adult ASD.

REFERENCES

American Psychiatric Association. (1994). *Diagnostic and statistical manual of mental disorders (4th ed.).* Washington, DC: Author.

American Psychiatric Association. (2000). Diagnostic *and statistical manual of mental disorders (4th ed., text revision).* Washington, DC: Author.

Aston, M. (2003). *Aspergers in love: Couple relationships and family affairs.* London: Jessica Kingsley Publishers.

Attwood, T. (1998). *Asperger's syndrome: A guide for parents and professionals.* London: Jessica Kingsley Publishers.

Attwood, T. (2004). Cognitive behaviour therapy for children and adults with Asperger's syndrome. *Behaviour Change, 21(3),* 147-162.

Attwood, T. (2006a). Asperger's syndrome and problems related to stress. In M.G. Baron, J. Groden, G. Groden, & L.P. Lipsitt (Eds.), *Stress and coping in autism* (pp. 351-370). New York: Oxford University Press.

Attwood, T. (2006b). *The complete guide to Asperger's syndrome.* London: Jessica Kingsley Publishers.

Beck, A.T. (1963). Thinking and depression. *Archives of General Psychiatry, 9,* 324-333.

Beck, A. T. (1976). *Cognitive therapy and the emotional disorders.* New York: International Universities Press.

Beck, J.S. (1995). *Cognitive therapy: Basics and beyond.* New York: Guilford Press.

Beebe, D. W. & Risi, S. (2003). Treatment of adolescents and young adults with high-functioning autism or Asperger syndrome. In F.M. Dattilio & M.A. Reinecke (Eds.), *Cognitive therapy with children and adolescents: A casebook for clinical practice* (pp. 369-401). New York, Guilford Press.

Bolton, P., Pickles, A., Murphy, M., & Rutter, M. (1998). Autism, affective and other psychiatric disorders; patterns of familial aggregation. *Psychological Medicine, 28,* 385-395.

Brugha, T., McManus, S., Meltzer, H., Smith, J., Scott, F.J., Purdon, S., et al. (2009). Autism spectrum disorders in adults living in households throughout England: Report from the adult psychiatric morbidity survey 2007. *The Health & Social Care Information Centre, Social Care Statistics.*

Butler, A.C., Chapman, J.E., Forman, E.M., & Beck, A.T. (2006). The empirical status of cognitive-behavior therapy: A review of meta-analyses. *Psychology Review, 26(1),* 17-31.

Cardaciotto, L. & Herbert, J. D. (2004). Cognitive behavior therapy for social anxiety disorder in the context of Asperger's syndrome: A single subject report. *Cognitive and Behavioral Practice, 11,* 75-81.

Centers for Disease Control and Prevention (2007a). Prevalence of autism spectrum disorders – Autism and developmental disabilities monitoring network, six sites, United States, 2000. *Morbidity and Mortality Weekly Report, 56, SS-1,* 1-11.

Centers for Disease Control and Prevention (2007b). Prevalence of autism spectrum disorders – Autism and developmental disabilities monitoring network, 14 sites, United States, 2002. *Morbidity and Mortality Weekly Report, 56, SS-1,* 12-28.

Chalfant, A.M., Rapee, R. & Carroll, L. (2007). Treatment anxiety disorders in children with high functioning autism spectrum disorders: A controlled trial. *Journal of Autism and Developmental Disorders, 37,* 1842-1857.

Cohen, S. & Wills, T.A. (1985). Stress, social support, and the buffering hypothesis. *Psychological Bulletin, 98(2),* 310-357.

Ellis, A. (1962). *Reason and emotion in psychotherapy.* New York: Lyle Stuart.

Fombonne, E. (1999). The epidemiology of autism: A review. *Psychological Medicine, 29,* 769-786.

Frith, U. (1989). *Autism: Explaining the enigma.* Oxford: Blackwell.

Gaus, V. (2000). "I feel like an alien": Individual psychotherapy for adults with Asperger's disorder using a cognitive behavioral approach. *NADD Bulletin, 3,* 62-65.

Gaus, V. L. (2007). *Cognitive-behavioral therapy for adult Asperger syndrome.* New York, Guilford Press.

Gaus, V.L. (in press*).* Adult Asperger syndrome and the utility of cognitive-behavioral therapy. *Journal of Contemporary Psychotherapy.*

Gerhardt, P.F. & Holmes, D.L. (2005). Employment: Options and issues for adolescents and adults with autism spectrum disorders. In F.R. Volkmar, R. Paul, A. Klin, & D. Cohen (Eds.), *Handbook of autism and pervasive developmental disorders: Vol. 2. Assessment, interventions and policy* (3rd ed., pp. 1087-1101). Hoboken, NJ: Wiley.

Ghaziuddin, M. (2005). *Mental health aspects of autism and Asperger's syndrome.* London: Jessica Kingsley Publishers.

Gray, C. (1995). *The original social story book.* Arlington: Future Horizons.

Gray, C. (1998). Social stories and comic strip conversations with students with Asperger syndrome and high-functioning autism. In E. Schopler, G.B. Mesibov, & L.J. Kunce (Eds.), *Asperger syndrome or high functioning autism?* (pp. 167-198). New York: Plenum Press.

Green, J., Gilchrist, A., Burton, D., & Cox, A. (2000). Social and psychiatric functioning in adolescents with Asperger syndrome compared with conduct disorder. *Journal of Autism and Developmental Disorders, 30,* 279-293.

Hare, D. J. (1997). The use of cognitive-behaviour therapy with people with Asperger's syndrome. *Autism, 1(2),* 215-225.

Hare, D. J. & Paine, C. (1997). Developing cognitive beahvioural treatments for people with Asperger's syndrome. *Clinical Psychology Forum, 110,* 5-8.

Hénault, I. (2005). *Asperger's syndrome and sexuality: From adolescence through adulthood.* London: Jessica Kingsley Publishers.

Jacobsen, P. (2003). *Asperger syndrome & psychotherapy.* London: Jessica Kingsley Publishers.

Jennes-Coussens, M, Magill-Evans, J, & Koning, C. (2006) The quality of life of young men with Asperger syndrome. *Autism, 10(4),* 403-414

Kim, J. A., Szatmari, P., Bryson, S. E., Streiner, D. L., & Wilson, F. J. (2000). The prevalence of anxiety and mood problems among children with autism and Asperger syndrome. *Autism, 4(2),* 117-132.

Kingdon, D.G. & Turkington, D. (2005). Cognitive therapy of schizophrenia. New York: Guildford Press.

Klin, A., Jones, W., Schultz, R., & Volkmar, F. (2005). The enactive mind - from actionsto cognition: Lessons from autism. In F.R. Volkmar, R. Paul, A. Klin, & D. Cohen (Eds.), *Handbook of autism and pervasive developmental disorders: Vol. 1. Diagnosis, development, neurobiology, and behavior* (3rd ed., pp. 682-703). Hoboken, NJ: Wiley.

Klin, A., Jones, W., Schultz, R., Volkmar, F., & Cohen, D. (2002a). Defining and quantifying the social phenotype in autism. *American Journal of Psychiatry, 159(6),* 895-908.

Klin, A., & Volkmar, F.R. (2003). Asperger syndrome: Diagnosis and external validity. *Child and Adolescent Psychiatric Clinics of North America, 12,* 1-13.

Klinger, L.G., & Williams, A. (2009). Cognitive-behavioral interventions for students with autism spectrum disorders. In M.J. Mayer, J.E. Lochman & R. Van Acker (Eds.), *Cognitive-behavioral interventions for emotional and behavioral disorders: School-based practice (pp. 328-362).* New York, NY: Guilford Press.

Kogan, M.D., Blumberg, S.J., Schieve, L.A., Boyle, C.A., Perrin, J.M., Ghandour, R.M., et al. (2009). Prevalence of parent-reported diagnosis of autism spectrum disorder among children in the US, 2007. *Pediatrics, 124,* 1395-1403.

Koller, R. (2000). Sexuality and adolescents with autism. *Sexuality and Disability, 18,* 125-135.

Kroese, B. S., Dagnan, D., & Loumidis, K (Eds.) (1997). *Cognitive-behaviour therapy for people with learning disabilities.* London: Routlege.

Myles, B.S., Trautman, M., & Schelvan, R.L. (2004). *The hidden curriculum: Practical solutions for understanding unstated rules in social situations.* Shawnee Mission, KS: Autism Asperger Publishing Company.

Nezu, C.M. & Nezu, A.M. (1994). Outpatient psychotherapy for adults with mental retardation and concomitant psychopathology: Research and clinical imperatives. *Journal of Consulting and Clinical Psychology, 62,* 34-42.

Ozonoff, S., & Griffith, E.M. (2000). Neuropsychological function and the external validity of Asperger syndrome. In. A. Klin, F.R. Volkmar, & S. S. Sparrow, (Eds.), *Asperger syndrome.* New York: Guilford Press.

Padesky, C.A. (1994). Schema change processes in cognitive therapy. *Clinical Psychology and Psychotherapy, 1,* 267-278.

Persons, J. B., Davidson, J. & Tompkins, M. A. (2000). *Essential components of cognitive-behavior therapy for depression.* Washington, D.C.: American Psychological Association.

Piven, J. & Palmer, R. (1999). Psychiatric disorder and the broad autism phenotype: Evidence from a family study of multiple incidence autism families. *American Journal of Psychiatry, 156,* 557-563.

Reaven, J.A., Blakeley-Smith, A., Nichols, S., Dasari, M., Flanigan, E., & Hepburn, S. (2009). Cognitive-Behavioral group treatment for anxiety symptoms in children with high-functioning autism spectrum disorders: A piolot study. *Focus on Autism and Other Developmental Disabilities. 24,* 27-37.

Reaven, J. & Hepburn, S. (2003). Cognitive-behavioral treatment of obsessive-compulsive disorder in a child with Asperger syndrome: A case report. *Autism, 7(2),* 145-164.

Sarason, I.G., & Sarason, B.R. (Eds.) (1985). *Social support: Theory, research and applications.* Dordrecht, The Netherlands: Martinus Nijhof.

Sofronoff, K., Attwood, T., & Hinton, S. (2005). A randomized controlled trial of CBT intervention for anxiety in children with Asperger syndrome. *Journal of Child Psychology and Psychiatry, 45,* 1-9.

Sofronoff, K., Attwood, T., Hinton, S. & Levin, I. (2007). A randomized controlled trial of cognitive-behavioral intervention for anger management in children diagnosed with Asperger Syndrome. *Journal of Autism and Developmental Disorders, 37(7),* 1203-1214.

Sterling, L., Dawson, G., Estes, A. & Greenson, J. (2008). Characteristics associated with the presence of depressive symptoms in adults with autism spectrum disorder. *Journal of Autism and Developmental Disorders, 38(6)*, 1011-1018.

Strohmer, D. C., & Prout, H. T. (Eds.) (1994). *Counseling and Psychotherapy with Persons with Mental Retardation and Borderline Intelligence*, Brondon, VT: CPPC.

Sze, K.M. & Wood, J.J. (2007). Cognitive behavioral treatment of comorbid anxiety disorders and social difficulties in children with high-functioning autism: A case report. *Journal of Contemporary Psychotherapy, 37,* 133-143.

Sze, K.M. & Wood, J.J. (2008). Enhancing CBT for the treatment of autism spectrum disorders and concurrent anxiety. *Behavioral and Cognitive Psychotherapy, 36,* 403-409.

Tsai, L. (2006). Diagnosis and treatment of anxiety disorders in individuals with autism spectrum disorder. In M. G. Baron, J. Groden, G. Groden, & L. P. Lipsitt (Eds.), *Stress and coping in autism* (pp. 388-440). New York: Oxford University Press.

Volkmar, F.R. & Klin, A. (2005). Issues in the classification of autism and related conditions. In F.R. Volkmar, R. Paul, A. Klin, & D. Cohen (Eds.), *Handbook of autism and pervasive developmental disorders: Vol. 1. Diagnosis, development, neurobiology, and behavior* (3rd ed., pp. 5-41). Hoboken, NJ: Wiley.

Volkmar, F.R., Klin, A., Siegel, B., Szatmari, P., Lord, C., Campbell, M., et al. (1994). DSM-IV Autism/Pervasive Developmental Disorder Field Trial. *American Journal of Psychiatry, 151,* 1361-1367.

Winner, M.G. (2000). *Inside out: What makes a person with social cognitive deficits tick?* San Jose, CA: Author.

Winner, M. G. (2002). *Thinking about you, thinking about me.* San Jose, CA: Author.

Wood, J.J., Drahota, A., Sze, K., Har, K., Chiu, A. & Langer, D.A. (2009). Cognitive behavioral therapy for anxiety in children with autism spectrum disorders: A randomized, controlled trial. *Journal of Child Psychology and Psychiatry, 50,* 224-234.

World Health Organization. (1992). *International classification of diseases: Tenth revision.* Geneva: Author.

CHAPTER 8

Psychotherapy for Individuals Who Have Intellectual Disabilities and Are Mourning

Jeffrey Kauffman, M.A., LCSW

INTRODUCTION

Experience and Expression: Respecting Individual Grief Experiences and Meanings

The death of an attachment object, a family member, a friend, or a staff person precipitates a grief reaction and in turn a need to reckon with, or mourn the loss. The loss of an attachment object may focus on the bond and the meaning of the bond that has been broken by death. However, when approaching treatment we do not begin by assuming that the meaning of the loss has to do specifically with attachment issues. Broken attachment anxiety grief may be part of a multi-factor clinical picture. It is possible, and not uncommon, that the meaning of grief reaction to the death of an attachment object has little or nothing to do specifically with broken attachment issues. For example, the loss may be experienced as a loss of routine and predictability, or the loss may be experienced as an accusation, or the loss may trigger a sense of not being safe. On the other hand, the locus of the grief experience may be a continuation and exacerbation of conflicts and wounded feelings in the relationship. Such loss experiences are prone to be more overwhelming among persons with intellectual disabilities than among persons who do not have an intellectual disability.

While separation anxiety is often an important part of the grief picture, it may not, in any given situation, be the key focus of the clinical picture and understanding of grief. When we approach a case with the grief assessment question, "What does the loss mean?" we are asking, "What does it mean *in the experience* of the person grieving?" To start with the grieving person's *experience* is basic clinical humility and respect for the client. Empathy is a receptivity and ability to enact within one's own mind (Titchner, 1909) the grief pain of the other, without interference by the projection of one's own anxieties into one's perceptions.

Since the communicative languages of grief in persons with intellectual disabilities are, as we will see, quite varied and not always self-evident, the construction of a narrative for one's own thinking about the person's loss experience may require patience. Focusing clinical attention on the *meaning* of the expressive grief language of the client is a clinical assessment practice which supports the client's humanity, dignity, autonomy and personal self-regulative identity. Our values are, in this sense, not in a separate compartment from our clinical framework for relating to and treating the client. How we clinically think about the client is implicitly an expression of values. The technique discussed in this chapter respects the subjective meaningfulness of the client's experience and selfhood. The approach has its roots in psychoanalytic psychotherapy and may be regarded as a type of psychoanalytic grief therapy grounded in empathy for the client's experience of grief.

To understand the client's grief one must pay careful empathic attention to what the person *expresses,* which, I will show, means interpreting the client's expressive grief language. Expressive languages include the use of speech, interpersonal expressiveness, actions and reenactments, behaviors and behavioral patterns, and fluctuations, such as increased compulsivity, aggression, somatization, isolation, or other behaviors that signify distress.

Our attention to the individual's experience and expressions of grief sees the person as a whole, into whose life loss has set off a disturbance. This *disturbance,* a subjective condition with a behavioral expression, is the object of clinical concern by which grief therapy takes its bearings.

Psychological Disturbance After a Loss Is Normal

In reaction to a loss, grief erupts from within a person. This is a disturbance which is normal. We especially note the normalcy of this reaction, because in our culture there is a strong current of opinion which cannot reckon with a psychological disturbance being normal. It can be difficult to integrate an awareness that a disturbance is normal. As one opens this up for reflection, it may require some rethinking of the line drawn in society and in clinical judgment between normal and not normal. In the general population throughout the modern world, societal tolerance of grief disturbance is painfully limited, a limitation which complicates the grief experience of many. The social non-recognition of grief (Doka, 1989, 2002; Walter, 1994) has been even more the case for persons with intellectual disabilities. Twenty-five years ago it was widely assumed that persons with intellectual disabilities did not experience grief. So, while social recognition and sanctioning of grief has been much too restrictive for the mental health of general population, the very existence of grief had not been recognized for persons with intellectual disabilities. In recent years the recognition of the grief of persons with intellectual disabilities has changed, and it is no longer widely assumed that persons with intellectual disabilities do not experience grief and mourn. However, while this is a significant advancement in understanding, there is a long way to go for this grief to be recognized in it's diverse and extended expressions, for disturbing grief behavior to be understood, and for there to be established standards of care for grief.

Grief support standards of care for support environments are in a very early stage of development, so that the psychotherapist treating grief needs to be aware that presenting grief may be complicated by its having not been recognized or supportively responded to, and the therapist may need to collaborate with the support environment in which the person lives about the person's grief support needs. This is not infrequently the case in situations where a referral for treatment is specifically for grief therapy as well as for situations where the referral is for behavioral problems which are assessed to be unrecognized expressions of grief.

We will look at grief disturbance as a type of anxiety. Grief is not often spoken about as a form of anxiety, but grief disturbance is an anxiety-reaction to a loss event. We do recognize this, however, when we understand grief to be a type of separation anxiety. We may also recognize anxiety in other ways in which grief occurs. In persons with intellectual disabilities there is, for example, a particular and noteworthy anxiety that is aroused, associated with a heightened tendency for compulsivity when experiencing distress; it is a reaction to *change*. This is a type of grief anxiety over the loss of the familiar, the routine, the predictable, etc. and the organization of one's sense of reality, or one's *assumptive world* (Kauffman, 2002) secured by familiarity, routine and predictability. While death is usually taken as the paradigm for understanding loss, change is a basic way that mortality is represented in the temporality of consciousness and is another basic modality of loss experience. Also, among persons with intellectual disabilities, the fragility of order maintained by familiarity is marked by the propensity for change to trigger significant anxiety reactions and drive heightened compulsivity. Compulsivity as a reaction to change is the action of repetition functioning to try to prevent the dangerous prospect or escalation of change. While compulsive repetition is a distress signal, its operation may have other dimensions and meanings. For example, a man who wanted to visit his family, but did not feel he had the power to directly ask for what he wanted, compulsively repeated that he was going to visit a relative. In this instance, the compulsive behavior was deployed as a communicative tool seeking to resolve the very anxiety it was expressing.

The expressive behavioral language of grief operates as a *distress signal*. Internal grief disturbances can be expressed by behaviors which create a disturbance in the social environment, most commonly increased aggression and increased compulsivity. The social environment disturbances of these behaviors makes it more difficult for some support environments to manage the grief supportively, and the narrative which accompanies a referral may disclose the frustrations of the support environment. Sometimes, the client is not only the grieving individual; for this person is grieving *in an environment*, and supporting the support environment may be part of the treatment of the individual. Even within a strict clinical frame for treatment, helping the support environment support the individual may be indicated.

The Need to Mourn

Mourning is the process of healing the grief wound inflicted by death and other losses. In the psychological literature the terms grief and mourning are used in diverse ways, and there are no agreed upon definitions.

In this chapter I use the term grief to mean the psychological wound of loss and mourning to mean the processing and healing of the wound. Whenever grief occurs a process of healing is needed. This process may be difficult and can be extended indefinitely. There is a widespread belief that mourning has a beginning, a middle, and an end, and this belief was expressed and advanced by "stage" and "task" theories of grief (Bowlby, 1980; Rando, 1993; Worden, 2009), which conceptualize mourning in this way. While there are many shortcomings of "stage" and "task" theories of mourning, key, I believe, to the design and appeal of these theories is their effort to contain the disturbances of grief by breaking it down into parts and organizing the series of stages around the idea of a final stage, an end to the disturbance. However, stage theory is not descriptively accurate of the ways in which many persons in the general population mourn. This is even more so among persons with intellectual disabilities. The final stage of grief is frequently not so "final." Grief and mourning may continue over the course of a person's life; this is not necessarily a type of pathological grief and mourning. The wound, and the processing/healing of the wound, may be open ended. Processing grief is part of an ongoing psychological dynamic of human identity and existence.

This is especially notable among persons with intellectual disabilities, where there are a number of distinct ways in which living with grief may be noticed. For one, old grief may be just beneath the surface. For example, in a grief support group for the death of a peer, group members went from discussing feelings about the death of this friend, to recollecting significant deaths that had occurred over the course of their lifetime. These memories emerge with grief that is right there, present just beneath the surface, full and meaningful, that then recedes right back into the background again. We can also see the presence of "old" grief in life in ongoing vulnerabilities that lead to periodic eruptions or old feelings flooding in when subsequent loss occurs. Also, grief may live in a person's very sense of identity as a sense of being tarnished, as self-negation, and as diminished sense of self; and these identity disordered conditions may become a part of the person's personality. The presence and influence of old grief and mourning may also be seen by following the traces of how loss experiences become more or less integrated into the self, as reckoning with or mourning a loss nurtures the sense of self. In this circumstance an amalgam of wound and healing forms within one's sense of self. The belief that mourning simply comes to an end may get in the way of recognizing the ways in which mourning becomes part of an ongoing life process. One reason that this perspective is so important for understanding the grief of persons with intellectual disabilities is that a lot of the suffering in the lives of persons with intellectual disabilities goes unrecognized for what it is. Understanding the ways that grief is integrated and is not integrated also helps one understand the person as a whole, for the subjective trajectory of loss experience is the core part of selfhood and a person's experience of him/herself and the world.

Grief After Non-Death Losses

Grief occurs in reaction not only to death, but to a broken relationship, to physical health problems, to changes in employment, residence, and, as already noted, to any change in a person's routine. Injuries experienced in interpersonal relationships are also a form of grief, and it is particularly evident among persons with intellectual disabilities that the grief wounds in non-death losses touch on the same vulnerabilities as death losses do. The same behavioral *distress signals* occur with death and non-death losses. So, while the psychotherapist needs knowledge of grief issues that are specific to death grief, we also need to understand grief language and mourning needs across the spectrum of loss experiences and to understand the range and pattern of loss experience in a given individual's life experience. With this awareness in hand the psychotherapist is in a position to begin to recognize and develop a clinical understanding of the functional meaning of behavioral disorder as an expressive language of grief.

LITERATURE REVIEW

It is recommended that the therapist treating grief issues be familiar with the broader grief and mourning literature and with the literature on psychotherapy for persons with intellectual disabilities who are mourning. Familiarity with the literature on agency and family support for persons with intellectual disabilities who are mourning in the context of a family or agency is also recommended.

With regard to broader grief literature, here is a list of recommended readings, selected to provide an introduction to contemporary grief and mourning theory. The basic distinction between normal and not normal mourning begins with Freud's "Mourning and Melancholia" (1917/1959). The distinction between normal and not normal mourning has become more problematic than ever, though it remains at the basis of much clinical thinking about mourning. In "Mourning and Melancholia," pathological mourning is when, in grief, the self turns against itself in a self-blaming self-preoccupation. This is often a key feature in the most persistent and disruptive grief behaviors.

Bowlby (1969, 1973, 1980) studied the attachment bond of mothers and infants and describes mourning as separation anxiety. This has been a predominant influence in understanding grief and mourning. In connection with this, I wish to point out that the developmental process which leads to autonomy can be complicated by dependency needs that exist independent of the developmental thrust towards autonomy and can stress the attachment bond, which is a presdispositional developmental event for later mourning dynamics. This dependency-based complication of attachment is often more strikingly the case among individuals with intellectual disabilities than with the general population.

Rando has made a substantial contribution to our understanding of grief and mourning. She integrates and synthesizes clinical and theoretical issues and formulates useful understandings of complicated grief and other topics. I recommend her book, *Complicated Mourning* (1993) as the most important and useful text for the clinician seeking to master grief and mourning theory.

Niemeyer's work (2001), from a narrative constructivist point of view, is the strongest theoretical influence operating today in the grief and mourning literature. His work focuses clinical attention on the individual process of (re-)constructing the self through narrative in the wake of a loss. Attig (1996), from a more spiritual than psychological stance, advances a very similar conceptual agenda. The outcome of mourning in these points of view is a new narrative identity.

Doka (1989, 2002) developed the theory of disenfranchised grief. Disenfranchised grief is grief which is not socially recognized nor permitted. This has been a useful concept in the grief and mourning literature as it conceptualizes a very powerful social force which operates in complicating the grief of individuals. This concept has particular pertinence to our understanding grief issues with persons with intellectual disabilities whose grief is often not recognized and is sometimes stigmatized as problem behavior.

Klass has articulated a grief concept that has had wide appeal. Social norms that advance an ardent social wish to keep death and grief out of social space, putting losses behind and moving on, has been most notably confronted by Klass's theory of continuing bonds, which says that some persons maintain a healthy and meaningful continuing emotional bond with a loved one who has died. The grief and mourning literature responded to this with an affirmation that the theory had recognized and sanctioned what was often experienced but had not been validated in this way. The meaningfulness of continuing bonds throughout the inner life of persons with intellectual disabilities is more notable and widespread than in the general population, and awareness of continuing inner relationships with persons who have died or are otherwise no longer in a person's life can be clinically very useful. The book usually recommended for continuing bonds theory is *Continuing Bonds* (Klass, Silverman, & Nickman, 1996). However I recommend another book in which Klass discusses the theory, *The Spiritual Lives of Bereaved Parents* (1999), both for the way it states the theory and the spiritual-psychological meaning context in which he discusses the bond.

Traumatic aspects of grief are becoming more important in the grief and mourning literature. Among a handful of books on traumatic grief, I recommend my *Loss of the Assumptive World* (Kauffman, 2002). The concept of traumatic grief is another concept from the grief and mourning literature which is particularly pertinent to the grief and mourning of persons with intellectual disabilities.

With regard to the psychotherapeutic treatment of grief for persons with intellectual disability, I recommend my *Guidebook for Helping Persons with Mental Retardation Mourn* (Kauffman, 2005). This book is written for all persons who provide grief support, including agencies, families, advocates, and mental health professionals and includes clinical discussions of psychological concerns and complications. It also contains discussions of a variety of grief support issues for agencies and families, which can be useful by the therapist working collaboratively with an agency or a family dealing with a person who is mourning.

I have appended to this chapter a selection of articles on diverse death and dying issues of persons with intellectual disabilities.

THEORETICAL FOUNDATION

Grief Language Theory

The starting place for treatment is in developing an understanding of what the "distress signal" behavior which precipitates treatment is saying. This is taken as the client's presenting complaint, and treatment begins with efforts to understand what the *meaning* of this complaint is. The starting place and a key ongoing concern for the grief therapist is the search for the meaning of distressing and other grief related behavior. The therapist can only know what the problem is that needs clinical attention by paying careful attention to the behavioral language in which grief is expressed.

Paying attention to grief distress signals is not just a part of the method for formulating the case. It is a way of communicating. It communicates interest in and concern about the person and their grief and in so doing helps define the therapeutic relationship. It contributes to the person's experience of him/herself in the therapeutic relationship. How the connection is made in this relationship contributes to how people experience themselves and their grief, and in some instances the clinical position of being attentive to the grief language and to the person is a key part of the therapeutic process.

The expressive languages of grief appear to demonstrate a need to express and communicate one's grief, to place it in the world where the person acts and relates and experiences him/herself. There are instances where distress from an old loss breaks through at some time way down the road from the time when the loss event occurred. This suggests that grief may, for unspecified periods of time, be underlying, but not pressuring for expression. In such situations, the disconnects with the support environment and within the person may make the therapeutic act of engaging the expressive language and responding to it particularly meaningful.

Attentiveness to and concern about a person's grief language can help a sense of connection, as the person may be disconnected from him or herself and from his or her environment in the inward eruption of grief and in the disruptions due to the behaviors that express grief. It is helpful to make the link explicit and to build an intervention strategy based upon the perceived *meaning* of the loss experience. Sometimes, when distress behavior is experienced as being understood, an underlying sense of self- blame for bad behavior, failure, alienation, and loss is relieved.

Sometimes the meaning of what is behaviorally communicated is clear, sometimes it is opaque, and sometimes it, or we, are dense, and no meaning is disclosed. When an expressive language meaning appears to be self-evident, there is sometimes more than meets the eye. The explanatory value of meanings may change as a situation becomes more clear. The loss meanings in a person's grief may shift over the course of treatment. The story we tell ourselves about what a behavior says is a hypothesis. No hypothesis about what is expressed in behavioral grief language ought to have a standing any greater than its capacity to give perspective on, understanding of, and attunement to the pain it expresses.

The Narcissistic Wound of Grief

In a broken attachment, from death or otherwise, separation anxiety involves anxiety about the loss of the attachment object *and* anxiety about the loss of self. This occurs, for example, in experiencing loss as abandonment and accusation, as a rejection and devaluation of self, as signifying the person to be bad, wrong, helpless or unable, or as frustrating a person's sense of autonomy and safety (Kauffman, 2010).

Loss of self anxiety aroused in reaction to object loss can, once it occurs, become a persistent vulnerability, re-experienced over and over again. This anxiety, once it have been deeply felt, can become a part of oneself, a narcissistic anxiety disorder as background in everyday life. A moderate degree of this woundedness can be tolerable, but intense grief reactions, expressed by intensely aggressive, compulsive or withdrawing behaviors are frequently expressing an injury to the sense of self.

This injury can occur in reaction to a broken relationship or other loss event, or it can occur over the course of development, so that a person experiences him/herself as not good enough, not able enough, not safe enough, not entitled or empowered enough and responds to the experience of a loss over the course of life with that predisposition. Injuries to the sense of self that occur while a person is growing up and developing a sense of identity are prone to be an acutely present force in reaction to losses throughout life.

Damage to self-concept, self-worth, self-confidence, sense of competence, sense of belonging, and self-cohesion are types of narcissistic injury and involve a loss of self anxiety. A weakened sense of self can complicate a loss experience, and grief may occur as a loss of self anxiety, which interferes with the mourning/healing process. Loss and change can also trigger loss of self or narcissistic anxiety.

Experiences that violate the self, such as abuse, neglect, violence, or any other changes that overwhelms the ego's adaptive ability, including experiencing loss as abandonment, set off a traumatic stress anxiety reaction. There appears to be a particular vulnerability among persons with intellectual disability for narcissistic injuries in grief to have these features.

Death and Other Losses

Death loss, because it appears to define what loss means in human experience, is sometimes taken as the paradigmatic case for a variety of types. This has to do with death being the ultimate loss and with some metapsychological assumptions related to the fear and shame of death, the inevitability of death, and the mystery of death. Grief experiences that occur in reaction to death are, however, not specific to death, but to loss in a broader sense. Broken attachments may trigger grief regardless of whether the loss is a death or the relationship is otherwise broken. Likewise, the death of a family member may trigger, for example, anxiety about life changes which are a consequence of the death, and the grief reaction will then be anxiety about change more than about the broken attachment. Broken attachment anxiety and change anxiety are, obviously, not specific to death, and the processing of and adaptation to the loss does not differ whether or not the loss is a death.

As noted above, change of residence or job, staff turnover, disconnects, or experienced abandonment by family or other attachment objects can trigger a grief reaction. Less eventful losses can also be just as wounding. Narcissistic wounds experienced in relationships with others or in some other way may be more difficult to identify and can be powerful. Intense reactions to perceived slights and other narcissistic wounds are often indicators of persistent loss anxiety.

The seeming magnitude of a loss event is not necessarily a reliable indicator of the magnitude of the grief reaction. Grief is better understood by starting with and focusing on the experience, rather than on the event. The clinical task is focused primarily on the experience of the loss. Our concern when approaching distress signal behavior is to evaluate if the distress signal is a expressing grief, and, if so, what the loss is or what the losses are and what the meaning or meanings of the loss are.

DESCRIPTION OF THERAPY TECHNIQUE

Loss Assessment

The loss assessment process is at the heart of this approach. The object of the assessment process, the experience of loss, which we simply call grief, is a multi-layered phenomena. While an understanding of grief may be formulated in terms of a predominant meaning of the loss, and this is often quite helpful, the experience of loss is not infrequently complicated by an interconnection of diverse meanings.

The meaning of the client's grief experience is examined by assessing two sets of information: the client's history and the meanings that are behaviorally expressed. Assessing a person's loss history, as it bears on the present, involves identifying what counts as a loss event and then reviewing accounts of the loss event. This includes examining the immediate behavioral expressions of the loss experience at the time of the loss event, over time, and in the present and examining the response of the support environment at the time of the loss, over time, and in the present. With regard to assessing the *meaning* of a loss experience, the process is more complex, as it centers on reading the signs of behavior rather than gathering the facts about what has happened which may be affecting the person's experience. The process of seeking the meaning of a loss is central to this approach and is discussed throughout this chapter. In this section we will look at historical information gathering and synthesizing. By 'synthesizing,' I mean seeing how what has happened over time in the person's experience is contributing to the meaning of the loss in the person's present experience. The task is to gather information that will shed light on the meaning of the present loss experience. A loss history may also tell the therapist about the experiential context in which the current loss occurs.

Take note that assessing a death loss requires some knowledge about death and dying in order to assess the facts involved in the event of a death. For example, it requires an awareness of the possible significance of attending the funeral or not and of being given an opportunity to feel oneself to be a connected and valued part of the grieving family or not. In order to consider these issues and weigh their significance, familiarity with the basic circumstances that effect grief from a death loss is useful.

One of the most significant areas for assessment in a death loss or any broken relationship is in the relationship itself, particularly injuries which have been experienced in the relationship with the deceased. The meaning of the loss, that is to say of the grief experience, is, as already noted, often entirely about the relationship, and the complications of grief are recapitulations of the injuries in the relationship. This is a basic feature of grief for all persons, though it is more distinctly so among persons with intellectual disabilities. Likewise, the grief experienced in the loss of a place, such as a place of work or of residence, expresses the nature of the attachment to the place. Negativity in a relationship, conflicts, frustrations, hurt, and anger may, in the loss of the other, be what needs to be mourned, reconciled, and adjusted to.

The assessment process composes a picture of what the griever is experiencing, the psychological story or meaning of their pain, *and* engages the griever, so far as possible, in the process of calling attention to and symbolizing the loss in words and actions. In the course of doing this the therapist engages the client with his or her concern about the distress which the client behaviorally expresses.

Symbolization

Persons with intellectual disabilities do not lack a capacity for creating or for recognizing symbolic representation. This is not the place to explore the symbolic thinking abilities and disabilities of persons with intellectual disability, but suffice it to note that persons with intellectual disabilities are fully capable of symbolic thinking involved in mourning, whether in ritual performances and artistic representations or in intrapsychic and spiritual symbolic representations integral to the mourning process. Symbolic thinking, involved in the organization of selfhood, a basic language of human identity and interaction, also appears to be a capacity through which mourning becomes possible. Persons with intellectual disabilities do transform the disturbing subjectivity aroused by death, loss, and trauma into the reality of symbolic representations.

The process of mourning draws together anxieties which are at the core of grief – such as annihilation, helplessness, and abandonment anxiety— into a symbolic reality in which the loss is integrated, even while aspects of grief continue to exist outside the symbolic reality constructed through mourning. Integration and non-integrated fragments are not mutually exclusive. Even as integrative symbolic representations are achieved, disturbances due to the loss are usually not thoroughly dissolved and may persist or may re-emerge in stressful times, particularly around subsequent loss.

Four Principles for Supporting Acute Grief from a Death Loss

With regard to the *supportive* aspect of the therapeutic process for a person who is mourning, I would like to point out four areas to keep in mind: the need for information, the need for connection to and involvement in the social context of the death, the need for cognitive and affective self expression, and the need for relationship security.

The first task in supporting a person who has experienced a recent death loss is to provide or help others to provide the facts about the loss. Giving information and helping the person process information can help reduce anxiety associated with not knowing the facts. Keeping a person in the dark, particularly about information related to a death, feeds anxiety and invalidates the person. A meaningful narrative that answers the person's questions about the loss and helps with coping supports a person's making sense out of the loss and is empowering. Factual information can have emotional meaning which the person needs to process. Not being told information or not being told information in a timely way excludes, and feeling excluded is a narcissistic wound or a wound to self-worth which complicates the mourning process and can be damaging.

Secondly, so far as possible, the therapist should support the person's having maximum involvement in the social environment surrounding the death. Full inclusion in family activities and connections in anticipating a death and in ritual and informal family activity after a death can be powerfully nurturing and can facilitate mourning. The therapist may be in a position to help families and agencies understand the importance and value of this and to allay any concerns that prevent this.

A third situation is that the death of an attachment object can damage a person's sense of security, increasing the need for interpersonal connection. This may especially be the case in situations in which behaviors are distancing or isolating. The therapeutic relationship with the grieving client may be of some benefit in this, but the primary relationships in the person's life are the site of the primary need for secure connection. The therapist may not only be able to forge a secure bond but also may be able to help family or residential supports to understand the person's needs, such as for enhanced connectedness. This may be especially indicated where the person's behaviors are difficult for the family or agency to handle. Day to day interpersonal situations where the person's expressions of grief are lived are a most appropriate context for clinical interventions aimed at helping the support environment respond to the person's grief needs.

And, fourth, the therapist aims to maximize the person's opportunities for self-expression. This, again, is not just by providing a safe place to express oneself in the therapeutic situation but by collaboration with the primary support environments to help staff, family, or others to understand the behavioral grief language expressed and the other grief support issues. The collaboration process with the support environment goes both ways. The therapist helps primary support environments to understand and respond helpfully to grief needs and behaviors, and the primary support environment provides the therapist with pertinent information and understanding at the outset of treatment and along the way.

A part of this collaboration may also involve supporting the support environment. In conjunction with this, the therapist may need to assess how the support environment is affected by the loss or by the person's expressive grief behavior and intervene supportively, on behalf of the client, with the support environment. The therapist establishes a collaborative relationship with the support environment and approaches the relationship with the support environment, so far as it is appropriate, with an expectation of mutual learning. In some situations it works best if the collaboration with support environment includes the development of a treatment plan.

Action Interventions

Psychotherapy for persons with intellectual disabilities who are mourning may include interventions which involve arranging for various types of grief and mourning-related activities. In some situations it may be indicated for the therapist to arrange for rituals or other grief related activity (for discussion of grief support activities for agencies see Lutcherhand and Murphy, 1998) or to arrange for visits to people or places, such as a cemetery or a place associated with meaningful memories and attachment associations. In most situations the client will be involved in the planning of the event, to the fullest degree possible, and will have an active part in the activity, such as carrying out ritual acts or speaking at a memorial. Actions set up as responses to the person's grief aim to facilitate mourning and can be an important part of treatment.

Key Role of Acceptance, Affirmation, and Validation of Grief

It has occurred to me that simple acts and basic clinical stances that serve to affirm and validate the person and the person's grief are particularly helpful and beneficial in facilitating mourning. However we may theorize the therapeutic meaning of this empathic, attentive approach, the positive self-regard it nurtures can sometimes have a significant benefit in helping to alleviate disturbing grief symptoms. It can also provide a context of safety and acceptance which increases the efficacy of other clinical interventions. Also, the pain of grief can be invalidating, and the painful meaning of being invalidated can be a significant part, and the most difficult or complicating part, of grief and mourning. The injury of invalidation of the grieving self is called a secondary wound of the loss, but it can be a primary aspect of the grief pain and a critical concern in the mourning/healing process.

APPLICATION OF THE TECHNIQUE

Basic Forms of Distress Language

The most frequently occurring expressions of grief distress are increased compulsivity and aggression. We also see, though not as often as compulsivity and aggression, isolation or withdrawal and somatization occurring. Each of these are reactions to the self's being overwhelmed by loss anxiety. When grief, beyond an initial period of time after the loss, is overwhelming, it is, among persons without an intellectual disability, generally regarded as complicated (Rando, 1993) or traumatic grief (Jacobs, 1999; Kauffman, 2002).

Aspects of a narrative meaning of compulsive and aggressive gestures are sometimes discernable in the particulars of the compulsive and aggressive gestures. As we come to understand a given gesture more fully, we may see the fuller story of which the gesture is a part. This may involve more guess work than one would prefer, as the therapist works to have as best an idea as he or she can of the grieving individual's experience. For example, after the death of his mother a young man began hitting women in his workshop. This increased aggression was selectively directed at women. Why? Does this selectivity say he is angry with his mother? If so, what is he angry with her about? Perhaps he is not angry with his mother, or even with himself, but he may be angry that she is absent, or frightened of her not being there or of death. It may be that the sight of women reminds him of his mother, and he is overwhelmed by a non-specific loss anxiety. In the ongoing assessment process in which a narrative account of the meaning of the loss is developed, the therapist stays open to possibilities of further clarification in the meaning of the person's experience. In so far as the meaning of the gesture is not sufficiently clear that there is reason to accept one possible interpretation over another, the therapist makes interventions based on trial assumptions.

I cannot repeat too often that turning against oneself, such as in guilt and shame, can be a powerful force in grief. The self is prone to turn against itself in the face of a painful loss and to blame itself for the loss, even as the person may strike out in anger at others. Conflicts in a relationship with strong dependency issues in play are especially likely to become prominent in grieving the death of the dependency object. This may involve significant guilt or shame, which can become exacerbated and be central to a person's experience of grief.

Managing the Therapist's Defenses Against Awareness of Mortality

The clinical wisdom of the psychoanalytic understanding of countertransference is that it recognizes the significance of the therapist's reactions in treatment. In the thanatological literature there is a widespread recognition of the critical value of being aware of one's own mortality as the foundation for understanding death and dying. These conceptualizations of self-knowledge are of basic value clinically. We, as therapists, do not come to know ourselves in a definitive and complete way. That is not the goal. The goal is to be aware to one's own reactions while being present with the grief of the client, and to take these multiple points of awareness into account in processing clinical material. We cultivate within ourselves an intention, a willingness and an openness to be aware of our emotions and cognitions and even elusive threads that appear in consciousness in the context of being with and experiencing the grieving client. Given this practice principle as a general guideline for the therapist, how does it apply specifically to treating persons with intellectual disabilities who are mourning?

If the therapist has overly protective tendencies, these will get in the way of supporting the person's experience of grief. Being overprotective supports denial, communicates that the person lacks the ability to be able to experience and go through the pain, and expresses the denial of issues in the therapist related to the overprotection. The therapist may experience pity or other distancing emotions which are hard to accept in oneself, but recognition of such tendencies is beneficial and can deepen and sharpen awareness and acceptance of the mourner and his/her grief. Such feelings are hard to recognize in oneself because one may disapprove of such feelings. The feelings and thoughts that one may disapprove of are likely to represent a blind spot and are most beneficial to consider. This process of clinical self-awareness is just as pertinent and valuable in the treatment of persons with an intellectual disability as it is in treating persons without an intellectual disability. Let's look a little closer at pity. Pity may function as a defense against unrecognized and despised vulnerability in oneself, vulnerability in just the sense in which the other is perceived to be pitiable, as if one is threatened by the perception of the other and deploys pity to bolster feelings of superiority. Like being overprotective, pity communicates and imposes invalidation. The vulnerability perceived in intellectual disability and in grief can be threatening to the therapist who may respond with a variety of defenses.

The touchstone for countertransference issues in the treatment of a person who is grieving has to do with how the grief anxiety of the client affects the therapist. In treating a person who is deeply affected by death, one's own awareness of mortality and personal grief history is the screen through which perceptions pass. The therapist's practice of monitoring his or her clinical experience in response to the client's grief is a cornerstone of practice.

Difficulty in being able to identify with a person with intellectual disabilities can indicate that the therapist is defended against the meaning that the disability has for the therapist. Sometimes a clinical strategy or intervention can mask *and* express the therapist's wish to control the grieving client, in order to protect him or herself from anxiety-producing aspects of the therapist's experience of the client's intellectual disability.

A person with intellectual disabilities may awaken in the therapist a sense of his or her own humanity, both in ways that feel fulfilling to the therapist and in ways that are experienced as threatening to the therapist's own sense of identity. Much of the intense behavioral grief language of persons with intellectual disabilities expresses in a direct, demonstrative, and sometimes exaggerated, potentially evocative, way underlying grief trends that may exist in the therapist. Awareness of this not only permits the therapist to experience and support the client more empathically, but also may allow the clinician to experience an enriched personal sense of what it means to be a human being. Finding the space within oneself as a therapist to accommodate the powerful grief language of the person with intellectual disabilities allows the therapist to receive a gift from the client which nurtures both clinical acuity and life.

I believe that I should account for myself here for shifting the frame of reference from an account of the psychology of grief in persons with intellectual disabilities using a strictly psychological language and explain, briefly, what I mean by *gift exchange* in the therapeutic relationship. The gift I have just described as a gift received by the therapist occurs in a system of gift exchange, the interpersonal space where the therapist and the client meet. In being present for this meeting with a consciousness and symbolic language of gift exchange the shared human bond becomes the nucleus of the therapeutic process. The language of gift exchange conceptualizes the basic human contact which occurs within the strictly psychological frame of treatment.

Sign Exchange

Frequently, treatment does not involve a significant meeting and gift exchange, and interventions involve only sign exchange through words and actions. An exchange of signs is a clinical exchange in which the client exhibits grief distress and the therapist responds with language which addresses, accepts, gives meaning, validates, or in other senses responds to the grief distress language of the client. Responses may involve speaking with the client and active intervention in the individual's life. Active intervention includes recommending and, when indicated, helping to set up trips, rituals, and other activities that support and help facilitate the mourning process. Active interventions also include interventions with the social support environment in which the person lives. These intervention are designed to help the support environment respond supportively to the individual's grief needs and grief behaviors.

There are diverse types of active grief interventions specifically fitting for different situations. In *acute grief* after the death of an attachment object the therapist may need to support the individual's maximum involvement in the informational, interpersonal, and ritual activities which surround the death. The therapist may need to help the social environment provide support through these activities. The person will be included in the sharing of information and in experiences around the death. Also, the support environment may need help in understanding how to respond to expressive grief language.

Persons with intellectual disabilities, particularly with mild to moderate disability, usually understand the meaning of death as irreversible. Nonetheless, sometimes an individual needs help in processing the realization that a death is irreversible. Holding simultaneously the belief that death is reversible and that it is not is not unusual, and, if there is not a recurring painful disappointment of expectations that the deceased is returning, holding opposite beliefs is not, clinically speaking, maladaptive. Helping a person to process a strengthened grasp that the deceased is not returning may involve clarification of irreversibility, but it is primarily a process of reckoning with an irreversibility that has registered but has not been reckoned with.

CASE EXAMPLES

Nicholas

When Nicholas's father died, Nicholas responded by looking for him in all the familiar places where he might be. As he searched for him, running from place to place, again and again, and not finding him, he became increasingly anxious and frantic. By these actions, he demonstrated Bowlby's middle stages of grief, yearning/searching and disorganization/despair, but he did not emerge into Bowlby's final stage, reorganization (1980). Through this literal enactment of his thoughts, we can see him saying, "Where is my father?" We can read his emotional state by the movements of his body and the intensity of his affect. His search for his missing father says, "He has got to be somewhere," enacts his sense that his father is gone, and his refusal to accept that this can be so. His searching appears to function to try to prove to himself that his father is there *somewhere*. He must be. Failure to find him intensifies his effort. He throws himself completely into the search.

We can read the meaning of Nicholas's action with clarity and reasonable certainty. What is so dramatically displayed in Nicholas's acute grief reaction can be carried out in imagination and cognition in more subtle and extended ways over the course of the mourning process. Nicholas's burst of intense loss anxiety bears somewhere within itself the history of his attachment to his father, but the story which Nicholas's actions tell is transparent in what it signifies. This is not often the case. Grief can be expressed in ways in which the narrative form is more complex and in which the meaning is not as self-evident as it is in Nicolas's case.

Jamie

Here is an example of a more complex narrative form. One day just before Thanksgiving Jamie put on his coat, packed his bag, and stood by the door of the residential facility where he lived. He stayed there all day and at night slept with his coat and bag. Approached by his staff he only said, "No show." In an assessment for treatment, the following story was put together. His father had come to visit him every weekend until Thanksgiving week the previous year. No one from his family came to see Jamie or called him until Christmas, when his family came and told him of his father death. When this behavior emerged, staff immediately recognized that his performance expressed an expectation that his father was coming and took this to mean that Jamie did not understand that his father was dead. In discussing this with me, Jamie showed me, in a dramatic gesture, where heaven is located, indicating that this is where his father is. His showing me the place where his father is, and my being attentive, being involved, and bearing witness was the core of our therapeutic relationship, that is, a strong sense of connection between us developed in the course of our discussing this.

Maintaining a sense of place for the deceased can quell anxiety about the death of an attachment object and the less specific anxiety about the intrusion of death into the person's life experience. This understanding supported a sense of connection to his father. To further support his symbolic connection to his father and his family, a trip with his sister to the family grave was arranged, and the sister was invited to meet with us to discuss the cemetery visit and the whole situation.

Jamie's grief distress language, his grief performance announcing that he was experiencing distress, was responded to by his staff's referral and by the set of interventions involved in treatment. As a result his confidence in being able to communicate his needs to others was also strengthened. Jamie's stunningly expressive grief language, a persistent enacting of a single scene in which he is expressing distress and making a request (an order, if he could), is a demonstration of impressive adaptive resourcefulness and directness of expression for a man who did not have the discursive language to say what was on his mind.

Mark

Mark's ability to walk was deteriorating, and, as a consequence, he was becoming overwhelmed by shame about himself. His much slowed walking pace caused him to fail to get to the bathroom on time, and anxiety about this happening began to consume him. An accident at night led to his bedroom becoming the scene for an escalation of self-loathing that culminated in the symbolic language ritual expression of piling his clothes on his bedroom floor into a mound, in wildly manic excitement humiliating himself by urinating on his clothes, and then falling into unmitigated self-loathing. In this disturbing grief language, a trend that is common in grief, feelings of shame spiral out of control. The self-destructive obsessive pull of Mark's shame of being disabled is a powerful symbolic expression of the psychological wound of his trauma of experiencing himself to be disabled.

Doris

We see narcissistic woundedness occurring in diverse and significant ways in grief reactions. Injuries to the sense of self due to experiencing oneself as disabled, or due to the frustrations related to dependency needs or other emotional complications of development, are often background vulnerabilities in the lives of a person with intellectual disabilities. These vulnerabilities are prone to be exacerbated in experiencing grief, and are likely to be the difficulty most recalcitrant to the inherent healing trends of mourning and the interventions of psychotherapy.

Doris had fits of rage when a request was made of her or when someone else got attention. Being asked to do something was experienced by her to be demeaning and critical. This reflected a struggle with autonomy. When someone else got attention, Doris experienced abandonment and criticism that she is not good enough. These experiences with others at her residence were a repetition of the narcissistic anxiety she experienced in her relationship with her mother, exacerbated in her grief over her mother's death, and displaced in the social dynamics of her residence.

There was a pattern to Doris's behavior after her rage episodes. After feeling abandoned and shamed, she expressed rage and *then* sought reconciliation. This also fit a pattern that was reportedly there in her relation with her mother— injury, rage, and then the search for reconciliation. It is suggested by this pattern that Doris did not become entirely absorbed in her narcissistic woundedness but that she also felt guilt, which functioned as an urge to restore her bond with her mother. Her injury persisted and the cycle repeated.

In treatment we talked about these matters in many different ways. Doris was engaged in this process of exploring feelings about missing her mother, feeling hurt and being angry at her mother, feeling bad about getting angry, wanting to make up, and also feelings of anger about a housemate, etc. These discussions continued weekly for about a year. Over this course of time this pattern of behavior abated, though I do not know what specific aspects of our work were helpful. The hurt and angry feelings were still present but in a more contained and less disruptive way. In place of the volatile pattern of hurt, anger, and reconciliation seeking, Doris developed the habit of calmly saying critical things about her housemates. There was a shift in the configuration of depressive patterns, and she was in much less distress.

Chad

Sometimes treatment is not much more than interpreting grief language for the support environment. Chad had been compulsively telling everyone that he was going to visit his aunt. The staff at his residence felt this to mean that he did not understand that his aunt was dead.

Chad understood the fact of his aunt's death perfectly well but felt unable to make a request. He wished to feel connected to his family. His aunt's home had been a family gathering place with very pleasurable memories for Chad, and she was the last family member visiting him when she'd died several years earlier. He was trying to make this happen by magical wish commands: bring me to my family. Treatment consisted of assessing what his grief distress language was saying and then carrying out his request.

AFTERWORD

While grief due to a death is the circumstance that especially concerns us in this chapter, the experience of grief can occur after any loss and can have a profound impact on a person's life. Losses affect behavior, self-experience, and identity. The far-reaching consequences of grief wounds on a person's well being and quality of life make understanding grief and mourning and developing therapeutic strategies for individuals who are mourning an especially important psychotherapeutic concern. Even in cases in which distress behaviors are connected to medication or brain chemistry issues, grief distress aspects may yet be a secondary factor and be psychologically significant.

REFERENCES

Attig, T. (1996). *How we grieve*. New York: Oxford.

Bowlby, J. (1969). *Attachment and loss. Vol. I. Attachment*. New York: Basic Books.

Bowlby, J. (1973). *Attachment and loss. Vol. II. Separation, attachment and loss*. New York: Basic Books.

Bowlby, J. (1980). *Attachment and loss. Vol. III. Sadness and depression*. New York: Basic Books.

Doka, K. (Ed.). (1989). *Disenfranchised grief*. New York: Lexington Books/D.C. Heath.

Doka, K. (Ed.). (2002). *Disenfranchised grief: New directions, challenges and strategies for practice*. Champaign, IL: Research Press.

Freud, S. (1959). Mourning and melancholia. In *Collected Papers*, vol. IV (J. Rivere, Trans.) (pp. 152-170). New York: Basic Books. (Original work published 1917).

Jacobs, S. (1999). *Traumatic grief.* New York: Brunner-Routledge.

Kauffman, J. (2002). The psychology of disenfranchised grief. In K. Doka (Ed.) *Disenfranchised grief: New directions, challenges and strategies for practice.* Champaign, IL: Research Press.

Kauffman, J. (Ed.). (2002). *Loss of the assumptive world.* New York: Brunner-Routledge.

Kauffman, J. (2005). *Guidebook on helping persons with mental retardation mourn.* Amittyille, NY: Baywood Publishing Co.

Kauffman, J. (2010). The primacy of shame. In. J. Kauffman (Ed.), *The shame of death grief, and trauma.* New York: Routledge.

Klass, D., Silverman, P., & Nickman, S.L. (1996). *Continuing bonds.* Philadelphia: Taylor & Francis.

Klass, D. (1999). *The spiritual life of bereaved parents.* New York: Brunner-Routledge.

Luchterhand, & Murphy, N. (1998). *Helping adults with mental retardation grieve a death loss.* Philadelphia: Accelerated Development Press.

Markell, M. (2005) *Helping people with developmental disabilities mourn: Practical rituals for caregivers.* Fort Collins, CO: Companion Press.

Neimeyer, R. (2001). *Meaning reconstruction and the meaning of loss.* Washington, D.C.: American Psychological Association

Rando, T. (2000). On the experience of traumatic stress in anticipatory and post-death mourning. In T. Rando (Ed.), *Clinical dimensions of anticipatory mourning.* Champaign, IL: Research Press.

Rando, T. (1993). *Treatment of complicated mourning.* Champaign, IL: Research Press.

Titchner, E. B. 1909: *Lectures on the experimental psychology of thought-processes.* New York: Macmillan.

Walter, T. (1994). *The revival of death.* London: Routledge.

Worden, W, (2009). *Grief counseling and grief therapy.* New York: Springer.

ARTICLES DEALING WITH DIVERSE DEATH AND DYING ISSUES OF PERSONS WITH INTELLECTUAL DISABILITIES

Barbara, T.V., Pitch, R.J., & Howell, M.C. (1986) *Death and dying: A guide for staff serving adults with mental retardation.* Boston: Exceptional Parents Press.

Bogden, R. & Taylor S.J. (1989). Relationships with severely disabled people: The social construction of humanness. *Social Problems, 36 (2),* 135-148.

Deutsch, H. (1985). Grief counseling with the mentally retarded client. *Psychiatric Aspects of Mental Retardation Reviews. 4*(5), 17-20.

Emerson, P. (1977). Covert grief reactions in mentally retarded clients. *Mental Retardation, 15(6),* 46-47.

Gaventa, W. (1988). On death and dying: A guide for staff serving developmentally disabled adults. *Mental Retardation. 25,* 387-388.

Hollins, S. (1995). Managing grief better: People with developmental disabilities. *The Holistic Healthcare Newsletter, 14*(3), 1-3.

Howell, M. (1989). Grief counseling. In M.C. Howell , D.G. Gavin, G.A. Cabrera, & H.A. Beyer (Eds.), *Serving the underserved: Caring for people who are both mentally ill and mentally retarded* (pp. 327-379). Boston: Exceptional Parents Press.

Hoover, J.H., Markell, M.A., & Wagner, P. (2004/2005) Death and grief as experienced by adults with developmental disabilities: Initial exploration. *OMEGA: The Journal of Death and Dying, 50* (3), 181 – 196.

Huston, L. (1992, Fall). Helping people with developmental delays to grieve and mourn. *NAPMR Quarterly,* 6-11.

James, I.A. Helping people with mental retardation cope with bereavement. *Mental Handicap, 23(2),* 74-78.

Kennedy, J. (1989). Bereavement and the person with a mental handicap. *Nursing Standard,* 4(6), 36-38.

Kloeppel, D. & Hollins, S. (1989). Double handicap: Mental retardation and death in the family. *Death Studies, 13,* 31-38.

Lavin, Claire (1989). Disenfranchised grief and the developmentally disabled. In K. Doka (Ed.), *Disenfranchised grief: Recognizing hidden sorrow* (pp. 229-237). New York: Lexington Books.

Lutcherhand C. (1998). *Mental retardation and grief following a death loss.* The Arc of the United States. www.thearc.org.

McLoughlin, I.J. (1996). Bereavement in the mentally retarded. *British Journal of Medicine, 36,* 256-260.

McLaughlin, I.J. & Bhate, M.S. (1987). A case of affective psychosis following bereavement in a mentally handicapped woman. *British Journal of Psychiatry, 151,* 552-554.

Naragon, P.J. (1994). Death and bereavement: Issues for older adults with mental retardation. *University of Missouri-Kansas City Institute of Human Development: Fast Facts on Aging, 11,* 1-7.

Nelson, M., & Febeis, A. (1988). *Grief, death and dying.* [Brochure]. St. Paul, MN: Community Health Education Network of the Association of Retarded Citizens Minnesota.

Oswin, M. (1985). Bereavement. In M. Craft, J. Bicknell & S. Hollins (Eds.), *Mental handicap.* London: Bailliere Tindall.

Oswin, M. (1989). Bereavement and mentally handicapped people. In T. Philpot (Ed.), *Last things: Social work with the dying.*

Singh, I., Jawed, S.H., & Wilson, S. (1988). Mania following bereavement in a mentally handicapped man. *British Journal of Psychiatry, 152,* 866-867.

Yanok, J., & Beifus, J. A. (1993). Communicating about loss and mourning: Death education for individuals with mental retardation. *Mental Retardation, 31,* 144-147.

SECTION II

GROUP THERAPY

CHAPTER 9

Group Psychotherapy with Trauma Survivors Who Have Intellectual Disabilities

Nancy J. Razza, Ph.D.
Daniel J. Tomasulo, Ph.D., M.F.A.

INTRODUCTION

Following a literature review on survivor treatment for people with DD, this chapter will take the reader through an application of the interactive-behavioral model of group psychotherapy (IBT) in the treatment of trauma survivors. The unique needs of survivors of sexual abuse and other interpersonal trauma will be discussed at length, along with therapeutic techniques that maximize the individual's sense of safety and trust.

A group psychotherapy session with trauma survivors will be presented in detail to provide the clinician with an in-depth feel for the process and techniques that enhance treatment efficacy for this vulnerable population.

LITERATURE REVIEW

Group psychotherapy has a well established history in the treatment of survivors of sexual and other forms of interpersonal violence (Foy, Eriksson, & Trice, 2001; Herman, 1992; van der Kolk, McFarlane, & van der Hart, 1996; Young & Blake, 1999). We will look at group psychotherapy's merits in the treatment of abuse survivors with ID and describe the IBT model of group psychotherapy (Razza & Tomasulo, 2005) in detail, walking the reader through an actual session.

While controlled outcome research on the efficacy of group psychotherapy with persons who have ID (along with any additional psychiatric diagnosis, not necessarily trauma-related) is limited, some research offers support for use of the IBT model (see, for example: Blaine, 1993; Carlin, 1998; Daniels, 1998; Kirchner & Mueth, 2000; Lundrigan, 2007; and Oliver-Brannon, 2000).

Foy et al. (2001) reviewed studies on the efficacy of three different models of group psychotherapy for trauma survivors. The authors noted that, because group psychotherapy is so widely used for treating survivors of trauma and is regarded as offering unique therapeutic benefits to such persons, research into the relative merits of various models is the next logical step. The authors point out that group psycho-therapy is able to address the profound sense of detachment and estrangement from others commonly seen in survivors. We might add that, for people with ID, the sense of being different than, and not connected to, larger society is already heightened.

Foy et al. (2001) compared three group therapy models – supportive, psychody-namic, and cognitive-behavioral – used with survivors from the general population and looked at studies with adults, studies with children, and studies with adolescents. The authors concluded that there is no evidence for the superiority of one particular model of group psychotherapy over another and that each had sufficient merit to warrant use. This is important research for us to make note of. It supports a larger body of meta-analytic research being done which finds that, despite therapist's beliefs and preferences for certain models of therapy, broad scale meta-analytic research comparing the relative efficacies of established models consistently finds no appreciable superiority of any one model over the others (see, for example: Asay, Lambert, Gregersen, & Goates, 2002; Wampold, 2001). In fact, the evidence suggests that it is not the particular model, but what the *client* brings to the therapy, that is most important to the final outcome. What successful therapies – and therapists – have in common is their ability to tolerate the client's pathology while mobilizing the client's strengths (Duncan, Miller, & Sparks, 2004). As we begin our work with abuse survivors who have ID, let us remember to pay great attention to what each client brings. Using a model such as IBT creates the environment in which healthy change can take place. The healthy change will be the unique evolution of each individual along a path that we do not predict or direct, but can, and should, support.

Because of the complexity of material related to working with survivors who have ID, the reader will be further informed by also reviewing this book's chapter by Razza and Sobsey on abuse survivors. It outlines the procedure for clinical assessment, and provides information that is essential to the initiation of the therapy process for survivors with ID.

THEORETICAL FOUNDATION: KEY ELEMENTS OF THE GROUP PROCESS WITH ABUSE SURVIVORS

Establishing Safety and Confidentiality

As stressed in Chapter 6 which presented the foundation of treatment with abuse survivors, establishing the safety of the therapeutic relationship is essential to the treatment's success. This is every bit as important when the therapy takes place in a group format and is, perhaps, even more challenging to establish and to maintain. As we walk through the very first steps a facilitator takes in a newly formed therapy group, note that each of the members should have already had a least one individual intake session like the one detailed in Chapter 6, establishing for the patient some sense of what therapy is about and what she can expect regarding how she will be treated.

At the start of the first session, group facilitators must take responsibility for making clear to the members that there are two unfailing rules that govern the group's work: safety and confidentiality. Safety refers to the fact that the group must be a safe place for each member. Members must not subject each other to physical or verbal aggression. Examples should be given, such as not hitting or cursing at each other and should be geared to the members' level of comprehension. It is important to point out that no one is expected to be perfect. Aggressive acts with other people outside of the group will not cause a member to be cast out of the group. In fact, members are encouraged to come in and discuss such problems when they have them. However, aggression against a fellow member, even during non-group hours, could result in the aggressor having to leave the group. This can be a difficult concept initially for some members. Keep checking back with the members, asking them to restate their understanding of these ideas in their own words.

Begin demonstrating the interactive nature of the group right away, by teaching members to listen to each other with the same dedication with which they listen to the facilitators. For example, when checking back on members' understanding, you may find one member who understands and can state the safety rule quite clearly and another who is confused. Ask the member who is clear to look at the other member and explain it to her. Be sure each member is listening, then thank each for the effort. Once the confused member has gotten something helpful from the first member, affirm each for their respective roles.

Once a therapy group is well established, explaining safety and confidentiality to each new member becomes a much easier task. When a new member enters, the facilitators can ask if some of the members would be willing to explain the rules to the new member. In this way, members are empowered with a sense of ownership for the group's procedures and get a sense of self-esteem by taking on an advisory role like that of the facilitators. Also, the new member immediately learns the importance of attending to the other members, not just to the facilitators.

Finally, be sure that members don't confuse aggression with anger. Behaving aggressively is sometimes what we do when we feel angry. Let members know that feelings –all feelings – including anger, are acceptable. We just cannot curse at or harm each other. Let the members know that they will be encouraged to talk about their anger with each other and that this is something we will regularly do in this group. I sometimes say, for example, "I may feel mad at Tanya (my co-facilitator). What should I do?" Then I encourage members to share their thoughts. Eventually, we get to the idea that I can talk to her about it. I can tell her I am angry. The issue of discussing anger is often difficult for survivors and especially difficult when it is felt in relation to other group members. It is, however, inevitable that some anger will be felt between some of the members at some point. It is necessary to be proactive and set the stage both for the acceptance of feelings and for a specific procedure for coping with them up front. It will be revisited many times.

Regarding confidentiality, members must come to understand that they cannot talk about each other outside of the confines of the group setting. The trade-off is, of course, that each member need not fear being talked about "behind her back" (a phrase that is meaningful for many, even very impaired, persons.) For people at very concrete levels of understanding, the issue can usually be clarified for them by stating that the rule is that no one mentions another member's *name* outside of the group.

In exploring members' comprehension, it is important to ask questions such as, "If your mother (or your job coach, or your boss) asks you who else is in the group and what they talk about, what should you do?" Members often get the idea that they shouldn't "tell tales" to other peers, but hesitate about what to do when someone in authority asks. Many members who understood the rule and didn't "talk behind anyone's back" have shared confidential information when such questions were posed by people in authority. They felt they had to answer them. For some members, this may be their first experience with having to hold a boundary against the wishes of authority figures.

Another point to make clear to members is that each person always has the right to talk about herself, if she would like. Members should not take confidentiality to mean "keeping secrets." In fact, sexual abuse and incest often involve the keeping of secrets, usually under threat of serious harm. In no way should members conclude that they need to keep secrets in order to stay in the group. Rather, confidentiality is about boundaries. My business is mine to discuss, with whomever I choose and whenever I choose. Other people's business is not mine to discuss. This is the essence of confidentiality. Work with many dozens of people with mild and moderate levels of ID over more than twenty years suggests that the majority are able to learn this distinction.

In explaining the limits of confidentiality, it is important to clarify the facilitator's role in this regard, as well. Having to breach confidentiality when there is a risk of homicide or suicide, or abuse of a minor, needs to be explained. Also, that the facilitators cannot give out information to third parties without the member's permission is important for members to know. When a third party request information, our first course of action is to inform the member and suggest to the member that we speak to that person along with her. This is far more empowering to the member and allows us, as facilitators, to play a role during the meeting which supports the direct communication between the member and this third party who is a part of her life. In addition, it allows the member a chance to hear positive comments about her efforts being shared with a key individual. Importantly, it guards against feelings of anxiety or paranoia that the member might have if she knows conversations between her therapist and someone else important in her life are taking place without her.

Session One

There is a world of difference between the first session of a newly formed group, and the first session for a new member in an ongoing group. Beginning a new therapy group for survivors with ID may be the most difficult task a facilitator faces. All of the members are symptomatic, are fearful of others to at least some degree, know nothing about the process of group psychotherapy, and tend to have very limited interpersonal skills owing to their ID. In addition, all of them have yet to learn the safety and confidentiality rules we covered in the previous section.

Most of the first session will be devoted to introducing members to each other and to the discussion of safety and confidentiality. Depending on the level of impairment of the members, the first session may cover only these issues. Some groups, however, will get enough understanding of the rules to proceed with member-generated material. In any case, the learning of each other's names and the discussion of the rules are all grist for the mill. During these discussions, facilitators use every opportunity to begin shaping good interpersonal behavior. Every effort, such as eye contact with the member who is speaking or being able to repeat back what another member said, is verbally praised. As much as possible, avoid addressing a member who is demonstrating poor social skills, such as talking over someone else or staring at the floor. Find positive models to reinforce and do so regularly and pointedly. Members learn fairly quickly what works.

In an ongoing group, the entrance of a new member occasions the revisiting of the rules, which is usually taken on voluntarily by the other members. It is quite easy to shape good interpersonal behavior, such as looking at and listening to each of the members when there is only one new person at a time. The new person has many models for good interpersonal behavior and is generally motivated to fit in. Along these lines, it is our recommendation that once a therapy group is established, it be kept running. Individual members can end their treatment ("graduate") when ready (which also builds a sense of hope in newer members).

Ongoing groups have many merits over time-limited groups. Time-limited groups necessitate a time-consuming rules discussion and shaping of interpersonal behavior. Moreover, time-limited groups have no one who is more "veteran" than the others. Veterans not only establish the norms for the group, conditioning the occasional new member with ease; they have the opportunity to share their recovery with members who are not as far along in the journey. A more veteran member can see the suffering in a new member and say, "I know; I used to hurt myself, too." The new member gets the gift of hope; the veteran, the gift of self-esteem. The veteran member reinforces her own awareness of her improvement. Further, she gets to be in the role of a helper or a support to another person. Very rarely do people with ID find themselves in this role, and it is a role with powerful esteem-building potential. It is a key component in well-established recovery programs such as AA and is a therapeutic component completely unavailable in individual psychotherapy.

DESCRIPTION AND APPLICATION OF TECHNIQUES USED IN IBT: A SINGLE SESSION WITH MULTIPLE CASE EXAMPLES

Let's examine the techniques used in IBT group psychotherapy with survivors who have ID. Each session is comprised of four stages: *Orientation; Warm-Up and Sharing; Enactment; and Affirmation.*

In the session we will examine a group, comprised of seven women with mild and moderate ID, with five of the women being veteran members. They each have some reduction in symptoms and some improvement in functioning. The sixth member, Kayla, still feels very new to the group although she has been coming fairly regularly for two months. She frequently arrives late, often midway through the hour, due to transportation problems beyond her control. The seventh member, Nicole, has come to the group for the first time.

During the first stage of the session, the *Orientation* stage, the members are asked to introduce themselves to Nicole. Each member looks at Nicole and tells her their name. Nicole does the same. One member spontaneously begins to explain what confidentiality is. The facilitator thanks her for taking this responsibility, then checks with Nicole, saying, "So Nicole, what do you hear Janine saying?" Whenever we check for a member's understanding, it is not enough to say, "Do you understand?" Rather, the member must be asked to repeat back, in her own words, her understanding of what was said. Then she must check with the speaker to see if her understanding is correct. If it's not, the speaker can repeat her statement, or another member who understood it can repeat it for the benefit of the member trying to understand it. In this session, the group goes through this process with Nicole, who, with one or two tries, is able to show that she has understood the group rules.

During the second stage of the session, the *Warm-up and Sharing*, group members take turns stating what they each would like to work on in the session that day. In practice, we refer to this as the "check-in." Usually one of the facilitators asks, "Who'd like to start the check-ins?" A member may volunteer herself or ask another member if she would like to start. Sometimes, two members both state that they would like to start. In this case, the facilitator asks them to speak with each other and come to a decision about who will go first. In most cases, one member easily gives the floor to the other member. The one who gave the opportunity to the other is roundly affirmed for her prosocial behavior. The facilitator usually stops the action momentarily, to highlight this good interpersonal behavior, asking if anyone else noticed what the member had done. Any member who saw and can describe the prosocial behavior is affirmed as well. Remember, every interaction is an opportunity for interpersonal learning and skill development, and every apparent problem is just more grist for the mill.

If the two members cannot agree, the facilitator can suggest asking the group for help. The facilitator can then slow down the debate by asking the other members, "Who understands what is going on right now?" Once some of the members can explain that two members are disagreeing about who should start first, the facilitator can bring the issue of starting back to the group, saying something such as, "How can we help Janine and Martha and get the check-ins started?" Although a belabored process, a great deal of interpersonal growth takes place. And this growth is exactly what abuse survivors, especially those with intellectual impairments, need. Only in new groups does this process tend to take so long, however. Because members receive so much consistent reinforcement for prosocial behavior, and because members, in time, learn that they will have plenty of opportunity to work on their issues, one member readily defers to another in ongoing groups.

Note that it is very, very important for facilitators to resist the urge to take over and direct or organize the process. However long the exchange may be, members are struggling to learn interpersonal skills they have not yet mastered. If we, as facilitators, usurp control because of our own intolerance of the process, we deprive members of much-needed learning experiences.

In this session, as the check-ins proceed, Mary, a young woman with severe PTSD symptoms, talks about starting a new part-time job. After someone questions her about her symptoms, she admits that she has been having nightmares about her rape. The fourth anniversary of her rape is coming up, and Mary has been hospitalized in the past around the anniversary date. Another member, Dawn, talks about a fight she had with her son, but also reports that her husband's brother, who has been staying with them temporarily, is "disrespecting" her.

The more experienced members proceed in this fashion. One of the facilitators responds to each member, clarifying what each wants to work on for that day. For example, with Mary, the facilitator is aware that she has become somewhat more stable and has increased her work tolerance. Because of her efforts and her requests for job coaching at her workshop, she is now getting an opportunity to start a part time job in the community. Mary is happy yet anxious about this. The facilitator also realizes that she still has some PTSD symptoms, yet notes Mary's desire to focus on the new job. The facilitator's job is twofold: first, she must let Mary know she has been heard, and, second, she must clarify her topic for the day. The facilitator says, "So, Mary, it sounds like you still have some problems with nightmares and feelings about the rape but that you are also focused on your new job. It sounds like, for today, you'd like to talk about your happiness about getting the job and also some worries you have about it. Is that right?" Once Mary's check-in is supported and clarified in this manner, the facilitator says, "Great check-in, Mary. Who would you like to hear from next?" In this way, members are helped to think about each other, about who has already checked in, and about who still needs an opportunity. Mary, not the facilitator, chooses the next person.

Note that in newer groups, or groups with more impaired members, facilitators typically have to provide more structure to help the members set agenda items. This is done by further questioning designed to help the member define an item for discussion. Also, if a facilitator notices that a member fails to bring up something salient, this is questioned. An example might be with a member who was highly distressed the week before over having been reprimanded at work but this week makes no mention of work. The facilitator would ask about how things went at work this week. If the member says things were ok and there were no problems, the facilitator needs to ask why this is. If things have gotten better, it is important that the member know why. For the member to figure out why things improved, and discover her role in the improvement, could be set as an agenda item.

The Heart of the Session: The Enactment

After each member has checked in (including, in this case, the new member, who is given a bit of extra time to tell the group a little about herself, as well as to set her check-in topic) the group decides on which member will begin working. In a more veteran group with mildly to moderately impaired members, members will often suggest a member whom they notice is particularly distressed or will volunteer themselves when they feel the need. In new groups, or groups with more impaired members, facilitators often need to structure this process more heavily with questions.

Facilitators should take note of the amount of connection members feel toward each other. Well functioning groups are cohesive; members are drawn to help other members in distress; similarly, members feel safe enough to ask for help when they need it. In any case, we need to focus our awareness on the process of the group: who shows interest in whom; who tends to take a leadership role, such as suggesting a member to go first or helping the session to get started; who tends to be the last person chosen to check in. Although a few members may get to discuss their issues in further depth after the check in, usually one member's issue ends up being the center of the enactment. The term *Enactment* is the name given to the third stage of the session in which a member's issue is explored in depth and moved into action through the use of psychodramatic techniques. Facilitators need to make sure that the member whose issue is chosen for this development has the interest and support of a majority of the other members. No matter how important a member's check in issue may seem to the facilitators, if that member is not well supported by the group, her work will fall flat. Neither she nor the group will benefit.

In the session we have started to look at, Mary and Janine start to talk at the same time. Mary suggests that Dawn be the one to begin working on her issue. Janine had started to nominate herself but quickly gave way and said she would be ok with Dawn starting. With coaching from the facilitator, Mary asks Dawn if she would like to begin. She says yes and then asks the rest of the members if this is all right. The members agree.

Dawn spends some time describing the "fight" with her son. The son she is referring to is her younger son, who is highly verbal and nondisabled. He is 13 years old and is the product of Dawn's having been raped by her cousin. Dawn's older son, who is the child of Dawn and her husband, has mild ID, like Dawn and her husband. Dawn and her husband, to their great credit, have taken on the raising of the younger son entirely as their own.

From Dawn's presentation, it is clear that although the "fight" with her son was distressing for her, she handled the interaction well. Dawn has made great strides in her ability to set healthy limits with her sons. In the past she would often back down and leave the scene in an effort to avoid "blowing up" (yelling and sometimes becoming physical). Dawn is affirmed for her efforts with her son and is encouraged to talk about the problem with her husband's brother. Dawn describes a few scenes in which she is mocked by her brother-in-law. In addition to this verbal abuse, the man defies her requests for him to clean up after himself. As she goes on, we check with other members to see if they are following the story and if they understand Dawn's feelings about it. Dawn has a good deal of detail to share. The facilitator's job, however, is to ensure the cohesiveness of the group; after all, this is what makes it a safe and therapeutic place to work. So as soon as Dawn describes the first scene with her brother-in-law, the facilitator gently breaks into her narrative, saying, "Dawn, who in here do you think gets how you felt when he did that?" Note whom Dawn chooses; this is information about whom she feels connected to. Note also if she is able to pick a member who truly does understand her feelings.

Dawn chooses Janine, who says, "She was pissed!" to which Dawn agrees. Another member, Corinne, spontaneously adds, "Hurt," and Dawn agrees with this also.

As we continue this process with Dawn and the group members, the facilitator probes Dawn about the role of her husband. As suspected, Dawn's husband has not protected her from his brother's insults. Rather, he enjoys "being cool" with his brother; he laughs off and minimizes his wife's distress. To her credit, Dawn has already spoken up assertively to the brother-in-law on more than one occasion, but it is clear that he is empowered by the husband. This is where the action is. Dawn is clearly very angry and hurt by her husband's behavior and is feeling at a loss as to how to engage his help.

The facilitator asks Dawn if it would be ok if the group did some doubling for her. Dawn agrees and moves her chair slightly into the middle of the group. The facilitator begins the doubling. She gets up and stands behind Dawn's chair. This is the position of the double and lets the person know you are endeavoring to see the problem as she sees it. Speaking in the first person as though she were Dawn, the facilitator says, "I'm so hurt. It isn't fair. I get disrespected [Dawn's word] by my husband's brother, and my husband won't even help me." The facilitator checks with Dawn to see if this is correct. The facilitator says to Dawn, "Is this right? If it's not, let me know so I can fix it." It is always necessary to see if the protagonist (Dawn, in this case) truly feels represented by the words of the double. Continual checking with the protagonist is a must. For someone with ID, who may be timid about telling an "authority figure" that she is wrong, we stress the helpfulness of their correcting us; she is giving us a chance to get it right.

Next, the facilitator asks Dawn if she would like to have another member come up and double for her. Dawn chooses Mary. Mary stands directly behind Dawn's chair, and the facilitator remains standing as well, at Mary's side. Mary is coached briefly by the facilitator to think about what Dawn might be feeling. "Really bad," Mary says. Dawn nods her assent. Mary continues, "You always stick up for your brother, not me." (Mary is expressing Dawn's feelings toward her husband.)

To involve all of the members and to increase the amount of support available for Dawn, each of the member's takes a turn at doubling. It is not necessary to have each of the members double, but it can help with cohesiveness and support for the protagonist. In this session, in which there is a brand new member, it is a good opportunity for her to learn how the process works. Also, Dawn and the other members will get to experience the new member as someone who can tune into them, which will aid her integration into the membership.

Doubling is the safest psychodramatic technique to use. In new groups, or, especially, for facilitators who are new to group work with this population, doubling is all that needs to be done until everyone is further along in treatment. In this group, with veteran members and a veteran protagonist, we were able to move the enactment to a deeper stage. We asked Dawn if we could put an empty chair across from her to represent her husband. Then we asked if she could verbalize some of her feelings to him, with our support. The facilitator asked Dawn if she would like a member behind her while she did this, and she again chose Mary. Mary stood behind her, and the facilitator stood at Mary's side. The facilitator asked Dawn to begin telling her husband how she felt, noting that she could ask for help from Mary, or any of us, if she wanted.

Dawn looked at the empty chair and said, "Your brother disrespected me. He called me a 'bitch' and he drank beers and left bottles and stuff all over the kitchen. He's *your* brother; you should tell him to get out."

Dawn did not ask for any help from Mary. She continued in this fashion for a few more minutes. Once she stopped, the facilitator asked her the usual question we employ to help bring enactments to some sense of closure. The facilitator said, "Dawn, say the last thing that you would like to say to your husband for now." Dawn faced the chair, and sat thinking for a minute. "I'm going to get really mad if you don't do something. If you don't get him out, we're going to have a meeting with Sara and everybody" (social workers involved with their case). The facilitator repeated Dawn's words exactly as she said them. Then she said to Dawn, "Is it ok to leave it here for now?" Dawn said yes, and everyone returned to their original seats in the circle.

Following the *Enactment* stage is the *Affirmation* stage. In this, the final stage of the session, each member is given feedback about the strengths and growth she exhibited that day. We start with affirming the protagonist. Because the protagonist has put herself on the line and exposed vulnerable material, it is essential that she be given feedback that is supportive. Facilitators give the other members opportunities, too, to affirm the protagonist. They are encouraged via questions that will elicit positive responding. For example, we might ask, "Corinne, what did you like best about what Dawn did today," but never, "What do you think of what Dawn did." This might elicit a critical response. After Dawn is affirmed by member and facilitators, the other members are affirmed for their support of Dawn through doubling and through creating a safe space for her to work. Be sure to affirm any member who did not double, or who was not part of the enactment in any way, so that they know they played an important part by giving their attention to the protagonist and being generous in allowing the time for the work.

In giving feedback to the protagonist, be sure to note each aspect of what she accomplished. Sometimes the protagonist may simply express her feelings. Other times, the protagonist may try out approaching a problem in a new way. In giving feedback to Dawn, the facilitator made the following comment, "Dawn, you did a great deal of work today. You shared a problem you had with your son and helped us to see how much better able you are to work with him. You also shared your feeling about your brother-in-law and helped each of us to understand how you feel. You let us double for you and accepted the group's support. You also practiced telling your feelings to your husband. You even came up with a plan for coping with the problem and practiced telling your husband the plan. Good work!" An example of giving feedback to Nicole, the new member, would be as follows: "Nicole, you did a great job for your very first day in group. You met everyone and told us a little bit about yourself, including the fact that you get mad at your father when he won't let you use the computer. You got up and doubled for Dawn and let her know you could understand her feelings. And you generously gave of your time to allow Dawn a chance to work on her problem. Thank you for your efforts today."

In giving affirmations, make a point of affirming both in-group behavior, as well as the material the member brought in. Also, we want members to leave with both a positive feeling about themselves and, connected with that, a positive self-thought. Never describe or comment on problematic behavior. For example, if a member typically has trouble looking at others while speaking, but made an effort to look another member in the eye when talking, you might say, "Corinne, you really did a good job of making eye contact today. It's clear that you are working hard to remember to do that, and you are really making progress."

A final thought about the group process is important to note. In using psychodramatic techniques, we are asking members to do lots of different things: move their chairs into the middle, speak to an empty chair, get up and stand behind someone else's chair, and so on. It is important to *ask*, always, if these requests are ok with the member. No one should feel she *has to* cooperate against her wishes. If, in fact, a member says she does not want to do something, affirm her for being able to say so. This is important in any therapy group, but all the more so with abuse survivors, who, in all likelihood, have not had their expressed feelings respected. Make a point of acknowledging the member for being able to say "no" when she needs to.

DISCUSSION

To review the key points of the IBT group process, note that the process describes a series of four stages that comprise a session and help to structure it. In addition, we employ ongoing positive feedback to shape prosocial interpersonal behavior. Members are not pressed to disclose information. Rather, each member is encouraged to provide her own check-in item or issue to work on that day. Some members may want to report on a positive experience they had, which is also accepted. The role of the facilitator is to create an environment in which the individual members can safely express their pain and, at the same time, discover and develop their resources and strengths.

REFERENCES

Asay, T.P., Lambert, M.J., Gregersen, A.T., & Goates, M.K. (2002). Using patient-focused research in evaluating treatment outcome in private practice. *Journal of Clinical Psychology, 58*, 1213-1225.

Blaine, C. (1993). *Interpersonal learning in short-term integrated group psychotherapy.* Unpublished master's thesis, University of Alberta, Alberta, Canada.

Carlin, M. (1998). *Death, bereavement, and grieving: A group intervention for bereaved individuals with cerebral palsy.* Unpublished doctoral dissertation, Long Island University, C.W. Post Campus.

Daniels, L. (1998). A group cognitive-behavioral and process-oriented approach to treating the social impairment and negative symptoms associated with chronic mental illness. *Journal of Psychotherapy Research and Practice, 7*, 167-176.

Duncan, B.L., Miller, S.D., & Sparks, J.A. (2004). *The heroic client: A revolutionary way to improve effectiveness through client-directed, outcome-informed therapy.* San Francisco: Jossey-Bass.

Foy, D.W., Eriksson, C.B., & Trice, G.A. (2001). Introduction to group interventions for trauma survivors. Group *Dynamics: Theory, Research and Practice, 5,* 246-251.

Herman, J.L. (1992). *Trauma and recovery.* New York: Basic Books.

Kirchner, L., & Mueth, M. (2000). Suicide in individuals with developmental disabilities. In R. Fletcher (Ed.), *Therapy approaches for persons with mental retardation* (pp. 127-150). Kingston, NY: NADD Press.

Lundrigan, M. (2007). Interactive Behavioral Therapy with intellectually disabled persons with psychiatric disorders: A pragmatic case study. Unpublished doctoral dissertation: Graduate School of Applied and Professional Psychology, Rutgers University, New Brunswick, NJ.

Oliver-Brannon, G. (2000). Counseling and psychotherapy in group treatment with the dually diagnosed (mental retardation and mental illness—MR/MI) (Doctoral dissertation, The Union Institute, 2000). *Dissertation Abstracts International,* 60(10-B), 5230.

Razza, N., & Tomasulo, D. (2005). *Healing trauma: The power of group treatment for people with intellectual disabilities.* Washington, DC: American Psychological Association.

Van der Kolk, B.A., McFarlane, A.C., & van der Hart, O. (1996). In B.A. van der Kolk, A.C. McFarlane, L. Weisaeth (Eds.), *Traumatic stress: The effects of overwhelming experience on mind, body, and society* (pp. 182-213). New York: Guilford Press.

Wampold, B.E. (2001). *The great psychotherapy debate: Models, methods, and findings.* Hillsdale, NJ: Erlbaum.

Young, B.H., & Blake, D.D. (1999). *Group treatments for post-traumatic stress disorder.* Philadelphia: Brunner/Mazel.

SECTION III

FAMILY AND COUPLE THERAPY

Psychotherapy with Families Impacted by Intellectual Disability, Throughout the Lifespan

Judith Hill-Weld, M.S., LMFT

Introduction

People living with intellectual and developmental disabilities (ID/DD) who also have mental health concerns can benefit from a wide variety of interventions and supports. One intervention, psychotherapy, offers a broad array of techniques and theoretical perspectives, as evidenced in this volume. However, one theoretical perspective within the world of psychotherapy – family systems theory – provides a filter through which many other models and interventions can be applied. This chapter establishes the value of utilizing family systems theory as a meta-theory in treating persons with intellectual and developmental disabilities, describes the current state of the literature about incorporating family systems theory into treatment of this population, and provides some case examples at different stages of the family life cycle.

Family systems theory prioritizes the reciprocal impact of the familial group and the individual. Because people with intellectual and developmental disabilities often sustain high involvement with their families throughout their lives, family systems theory might be especially relevant to their treatment. In addition, because people with intellectual and developmental disabilities often live in group settings and family systems theory can be applied to family-like groups, the theory is even more widely relevant. As Levitas and Gilson (1999) have said, "many people with MR [mental retardation] live...in a persistent web of relationships in which their ability to change their perceptions and behavior is limited by the capacity of their caregivers (families, counselors, case managers, supervisors, or employers) to share or respond to such changes..." While experts might debate the ability of individuals with ID/DD to independently change their perceptions and behavior, there is no doubt that families, counselors, case managers, supervisors, employers, and others in that persistent web affect individuals' lives, their choices, and their perceptions. This view is the primary focus of family systems theory: that all individuals exist interdependently with others in systems of influence and interaction, and that the systems influence the individual and the individual influences the systems.

This chapter provides an overview of the historical relationship of family systems theory and psychotherapeutic treatment of families living with ID/DD. The target audience is both those therapists who work with persons with ID/DD and have not yet considered the advantages of applying family systems theory, as well as therapists who commonly utilize family systems theory and are unfamiliar with ways to apply it to the population in question.

LITERATURE REVIEW

Efficacy Research on Family Systems Therapies

Researching the effectiveness of family therapy is fraught with difficulties. The size and complexity of the participant group being studied, the variety of modalities, the struggle to measure systemic and not just individual change, and the overly broad definitions of family therapy, all contribute to a paucity of large scale studies. However, specific manualized models have been evaluated effectively and a handful of ambitious authors have attempted meta-analyses and surveys to provide an overview of the efficacy research.

In 1995, Jay Lebow and Alan Gurman completed a comprehensive summary of research assessing both couple and family therapies. They concluded that structural family therapies had a "small, long-standing base of empirical support" (p. 36) while strategic therapies had seldom been assessed. They also noted that there were far more studies of behavioral methods than other approaches and therefore better evidence supporting the effectiveness of those methods. Overall they commented that "almost without exception outcomes achieved by treatment groups have exceeded those of control groups." (p. 32). In 1995, they concluded that due to the improvements in research methodology over the previous 30 years the evidence for overall effectiveness was probable. They summarized some prior meta-analyses in the 10 previous years that found impressive effect sizes, concluding that statistically significant results were emerging in couple and family therapies as the field grew.

In 1997 Sandberg et al., and again in 2000 Miller et al., published an article and accompanying chart regarding the existence of quality efficacy research of specific approaches of marriage and family therapy in treating certain disorders. Behavioral Family Therapy was found to have been researched the most frequently and its efficacy most firmly established for multiple disorders and problems. However, their review indicated strong support for Functional Family Therapy as a treatment for at least one disorder, for Structural Family Therapy for treatment of one disorder, and for Multi-Systemic treatment for at least one disorder, strengthening the support for systemic therapies.

Cottrell and Boston of the University of Leeds (2002) reviewed the development of systemic family therapy and examined the empirical basis for using systemic family therapies with children and adolescents. While they concluded that sufficient well-designed randomized controlled trials were lacking, they also determined that there was support in the research for the effectiveness of systemic family therapies in the treatment of conduct disorders, substance abuse, and eating disorders and some basis for using this approach as second-line treatments in depression and chronic illness. The authors described prior meta-analyses which indicated a positive effect on family interaction measures and a lower but also positive effect on behavioral measures. In particular they noted the positive effect of family therapy versus the no-treatment controls on behavioral measures. Cottrell and Boston called for improved research and also suggested that "practitioners should already be examining the contribution that systemic ideas can make to other therapeutic models. There is evidence that systemic therapies may reduce drop-out and increase engagement and consumer satisfaction…[and that] Systemic Interventions may also have positive effects that are maintained and even increase with time" (p. 582).

Recently, Alan Carr at University College Dublin updated previous analyses regarding the effectiveness of family therapy and systemic interventions for adult-focused and child-focused problems (2009a and 2009b). He noted (2009b) that the evidence reviewed indicates that systemic interventions are effective for a wide range of child-focused problems. Carr concluded that the evidence also supported the effectiveness of systemic interventions for a variety of adult focused problems as well. In both cases he suggested that the systemic interventions might be provided alone or as part of a multi-modal program. He also noted that more recently many of these interventions have been manualized, making them more replicable and accessible to clinicians. He also concluded that most evidence- based systemic interventions had been developed within the cognitive behavioral, structural-strategic, and psycho-educational traditions. It is important to note that Carr's review includes not only family therapy but other family based approaches such as parent training.

Efficacy Research in Family Systems Therapy with Persons with DD/ID

Very little past research has been completed that evaluates the efficacy of any type of psychotherapy for people with ID/DD. Prout and Nowak-Drabik (2003) reviewed studies conducted over the prior thirty years of psychotherapy with persons who have intellectual disability. They conducted both an expert consensus review and a small meta-analysis (small because of the diversity of the literature and the number of studies that qualified for a meta-analysis). They note a history of past reviewers concluding that psychotherapy is not generally effective with this population, and that historically many general books and resources on counseling and psychotherapy do not address issues related to ID/DD. Overall their review suggested that psychotherapy with people who have ID/DD actually produces a moderate amount of change and is moderately effective or beneficial. Prout and Nowak-Drabik concluded that their analysis also demonstrated that this effectiveness is not significantly impacted by age, level of impairment, technique, or theoretical approach. They noted that group, behavioral, and cognitive behavioral interventions were the most heavily researched modalities. Preliminarily they suggest that the data favors individual and clinic-based treatments. The Prout and Nowak-Drabik review does not cite a single study of family therapy. (See Prout's chapter in this book for updated information regarding research on therapy for people with ID/DD.)

Other Literature on Family Systems Therapy with ID/DD

Standard texts on family therapy for graduate students in marriage and family therapy did not historically do more than merely mention disability. Increasingly these texts have begun to explicitly acknowledge family constellations which include developmental or intellectual disability (e.g., Goldenberg & Goldenberg, 2007). Several texts exist which discuss family needs in the context of chronic illness or disability but not specifically focused on developmental or intellectual disability. Also numerous authors have written about the impact of disability on families, the types of support and assistance those families need, and the specific challenges and rewards that disability brings them but these texts rarely mention family therapy, nor family systems theory (e.g., Power & Dell Orto, 2004). Research and writing on families living with ID/DD has tended to focus on families with young children and has provided a rich resource of understanding the experience of raising children with ID/DD, the specific stresses and rewards involved, the evolution of strengths resulting from the experience, and the supports needed.

While there is little efficacy research on family therapy with people with ID/DD, there is literature describing the integration of family systems theory with theories of disability and family life, case studies, ethical considerations, and proposed approaches or models to provide family therapy for people with ID/DD.

As early as 1988, Martha Foster of Georgia State University wrote an article challenging the notion that dysfunction is to be expected in families living with ID/DD and that emotional distress in these families necessarily signifies pathology. She also noted an evolution towards an "ecosystemic framework" in thinking about families and ID/DD but commented that most of the empirical work had not been from a systems framework. She also noted:

> Models for how to work with these families, in addition to behavior
> modification with children, parent education, and crisis intervention, are sorely
> needed. Although family therapists are increasingly sophisticated about how to
> use systems constructs in the change process, most families with handicapped
> children do not seek family therapy. Clinical services are more often rendered,
> if at all, in conjunction with educational programs or through the medical
> system (p. 55).

Foster advocates for a conceptual framework that recognizes strength and competence in families, and views the family's current behavior from a life cycle and multigenerational perspective.

Ann Turnbull and colleagues wrote a book on cognitive coping (1993) which addresses the impact of giving birth to and/or raising a child with a developmental disability and finding ways to improve family members' self esteem, feelings of control, and a sense of meaning. The focus of this volume is on cognitive coping techniques that support resilient family patterns of stress, coping, and adaptation. While much of the writing could be of value to a systemic therapist, the book does not address family systems theory or therapy directly.

In 1994 John S. Rolland published his well known book *Families, Illness, and Disability: An Integrative Treatment Model.* His book filled a gap for health and mental health professionals dealing with families facing illness and disability. His model was explicitly based on systems theory, and it prioritized interaction and context as the dominant concepts. He considered transactional patterns within a family and between a family and other systems as central in shaping individual behavior. Rolland specifically stated that therapeutic interventions should be targeted at modifying dysfunctional family patterns (page 11). This seminal work outlines the biopsychosocial demands of different illnesses and disabilities, how the different stages of an illness affect a family, and how family belief systems significantly impact the ability to manage health and illness. Therefore his model examined the intersection of a series of life cycle and illness cycle variables. Although he mentions mental retardation several times, the book is largely focused on illness and injury that leads to disability rather than developmental disabilities that are lifelong, genetically based, or that begin in early childhood and maintain a stable pattern of impairment. He acknowledges that with intellectual disability that "the need for high cohesion may be permanent, derailing family members from normative developmental shifts" (page 68).

In 1996, Arlene Vetere of Reading University in the United Kingdom wrote an essay for *Clinical Child Psychology and Psychiatry* about the neglect of family systems ideas in working with intellectual and developmental disabilities. Although her focus was the United Kingdom, she pointed out that while there was, in 1996, an increasing amount of literature exploring the coping and adaptation of families living with intellectual disability that the literature was not quite systemic in conception and orientation. She felt the Beavers team in Dallas (1986) presented an exception in their study on coping in families living with disabilities. She did not acknowledge Rolland's contributions to systemic thinking about such families.

Laura Marshak, Milton Seligman, and Fran Prezant collaborated on a book in 1999, *Disability and the Family Life Cycle*, which incorporated some of Rolland's theory, focused more exclusively on disability that begins in infancy or early childhood and sustains throughout the lifespan. Marshak, Seligman and Prezant outline the stages and cycles in family life when disability is a variable, and their book is premised on the importance of interdependence, family structure and functions. Pages 271 through 277 describe possible uses of marital and family counseling, including marital counseling, medical family counseling, behavioral parent training, and family therapy. The family therapy themes and interventions emphasized include an emphasis on roles, functioning, boundaries, normalizing struggles, reframing, communications, triangulations, control issues, and sexual functioning. These are all areas of focus and intervention common to family systems therapy.

NADD itself contributed to the discussion of family systems theory with its publication in 1999 of Louis Lindebaum's chapter on family therapy (Fletcher, 1999). Lindebaum specifically addresses the systemic approach to family therapy and the value in incorporating it into family therapy with persons with developmental disabilities. He quotes the work of Hennicke and Bradl (1990), which describes the structural nature of problems in families including tendencies to scapegoat or overprotect the person with developmental disabilities.

Beverly Fidell, a clinical psychologist in the United Kingdom, wrote a lengthy essay exploring the use of family therapy with adults with intellectual disability (2000). Although she is focusing on lack of family systems focus in mental health services in Britain, she describes the use of this theoretical perspective in her clinic. She also outlines the pros and cons of both structural and brief family therapy, concluding that when family therapists work systemically with families living with DD/ID the complexity of the systems involved increases.

Also in 1999 Nick Bouras edited an overview of psychiatric and behavioral disorders in intellectual disability which does not address family systems theory. However the 2007 update of this book does include some material on family systems treatment, perhaps reflecting the growing interest in applying family systems theory to families living with ID/DD.

In 2001, Wilhelm Rotthaus contributed an entire chapter on Systemic Therapy in Dosen and Day's comprehensive text *Treating Mental Illness and Behavior Disorders in Children and Adults with Mental Retardation*. In his conclusion he points out that the therapist should avoid one-sided coalitions, and should focus on the exceptions to the problems so that they become the norm. He suggests that the systemic approach has been in use in Germany since the 1980's and recommends it as an effective approach for persons with ID/DD.

Christopher Lynch (2004) summarized the varied uses of psychotherapy with persons with ID/DD. He briefly mentions family therapy, but not in any detail. However, Lynch points out that although psychotherapy has generally been accepted to be moderately effective for persons with intellectual disability, providing that therapy often requires more time for the client to learn and incorporate coping strategies, availability of booster sessions, and more use of indirect services than perhaps typically developing clients utilize. He rightly concludes that "such services are not typically reimbursed in the current cost-cutting environment" (p. 402). Just as family systems therapy is complex to research (in terms of operational process and in terms of effectiveness), so family systems therapy is difficult to fund since the measurement of outcome and the identification of the patient unit do not easily fit into funding scheme requirements.

Goldberg et al. (2005) describe a method of working with ID/DD adults and their families focusing on life-cycle transitions and the recurring of grief. Their approach includes basic family systems approaches including joining the family, developing hypotheses, and recognizing universal and unifying themes among family members.

Thomas and Ray (2006), while writing for a school counseling journal, described the use of systems theory applied to "exceptional students" including children with ID/DD. They argue that the focus is to improve relationships and to change the context of a problem, not necessarily to change the presenting problem itself. They describe three possible models – 1) The Belin-Blank Center Model, 2) Structural-Strategic Model, and 3) Imaginative-Postmodern model – and provide case examples of applying these models. The Belin-Blank Center model is a brief approach, focusing on family dynamics related to inclusion, control, and intimacy, but is largely intended for families with gifted children. The Structural-Strategic Model teaches family members to see relational issues systemically, and the therapist uses techniques of joining and matching, working in the present, reframing, and working with boundaries and alliances. The Imaginative-Postmodern Model incorporates concepts from narrative and solution-focused therapies, such as changing the stories people tell about their problems and identifying how solutions already exist in the apparently problematic situation.

In 2006, Sandra Baum and Henrik Lynggaard edited a volume remarkable for its persistent and thorough focus on ID/DD and the systemic approach (2006). Their primary focus is work in the United Kingdom, reflecting a movement in that country to apply systemic thinking more widely in clinical work with persons with ID/DD. In addition, while some of the writers in this volume may follow a specific manualized model of family systems therapy, many also advocate for the meta-theory approach, arguing that the focus on relationships and interactions shifts the clinical focus away from automatically pathologizing the individual with ID/DD. They also emphasize the importance of identifying circular patterns in case formulation and of remaining open to multiple realities and meanings constructed by different subsystems.

In their book *Ordinary Families, Special Children* (2007), Milton Seligman and Rosalyn Benjamin Darling use Family Systems Theory as one of two conceptual bases underlying their work. They explicate such important concepts as subsystems, cohesion (and enmeshment and disengagement), and adaptability, as well as resilience, social support, and developmental transitions. The authors also describe in detail the many types of stressors and factors which may be unique to living with DD/ID in the family and the possible effects of these on each family member. While they describe several models of counseling intervention, they generally do not describe the specifics of family systems interventions but are clearly advocating for a systems understanding of family issues in ID/DD.

Julie Ramisch and colleagues (2009) recently explored the impact on families with children with disabilities of a concurrent diagnosis of severe emotional disturbance. They noted that the frequent and challenging behaviors presented by dually diagnosed children produce greater caregiver strain and may trigger a negative pattern of interaction between parent and child. Additionally, these authors note that such negative patterns of interaction may cause the parents greater difficulty in redefining and reframing their problems as a means to cope with difficult feelings and events. One possible implication is that interrupting the negative patterns of interaction, and supporting efforts to redefine and reframe problems, could strengthen family coping.

One final article deserves mention. Julie Ramisch and Darrell Franklin wrote an article for the *American Journal of Family Therapy* (2008) which described ethical issues in family therapy when ID/DD is involved. While they raise numerous important issues, one stands out as relevant to this chapter. They point out that "the goal of family therapy is not to elevate either family or individual rights over one another, but to achieve a balance where individual and family rights are mutually accommodated" (p. 319). Family systems theory may be uniquely suited to the pursuit of that balance in the context of therapy.

THEORETICAL FOUNDATION

Family Systems Theory as a Meta-Theory

Family systems theory evolved out of the fields of biology and engineering to explain patterns of escalation (in families this is the escalation of symptoms or problem behaviors) and homeostasis (or the tendency to reach a state of equilibrium). The literature review presented in this chapter has already mentioned many of the significant concepts within the theory, but the primary ones include:

- the problem behavior or symptom as a function of the family system;
- patterns of belief and levels of meaning in the interacting subsystems of the family;
- circular patterns of escalation and feedback;
- focus on relationships and interactions rather than isolated pathology;
- family roles and boundaries;
- degrees of engagement, individuation, disengagement, and enmeshment

Gwyn Daniel (in Vetere & Dallos, 2003, p. viii) suggests that systemic therapy can be viewed as a treatment model (or models), which can be manualized and replicated and researched, *and* as a meta-theory "which can encompass and engage with many perspectives simultaneously without losing intellectual rigor." The meta-theory approach is applied in the case examples discussed later in this chapter.

History of Concept and Types of Therapy

The scope and size of this chapter do not support a complete history of the evolution of family systems theory and the numerous treatment models which have emerged over the decades. However, a brief listing of some of the best known models may be useful: Structural, Strategic, Brief, Milan, Family Construct, Solution Focused, Feminist, Narrative, and Post-Milan models have been written about at length and should be familiar to most students of family therapy. Some of these models or related interventions are manualized and replicable. This chapter does not present any particular manualized model; instead it explores using the systems meta-theory as a lens through which to view the family and the individual, while retaining access to a wide variety of intervention techniques including many of those mentioned here as well as standard cognitive behavioral and psychodynamic strategies.

Change in Family Systems Theory

Much of individual therapy is designed to produce change within the presenting individual. In family systems theory, change in individual problem behavior, while sometimes desirable, is not the primary goal. Instead the therapist looks to produce a reorganization of what the problem means and the dynamic patterns that have evolved around and with the problem (Vetere & Dallos, 2003). Change can occur on a behavioral level, in cognitions and beliefs, as well as in family members' emotional experiences, but it is the shifting of patterns and meanings that counts as success. Family systems theory posits that this "second order" change will result in longer term improvement in closeness, functioning, and well-being for the family and the individuals.

Additionally, family systems theory accepts the difficulty of producing change and theorizes that this is due in part to the system's tendency to seek homeostasis or equilibrium, even if this means sustaining the problem behavior. The family systems therapist general attributes positive connotations to this tendency and may not initially seek to unbalance the pattern. Eventually however, the goal is to shift the interactions to achieve a new, more functional equilibrium.

A final significant concept in this chapter is the notion of family life cycles. Numerous writings on family life cycles have posited a fixed and normative progression of stages through the chronological age of the family members, linking individual developmental cycles to those of the group. Other authors have written about the stages and cycles inherent in experiences of illness and disability, such as the stages of loss and grief, the crises of medical intervention and adaptation, and the progression of responses to a disability diagnosis in the family. With the diversity of the word "family" becoming more evident in society every day, the notion that we can impose a particular expectation of developmental stages or tasks on every family without consideration of their cultural values, multi-generational traditions, or disability experience is unworkable. Rather, we must use the excellent thinking about life cycles as a gentle reminder that some dysfunctional dynamics occur simply because a family is attempting to develop in a healthy direction and has become stuck. If we can reframe the problem a family experiences as a problem that the system has accommodating the disability (and the disability in conjunction with the developmental tasks that are present for the individual), rather than simply a problem of the disability itself, we can depathologize the individual with ID/DD and acknowledge his or her value as a member of the system. (On the other hand, there are times when a family struggles simply because living with the disability itself is difficult.) Sometimes introducing the life cycle concept to a family will help them normalize their struggles and thus remove them from the realm of dysfunction simply by this shift in perspective.

THERAPY TECHNIQUE

The case examples presented in this chapter do not follow a manualized model of family systems theory, and therefore the list of possible techniques is large. Rather these cases are presented as examples of seeing through the family systems lens, utilizing some of the standard family systems techniques but also relying on techniques from cognitive-behavioral and psychodynamic approaches. This is a fluid approach, designed to simply remind (or awaken) readers of the possible values and applications of family systems theory, rather than a prescription for proper technique.

Some of the many techniques used in family systems therapy include the following:
- Joining through pacing and matching a family's tone and tempo
- Assigning therapeutic tasks
- Altering patterns through direction and redirection
- Describing hypotheses about circularities
- Re-framing the function of symptomatic behavior in either a positive or a startling manner
- Unbalancing the system through assigning unfamiliar tasks, positions, and rules
- Enactment of typical circularities
- Re-storying the narrative of the family problem to be more accurate, inclusive and systemic
- Identifying the co-construction of shared stories
- Circular questioning designed to help individuals step outside the patterns in order to observe them
- Using reflecting teams in a variety of formats

- Externalizing problems (through circular questioning or other cognitive means)
- Writing tasks to engage observation and narrative
- Genograms to explore the multi-generational transmission of roles and boundaries
- Using paradoxical assignments to increase a sense of control and choice, but also create a bind from which the system seeks escape

In the case examples described below, therapy is provided in a private outpatient psychotherapy office by an individual practitioner. Due to the constraints of this setting, none of the cases include reflecting teams or other interventions that require multiple clinicians.

CASE EXAMPLES

Case #1

John and Cassie are a Caucasian couple adjusting to the diagnosis of an Autistic Spectrum Disorder for their 3 year old son, Dustin. Dustin has a big brother, Jordan, who was 4 and half and one year away from entering kindergarten. John was in his late forties and taught high school science, while Cassie was in her early thirties and had become a stay at home mom after a successful career in advertising. Neither John nor Cassie has any family members with autism or any other experience with developmental disability.

John and Cassie were referred to therapy by the early childhood intervention program when the couple expressed concerns about coping with the world of autism interventions. In person, Cassie reported that over the previous year the couple had dived into early childhood interventions, taking Dustin to Speech and Occupational Therapy, seeking an assessment for a 40 hour per week ABA program, and researching dietary interventions. However, she expressed a strong degree of anxiety, as well as dismay at what she perceived as John's detached, unemotional attitude. John said he was affected by Dustin's diagnosis but was more focused on financially supporting the family and so wasn't able to be as animated or as involved in worrying about Dustin as Cassie.

The therapist held a family session including the children and observed a similar degree of involvement, although with different styles, by both parents. Both parents interacted skillfully with the children, had clearly learned some floor time techniques, and made a strong effort to be attuned to and to engage both their children. Interviewing Jordan, who was quite articulate, it was revealed that "Daddy slept with Dustin." When the therapist asked Cassie and John about this they explained that Dustin had great difficulty staying asleep but would settle back down if John was in the bed with him. So John had taken to sleeping every night with Dustin to prevent nighttime activity and wandering. It worked effectively and allowed Cassie to get a full night's sleep, although John was a little bit sleep deprived.

In subsequent sessions the therapist joined the family through empathy and reflective listening. Cassie's anxiety appeared to become quite overwhelming, and she was referred to an individual therapist and to her doctor for a medication evaluation. While John's style seemed detached and distant, his actual behavior regarding Dustin was quite engaged. In addition to sleeping with Dustin nightly, he had read books about autism, researched dietary issues on the internet, and attempted to provide Cassie with one night out per week on her own as relief from parenting. Cassie was able to affirm John's involvement and express appreciation for it but her frustration over his low emotionality continued.

Therapy continued, focused on grief resolution (a common developmental stage for young families facing a new diagnosis) and couples communication. At one session it became clear that the couple had some conflicts about spending and budgeting, and the therapist introduced the idea of a weekly couples' business meeting. The couple was unable, or unwilling, to implement this technique at home and reported that it was just too uncomfortable. In processing their experience the therapist discovered that in the previous year the couple had spent large amounts of money on specialized food for Dustin, purchased a hyperbaric chamber and paid out of pocket for an expensive specialized doctor, and were now in heavy debt. They also reported that this was not the first time they had incurred significant debt and described how they had overspent approximately eight years earlier and had then gotten themselves out of debt by severely restricting their spending for a couple of years. The therapist enquired if this approach might not be used again but Cassie insisted that they needed to spend whatever it took to help Dustin.

Through a family systems theory lens, the therapist noticed that Cassie was highly defensive and emotional about the money and about Dustin while John seemed to recede into himself becoming quieter and more intellectual in his few responses. The system continuing to operate seemed dependent on this polarity of high activation and low activation, with Cassie getting louder and more emotional in response to John's withdrawal which was his response to Cassie's anxiety. The therapist theorized that some of Cassie's anxiety was due to her awareness of the financial liability being created without any solution planned to manage the debt. Maintaining this dynamic required not talking about money in too much detail and generally avoiding confrontation of the money problems. However, such avoidance also increased anxiety and withdrawal within the system.

The therapist dove into this dynamic with the couple by not talking about the current situation and instead helping them explore the meaning of money in their families of origin, the narrative of money in their marriage, and their visions for how they hoped their children would manage money as adults. This approach allowed them to begin to externalize the problem and uncovered a multi-generational pattern of poor financial management which the couple wanted to interrupt. Over time, John confessed that he was managing the family's debt by shifting from credit card to credit card and was anticipating running out of credit and options. He could see the point coming when the minimum payments would outstrip the available cash flow. He also explained how reluctant he had been to discuss any of this with Cassie because he saw her as the "autism hero" of the family dedicated to Dustin's improvement and deserving of luxuries and indulgences as her reward for working so hard. Cassie confessed that she knew she was overspending on herself and couldn't bear to be the source of the problem and so had wanted to avoid thinking about it. Both parents admitted deep fear at "doing less" for Dustin. They equated spending money with "doing more" and felt panicked at the thought of "doing" any less for him than they had been for the previous year.

The therapist articulated the vicious circle she saw happening within this family. She helped them further externalize this dynamic so they could begin to imagine joining together as a team to fight it. She made paradoxical assignments, such as intentionally "spending more to do more" for Dustin. When the couple experienced the sense of control this gave them, they found themselves choosing to spend less, and feeling less frightened of spending less. Cassie began to notice how much John did for Dustin and Jordan that was not about spending. Tentatively, John began to speak up about expenses and an informal "business meeting" evolved on an almost weekly basis. Cassie developed a sense of pride in her newfound frugality.

Like many parents of young children with Autistic Spectrum Disorders, Cassie and John heard the message that they needed to intervene with Dustin early and intensively to make the greatest impact. They also felt pulled in multiple directions by the variety of interventions available and the sense that they must try all of them if they were to be "good enough" parents. Many parents of young children with autism experience these pressures. No one else can determine for them which is the best investment of their time and money. However it is clear that family sanity and financial stability have to be part of the equation. For Cassie and John, in the context of their histories, the dynamic of "spend more to do more" was destructive.

Being willing to spend some time focused on the origins of John and Cassie's "money narrative" helped each of them let go of some of their defensiveness and fear and begin to disclose the truth. Externalizing the problem, intervening to give them control over the behavior, and placing the patterns in a multi-generational lifetime context allowed them to grow confidence in their ability to make more conscious choices. Ironically, as they began to spend less, they also could notice each other's efforts to help Dustin more readily.

Case #2

Grace was a 19 year old, athletic Caucasian woman who had been diagnosed with an Autistic Spectrum Disorder at age 15. Prior to that diagnosis she had seen multiple experts and variously been diagnosed with Tourette Syndrome, Attention Deficit Hyperactivity Disorder, and Obsessive-Compulsive Disorder. She had low-average IQ but had trouble performing well academically due to haste, impulsivity, difficulty following directions, and some receptive and expressive language impairment. She and her family had worked successfully for several years with a psychiatrist to manage medications that reduced the worst of her tics, anxiety, impulsivity and obsessive thinking. She knew very little about ASD, and because of her very late diagnosis had not participated in any of the standard early childhood treatments or educational interventions for ASD. Grace was referred to therapy by her social worker at the regional disability services office due to problems with overspending, failures in job settings due to haste and impulsivity, and emotional reactivity and acting out in the form of ordering, purging, or selling others' belongings without permission. She attended junior college and wanted to become a marine biologist, due to her love of sharks.

Grace lived, curiously, in her father's home while he lived there only part-time and increasingly lived with his new wife in a separate house. Her parents had divorced early in her adolescence, her mother had remarried, and Grace remained living with her father. Because Grace was completely dependent on her father financially, and her living situation was so unusual, the therapist theorized that this might be part of the dynamic underlying Grace's problem behaviors. Once basic rapport had been established, with Grace's consent the therapist invited her parents to attend the next session.

Grace's mother, Stella, was a 55 year old, athletic, fit visual artist remarried to a sculptor. She also had an older child from a previous marriage. Grace had not lived with Stella since the divorce, but they regularly had dinner together at Stella's home or went out to lunch or shopping together. Stella's current husband had limited involvement in Grace's life. Stella displayed a tendency prior to therapy to frequently call the social worker in a panic anytime Grace displayed any anxiety or her problem behaviors began to escalate. She reported being angry with Grace's father for not being more strict and consistent. She herself had established very firm boundaries in her home for Grace, intended to protect her belongings from Grace's acting out. She viewed Grace's career aspirations as unrealistic and felt that the academic curriculum was highly stressful and damaging for Grace. Stella was also under multiple stressors herself, including financial and health related issues as well as concerns about an aging parent.

Grace's father, Ike, was a 60 year old scientist who had recently remarried and had other adult children from a prior marriage. Ike's responses to Grace's problem behaviors were often somewhat passive, intellectual, and short-lived. He was reluctant to set strict limits with her, had provided her with a credit card and funded her bank account, and, while he asked her to do chores, he rarely followed through if she did not complete them. He respected her intellectual abilities and wanted her to be able to pursue her career goals unfettered and often expressed faith in her ability to achieve them. Ike's wife wanted to be active in Grace's life but Grace resisted this involvement.

Multiple approaches to Grace's problems were available. The therapist could have referred the case for behavioral analysis. The therapist could have conducted psychodynamic therapy with Grace to help her grow her insight into her behaviors and heal the psychological wounds of her repeated failures and her parents' divorce. The therapist could have engaged Grace in cognitive therapy designed to help her gain understanding and control over her assumptions and choices and notice the triggers that lead to her acting out behaviors. To some degree the therapist engaged in all of these approaches. However, it turned out that the family systems filter provided the best opportunity for Grace to make change.

Using techniques such as circular questioning and enactment, and through repeated attempts to help Grace's parents implement behavior plans and family meetings, the therapist uncovered the following family dynamic: Grace would begin to obsess on a particular topic, such as her desire to attend a world class sports event at a great distance or her plan to take a large and rigorous course load during the next semester. She would not discuss this desire with anyone because she believed, correctly, that her parents' first response would be discouraging. She would then begin to worry about not having enough money to accomplish her plan. As her anxiety would build she would act more erratically, which her mother noticed. Her mother's anxiety would build as well, which Grace noticed and which served to stimulate her more. Then Grace would act out: for example, she would purchase very expensive plane tickets on her father's credit card or steal something from her parents and try to sell it, or simply become so overwrought she was unable to cope and made unsafe decisions or stopped sleeping. Eventually the acting out would be discovered, Stella would become highly distressed and almost histrionic and call the therapist or the social worker, and a family session would be held. Ike would express deep concern and question Grace about her motives but also appeared irritated with Stella's emotionality. Grace would become tearful and apologize, feel ashamed of her perceived failure, then shut down and become even more obsessed with her original plan. These events sometimes resulted in agreements about logical consequences proposed by Stella and reluctantly agreed to by Ike, but implementation and follow through usually did not occur.

The therapist first joined the family. She attempted to help each person feel heard and seen, and she acknowledged and validated their distress. She agreed there were serious problems that needed help and created a safe enough environment for Grace to admit this as well. Then she began to reframe the situation. She noted that Grace was attempting to act as an independent adult via trial and error forays into adult decision-making, that her mother Stella was kindly trying to protect Grace from failure, and that her father Ike was sympathetically trying to support Grace's forays into the adult world by not setting too many limits on her. By attributing positive intention to each person the therapist interrupted the cycle of blame that helped perpetuate the problems.

The therapist then clarified with Grace that she did indeed want to be more independent, although she was frightened about changes such as moving out of her father's home. The therapist provided the family with education about the characteristics of adult decision-making, which involves brainstorming, research, planning, and problem-solving. She asked if each person would be willing to participate in learning a technique for adult decision-making that would support Grace, increase her confidence, and help her achieve her goal of becoming more independent. All agreed.

At about this time Grace developed a good working relationship with her new independent living skills (ILS) specialist. The therapist proposed some sessions with Grace and the ILS specialist, partly as an effort to join Grace's developmental need to find appropriate separation from her parents. Grace agreed to this, and her parents agreed to return to therapy when invited by Grace. The therapist and the ILS specialist designed a planning form which she then trained Grace to use. The form required Grace to write down any desires she had for major purchases, travel, career, or educational plans. The next step on the form required Grace to have a conversation with someone (her father, mother, ILS specialist, social worker, or therapist) about her plan and to brainstorm with that person all the steps needed for research and information gathering. Grace was asked to promise not to spend any money before the entire form and process was completed, to which she agreed. The therapist and the ILS specialist reviewed the form in session with Grace with low level targets multiple times in session. Then the ILS specialist and Grace practiced using the form together on a weekly basis until she was very familiar with it and could overcome her impulses to skip ahead or not complete the process correctly. The clinical focus on thoroughness, routine, and success appealed to Grace's tendency toward obsessive thinking, need for familiarity, and predictability and gave her repeated experiences of success to build her confidence.

Subsequently, with Grace's permission, the therapist invited Grace's parents back to therapy. She reviewed the form with them, described Grace's excellent progress in learning to use it, and asked if they would be willing to follow the process if Grace initiated discussions with them about her desires and plans. They agreed to do so. The therapist also agreed that these discussions could happen in therapy if Grace chose. The therapist also, at this time, recommended that from now on therapy sessions be initiated only by Grace and that Grace determine who to invite to attend each session. Without explicitly using an externalizing approach, this last arrangement allowed Grace to imagine herself as a person with control over her problems and with control over the approach to solving them. The therapist and Grace also identified probable cues for scheduling a therapy appointment.

Grace became an expert with the planning form. Since her ambitions often involved money and her father was her primary source of financial support, she usually invited her father to a session to discuss an idea. Her father, because he was inclined to be sympathetic, did not initially discourage her and soon learned to ask her to do research on costs and logistics before he decided whether to fund a project. These conversations over time allowed both Grace and her father to speak more honestly about his financial limitations, as well as the realities of young adult responsibilities and privileges. Also, when Grace had crisis periods where her anxiety escalated she became very skillful at seeking help from the psychiatrist or the therapist without waiting for things to explode and her mother to initiate help-seeking. She seemed to enjoy more social contact with her mother, with less escalation, and invited her mother to sessions periodically when she knew her mother was worried about her. Grace no longer incurred large debts. Her interference with other people's belongings continued but on a much smaller and less damaging scale. And, she was able to delay gratification more successfully as she engaged in this planning process as well as to participate in brainstorming more reasonable and affordable plans. Ike began to set limits and impose consequences more readily without encouragement, and Stella panicked less and enjoyed her daughter's changes, trusting her daughter would speak up when troubled.

This approach to family therapy addressed a major structural problem: Grace was caught in a triangle with her divorced parents over how to parent her through the transition to adulthood. Therapy shifted the responsibility for problem solving to Grace, while placing her parents in the more developmentally appropriate position of being resources and consistent sources of feedback. In addition, it addressed a developmental problem: how to support Grace in her appropriate transition to a greater degree of independence while addressing the real dangers of her problem behaviors, as well as support her parents in stepping back a bit while providing the structure and support Grace needed due to her disability.

Viewing this case through the rubric of family systems theory allowed each family member to retain dignity, to feel heard and acknowledged, and to shift his or her patterns of behavior to make room for change. Disability can frighten parents because it implies vulnerability, and the transition to adulthood exacerbates this fear with a pressure to allow for greater autonomy with no guarantee that past problems will not recur. Using a family systems theory approach gave Grace's parents the breathing room to try other, less triangulating approaches. And, reframing Grace's problem behaviors as a positively intentioned reach for independence opened a door for her to view her next step as skill-building rather than any intervention as punishment for her failures. It also allowed her to develop a new repertoire of cognitive skills which will be applicable in multiple situations.

Other, equally valid approaches to Grace's problem behaviors might be used by other clinicians. In this case, the family systems perspective created a shift in perspective and behavior by all family members that successfully resulted in Grace's next step toward maturity.

Case #3

Frederica was a 62 year old, Caucasian woman living with her 84 year old mother, Frances, in their small family home. Her father had died many years previously, but her older sister Jody lived nearby and was closely involved in their lives. Frederica had been diagnosed with mild intellectual disability of unknown etiology and also had scoliosis and arthritis. She had been quite ill the previous winter and had lost a lot of mobility which was only slowly returning and her doctors speculated it might not return fully. They also suggested that this was the beginning of a degenerative process of premature aging. Her mother, Frances, was seeking therapy for Frederica because she displayed a high degree of irritability and had become quite demanding. Frances wondered if Frederica was depressed about her physical condition. Simultaneously, Frances had developed macular degeneration and was rapidly losing her eyesight. She, too, had severe arthritis and several other medical problems that caused her chronic low grade pain.

Frederica had lived most of her life with her mother, with two exceptions: once as an adolescent she had been placed in a large institution for people with developmental disabilities for a year, and once later in adulthood she had tried living in a group home but was very unhappy and missed her mother and so returned home. The adolescent placement had been traumatic for the family and was only pursued because Frederica had become aggressive and unmanageable at home.

Frederica and Frances had some in-home care, primarily to assist with cleaning, and someone to take Frederica out for social activities once per week. Frederica also attended a day program with an arts focus four days a week which she enjoyed, but staff there had also told Frances they had noticed an increase in Frederica's irritability. She had previously been a sweet and pleasant person with many kind words for others; now she more often snapped or barked at people, complained about others' behaviors, and often blamed others when explaining her feelings.

The therapist initially worked with Frederica alone to explore the possibility she was depressed and possible courses of treatment. However, there were insufficient symptoms of depression, as Frederica continued to eat and sleep normally, said she felt hopeful about the future, and was not excessively tearful. The therapist noticed that Frederica often accused her mother of starting their arguments and not being nice enough to her. She also accused her sister of being bossy. With Frederica's agreement, the therapist invited Frances and Jody into the sessions. While Jody did not use bossy or controlling language or behavior in sessions, she did express her opinion about how her mother and sister treated each other and appeared to be very protective of her mother. In sessions, Frances alternated between tearfulness, irritation with Frederica and a strongly expressed desire to mother Frederica as she always had done.

The therapist theorized that this family had reached a developmental transition which challenged their typical coping techniques. Frances was experiencing many difficult symptoms of aging and was feeling less competent to care for herself. In the typical developmental cycle this might result in Frances's daughters stepping in to help care for her to compensate for the changes of aging and illness. Jody was doing this. However, Frederica herself was experiencing problems with illness and aging that seemed to parallel if not exceed her mother's and was unable to put her mother's needs first or offer her usual cheerful kind persona as help. The therapist shared this theory with the family. Frances acknowledged that she felt resentful that after all her years of caring for Frederica that she was unable to reciprocate when Frances needed it. Frances also realized she was frightened of the changes her body was facing, particularly her growing blindness and that this made her more short-tempered with what had previously been typical and tolerated demands from Frederica. Lastly, Frances felt heart-broken to experience herself no longer able to be patient and loving with Frederica as she always had been, particularly when Frederica was going through her own difficult physical challenges. For her part, Frederica admitted she was scared to see her mother change so dramatically and be at all helpless. She was mad at her mother for being sick. She also felt mad at herself for not being able to help more but found it difficult to admit this. Jody admitted she felt very protective of her mother, since she saw the changes aging was bringing and felt that Frederica's demands and temper were unfair to Frances.

From a family systems perspective, overlaid with a life cycle perspective, this family was caught in a dynamic which scapegoated Frederica as "the irritable one" rather than look directly at the fears raised by aging and illness – and since Frederica was indeed being irritable, everyone bought into this narrative. Simply identifying the dynamic helped relieve some pressure for a time. However, eventually Frances realized she would need to make some changes to benefit both herself and Frederica. Jody was reluctant to make any suggestions for fear of appearing "bossy." The therapist suggested to Frances that perhaps both Frances and Frederica needed more care as part of aging than their three person system had in its capacity. To Frederica, the therapist suggested that the best way to help her mother would be 1) to get help for herself; and 2) to focus her energy on having loving social times with her mother rather than focus on taking care of a household together. The therapist raised the possibility of a nearby senior living setting for Frederica, where there would be medical staff prepared to cope with her declining health, with regular visits with Frances and Jody at weekends. Both Frances and Frederica were highly anxious about this idea at first due to their prior experiences with Frederica in residential placement. The therapist recommended they attempt a trial period of living apart for 3 months and then re-evaluate to determine if the new arrangement was meeting their needs. Framing the move as Frederica's choice of how to best help her mother addressed some of the family's fear of re-traumatization, and agreeing to a trial period allowed them all to maintain a sense of control and choice.

When Frederica moved she continued to engage in blaming communications for a while. Jody attempted to make some changes by soliciting Frederica's ideas about how to best help their mother and this approach reduced Frederica's fear of Jody being bossy. Frances felt guilty but also relieved and began to engage in realistic planning for her own care as her eyesight deteriorated. Frederica was observed at her day program and in the nursing home to return to her kind and sweet personality, although when her physical pain increased she would temporarily become more irritable. However, at these times she had care staff at home who were equipped to provide additional care and patience as well as medical intervention when appropriate. Frances began to feel more secure seeing that Frederica had adequate support

Frederica's family needed to re-interpret the meaning of their irritability in order to envision possible solutions and be open to trying them. Re-framing the problem as a desire to care for and protect each other helped them restructure their approach to mutual care to allow more caregivers into their family system and to deal more realistically with each person's limitations.

DISCUSSION AND CONCLUSION

Discussion of Cases

In the case of John and Cassie, a family systems perspective allowed them to recognize and interrupt the vicious circle of anxiety, avoidance, and withdrawal that undermined their marital happiness and their financial stability. Multi-generational exploration of beliefs about money combined with acknowledgement of the role money can play in autism intervention freed them to observe their patterns and make new choices. A paradoxical intervention escalated their experience of the looming financial crisis and unbalanced the system in order to make room for change. The result was an increase in financial stability and marital closeness as well as improved communication and teamwork as parents of a child with autism.

Grace was caught in a triangle with her parents, generated by the combination of their divorce, her life cycle stage (launching), their genuinely positive intentions toward her, and the nature of her disability. Reframing her problem behaviors as a systemic problem reduced her sense of shame, while assigning her the task of initiating sessions increased her sense of competence. Subsequently teaching her a cognitively based planning process without negatively judging her desires allowed her to learn the skills she needed to move toward the independence everyone in the family desired for her, including Grace herself. These changes resulted in a decrease of the severity of her problem behaviors because the patterns of interaction no longer maintained them as successfully.

Frederica, her mother, and her sister were caught in a time of life that is stressful for many families – aging and later life dependency. Due to the family's long-held beliefs about their roles and, more importantly, how to manifest those roles, they were unable prior to therapy to step out of the destructive pattern of irritability and unmet needs for closeness. Re-framing their struggle as part of a natural developmental process, uncovering their unspoken desires and needs, and offering a way to meet those needs allowed them to find greater emotional closeness through greater physical separation.

In all these cases the families' ability to use therapy effectively also depended on their strengths and resilience. John and Cassie were close and committed to the marriage and their children, actively involved in learning about autism and had previously overcome debt. Grace had two parents who spoke to each other regularly despite divorce, tried to collaborate in supporting her, and had a great deal of empathy and sympathy for her experience. Grace herself had the intellect and the reading skills to learn the new planning techniques, a track record of being resourceful and assertive with her support team, as well as a strong desire to eliminate her problem behaviors. Frances and Frederica had a long history of companionship and successful care giving, as well as a reliable and available support person, Jody. These strengths and resources enabled these families to utilize therapy more fully, and acknowledging and building on them enabled the therapist to be more effective.

None of these cases specifically illustrate the manner in which concentrically expanding systems beyond the primary family system might also require systemic intervention. Sometimes such intervention is beyond the capacity of an individual therapist, but it is essential at a minimum for the therapist to know about and identify the impact of systems of care and support on individuals with ID/DD and their families. For example, the therapist's familiarity with the external system of autism intervention was a significant part of building a hypothesis in John and Cassie's case; in Grace's case a similar familiarity provided awareness of the absence of early intervention due to her late diagnosis, delineating a possible gap in individual and family skill relative to Grace's disability.

Conclusions

For families living with ID/DD, psychotherapy can be an effective option for support and solution. Systems theory can strengthen the family and the individual's receptivity to psychotherapeutic intervention, as well as strengthen the success of the intervention. Systems theory acknowledges and works with the reality of interdependence which affects all individuals and more profoundly affects the lives of those with ID/DD.

Systems theory enlivened many fields of endeavor when it emerged. Unfortunately, the application of family systems theory in therapy has often proved difficult to study, whether measuring outcome or process. To gather the literature, even on non-empirical research, that combines family systems theory with ID/DD families is complicated because it comes from multiple fields and genres.

The best approach to future research on applying family systems theory with families with ID/DD will be to attempt descriptive process research first, in order to clarify the terms of measurement and accurately describe the process of family systems therapy. This information could then be applied to experimental studies and outcome research using multiple models with narrow subsets of populations or specific manualized models with multiple populations. If even a few researchers in family therapy will bravely accept the added complication of developmental or intellectual disability, through a patient accumulation of such research the field will eventually be able to demonstrate more specifically which families, which disabilities, which problems, and which intervention models are best served by family systems theory.

In the meantime the option of using family systems theory as a meta-theory continues to provide a creative option for therapists working with ID/DD issues. For family therapists who would like to work more effectively with clients with developmental and intellectual disabilities, family systems theory offers a viable alternative, particular as a filter or lens for viewing the problems. For clinicians already working with clients with developmental and intellectual disabilities, family systems theory offers a way to conceptualize presenting problems in light of the "persistent web" in which our clients live. This perspective can be applied alongside other theoretical perspectives, to enrich understanding of the problem and to expand opportunities for change.

REFERENCES

Baum, S., & Lynggaard, H. (Eds.). (2006). *Intellectual disabilities: A systemic approach*. London: Karnac.

Beavers, J., Hampson, R.B., Hulgus, Y.F., & Beavers, W.R. (1986). Coping in families with a retarded child. *Family Process, 25*, 365-378.

Bouras, N. (Ed.). (1999). *Psychiatric and behavioral disorders in developmental disabilities and mental retardation*. Cambridge: Cambridge University Press.

Bouras, N. (Ed.). (2007). *Psychiatric and behavioral disorders in intellectual and developmental disabilities.* Cambridge: Cambridge University Press.

Carr, A. (2009a). The effectiveness of family therapy and systemic interventions for adult-focused problems. *Journal of Family Therapy, 31,* 46-74.

Carr, A. (2009b). The effectiveness of family therapy and systemic interventions for child-focused problems. *Journal of Family Therapy, 31,* 3-45.

Cottrell, D., & Boston, P. (2002). Practitioner review: The effectiveness of systemic family therapy for children and adolescents. *Journal of Child Psychology and Psychiatry, 43(5),* 573-586.

Dosen, A., Leibenluft, E., & Day, K. (Eds.). (2001). *Treating mental illness and behavior disorders in children and adults with mental retardation.* Arlington, VA: American Psychiatric Publishing, Inc.

Fiddell, B. (2000). Exploring the use of family therapy with adults with a learning disability. *Journal of Family Therapy, 22,* 308-323.

Fletcher, R. J. (Ed.). (1999). *Therapy approaches for persons with mental retardation.* Kingston, NY: The NADD Press.

Foster, M. A. (1988) A systems perspective and families of handicapped children. *Journal of Family Psychology, (*September), 54-56.

Goldberg, D., Magrill, L., Hale, J., Damaskinidou, K., Paul, J., & Tham, S. (2005). Protection and loss: Working with learning-disabled adults and their families. *Journal of Family Therapy, 17,* 263-280.

Goldenberg, I., & Goldenberg, H. (2007). *Family therapy: An overview.* Belmont, CA: Brooks Cole.

Hennicke, K., & Bradl, C. (1990). Systemic family therapy and mental retardation. In A. Dosen, A. Van Gennep, G.J. Zwanniken, G.J. (Eds.), *Treatment of Mental Illness and Behavioral Disorder in the Mentally Retarded. Proceedings of the International Congress, May 3rd and May 4th, 1990. Amsterdam, the Netherlands.* Leiden, the Netherlands: Logon Publications.

Lebow, J. L., & Gurman, A.S. (1995). Research assessing couple and family therapy. *Annual Review of Psychology, 46,* 27-57.

Lindebaum, L. (1999). Family therapy supporting parents of a young adult with dual diagnosis during the transition to adulthood. In Fletcher, R. (Ed.), *Therapy approaches for persons with mental retardation* (pp. 113-126). Kingston, NY: The NADD Press.

Lynch, C. (2004). Psychotherapy for persons with mental retardation. *Mental Retardation, 42 (5),* 399-405.

Marshak, L. E., Seligman, M., & Prezant, F. (1999). *Disability and the family life cycle.* New York, NY: Basic Books.

Miller, R., Johnson, L., Sandberg, J.G., Stringer-Seibold, T.A., & Gfeller-Strouts, L. (2000). An addendum to the 1997 outcome research chart. *The American Journal of Family Therapy, 28*, 347-354.

Power, P. W., & Dell Orto, A. E. (2004). *Families living with chronic illness and disability.* New York, NY: Springer Publishing Company.

Prout, H. T., & Nowak-Drabik, K. M. (2003). Psychotherapy with persons who have mental retardation: An evaluation of effectiveness. *American Journal on Mental Retardation, 108*(2), 82-93.

Ramisch, J. L., & Franklin, D. (2008). Families with a member with mental retardation and the ethical implications of therapeutic treatment by marriage and family therapists. *The American Journal of Family Therapy, 36*, 312-322.

Ramisch, J. L., Pavkov, T., Negash, S., & Wetchler, J. (2009). Parental burden among families with children having disabilities: The role of ADHD and mental health disorders. *The NADD Bulletin, 12*, 67-73.

Rolland, J. S. (1994). *Families, illness and disability: An integrative treatment model.* New York: Basic Books.

Rotthaus, W. (2001). Systemic therapy. In A. Dosen, E. Leibenluft, and K. Day (Eds.), *Treating mental illness and behavior disorders in children and adults with mental retardation* (pp. 167-180). Arlington, VA: American Psychiatric Publishing, Inc.

Sandberg, J.G., Johnson, L.N., Dermber, S.B., Gfeler-Strouts, L.L., Seibold, J.M., Stringer-Seibold, T.A., et al. (1997). Demonstrated efficacy of models of marriage and family therapy: An update of Gurman, Kniskern, and Pinsolf's chart. *The American Journal of Family Therapy, 25*, 121-137.

Seligman, M., & Darling, R. B. (2007). *Ordinary families, special children: A systems approach to childhood disability* (3rd ed.). New York: The Guilford Press.

Thomas, V., & Ray, K. (2006). Counseling exceptional individuals and their families: A systems perspective. *Professional School Counseling 10*, 58-65.

Turnbull, A. P., Patterson, J.M., Behr, S.K., Murphy, D.L., Marquis, J.G., & Blue-Banning, M.J. (1993). *Cognitive coping, families and disability.* Baltimore: Paul H. Brookes Publishing Co.

Vetere, A. (1996). The neglect of family systems ideas and practice in services for children and young people with learning disabilities. *Clinical Child Psychology and Psychiatry, 1*, 485-488.

Vetere, A., & Dallos, R. (2003). *Working systemically with families: Formulation, intervention and evaluation.* London: Karnac.

CHAPTER 11

Couple Therapy for People with Intellectual Disabilities: A Positive Treatment Model[1]

J. Dale Munro, M.S.W., RSW, FAAIDD

"There ain't no cure for love!"
Leonard Cohen (1988)

INTRODUCTION

Teenagers and adults with intellectual disabilities often dream about finding love, moving in together, getting married and having children. Even in our post modern society, marriage and parenthood still constitute two of the defining stages in the journey from childhood to adulthood (May & Simpson, 2003). Yet, when considering people with intellectual disabilities, this topic can raise deep anxieties, confusion and misunderstanding in family members, professionals, the general public, and the individuals themselves. Historically, there has been resistance to people with intellectual disabilities becoming companions, living together, or marrying, due in large part to fears about them procreating and "contaminating the gene pool". This resistance took the form of legal restrictions on marriage, eugenic laws leading to forced sterilizations, and at one time, many admissions to institutions (Kempton & Kahn, 1991). However, throughout history, many individuals married, raised children and did not come to the attention of service providers because they were able to manage (Koller, Richardson & Katz, 1988).

In the early 1960's, attitudes started to change. Society began to more openly discuss the topic of sexual expression, love, and marriage concerning people with intellectual disabilities. In the United States, the President's Task Force on Law (1963) emphasized that marriage should not be categorically denied for people with intellectual disabilities. By then, most people with disabilities were living longer; and their adulthood, at least in a biological sense, could no longer be denied. The sexual revolution of the 1960s, along with advances in birth control methods, had the effect

---

[1]Revision and expansion of an article published in *The NADD Bulletin*, September/October 2007.

of decoupling sex from procreation. This removed one of the principle objections to love relationships and marriage for people with intellectual disabilities (May & Simpson, 2003). Also, research demonstrated that the eugenics fear about an exponential increase in, and overpopulation by, people with disabilities just had not occurred (Cochran, 1974). By the 1980s, spiritual leaders such as Jean Vanier, had begun to suggest that some people with intellectual disabilities could be "married more or less successfully" and could find inner stability and peace in a committed relationship (Vanier, 1985).

Unfortunately today, even with these societal advances, many couples with intellectual disabilities have problems accessing counseling services because therapists often assume that "they are not good counseling candidates". Based on four decades of work as a couple and family therapist, the author believes that no clinical work is as exciting and rewarding – or as potentially challenging – as counseling and trying to improve the emotional functioning and relationships of couples with intellectual disabilities. The purpose of this chapter is to review literature on the topic of marriage and committed relationships for people with intellectual disabilities, offer case examples, and present an effective couple intervention model. *"A couple" is defined as two people closely associated, bonded, or paired with each other, at least one of whom functions in the mild or moderate range of intellectual disability. A couple can be a man and a woman—or a same-sex relationship – engaged, married, living together or in a committed love relationship.*[2]

Reviewing Marital Research

One of the most heavily discussed, written about, and researched topics in the history of the intellectual disability field relates to marriage and parenting. Despite methodological weaknesses in many studies (e.g., one versus both members of the couple having an intellectual disability), the findings are still interesting. Hall (1974) reviewed fifteen studies going as far back as the1920's and concluded there was considerable evidence that people with intellectual disabilities frequently had "successful marriages" (i.e., no separations or divorces). Bass (1964) reviewed literature beginning in the 1940s and noted there was an increasing recognition of the ability of many people with intellectual disabilities to hold a job, marry, and support themselves. She made a strong case for voluntary sterilization and no children.

Andron and Sturm (1973) surveyed 12 couples and found that they overwhelmingly felt that the companionship of marriage was much better than single life. Mattinson (1973) completed one of the most frequently quoted studies. Her research in-

---

[2] Although not the main focus of this article, it is worth noting that many of the counselling and support approaches described here often can benefit other configurations of "couples," such as resolving conflict or other issues between an individual with a disability and a parent or sibling; between roommates living in supported living settings, or between parents of individuals with intellectual disabilities.

vestigated 36 marriages where both partners had intellectual disabilities, many of whom had been previously institutionalized. The majority of the couples (25) were affectionate, happy, and felt their lives were better married than single. Most helped each other and worked on a complementary basis, where the skill of one partner supplemented an inability of the other ["He does the reading , and I do the writing."]. Edgerton (1967) reported that a striking feature of the lives of people formerly institutionalized was that being married was perceived as "a highly meaningful status to achieve". Thirty of the 48 individuals studied were married, 18 were married to non-disabled individuals, and only 4 were divorced or separated. Most of the individuals held strongly negative feelings about being involuntarily sterilized when institutionalized.

Floor, Baxter, Rosen, and Zisfein (1975) did a follow-up study of previously institutionalized people regarding marriage and children. They found the children were fairly well cared for, at least in their early years. Frequent couple problems included chronically poor health of one partner, erratic employment, money management, and interference from "demanding relatives". Marriages did better when one partner had average intelligence and when a relative, landlord, or employer supported them. Married people showed fewer social and personal problems (e.g., lawbreaking, work or alcohol-related problems) than single adults. The study concluded that couples needed practical training in budgeting and money management, basic sex education, birth control, and the availability of a community advocate.

Munro (1977) surveyed adults with intellectual disabilities residing in a large institution. In terms of discharge planning, most respondents expressed a strong desire to learn more about marriage, second only in importance to finding a community job. Ann and Michael Craft (1979) completed a pilot study of 25 marriages and a more detailed investigation of 45 other couples. Length of marriages had lasted up to 25 years. Findings suggested a better marital "success rate" and chance of happiness than the population at large.

Timmers, DuCharme, and Jacob (1981) found that the majority of surveyed adults with intellectual disabilities wanted to be married and have children. Koller et al. (1988) concluded that about half of the adults were in marriages that "appear to be going well." Kempton and Kahn (1991) found that married couples with intellectual disabilities had about the same chance of divorcing as non-disabled couples, and they preferred marriage over single life. They argued that while community integration for people with intellectual disabilities is typically narrowly defined in terms of vocational and residential placement, integration needs to be broadened to consider companionship and love.

What Brings Couples Together?

Modern society sometimes has been associated with alienation and loneliness, with an overemphasis on materialism, individuality, and the breakdown of traditional social institutions and support networks (Keefe, 1984). This sense of aloneness may be particularly intense for people with disabilities who too often have experienced rejection, isolation, abuse, economic deprivation, and marginalization. Almost everyone, including people with intellectual disabilities, on some level probably craves close intimate relationships and the possibility of a committed relationship with someone special. Many of these individuals fantasize about moving in together. Others dream about a grand marriage ceremony, a big reception, and maybe even wedding gifts, being the center of attention, and having "someone to call their own." Despite high separation and divorce rates (in the general population) and many people choosing to "live together," our society is still geared towards marriage, not only as the major expression of our gender roles, but also as the only fully accepted vehicle for parenthood and sexual expression (Bidgood, 1975). Recent, intense advocacy for legally-recognized marriage within the gay and lesbian community further supports this notion.

For many people (disabled and able), marriage is the most important developmental milestone in life. It signifies admission into adulthood, affirmation or competency as a sexual person, and becoming part of the cultural tapestry of society (Bernardo, 1981). As well, some studies in the general population suggest that married life contributes to one's overall well-being and psychological health, and married people tend to live longer, have better mental health and have a richer quality of life (Waite & Gallagher, 1981). For people with intellectual disabilities, marriage sometimes can offer richer and more satisfying companionship, an expanded social support network, and a channel for socially acceptable sexual expression. Close intimate relationships can act as a 'shock absorber' to help cope with frustrations, disappointments, and the insensitivity of others. Research suggests that increased social support for people with disabilities is positively correlated with an improved quality of life and mental health (Lunsky & Neely, 2002).

It is worth noting that people (disabled and able) often select partners they hope will be selfless, strong, and the "good parent" they once had or wished they had. There are often unconscious attractions that result in people tending to select partners that recreate their family of origin, or one that is diametrically opposed (Satir, 1967). There are sexual and biological attractions, as well as shared (good and painful) experiences, that lead to further bonding (Toufexis, 1993). All these factors together are sometimes referred to as 'chemistry.' As with all couples, but particularly among couples with disabilities, partners frequently compensate for the other person's weaknesses or vulnerabilities (e.g., a blind person is a good money-handler, while the sighted partner is able to drive). Other people can share expenses and combine disability pensions, so they have a better quality of life (Mattinson, 1970). Such sharing and mutual support tends to strengthen couples and helps empower them to become better connected and self-reliant.

THE "POSITIVE SUPPORT-COUPLE THERAPY" MODEL

As noted above, there is a wealth of research suggesting that couples with intellectual disabilities can have successful love relationships. Surprisingly, however, little literature exists regarding clinical interventions for these couples. Couples, themselves, along with their families, frequently report difficulties in finding therapists willing to work with them. With this in mind, the author has developed an intervention model that combines many of the best elements of established therapy approaches, with strategies that recognize the complexity of these couples and their support systems. The author calls this the "Positive Support-Couple Therapy" Model (PSCT Model). It is particularly helpful where there is a great need for collaboration among the couple, the extended family, and the service system. This level of collaboration is typically needed by couples with intellectual disabilities to maintain successful relationships. By proposing this model, the author wishes to make a strong case for generic community therapists to become more open to working with these couples.

Therapeutic Stance: Being Unconditionally Positive

The PSCT Model incorporates many elements of the "strength-based social work perspective" (Russo, 1999; Saleeby, 1992), "positive psychology" (Seligman & Csikszentmihalyi, 2000) and "unconditionally constructive mediation" (Munro, 1997). This model provides a positive foundation from which to build effective working relationships with the couple, their extended families and service system representatives. Real problems are not ignored. But *this perspective focuses on what is right, rather than what is wrong with the couple and other significant people in their lives.* Couple resilience, resourcefulness, and one's ability to rebound from past trauma, rejection, and ostracism are emphasized. The PSCT Model also draws ideas from Integrative Couple Therapy with its emphasis on cognitive-behavioral strategies, support, empathy, no-violence contracts, and acceptance of partner traits that cannot be changed (Jacobson & Christensen, 1996). Another contributor to the PSCT Model is Narrative Therapy with a focus on social justice and liberation through the development of alternative, empowering stories (White, 1995). It also draws upon traditional couple treatment stressing a conjoint, social systems orientation, along with efforts to improve interpersonal communication (Satir, 1967).

To a large extent, treatment success depends on the therapist's persistence, high energy, unflappable optimism, flexibility, knowledge of community resources, persuasiveness, and sometimes the ability to be satisfied with small gains. Interviews and meetings should focus on "here and now" issues. Even more so than with other populations, professionals should use words and phrases already part of the couple's vocabulary: speak in a simpler, more concrete manner, and avoid using jargon. Therapists must show patience and understanding, since these individuals quite frequently show up for appointments too early, or late, because precise time-telling is sometimes difficult for some of them. As well, the hygiene, etiquette, and clothing of these couples may not always be up to 'nice middleclass standards'. But this does not mean that their love is unreal or that their desire to be closer and happier, is not genuine.

In working with these couples, professionals must recognize *the power of casual small talk, simple kindness, empathic listening, a sense of humor, and sharing a coffee together* as a low-key starting point in building a positive relationship and therapeutic alliance. Because these individuals frequently have faced social ostracism and rejection, this can result in a greater tendency for approval-seeking. Therefore, therapists must try to ensure that couple assertiveness and empowerment, community integration, and the pursuit of *their* dreams and liberation is a real therapy outcome.

Four Alternative Roles for the Couple Therapist

Therapists using the PSCT Model must determine which role they might play, to better manage their professional time and to best help the couple and the people around them:

1. The couple therapist may play *a consultant role*, providing formal educational presentations or offering clinical advice to other couple therapists, community agencies, clergyor family representatives. This involves little face-to-face involvement with the couple and usually involves the smallest time commitment.

2. The therapist can act as *an outside mediator* who is brought in as an impartial third party to meet with key people and to help resolve complicated couple-family, couple-agency or agency-family disputes (Munro, 1997).

3. The professional may work directly with the couple -- playing *a role similar to more traditional couple therapists* with a contracted number of conjoint sessions. Since the self-reports of people with cognitive limitations at times can be somewhat misleading, a key feature of the PSCT Model is that *a trusted staff from a local support agency who knows the partners well is often asked to act as a co-therapist.* This helps monitor whether what is learned in the therapy is generalizing outside the professional's office and can contribute to real and positive change in the couple's relationship, their coping skills, and everyday life. For instance, in one case, the co-therapist followed-up a partner's complaint and found bird-droppings and feathers in every room, over every square foot of the couple's apartment. This became a prime counselling issue and in the end resolving this problem was significant in furthering the couple's emotional and developmental growth.

4. On occasion, the couple therapist may provide *individual counseling to one of the partner, or make a referral to a clinical specialist* to deal with serious individual concerns that impact the relationship (e.g., past trauma, sexuality concerns, substance abuse, serious anger, or grief issues).

Assessing the Couple, the Extended Family, and the Service System

Utilizing the PSCT Model, referrals are welcomed from the couple, professionals, clergy, or family. The assessment process usually begins over the telephone when arranging for the first interview. Clues can be picked up regarding couple and family hostility, potential for cooperation, and the nature of the couple's previous contact with agencies or professionals. From the very beginning, professionals must show empathy and sensitivity and present themselves as people who have knowledge, hopefulness, and compassion.

In contrast to assessment methods utilized by most couple therapists, the PSCT Model suggests some differences for people with intellectual disabilities. For instance, *besides assessing the couple, the therapist sometimes asks the couple's permission to meet with the extended family and the support agencies involved* to determine how helpful these 'outsiders' are in the everyday life of the couple. Some family members (particularly parents or adult siblings) may exert powerful influence over the couple, to the point of overcontrol, overinvolvement, even sabotage (Munro, 2007). As well, since women and men with intellectual disabilities are much more susceptible to sexual abuse (Barger, Wacker, Macy & Parish, 2009; Randall, Parrila & Sobsey, 2000), and women more prone to domestic abuse (Welner, 1999), professionals must be sensitive to this possibility during the assessment process. Gathering a thorough biopsychosocial history (including knowledge about past love relationships and counseling successes) of each partner is recommended.

During interviews, careful attention should be paid to couple and family dynamics (i.e., potent underlying forces), the clarity of family roles, and the effectiveness of boundary-setting; problem-solving and decision-making patterns; feelings of safety; housing and financial stability; family discord and past problems and the current health of the couple and the extended family, including psychiatric difficulties. Professionals must *listen with a "third ear"* – not only to what is being said, but also to what people are really saying (i.e., nonverbal meta-communication). Throughout, the therapist and co-therapist must be sensitive to the cultural or religious backgrounds of the partners and other significant people in their lives.

A useful focal point for initial assessment interviews with the couple, and possibly the extended family, may include exploring family photo albums. This can act as a catalyst for discussion and can give therapists a glimpse of how the couple and the extended family relate to each other. The assessment should note areas of couple and extended family strength, cohesion, affection, mutual support, and how well the couple is integrated into the everyday lives of their families and community. The therapist, with the help of the co-therapist, must also assess the level of agency support the couple receives, with attention to the attitude, accessibility, and availability of needed services.

Throughout the helping process, *professionals must remain in tune with intervention outcomes important to the couple* ["What outcome would you like to see by the time we are done working together?"]. After carefully analyzing the couple, their families, and the support system, professionals should begin to *develop working hypotheses* (to be continually updated and revised throughout the intervention process) about what may be contributing to the couple's current difficulties and what might be done to resolve them. Also, as clinical information is gathered, the couple's potential for a "successful" relationship can be estimated in a general sense, by comparing the couple's history and current situation against the checklist found in Figure 1.

Figure 1. Assessing Couples: Check Marks for 'Successful' Relationships

Many couples with intellectual disabilities have long, happy and satisfying relationships. Others do not. What really contributes to successful couple relationships? Billingsley et al. (2005) reviewed five decades of couple research regarding criteria for marital success in the general population. With these studies in mind, combined with the author's extensive clinical experience, the checklist below can begin to suggest what constitutes a successful relationship. **Think of a specific couple that you want to assess. Compare them against each of the factors listed below. More checkmarks suggest a happier, more stable and successful relationship.**

------✓There is no couple violence, over-control, or fear of partner (i.e., partners feel safe).
------✓Both partners perceive their relationship as "special."
------✓There is a sense of commitment, loyalty, and permanence to the relationship.
------✓They have similar values regarding sexual fidelity.
------✓There are physical and verbal expressions of love, affection, and intimacy.
------✓They have shared expectations about the frequency and type of sexual relations.
------✓Good couple teamwork and problem-solving is demonstrated.
------✓The partners are compatible in terms of temperament and personality.
------✓Mental health concerns are absent or successfully treated.
------✓They agree about whether to have children, birth control, and family planning
------✓They share some similar interests, activities, and personal values.
------✓They maintain some separate interests and activities from their partner.
------✓They are positive with, and show appreciation towards, each other.
------✓They have stable and supportive family and friendship networks.
------✓They have adequate agency and professional supports, when needed.
------✓They are 'best friends' and good companions.
------✓They respect each other's spiritual convictions (or lack of belief).
------✓They have a steady income and manage finances well (sometimes with support).
------✓They had a significant courtship (e.g., 3 years) before marriage, or moving-in together.
------✓They have a 'spark' or 'chemistry' that holds couple together during "difficult times".
------✓They demonstrate good conflict resolution and anger management skills.
------✓They like to celebrate special occasions (e.g., birthdays, anniversaries, religious events).
------✓They exhibit good parenting skills and enjoy being around their children.
------✓They divide-up household responsibilities, chores, and child-care.
------✓They complement each other by compensating for the other's weaknesses or vulnerabilities.
------✓They can effectively "stand up to" disapproval from strong-willed family or others.
------✓They are willing to go for counselling, parenting help, or mental health treatment, if needed.
------✓They do not abuse alcohol or illegal drugs.
------✓They are not addicted to gambling, Internet use, or video games.
------✓They have never faced eviction because of noise, property destruction, or hygiene complaints.
------✓They have some fun together almost every day.

Intervening with Couples, Extended Family and Service Systems

Because people with intellectual disabilities often have very involved families, upon whom they can be very dependent, *separate sessions with concerned relatives may be a significant part of the therapeutic process to help the couple.* The couple's parents, siblings, or grandparents may have many strong (sometimes misguided) opinions about the couple and their suitability for each other: whether they should go out, move in together, marry, or have children. Families may also be concerned about wills and estate planning; budgeting and money management; housekeeping, hygiene, proper food preparation and refrigeration; the partner's physical health; or the partner's propensity for genetic problems (e.g., Down Syndrome leading to early onset dementia). Families may worry that one of the partners is sexually 'promiscuous' or shows other 'high-risk behavior' (e.g., hanging out at strip clubs, unprotected sex) or criminal or abusive tendencies.

Therapists should view the strategic use of (well-timed and appropriate) humor, frankness, cheerleading, and brief inspirational or motivational talks as important tools for reducing anxiety and defensiveness when working with couples, their families, or service system representatives. Also, family representatives will need honest feedback and reassurance from therapists and agencies around five critical questions concerning the couple: (1) Is my adult child/relative physically and emotionally safe in this relationship? (2) Is my adult child/relative really happy with this partner? (3) Are money management, daily living, and health needs going to be properly met? (4) Is reliable birth control in place to prevent unwanted pregnancy? (5) Are they receiving enough, and the right kind, of agency support?

At the same time, if a couple is experiencing serious problems accessing services or supports, the therapist and co-therapist may combine forces with the couple and other significant people including family and local agencies to organize special *"couple-centered planning"* meetings. These meetings are held regularly (e.g., every 4-8 weeks) for several months or much longer if needed, to address practical problems. Planning meetings can help to improve networking, information sharing, and communication among key people and encourage creative problem-solving while permitting the expression of deeply-held concerns. Advocacy for improving clinical services and agency and "instrumental" supports (e.g., housing, child-care, reliable transportation, employment, budgeting, etc.) for the couple also may be organized. Figure 2 outlines some of the "points of intervention," including the possibility of couple-centered planning meetings, that can greatly improve a couple's life together.

Figure 2. Helping Couples: Points of Intervention

There are several points of clinical, agency or "instrumental" intervention that can have a dramatic affect in improving the lives of couples with intellectual disabilities. As well, regular "Couple-Centered Planning Meetings" can help strengthen the overall planning and advocacy process.

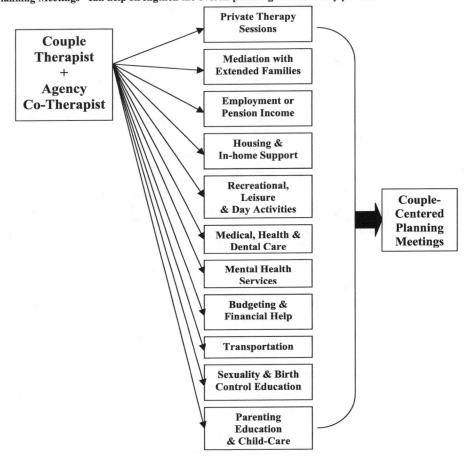

Ethics, Self-Determination, and Decision-Making

The principle of self-determination is an ubiquitous ethical thread that weaves its way through almost every issue relating to decision-making by people with intellectual disabilities (Munro, 1982). Frequently, individuals with disabilities request help from therapists, agency professionals, or family members to assist them in making relationship and sexuality-related decisions. At other times, couples unilaterally make what appear to be unsafe, uninformed, seemingly irresponsible, or emotionally destructive decisions. Classic examples include partners who abuse alcohol or illegal drugs; demand unsafe or unprotected sex; misuse power or are violent with their partner; neglect or mistreat their children; exhibit suicidal or dangerous attention-seeking behavior; spend inordinate amounts of time and money in strip-clubs or on phone sex lines; face eviction because of excessive noise, property destruction or hygiene complaints; or chronically overspend and run into serious financial difficulties.

Figure 3 illustrates that when counselling or supporting couples with intellectual disabilities, it may at times be necessary from an ethical perspective to question the behavior of one or both partners, if extremely unhealthy or dangerous choices are being made. People with intellectual disabilities (like the rest of us) have a right to learn from mistakes, make ill-informed decisions, and experience the "dignity of risk" (Perske, 1972). But a person's right to self-determination and freedom must be counterbalanced against an individual's willingness and ability to act responsibly in respecting the law, consequences to others, and reasonable societal norms (Thiroux, 2004). In fact, emphasizing rights without responsibility can be a professional excuse to abandon couples to dangerous, socially inappropriate, and unhealthy choices. Ethically, "where to draw the line" is an issue every professional, agency representative, and family member must struggle with each and every day.

Figure 3. Couple Decision-Making: Balancing Rights with Responsibility

One area of decision-making with which individuals or couples commonly request help is in choosing their "best" relationship option. As a starting point, the couple therapists and agency representatives working with adults with intellectual disabilities need to recognize that marriage and living or being together are not for everyone (as is the case with the general population). The PSCT Model focuses on helping couples (often with input from extended families and agency support staff) to determine what relationship option best suits their needs and wishes. Decision-making in this area is often influenced by the degree of intellectual disability, whether one or both partners have serious physical or mental health concerns, ability to communicate, the passivity versus the natural assertiveness of the partners, or if there is potential for partner abuse or a misuse of power.

An ethical issue that often must be addressed is to determine if each partner can provide informed consent to become involved in a close, intimate, and often sexual relationship. To help clarify this, the PSCT Model makes use of the excellent guidelines outlined in "Policy for Determining Sexual Consent" created by YAI/National Institute for People with Disabilities Network (2004) and related information developed by Taverner and Demarco (2006). Agencies, professionals, and families face a delicate balancing act, as they try to ensure a person's right to sexual expression and relationship choice, while ensuring each partner's safety and well-being. When meeting with individuals or couples with disabilities, relationship options may include:

- Highly satisfying, platonic relationships involving someone more special than a friend (e.g., "boyfriend" or "girlfriend").
- A long-term sexual and intimate relationship, but living apart, may meet the needs of committed couples, when one or both partners have deep-seated issues relating to trust, autonomy, control, past trauma, or fears of abandonment.
- Marriage or 'common-law' relationships (with or without children) may work well for more independent and capable couples.
- Separation or divorce may be the best outcome in cases of couple incompatibility, abuse, or relentless family interference.
- At times, emotional relationships with imaginary friends or fantasies about certain people (e.g., famous celebrities or people in authority) may be quite healthy and life-giving. Except in extreme situations, this does not reflect mental illness, but simply a response to loneliness, isolation, or a vivid imagination. It has been noted that this is sometimes found in individuals with Down Syndrome (Hurley, 2008).

A meaningful life spent as a single person may be the only, or best, alternative for some individuals. Maintaining a relationship or finding a committed partner is not always possible. Sometimes it is necessary for professionals to help individuals reframe and accept their single lives and begin to perceive this as a positive and fairly common option for people in our society. Masturbation can be encouraged as a pleasurable sexual alternative when finding a partner is not possible (Hingsburger, 1995; Hingsburger & Haar, 2000). There are now some sex stores offering specialized consultation into the use of sex toys that are meaningful and healthy for people with disabilities (e.g., Cory Silverberg, info@comeasyouare.com). Also, for single individuals, agencies should focus on helping the person expand their social support network to compensate for their lack of a partner or possibly connect them with a friendship and partner introduction service for people with disabilities such as is offered by Soulful Encounters (www.soulfulencounters.com).

The Rainbow Connection

As in society in general, not all love relationships for people with intellectual disabilities are heterosexual. In recent years, professionals have noted that couples requesting or reaching out for support represent a wide spectrum of sexual expression. Partners are not only are straight, but gay, lesbian, bisexual, transgender, or questioning (GLBTQ). Many of the GLBTQ individuals report a history of harassment, discrimination, and bullying as a direct result of their sexuality and past relationships. Recent research from Britain has emphasized that the emotional and sexual health of people with intellectual disabilities who are GLBTQ is being jeopardized by the failure of many services to provide support (Abbott & Howarth, 2005, 2007).

Consider the case of Bill and Gord, both with a mild intellectual disability, who have lived together in a committed relationship for the past 6 years. They were very cautious about going for counselling because of many 'bad experiences' in the past with people in authority in school and agency systems. Finally, however, they referred themselves because "our fighting is getting out of hand." In approaching this couple, the therapists used a GLBTQ-affirmative therapeutic approach that does not pathologize alternative lifestyles; that recognizes heterosexual privilege (often resulting in shame for many GLBTQ individuals) in societal institutions, laws and customs; that informs couples of supportive community services and resources; and that requires that therapists continually screen themselves for covert homophobia (Kort, 2008). In Bill and Gord's case, it took 12 private couple sessions spaced-out over 30 weeks to help them. The therapists used a "Stop, Think, and Go" anger and jealousy management strategy (described later in Figure 4) and focused on helping each partner become more assertive, while learning to label and communicate feelings better.

Another approach that helped was to have three private mediation sessions with Bill's family who historically had been very rejecting towards Bill's gay orientation and his relationship with Gord. These sessions had a profound effect in helping Bill's family (especially his father and a brother) begin to accept and perceive the relationship as being healthy and positive. After this, for the first time, Bill and Gord started to enjoy going together to some family gatherings. As well, an effort was made to encourage the couple to expand their leisure and social network, with a special focus on connecting them with the innovative sprOUT Program at the Griffin Centre in Toronto which serves GLBTQ people with intellectual disabilities (www.griffin-centre.org). These strategies helped to reduce much of Bill and Gord's arguing, and their overall quality of life and ability to communicate with each other improved. Together they started to have more fun, they felt less isolated, and they began to reclaim their love for each other.

Violent and Abusive Relationships

Although many couples with intellectual disabilities have happy, peaceful, and loving relationships, there are situations where couples have acrimonious relationships which involve abuse and violence. Consider Mildred and Jack. They were married 19 years ago, right after being discharged from a large institution. Mildred (high borderline range of intelligence) had a history of early childhood abuse and serious mental health problems. Their relationship was marked by periods of calm, real affection and love for each other followed by extremely violent exchanges which would escalate to the point that Mildred would call the police. On three occasions, the courts convicted Jack of assault, and he was ordered to take part in anger-management classes offered by a local program for abusive men along with some individual counselling sessions. Unfortunately, Jack (a highly anxious and "stubborn" man) seemed to gain little from these sessions.

The anger between Mildred and Jack seemed fuelled by their complete inability to manage money and their overspending, as well as by violent mood swings and alcohol binges on Mildred's part. Agency personnel on several occasions tried to provide them with budgeting assistance; couple counseling was arranged, but they failed to show up for sessions; and they became more and more secretive and refused to answer the door or phone, when contacted by agency staff. Mildred received a disability pension, while Jack worked almost full-time at a local grocery store. Mildred could not stick with any employment but felt slighted when Jack came home tired from work and did not want to talk or do much with her. Their arguing seemed to grow worse on the weekends when they spent more time together. Mildred became very suspicious about how Jack spent money or how he spent his spare time, and their financial debt was creating tremendous animosity between them. About a year ago, their situation deteriorated to the point that Mildred was screaming and started to strike out at Jack, and, after absorbing this for several minutes, Jack struck back. Both bruised and bloodied, Mildred called the police. Jack was again handcuffed by police and taken away to jail for the fourth time in the last three years. The police explained that, as a feminist organization, they had been instructed to always arrest the man in these situations.

This last time, the judge threw the book at Jack. The judge put a restraining order on Jack to stay completely away from Mildred or face some "real" jail time.

The service agencies in the community then came to an agreement. The community mental health agency would monitor Mildred's situation; help her with medication, money management, counseling; and try to ensure that she attend social activities and psychiatric appointments. The developmental service agency agreed to work with Jack by helping him find another apartment; start working at another grocery store (unknown to Mildred); get his debt under control; and go for some court-ordered counseling.

Over the next two years, Mildred refused almost all of the mental health and support services offered to her. Jack still seemed secretive and begrudgingly attended counseling. He complained constantly about how Mildred was calling his relatives to try to learn where he now was living, and she was relentlessly doing everything possible to re-connect with him. The therapists constantly and firmly reminded Jack that if he did re-connect with Mildred, he would be facing extended jail time. This black and white consequence was clear enough that Jack really understood that this time, "the judge will come down hard on me." He became frightened that Mildred would find him, but deep inside he still dreamed about seeing her again. The therapists repeatedly explained that Jack had to build a solid wall ("a rigid boundary") between himself and Mildred, and Jack did a fairly good job of distancing himself from her and widening his social support network.

Recently, Jack showed up unannounced at the therapist's office. He was in tears. He explained that he had just learned that Mildred had been found dead (apparently from natural causes). Tragically, in so many ways, the only woman he ever really loved was gone. Grief counseling was offered Jack, but he failed to show up for any of the sessions. Sadly, there are some couples who are very difficult to help.

To Parent or Not to Parent? That Is the Question!

For couples seriously considering pregnancy, the PSCT Model neither encourages nor discourages this possibility. Parenthood, as a personal right, has been gaining ground over the past two decades (May & Simpson, 2003) – and it is assumed that there are competent and inadequate parents in both the disabled and the general populations. Research has demonstrated that many parents with intellectual disabilities can learn parenting skills and provide acceptable child-care, if given appropriate training and support (Aunos & Feldman, 2007).

It is not unusual for couples with intellectual disabilities requesting premarital or marriage counselling, to have already decided that they do not want children (Craft & Craft, 1979). However, couples seeking counselling around this issue should be *fully informed* about the responsibilities, challenges, and skills required to be adequate parents. Birth control and family planning options should also be presented -- and the couple's physician or public health nursemay be of assistance. For couples needing considerable support to ensure proper parenting, it is both ethical and necessary (with the couple's permission) for therapists to interview the couple's parents (potential grandparents), other involved family, and agency representatives to realistically determine how much support might be available and needed. Too often, families (especially potential grandparents) are already overwhelmed by responsibilities involved in supporting one or both of the partners. Facing the possibility of having to nurture a small child (along with the child's parents) can create a formidable challenge (Parr-Paulson, 1998).

In situations where there is suspicion that a child may be neglected or abused, it is imperative that professionals inform child protection authorities. The couple should know that this is a possibility – before conception, if possible. Couples who unrelentingly want children, still probably will have them regardless of the views of others. In the end, if the couple unilaterally moves ahead with pregnancy, professionals and agencies should do everything possible to ensure proper parenting and child-care.

Premarital Preparation

The PSCT Model recommends that couples with intellectual disabilities contemplating marriage should take part in some formal preparation. Generally speaking, after some initial anxiety, many individuals with intellectual disabilities tend to thoroughly enjoy and are highly motivated to take part. Couple therapists experienced with people with intellectual disabilities may provide this service themselves, or they can make themselves available as consultants to other therapists, educators, agencies, clergy, or faith groups involved in this kind of work.

Two approaches to premarital preparation and marriage education have been traditionally used with people with disabilities, sometimes in combination with each other (Bernardo 1981):

1. Individual-Conjoint Premarital Counselling is the most common approach used with couples with intellectual disabilities. This method utilizes a combination of individual and couple counselling sessions. *This approach is the method most often used with couples with intellectual disabilities and by this author.*

2. Group Marriage Preparation may also be available. These groups, made up of a series of sessions structured around specific topics, are often available through faith communities or some agencies. It is worth noting that group approaches may be rather intimidating for some individuals with intellectual disabilities, especially if the group is made up of people with average intelligence who may seem economically, verbally, and intellectually "superior" to them. There may be less of a problem, and often it is very well received, if the "marriage preparation" is offered by a faith group or agency with whom the couple is already familiar or if a support person accompanies them. Role-play, artwork exercises (e.g., making a collage of magazine pictures of "What marriage will look like"), guest speakers, and homework assignments are sometimes utilized (Hartman & Hynes, 1975).

Premarital counselling and education must be supportive, use sexuality-positive language, and discuss issues in a highly concrete and pragmatic manner. Topics discussed should include the joys, as well as one's readiness for the responsibilities, of marriage; sexuality education and discussion of related concerns; birth control and parenting responsibilities; necessary income and money management; couple decision-making and divisions of labor; conflict management, learning to label feelings, self-assertion and stress management; housekeeping, cleanliness and hygiene issues; health, diet, food preparation and refrigeration; and leisure activities together and apart (Hartman & Hynes 1975; Walker 1977):

Private Sessions: What Couple Therapists Need to Know!

There appears to be systemic biases among many experienced therapists to work with couples with intellectual disabilities. It is not uncommon to hear therapists make erroneous statements that these couples are "too low functioning" or "lack the insight to be good counselling candidates." Yet, nothing could be further from the truth, especially for many adults functioning in the moderate or mild range of intellectual disability.

Private couple sessions are an important part of the PSCT Model. Therapy usually involves a short-term, action-oriented, contracted approach of six to twelve sessions spaced out every two to four weeks -- later augmented by occasional "booster sessions", if needed. On occasion, longer-term therapy might be required. Biased therapists may assume that these individuals are incapable of "insight" (i.e., affecting action through understanding). In fact, many adults have some capacity to consciously change behavioral and cognitive patterns as a result of psychodynamic and behavioral insight, at least on a basic and practical level. Some have wisdom, intuition, and verbal and memory skills well beyond assessed intellectual functioning, and these couples are often refreshingly honest and motivated to accept help.

Private sessions, along with therapeutic listening and clinical note-taking, can reinforce for couple's the notion that their relationship is special and significant. *Being really listened to ("active" or "empathic listening") is a powerful therapeutic tool*, since individuals with intellectual disabilities often have a history of being ignored, put off, or not being taken seriously by others. Couples can improve communication, self-assertion, problem-solving, and coping skills; develop better teamwork and cohesion with their partner; resolve deep hurts and misunderstandings; and with extra practice can become more skilled at clarifying, labelling, and channelling intense feelings.

Couples with intellectual disabilities tend to distrust clinicians who are too formal, pedantic, patronizing, and serious. A therapist axiom for "hooking" couples into the counseling process might be: *"Make sessions positive and fun, and half the work is done!"* Most individuals with intellectual disabilities have a great sense of humor and love to learn, but on their terms and often at a slower pace. With this in mind, the following strategies (sometimes skilfully modified from traditional counselling methods) can be helpful:

1. *Interviews usually should be held in the privacy of a therapist's office.* Because these individuals may have memory and scheduling difficulties, it is usually wise to call the couple ahead of time to remind them of the next session. Sometimes couples ask the therapist to come to their apartment or home for sessions, since many support agencies provide service in this manner. The therapist may do this, if the couple presents serious physical and mobility challenges. However, showing a willingness to come to the therapist's office can provide a general clue as to the couple's motivation for accepting help can nudge them away from the rigidity of their daily routines, and avoids in-home distractions.

2. When interviewing people with cognitive limitations, *frequent repetition of clinical impressions and advice* is often necessary, followed by a request that the couple repeat what has been said to ensure they understand. If individuals still seem confused, therapists should speak in a slower, clearer, more succinct manner, and request eye contact. Because generalization of learning for these individuals can disappear between sessions (especially at first), it is helpful to review the content of previous sessions at the start of each interview. Over time, as the information is repeated again and again, messages usually are retained.

3. The structured, specific, more directive nature of *cognitive-behavioral counseling strategies* (Burns, 1980; Jacobson & Christensen, 1996) seem particularly well suited for working with couples with intellectual disabilities. "Cognitive distortions" (e.g., "catastrophizing") can be explained simply as "ways your thoughts are playing tricks on you." *Behavioral rehearsal or role-play,* used in conjunction with *relaxation training,* can be a particularly effective and often enjoyable learning tool. Couples can rehearse ways of improving interactional skills with partners (e.g., appropriate sexual advances), learn to deal with anxiety-producing situations (e.g., meeting the inlaws, gay couples 'coming out' to their family), or practice self-assertion strategies for coping with domineering relatives or friends.

4. Better *management of anger, jealousy, and conflict* is a therapy outcome frequently requested by one or both partners, or their extended families. The PSCT Model supports the feminist belief that couple therapy not continue when one partner presents extreme abuse or battering. Yet, with "low-level violence" (e.g., threats, pushing, and other physical aggression without battering), there is often value in treating the couple together (Jacobson & Christensen, 1996; Nichols & Swartz, 2004). As illustrated in Figure 4, partners can be taught simple but effective strategies, such as the *"Stoplight: STOP/THINK/GO Approach"* of anger and jealousy management. As well, couples can be taught concrete "rules for fair fighting" (Bach & Wynden, 1968), such as no physical violence, focus on the "here and now" (not old hurts), and avoid global terms (e.g., "bitch", "jerk").

Figure 4. Anger & Jealousy: The "Stop, Think & Go Approach"

Anger and jealousy can be a persistent and damaging dynamic in the relationships of couples with intellectual disabilities. One strategy that can really help is the "Stoplight: STOP, THINK & GO Approach." First, the partner or couple is given a stoplight picture to visualize, similar to the one below. Then the therapist supports the individual or couple through the process described in Steps 1 through 6. Couples often find this strategy simple to learn and very helpful.

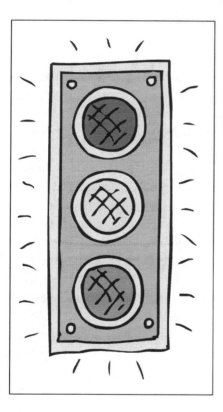

Step 1
Assist the partner or couple to identify times, situations, feelings & other signs that she or he is becoming enraged or jealous.

Step 2
Role-play or practice in a mirror what it looks like to be angry or jealous, focusing on the tension in the body (e.g., clenched fists, facial expressions, etc.).

Step 3
Role-play or practice in a mirror what it looks like to be relaxed (e.g., loose like a rag doll).

Step 4
Ask the partner or couple to visualize a traffic light with signals: Stop (red), Think (amber) & Go (green).

Step 5
Teach the partner or couple the words "Stop & Think" as a cognitive cue that the anger or jealousy is escalating; that 'bad' consequences could occur; & that calmness is needed.

Step 6
"Go" means disengage (Wolf, 2006), physically remove yourself from your partner, leave, & redirect yourself into an alternative activity (e.g., withdraw to a private place, go for an energetic walk, or do some other vigorous activity) or use various relaxation methods.

[Appreciation is expressed to Peggy Corrigan-Dench and Valerie Price for their consultation]

5. *Reframing* can be used to teach couples to re-think, change their perception, and reinterpret people or situations in a less emotional, more constructive, and rational manner. For instance, a man became uncharacteristically hostile towards his "stupid, retarded wife" after she was diagnosed with diabetes. During counseling, the therapist reframed this concern by suggesting the diabetes was "actually an advantage," because now for the first time, they both would have to exercise, watch their diet, and take better care of themselves. After several reframing repetitions over several ses-

sions, the couple accepted this explanation, lost weight, tension disappeared, and their love returned. On another occasion, a couple came in for a session and went on and on about what "terrible parents" they were. In fact, these people were very committed, loving, and motivated parents who were using every available child-related support for their child. The therapst's reframing helped the couple to proudly re-interpret their parenting ability as positive, loving, and growth-enhancing for their child.

6. Satisfying sexual relations can be an important aspect of couple harmony. Yet, Koller et al. (1988) have report that sexual difficulties are more common in couples with intellectual disabilities. Sometimes it is helpful to assess the social-sexual knowledge of each partner using a tool such as the

SSKATT-R before sexuality education or counselling is initiated (Griffiths and Lunsky, 2003). *Educating couples about (1) abuse prevention, (2) sexuality, intimacy, and relationships, and (3) safe sex, AIDS, and related health and hygiene issues* may be an important aspect of the counselling (Champagne & Walker-Hirsh, 1993). Some couples struggle with *sexual dysfunction* and need help in order to enhance pleasure, reduce tension, and increase intimacy. "Sensate focus" exercises are quite simple to teach (Masters & Johnson, 1970). This approach can greatly improve couple intimacy with the emphasis initially on slow, comfortable, and joyful opportunities for "cuddle sessions" and giving and receiving pleasure, without the "performance" pressure to have sexual intercourse. *Masturbation can be suggested* as 'sexual insurance' for either partner, if intercourse is not an option (Hingsburger, 1995; Hingsburger and Haar, 2000). Medications such as Viagara are now occasionally being prescribed for men with intellectual disabilities experiencing problems with erectile dysfunction. Couples can be taught to *make behavioral requests* of each other, to increase demonstrations of affection (e.g., "Give me a hug, you big lug!")

7. Mattinson (1973) noted that most couples with intellectual disabilities function on a complementary basis -- i.e., the skill of one partner supplements a weakness in the other. Therapists can *help couples to identify specific ways to better complement each other's weaknesses or stated desires* – keeping in mind emotional and physical limitations. For instance, a man with severe speech difficulties was encouraged to use his wife as his interpreter, since she had an uncanny ability to understand him. In return, she asked him to accompany her for frequent doctors' appointments, which she found very anxiety-producing. In another case, the illiterate husband of a woman with physical challenges was able to run errands and feed and bathe her, while she agreed to read and write for him.

8. *Healthy boundary-setting* (Minuchin, 1974) is a strategy that can be easily understood by most couples with intellectual disabilities. Strengthening boundaries may involve establishing conversational rules (e.g. only one person speaks at a time), insisting on less interference from inlaws (e.g., refusing visits with relatives who demean them); or encouraging more distance between a passive woman and her domi-

nating partner (e.g., an evening out each week with her friends). On the other hand, relaxing boundaries may involve "giving permission" to isolated couples to get out more (e.g., cheap dates or vacations, join a fitness club), pursue separate interests, or increase their social network (e.g., joining Special Olympics bowling, People First advocacy meetings). In addition, the CIRCLES Program can be a useful tool for couples to establish appropriate levels of intimacy and social distance with various people in their lives (Champagne & Walker-Hirsh, 1993).

9. For couples unable to read and write, therapists must be flexible in coming up with *creative, practical approaches.* One couple created (with the therapists' help) a song with pragmatic coping strategies outlined in the lyrics. Near the end of each session, the therapists and the couple sang the song together (with much enjoyment) to remind the couple of specific coping strategies -- updating and improving the strategies/song, when needed. For people with serious communication deficits, augmentative communication devices or visual tools (e.g., picture or symbol systems) can be used to improve specific skills (e.g., hygiene, basic cooking, manners and politeness, anger management, understanding public transportation schedules). The key is to be inventive and have fun with it.

10. Bibliotherapy (using self-help books as 'homework' to teach therapeutic insights and skills) is very common in general counselling practice. However, since many individuals with intellectual disabilities may have little or no reading skills, books are often overlooked as a therapeutic tool. However, the PSCT Model often uses books as teaching tools but in a modified way. For instance, a therapist may read aloud key passages from self-help books or may summarize or simplify passages in more simple English. For instance, *The Five Love Languages,* a popular book used in general therapy practice (Chapman, 2004), can be "translated" into simpler language, so that the couple can benefit from the practical ideas described.

11. When appropriate, therapists can suggest that one or both partners might benefit from *a psychiatric consultation, or from meeting with their physician regarding psychotropic medication,* to help treat mental health concerns. This, ultimately, can greatly improve couple relations (Carver, et al., 1987). Other times, with particularly complex individuals, treatment can be enhanced by having a psychologist provide *a thorough psychodiagnostic assessment*, in order to provide further understanding of underlying personality, learning or psychological disorders in one or both partners.

CASE ILLUSTRATION OF THE FULL INTERVENTION MODEL

Margaret (33) has Down Syndrome and John (35) functions in the mild range of intellectual disability. They recently began talking seriously about getting married and spend a great deal of time together. Mrs. Smith, Margaret's mother, contacted a clinical social worker specializing in intellectual disabilities and requested couple counselling for Margaret and John. Mrs. Smith explained that they had been turned down by every other counselling program and clinician in the community. Mrs. Smith said that her husband was concerned that John had "anger issues." With this in mind, the social worker contacted John and Margaret about coming in for a private session. Margaret was more than willing to come in for the first session, but John was somewhat reluctant ("Am I in trouble?").

During the first three couple sessions (which included an agency co-therapist familiar with the couple), it became clear that Margaret was not afraid of John's anger, and they complemented each other's limitations (e.g., John could read, but Margaret made friends easier). The therapy outcome most important to them was to get married. They had already decided that they did not want children, and (with maternal and public health support) they were using reliable birth control. Along with receiving a disability pension, they both worked a few hours a week in supported employment. John admitted that he had a tendency towards becoming irritable and frequently did not sleep well, and he felt strongly that Margaret's father was "rude" and "bossy." Such talk clearly upset Margaret.

Following these early sessions, the therapist arranged a session with Margaret's parents. Mr. Smith expressed extreme hostility towards John. He suggested that John was always snubbing and insulting family members and John's only reason to get married was: "The bum and his family know we're well off!" In actual fact, John had little contact with his family. Rather surprisingly, Mrs. Smith admitted that she had initially introduced the couple to each other because Margaret had been "somewhat promiscuous" and "John seemed like a pretty nice guy who could keep her out of trouble."

Soon after, the therapist received a phone call from Margaret's brother (Steve), a police officer. He threatened to sue the therapist and co-therapist, if they continued to see the couple. At this point, the therapist contacted Mrs. Smith and had a private session with her. He explained that it appeared that her husband and Steve also had "anger issues." The therapist noted that this situation needed to be ameliorated quickly or John and Margaret's relationship (potentially happy) might not last. He asked Mrs. Smith to instruct her husband and son to "back off," so they could explore if marriage was the right path for John and Margaret. With much finesse, she was able to get them to lower the intensity of their disapproval.

The therapist and co-therapist again met with John and Margaret, and they concluded that John's moodiness was a concern and that he would have to change his perception of his possible future father-in-law, if the marriage had any chance of succeeding. John really wanted to get married. Six more couple sessions occurred in which the therapist helped John "reframe" his perception of Mr. Smith into that of "a very concerned and protective father." John (using role-play) was taught the "Stoplight: Stop/Think/Go Method" of anger management (described earlier) when around Mr. Smith and Steve. The therapist encouraged John to go for a psychiatric consultation, where it was determined that he suffered from chronic, low-grade depression ("dysthymia") and medication was prescribed. This produced a marked improvement in his moods and sleeping pattern.

Subsequent sessions focused on building relationship skills and possible marriage preparation (sexuality, money management, assertiveness with domineering friends and relatives). The therapist and co-therapist convinced the couple to postpone the wedding for a year, so that current problems could be more fully resolved. As well, by then, they would have gone out for three full years ["Munro's three year rule!" encourages (able and disabled) couples not to rush into marriage, but to get to really know each other first]. At the same time, the therapist and co-therapist met on two occasions with Margaret's parents to help Mr. Smith gradually "reframe" John as "actually very good for Margaret." The agency co-therapist organized some "client-centered planning meetings," where other supports were discussed (e.g., marriage preparation classes with the couple's faith community, expanding leisure activities together *and apart*, finding an apartment, increasing John's employment hours for extra income).

About a year later, John and Margaret had a lovely wedding. Mr. Smith proudly walked his daughter down the aisle, and he 'sprang' for the cost of a honeymoon in Niagara Falls. The therapist used John and Margaret's case example for training seminars for local couple therapists in generic practice to try to encourage their involvement with couples with intellectual disabilities. Ten years later, John and Margaret are still happily married; they have a lot of fun together; and once or twice a year they call the therapists for a "booster session" around troubling issues.

CONCLUSIONS

Despite social, economic, and intellectual disadvantages, research and anecdotal evidence (Schwier, 1994) suggest that love relationships and marriage for couples with intellectual disabilities can be just as happy and meaningful as for the general population. As surprising as it may sound at first, in many ways, the example set by many couples with intellectual disabilities actually can offer life lessons for couples in the general population. For instance, these couples can teach others that relationship happiness is often based on lowering one's expectations about materialism and outward appearances; finding good companionship and simply sharing one's life with another; demonstrating loyalty and gentleness; recognizing that beauty truly is in the eye of the beholder; and reminding us that having fun should always be the first rule of committed relationships.

Much professional work still remains concerning understanding couple relationships, marriage, and parenting for people with intellectual disabilities. There is a need for well-designed research in this area, first called for about forty years ago (Katz, 1968). There also is a need for much more clinical literature concerning methods, strategies, and models of couple therapy with this important population, and for therapists, in general, to expand their practice to include these wonderful, but under-serviced, people.

REFERENCES

Abbott, D., & Howarth, J. (2007). Still off-limits? Staff views on supporting gay, lesbian and bisexual people with intellectual disabilities to develop sexual and intimate relationships. *Journal of Applied Research in Intellectual Disabilities, 20*, 116-126.

Abbott, D., & Howarth, J. (2005). *Secret loves, hidden lives? Exploring issues for people with learning disabilities who are gay, lesbian or bisexual.* Bristol: The Policy Press.

Andron, L., & Sturm, M.L. (1973). Is 'I do' in the repertoire of the retarded? A study of the functioning of mentally retarded couples. *Mental Retardation, 11*, 31-34.

Aunos, M., & Feldman, M. (2007). Parenting by people with intellectual disabilities. In I. Brown & M. Percy (Eds.), *A comprehensive guide to intellectual & developmental disabilities* (pp. 595-605). Baltimore, Brookes.

Bach, G.R., & Wyden, P. (1968). *The intimate enemy: How to fight fair in love and marriage.* New York: Avon.

Barger, E., Wacker, J., Macy, R., & Parish, S. (2009). Sexual assault prevention for women with intellectual disabilities: A critical review of the evidence. *Intellectual and Developmental Disabilities, 47*, 249-262.

Bass, M.S. (1964). Marriage for the mental deficient. *Mental Retardation, 2*, 198-202.

Bernardo, M.L. (1981). Premarital counseling and the couple with disabilities: A review and recommendations. *Rehabilitation Literature, 42*, 213-217.

Bidgood, F.E. (1975). Sexuality and the handicapped. *The Journal for Special Educators of the Mentally Retarded, 11*, 199-203.

Burns, D.D. (1980). *Feeling good: The new mood therapy.* New York: Avon.

Carver, C.M., Waring, E.M., Chamberlaine, C.H., McCrank, E.W., Stalker, C.A., & Fry, R. (1987). Detection of depression in couples in conflict. *Canada's Mental Health, 35*, 2-5.

Champagne, M.P., & Walker-Hirsch, L. (1993). *Circles I. Intimacy & relationships. II. Stop abuse. III. AIDS: Safer ways.* Santa Barbara: James Stanfield.

Chapman, G. (2004). *The five love languages: How to express heartfelt commitment to your mate.* Chicago: Northfield Publishing.

Craft, A., & Craft, M. (1979). *Handicapped married couples* . London: Routledge & Kegan Paul.

Cochran, B. (1974). Conception, coercion and control: Symposium on reproductive rights of the mental retarded. *Hospital & Community Psychiatry, 25*, 283-293.

Edgerton, R.B. (1967). *The cloak of competence: Stigma in the lives of the mentally retarded.* Berkeley: University of California Press.

Floor, L., Baxter, D., Rosen, M., & Zisfein, L. (1975). A survey of marriages among previously institutionalized retardates. *Mental Retardation, 13,* 33-37.

Griffiths, D.M., & Lunsky, Y. (2003). *SSKAAT-R: Socio-sexual Knowledge and Attitudes Assessment Tool-Revised.* Wood Dale, Illinois: Stoelting.

Hall, J. E. (1974). Sexual Behavior. In J. Wortis (Ed.), *Mental retardation and developmental disabilities: An annual review* (pp. 178-212). New York: Brunner/ Mazel.

Hartman, S.S., & Hyynes, J. (1975). Marriage education for mentally retarded adults. *Social Casework, 56,* 280-284.

Hingsburger, D. (1995). *Hand made love: A guide to teaching about male masturbation through understanding and video.* Newmarket, Ontario: Diverse City Press.

Hingsburger, D., & Haar, S. (2000). *Finger tips: Teaching women with disabilities about masturbation through understanding and video.* Eastman, Quebec: Diverse City Press.

Hurley, A. (2008, November). *Diagnosis and treatment of psychotic disorders in intellectual disabilities.* Paper presented at the 25th Annual Conference of the National Association for the Dually Diagnosed, Niagara Falls, Canada.

Jacobson, N., & Christensen, A. (1996). *Integrative couple therapy.* New York: Norton.

Katz, E. (1968). *The retarded adult in the community.* Springfield: Thomas.

Keefe, T. (1984). Alienation and social work practice. *Social Casework, 65,* 145-153.

Kempton, W., & Kahn, E. (1991). Sexuality and people with intellectual disabilities: A historical perspective. *Sexuality and Disability, 9,* 93-111.

Koller, H., Richardson, S.A., & Katz, M. (1988). Marriage in a Young adult mentally retarded population. *Journal of Mental Deficiency Research, 32,* 93-102.

Kort, J. (2008). *Gay affirmative therapy for the straight clinician.* New York, Norton.

Lunsky, Y., & Neely, L.C. (2002). Extra-individual sources of social support as described by adults with mild intellectual disabilities. *Mental Retardation, 40,* 269-277.

Masters, W.H., & Johnson, V.E. (1970). *Human sexual inadequacy.* Boston: Little, Brown.

Mattinson, J. (1973). Marriage and mental handicap. In F.F.de la Cruz (Ed.), *Human sexuality and the mentally retarded* (pp. 169-185). New York: Brunner/Mazel.

May, D., & Simpson, M.K. (2003). The parent trap: Marriage, parenthood and adulthood for people with intellectual disabilities. *Critical Social Policy, 23,* 286-296.

Minuchin, S. (1974). *Families and family therapy.* Cambridge: Harvard University Press.

Munro, J.D. (1977). Attitudes of institutionalized retardates toward living in the community. *The Social Worker/Le Travailleur Social, 45*, 130-136.

Munro, J.D. (1982). Developmentally disabled individuals. In S.A. Yelaja (Ed.), *Ethical issues in social work* (pp. 156-182). Springfield: Charles C. Thomas.

Munro, J. D. (1997). Using unconditionally constructive mediation to resolve family-system disputes related to persons with disabilities. *Families in Society, 78*, 609-616.

Munro, J. D. (2007). A positive intervention model for understanding, helping and coping with "challenging" families. In I. Brown and Maire Percy (Eds.), *A comprehensive guide to intellectual and developmental disabilities* (pp. 24, 373-382). Baltimore: Brookes.

Nichols, M.P., & Schwartz, R.C. (2004). *Family therapy: Concepts and methods (6th ed.).* Boston: Pearson.

Parr-Paulson, M. (1998, Fall). On marriage and mental retardation. *HARC Today.* [Greater Hartford Association for Retarded Citizens].

Perske, R. (1972). The dignity of risk and the mentally retarded. *Mental Retardation, 10*, 24-26.

President's Panel on Mental Retardation (1963). *Report of the Task Force on Law.* Washington: U.S. Government Printing Office.

Randall, W., Parrila, R., & Sobsey, D. (2000). Gender, disability status and risk for sexual abuse in children. *Journal of Developmental Disability, 7*, 1-15.

Russo, R.J. (1999). Applying a strengths-based practice approach in working with people with developmental disabilities and their families. *Families in Society, 80*, 25-33.

Saleeby, D. (1992). *The strength perspective in social work practice.* New York: Basic Books.

Satir, V. (1967). *Conjoint family therapy: A guide to theory and technique.* Palo Alto, CA: Science and Behavior Books.

Seligman, M.E.P., & Csikszentmihalyi, M. (2000). Positive psychology: An introduction. *American Psychologist, 55*, 5-14.

Schwier, K.M. (1994). *Couples with intellectual disabilities talk about living & loving.* New York: Woodbine.

Taverner, W.J., & DeMarco, C. (2006). *Verbal Informed Sexual Consent Assessment Tool.* Easton, PA: Center for Family Life Education.

Thiroux, J.P. (2004). *Ethics: Theory and practice.* Upper Saddle River, NJ: Prentice Hall.

Timmers, R.L., DuCharme, P., & Jacob, G. (1981). Sexual Knowledge, attitudes and behaviors of developmentally disabled adults living in a normalized apartment setting, *Sexuality and Disability, 4*, 27-39.

Toufexis, A. (1993, February 13)). The right chemistry: Evolutionary roots, brain imprints, biological secretions. That's the story of love. *Time,* 141, 39-41.

Vanier, J. (1985). *Man and woman he made them.* Toronto: Anglican Book Centre.

Waite, L.J., & Gallagher, M. (1981). *The case for marriage: Why married people are happier, healthier and better off financially.* New York: Broadway Books.

Walker, P.W. (1977). Premarital counseling for the developmentally disabled. *Social Casework, 58,* 475-479.

Welner, S.L. (1999). Contraceptive choices for women with disabilities. *Sexuality and Disability, 17,* 209-214.

White, M. (1995). *Re-authoring lives: Interviews and essays.* Adelaide, Australia: Dulwich Centre Publications.

YAI (2004). *Relationship and sexuality policy: The YAI policy for determining sexual consent.* New York: National Institute for People with Disabilities.

SECTION IV

OTHER ISSUES

The Effectiveness of Psychotherapy with Persons with Intellectual Disabilities[1]

H. Thompson Prout, Ph.D.
Brooke K. Browning, M.S.

INTRODUCTION

The effectiveness of psychotherapy has long been an issue of debate among mental health researchers and professionals. With increasing utilization of psychotropic medications to treat a wide range of mental disorders, there is even more pressure to identify effective treatments that offer advantages over medication or enhance the effectiveness of medical treatments. Psychotherapy outcome studies have become the focal point of these debates.

The early research views on the effectiveness of psychotherapy were not very positive. Eysenck (1952) published a classic and controversial review on the effectiveness of psychotherapy with adults, mostly described as neurotic. He reviewed a number of studies and concluded that the number of individuals who improved with treatment was not substantially different from those who experienced improvement without treatment, i.e., "spontaneous remission." He found that roughly two-thirds of each group improved, leading to an overall conclusion that the outcome research at that time provided little evidence of the effectiveness of psychotherapy with adult neurotics. Eysenck (1965) published a follow-up review, and Rachman (1971) published a book, *The Effects of Psychotherapy,* both questioning the effectiveness of therapeutic interventions. Levitt (1957, 1963, 1971) used a similar approach in evaluating the effectiveness of psychotherapy with children and found no substantial outcome differences between treated and untreated children at the conclusion of therapy and at follow-up. Thus, the primary research reviews through the mid 1970's indicated that psychotherapy was generally no more beneficial than no treatment. Interestingly, the period of the 1950's to the 1970'showed rapid development of various therapeutic perspectives (e.g., client-centered, rational-emotive, reality therapy, Gestalt).

---

[1] With the exception of direct quotes, the term intellectual disability will be used throughout this chapter although much of the literature reviewed utilizes the term mental retardation.

The landscape of the psychotherapy debate changed dramatically with the publication of the Smith and Glass (1977, 1980) meta-analyses of psychotherapy outcome studies. Meta-analysis is essentially a quantitative literature methodology comparing treated and untreated individuals on specific outcome measures. It differed from the Eysenck and Levitt approaches in that it examined more specific changes rather than more global "improved" or "not improved." Smith and Glass were able to demonstrate a moderate degree of effectiveness of psychotherapy across a wide array on types of treatments. Meta-analysis has now become the standard method of evaluating the effectiveness of psychotherapy. Of note, meta-analysis is now utilized by many disciplines including education, psychology, and medicine. The Smith and Glass meta-analyses spawned many, many subsequent analyses. To summarize these analyses is well beyond the scope of this chapter, but the prevailing view is that psychotherapy in general appears to be at least moderately effective.

The purpose of this chapter is to provide an overview of the current status of psychotherapy outcome research with persons with intellectual disabilities. To say the least, this area has not received anywhere near the attention of outcome studies with persons without intellectual disabilities. This chapter will focus on four areas: 1) general issues in psychotherapy research and their relevance for professionals who work with persons with intellectual disabilities; 2) a review of several published reviews on the effectiveness of psychotherapy with persons with intellectual disabilities; 3) a general review of published studies on psychotherapy with persons with intellectual disabilities in approximately the last ten years (i.e., since approximately 1998); and 4) a review of dissertations that focused on psychotherapy with persons with intellectual disabilities, also in the same time frame. In some cases, we included studies and dissertations before 1998 if they had not been included in prior reviews.

ISSUES IN PSYCHOTHERAPY RESEARCH

Psychotherapy research has become increasingly complex since the early reviews of effectiveness examined improvement vs. no improvement. More sophisticated study designs, treatment specification, population and treatment target definitions, and attempts to delineate treatment components have now become the focus of research. A number of issues are relevant for examining the research with persons with intellectual disabilities.

Definition of Psychotherapy

For the purposes of this chapter, we will not make a distinction between "counseling" and "psychotherapy" as long as the intervention meets certain criteria. In their review, Prout and Nowak-Drabik (2003) used a definition of psychotherapy adapted from Meltzoff and Kornreich (1970). That particular definition has long been used by other psychotherapy researchers (e.g., Smith & Glass, 1977, 1980). The definition included a number of components:

- Planned direct face-to-face application of psychological techniques was utilized with the techniques derived from established psychological principles and theories.
- The therapist or counselor was qualified by training and experience to understand and apply the techniques.
- The intention was to assist individuals to modify such personal characteristics as feelings, values, attitudes, and behaviors.
- Psychotherapy did **not** include interventions that are primarily conducted by teachers or paraprofessionals (e.g., behavior modification, classroom interventions, consultation).
- Psychotherapy **did** include interventions labeled as "counseling" or "training" that met the other definitional criteria.

The importance of this definition for professionals in the field of intellectual disabilities lies in what is not included. Interventions for persons with intellectual disabilities have been dominated by behavior modification or applied behavior analysis. These intervention, in most cases, would not be considered to represent psychotherapy. Additionally, interventions that are conducted by persons who do not have advanced degrees in a mental health discipline would also not fit the definition, even if they have the title of "counselor." Often, "counselors" in many human service settings are direct care professionals. While many of these professionals may conduct very effective direct interventions, these interventions would not represent psychotherapy from a research perspective.

Effectiveness vs. Efficacy

The terms effectiveness and efficacy are sometime used interchangeably. However, the terms do represent different constructs (Chorpita, 2003). Efficacy refers to the demonstration that specific techniques are demonstrated to have positive impact on specific problems, albeit often in a more controlled situation. Effectiveness includes "transportability" aspects of the treatment: Do treatments generalize to other settings? Are the treatments feasible? Are the associated costs reasonable for the expected effects and outcomes? Efficacy is the first level of evidence, i.e., does it work? Effectiveness aspects become more important for clinical practice. In the field of intellectual disabilities, effectiveness is important for treatments generalizing to a range of settings. Empirically Supported Treatments (EST's) are discussed later in this section of the chapter. Effectiveness becomes an issue in whether treatments shown to be efficacious or effective with persons without intellectual disabilities are also effective with persons with intellectual disabilities.

Therapist Characteristics

The general psychotherapy research literature has examined a wide variety of counselor/therapist characteristics. Studies have examined age, gender, years of experience, theoretical orientation, etc. In this area, probably the key factor would be years of experience in working with persons who have intellectual disabilities. This variable and the other therapist characteristic variables have not been closely examined with persons with intellectual disabilities.

Client Characteristics

Psychotherapy outcome studies have similarly examined an array of client or patient characteristics. Studies and reviews have routinely examined age, children and adolescents vs. adults, specific diagnoses, setting where client is served, level of disturbance, etc. Generally, the psychotherapy outcome literature for persons with intellectual disabilities does delineate age, setting, and level of intellectual disability. Specific diagnoses should be viewed within the context of some of the issues in diagnosing mental disorders in person with intellectual disabilities; e.g., diagnostic overshadowing. The relatively new *Diagnostic Manual - Intellectual Disability: A Textbook of Diagnosis of Mental Disorders in Persons with Intellectual Disability* (Fletcher, Loschen, Stavrakaki, & First, 2007) should not only facilitate treatment but should also improve research with regard to more clearly defining diagnoses in outcome studies.

Outcome Measures

The field of intellectual disabilities still lacks the range of personality and social-emotional measures available to researchers who study psychotherapy in persons without disabilities. There have been a number of scales developed that have been specifically developed for persons with intellectual disabilities (e.g. *Emotional Problems Scales*: *Self-Report Inventory and Behavior Rating Scale,* Prout & Strohmer, 1991; *Reiss Screen*, Reiss, 1988; *Psychopathology Instrument for Mentally Retarded Adults*, J. L., Matson, Kazdin, & Senatore, 1984). However, many studies employ measures or versions of measures (e.g., the Beck inventories, MMPI) not intended for use with persons with intellectual disabilities. This does add concern about the overall validity of studies in terms or adding error variance to the outcome measures.

Type of Design

As with other areas of intervention research, studies of psychotherapy effectiveness with persons with intellectual disabilities have utilized a variety of designs including case studies, single subject or N=1 designs, pre-post studies, and control group designs. Many reviewers (e.g., Prout and Nowak-Drabik, 2003) have noted that research with persons with intellectual disabilities have tended not to use the most rigorous research methodology.

Evidence Based, Empirically Supported Treatments

Since a task force of the Division 12 (Clinical Psychology) of the American Psychological Association issued their initial report on empirically supported treatments in 1995, there has been a focus on establishing treatments that appear efficacious or effective for dealing with specific disorders (Chambless and Hollon, 1998). The Division 12 websites with links (www.div12.org and www.PsychologicalTreatments.org) maintain a list of treatments that have reached various levels of empirical support. These lists include both treatments that meet the definition of psychotherapy and those that represent other types of psychological interventions (e.g., applied behavior analysis, biofeedback).

The definitions of empirically supported treatments (EST) considers whether the treatment showed statistically significant superiority compared to no-treatment control group, alternative treatment group, or placebo, and also if the studies represented a randomized control trial, controlled single case experiment, or other equivalent design. Stronger research support is indicated by studies with larger sample sizes and demonstration of effectiveness in more than one independent research setting. Studies must either have a treatment manual or provide enough detailed description of the intervention for replication and must provide a specific and reliable description of the population, inclusion criteria, and clinical problem. Additionally, the studies must include reliable and valid outcome measures and appropriate data analysis. Treatments are designated at three levels of support: possibly efficacious, efficacious, or efficacious and specific. The Division 12 listing now uses the terms as demonstrating either modest or strong research support.

In terms of psychotherapy with persons with intellectual disabilities, there do not appear to be any treatments that would currently meet the EST designations. A perusal of the Division 12 website (www.PsychologicalTreatments.org) at the time of the writing of this chapter shows over 60 treatments for specific disorders that have achieved either modest or strong research support. However, the studies cited in support of the various psychotherapeutic treatments show virtually no mention of persons with intellectual disabilities. The issue for professionals who deal with person with intellectual disabilities is whether the treatment could reasonably generalize or be adapted for persons with intellectual disabilities.

Therapeutic Alliance

Therapeutic alliance refers to the variety of interpersonal processes in play during psychotherapy that appear to impact outcome (Elvins & Green, 2008). Alliance is viewed as a parallel process, yet independent of structured or manualized treatment in effecting outcome. Alliance includes such constructs as rapport, empathy, client and therapist investment, therapeutic bond, etc. While therapeutic alliance has received more attention from researchers in the last few years (see the Elvins & Green review), there has been little attention in intellectual disability research.

A REVIEW OF THE REVIEWS

Nezu and Nezu (1994) observed that there were relevant studies that suggested that psychotherapy should be considered as an alternative for serving adults with intellectual disabilities and psychological problems in outpatient settings. At the time, there were only a limited number of strategies that had been tested and examined in a research context. In the last decade, there have been several reviews of counseling and pyshcotherapeutic interventions for persons with intellectual disabilities. These reviews include:

Prout and Nowak-Drabik (2003)

The Prout and Nowak-Drabik (2003) review probably represents the most comprehensive and systematic review of the literature for studies conducted prior to 1998. Prout and Nowak-Drabik searched the literature from 1968 to 1998 to identify studies that met the criteria of psychotherapy delineated earlier in this chapter; i.e., the Meltzoff and Kornreich (1970) definition. Their intent was to take a broad view of the literature and they included control group designs, pre-post designs, single subject studies, and case studies. They identified 92 studies from that period that met the psychotherapy definition. Both published studies and dissertations were included.

Because the literature at the time included a variety of reports and studies, it was not possible to apply standard meta-analytic procedures to all of the identified studies. Additionally, the research literature at the time could be best described as less than rigorous. Given this, they employed an expert consensus rating method to evaluate the identified studies. A panel of three experts who had strong background in research methodology applied to outcome research evaluated each study with respect to outcome/results/findings and overall effectiveness/benefits. Outcome was rated on a 1 to 5 scale: *no change*(no change on any measures), *minimal change*(change on one-third or less of the measures), *moderate change*(change on one-third to two-thirds of the measures), *significant change* (change on more than two-thirds of the measures), and *marked change*(change on all measures). Effectiveness was also rated on a 1 to 5 scale: *no effectiveness, minimal effectiveness, moderate effectiveness, significant effectiveness,* and *marked effectiveness.* Their procedures included reliability checks, and there was a procedure for reaching consensus or resolving discrepancies among the raters. The authors noted limitations with their expert consensus approach due to some degree of subjectivity and making comparisons between the wide range of research methodologies (e.g., comparing case studies with control group designs). Nonetheless, the consensus approach did allow for a systematic review of the literature. A few studies (N=9) had the required data for a meta-analysis, and this allowed for a small meta-analysis.

Prout and Nowak-Drabik found that the overall rating of change across studies was slightly above the moderate change rating and the effectiveness rating was just slightly below the moderate effectiveness rating. Where there were enough studies (N of at least 10), there were a number of comparisons on variables delineated in the studies. Among the findings:

- Published studies yielded higher ratings for both outcome and effectiveness.
- Individual treatments yielded higher ratings for both outcome and effectiveness.
- Clinic-based (vs. community or residential settings) treatments yielded higher ratings for effectiveness.
- Behavioral treatments yielded higher ratings for both outcome and effectiveness.

Among some of the other comparisons, there were not significant differences based on client age, level of intellectual disability, or type of design. The meta-analysis yielded an overall effect size of 1.01 for the nine studies. An effect size of 1.01 would be considered an "excellent" level of effect (Cohen, 1992). Again, this was a very small number of studies for a meta-analysis. The author's also concluded that the literature base was relatively weak. There was a large number of case studies or N=1 studies, too few studies had control group designs, there was almost no use of treatment manuals, few studies addressed treatment integrity issues, and outcome data, particularly in the case studies, was often vaguely described or omitted.

Despite the various cautions noted by the authors, Prout and Nowak-Drabik supported the notion that psychotherapy for persons with intellectual disabilities is moderately beneficial and effective. This conclusion is consistent with the earlier observations of Nezu and Nezu (1994). Prout and Nowak-Drabik further concluded that psychotherapy should more frequently be included in treatment and service plans for persons with intellectual disabilities and that community agencies should be more open to providing counseling and psychotherapy services to these consumers.

The findings and conclusions of Prout and Nowak-Drabik were not met with acceptance by some in the field and a bit of controversy was stimulated by the research. Sturmey (2005) wrote an article "Against Psychotherapy with People Who Have Mental Retardation" where he criticized the meta-analysis portion of the study as well as some aspects of the expert consensus methodology. His interpretation of the findings was that the analyses supported behavioral interventions. Sturmey was also critical of psychodynamic perspectives and the lack of well-conducted research on effectiveness. He concluded that there was no scientific basis to conclude effectiveness or ineffectiveness, as well as no basis to assess potential harmful effects. He concluded that behavioral approaches should remain the preferred treatment option for persons with intellectual disabilities. *(Note: the "behavioral" studies of psychotherapy met the research definition of psychotherapy for the Prout and Nowak-Drabik analysis)* Several professionals responded to Sturmey's analysis and essay. Beail (2005) and Taylor (2005) argued that there are some limitations in the evidence base for behavioral interventions and that the literature base for behavioral interventions does not address the full array of problems, settings, and issues for persons with intellectual disabilities. Hurley (2005) also noted that the behavioral approach does not address the full range of problems and further delineated some flaws in Sturmey's definition of psychotherapy. Hurley noted her own experience as a cognitive-behavioral therapist providing services for persons with mild intellectual disabilities, describing psychotherapy as an "essential tool" in treating psychiatric disorders in person with intellectual disabilities. King (2005) suggested that professionals should proceed with "compassion" while waiting for the evidence of effectiveness of psychotherapy with persons with intellectual disabilities. Not surprisingly, Sturmey (2006a) responded to the responses and defended his position.

The first author of this chapter and of the Prout and Nowak-Drabik study has to admit to being a bit amused by the discussion/debate that followed the presentation of our findings. Without fueling the controversy further, this author feels that some of the response appeared to be semantics related to the term psychotherapy and the implication that psychotherapy was tied to certain theoretical perspectives. "Psychotherapy" involves a wide variety of techniques and strategies. Interestingly, Sturmey (2006a) cites the Prout and Nowak-Drabik analysis as being supportive of psychodynamic psychotherapy. Obviously, the interpretation of the research literature base can be somewhat subjective. It would not be unreasonable to conclude that there is presently enough evidence to support psychotherapy in the provision of services for persons with intellectual disabilities. I would also agree with King's notion of not necessarily waiting for definitive evidence before deciding to serve our consumers. Had professionals in the 1950's to the early 1970's followed the conclusions of Eysenck (1952, 1965), Rachman (1971), and Levitt (1957, 1963, 1971), the field of counseling and psychotherapy would have shut down due to lack of clear evidence of effectiveness. Hopefully, continued research will provide a stronger research base with clearer conclusions.

Butz, Bowling and Bliss (2000)

Butz, Bowling, and Bliss (2000) reviewed 30+ years of literature. As others have noted, they found a paucity of research and felt that this contributed to the perspective among many general mental health practitioners that persons with intellectual disabilities could not benefit from psychotherapy. Additionally, Butz and his colleagues noted the phenomena of diagnostic overshadowing and the associated ignoring of indications of mental illness. They also cited the dichotimization of the intellectual disability and mental health service delivery systems. Their review delineated many of the barriers to providing psychotherapy services to persons with intellectual disability. However, they did note that there is a body of literature that provides some support for these services. They noted that the literature goes back at least thirty years and in some cases as far back as sixty years. The literature is hampered by its descriptive and qualitative nature, but they argued for continuing research as a mode for reducing some of the barriers in the area.

Whitehouse, Tudway, Look, and Kroese (2006)

Whitehouse, Tudway, Look, and Kroese (2006) specifically addressed adaptations in individual psychotherapy utilized in studies of cognitive-behavioral and psychodynamic therapies. These authors reviewed 10 cognitive-behavioral studies and 15 psychodynamic studies and were primarily interested in the types and frequencies of adaptations reported in the studies. Adaptations included simplification of the techniques (e.g., less complexity, smaller chunks, shorter sessions), altering language (e.g., lower level vocabulary, shorter sentences, simpler words), more use of activities (homework assignments, drawings), use of materials (e.g., games) at developmental level, being more directive (e.g., visual cues, more direct specification of goals), involvement of caregivers (e.g., family, support staff), being flexible (adjusting to developmental level), dealing with transference/countertransference (e.g., being reactive to attachment, setting boundaries), and disability/rehabilitation issues (e.g., addressing disability specifically within treatment, supporting positive self-view). Their findings showed that being flexible was the most common adaptation and the most frequent in the cognitive-behavioral studies, while transference/countertransference was the most frequently used technique in the psychodynamic studies. Directive and simplification adaptations were more frequently noted in the cognitive-behavioral studies. Psychodynamic studies were more likely to include care-givers. Disability/ rehabilitation issues were infrequently addressed in both approaches. The authors concluded that the differences in the utilizations of adaptations were not surprising given the tenets of the different theoretical perspectives. The review also noted that many of the adaptations were not adequately described in the literature as well as other aspects of the techniques and study. Additionally, most of the studies were case or single subject reports. Whitehouse and his colleagues did not directly address the issue of whether the adaptations yield more positive outcomes. Rather, they suggested that future research specifically delineate and describe the adaptations and assess the contribution to outcome.

Willner (2005)

Willner (2005) reviewed the available research literature and delineated among treatments by theoretical perspective, as well as examining outcome vs. process-outcome variables. Willner's review of the psychodynamic literature suggested that approaches from this theoretical perspective appeared to yield beneficial effects both in the short-term and slightly longer term. Willner hypothesized that there may be some general effects of providing individual attention with some focus on feelings.

Willner, while noting that the cognitive-behavioral approaches are now the primary theoretical perspective among general mental health practitioners, reviewed a variety of techniques including those that emphasized improvement in cognitive skill deficits (e.g., problem solving, self-instructional/management strategies) and those that emphasized dealing with cognitive distortions. There appear to be some benefits of both types of techniques, but Willner highlighted the need to consider language issues to effectively implement the "cognitive" aspects of the interventions. Process variables such as relationship issues need to be further examined and are likely to influence outcome. Willner concluded that many individuals with intellectual disabilities can engage in the psychotherapeutic process. Willner also cautioned that some purely behavioral approaches may not address the array of problems presented by persons with intellectual disabilities. He did acknowledge that behavioral approaches may be the only option for persons at the lower levels (i.e, severe/profound) of intellectual disability.

Sturmey (2004, 2006)

In these two reviews, Sturmey (2004, 2006b) continued to argue that there are differences between behavioral and cognitive therapies and that many cognitive therapies were mislabeled and actually represented behavioral therapies. In 2004, Sturmey detailed the deficits associated with persons with intellectual disabilities and posited that these deficits present barriers to effective cognitive therapy. He further concluded that there was not adequate evidence to establish a causative link between cognitions and psychopathology such as aggression and anger. Although Sturmey noted some indications of effectiveness, he felt that the cognitive aspect of the interventions could not be isolated from other components as many treatment packages have multiple components. The lack of well-conducted experimental studies hampered further delineation of specific effects. In 2006 (b), Sturmey continued to question the labeling of interventions and the misrepresentation of applied behavior analysis, reiterating the idea that the efficacy of cognitive therapies had not been established. Further, he posited: "The ethical imperative of beneficence requires that people, including people with intellectual disabilities receive known effective treatments. Those effective treatments are based on ABA" (p. 115). One can easily question the validity of that generalized notion.

We do agree with Sturmey that the overall research literature remains weak in the psychotherapy area. Much of Sturmey's position is based on a continuing misunderstanding of the definition of psychotherapy. However, the need to parse out behavioral vs. cognitive aspects of treatments appears based more on a need to defend a theoretical perspective. Clearly, "cognitive-behavioral" therapies represent treatments that can have components that are both behavioral and cognitive. It is noted that the Association for Advancement of Behavior Therapies changed their name to

Association for Behavioral and Cognitive Therapies in 2005. Prout, Chard, Nowak-Drabik, and Johnson (2000) argued that psychotherapy with persons with intellectual disabilities needed to move to the development of more empirically supported treatments, both for clinical practice and research purposes. They also cited the need for more manualized treatments. Manualized treatments, to an extent, negate the need to label an intervention. If a treatment includes relaxation training (a behavioral intervention per Sturmey, 2004) and a cognitive intervention, and both aspects of treatment are adequately described in a manual, the "correct" labeling of the treatment becomes superfluous. Admittedly, the field has not made as much progress in that and we do concur with the need for more and better research.

Summary

Using the broad definition of psychotherapy, these reviews would appear to lend general support that psychotherapeutic treatments offer some degree of benefit to persons with intellectual disabilities. Clearly, there needs to be more rigorous research with more detailed description of treatments, variables, and techniques. Additionally, further research needs to delineate the "ingredients" (e.g., adaptations, process variables) that contribute to successful treatments.

PUBLISHED STUDIES

Researchers have evaluated the use of psychotherapy for individuals with intellectual disabilities to treat a variety of issues and with numerous techniques. Psychodynamic (Beail, Kellett, Newman, & Warden, 2007; Beail, Warden, Morsley, & Newman, 2005), group (Crowley, Rose, Smith, Hobster, & Ansell, 2008; Hays, Murphy, Langdon, Rose, & Reed, 2007; Peckham, Howlett, & Corbett, 2007; McCabe, McGillivray, & Newton, 2006; Lindsay, Olley, Baillie, & Smith, 1999), cognitive behavioral (Murphy, Powell, Guzman, & Hays, 2007; Taylor, Novaco, Gillmer, Robertson, & Thorne, 2005; King, Lancaster, Wynne, Nettleton, & Davis, 1999), and behavior (Sterkenburg, Janssen, & Schuengel, 2008) therapy are some of the techniques that were evaluated for treating individuals with intellectual disabilities. Although researchers have demonstrated that therapy can be effective for individuals with intellectual disabilities, many questions about which techniques are most appropriate, who should conduct therapy sessions, and specific outcomes for children, adolescents and adults remain unanswered. It is important to know which individuals are likely to benefit from therapy and the techniques that work best. Knowing which programs are effectively treating individuals with intellectual disabilities is valuable information when evaluating specific interventions.

In an attempt to answer some of these questions about psychotherapy for children and adults with intellectual disabilities, published studies from the past 10 years that evaluated psychotherapy interventions for individuals with intellectual disabilities were selected for review. The authors categorized each study as evaluating psychotherapy services for either children and adolescents or adults.

Children & Adolescents

The studies that evaluated treatments for children and adolescents with intellectual disabilities utilized specific interventions. For example, Sterkenburg and colleagues (2008) examined the use of an attachment-based behavior therapy to reduce severe challenging behaviors (e.g. self-injurious behavior, aggression, disruption). The 6 participants had a severe intellectual disability and a visual impairment. The Attachment-based Behavior Modification Treatment occurred in the residential environment of each client. The researchers used standardized instruments to assess the challenging behavior prior to the intervention and after its completion. Additionally, professional caregivers recorded the frequency of the challenging behaviors every hour for 12 months. The totals for each day were combined into weekly average scores for data analysis. The findings of the six single cases were combined into an average effect size. The effects showed that during behavior modification, the attachment therapist was significantly more effective in stimulating adaptive behavior. The challenging behavior in the residential home also decreased during the intervention. According to this study, attachment-based behavior therapy can be an effective treatment to increase adaptive behavior for children with severe intellectual disabilities (Sterkenburg et al., 2008).

A group cognitive behavioral treatment for adolescent sex offenders focused on changing thinking errors related to sex offending, problem-solving in offending situations, and analyzing behavior and routines consistent with offending (Lindsay et al., 1999). The researchers followed the participants for 4 years to determine whether they committed additional sex offenses. The group sessions focused on teaching appropriate behavior in various situations and replacing offending cognitions with appropriate socialized thoughts derived through the participant's own logical analysis. The four adolescents responded positively to treatment and changed their attitudes about sexual offending. Three of the four denied the offense for up to 6 months, but eventually accepted responsibility for the offense. One limitation of the study is that the measure assessing attitudes consistent with offending against children did not have established reliability or validity. However, none of the adolescents had been accused of another sexual offense 3 or 4 years (depending on the participant) after receiving the cognitive behavioral therapy.

Another case study examined the influence of imagery rehearsal treatment (IRT) on a ten year old boy with an intellectual disability and psychiatric illness (Peirce, 2006). IRT focuses on helping clients change the endings of their nightmares while they are awake so that the ending is no longer upsetting. After five IRT sessions, the client was having a nightmare once every 2 weeks, on average, compared to every night prior to the intervention. Although the research with this population is limited, these case studies show that psychotherapy can be effective in treating some children and adolescents with intellectual disabilities. Controlled studies with larger sample sizes and diverse populations are needed to determine the overall effectiveness of psychotherapy for children and adolescents with intellectual disabilities.

Adults

The literature base evaluating the use of psychotherapy for adults with intellectual disabilities is more established than the studies for children and adolescents. The majority of the studies either examined the effectiveness of reducing anger and aggression or of group therapy interventions.

Common characteristics of individuals with intellectual disabilities are displaying anger and aggression (Willner, Brace, & Phillips, 2005). King and colleagues (1999) evaluated the efficacy of cognitive-behavioral anger management training for 11 adults with mild intellectual disabilities. Findings indicated that participants improved anger control and self-esteem. According to caregiver ratings, there were significant reductions from pre-treatment to post-treatment on a measure of undesirable behaviors. The researchers suggested a higher level of caregiver involvement to contribute to greater improvements in anger control. A limitation of this study is that there was not a control group.

Three researchers implemented controlled studies to evaluate anger management treatment (Taylor et al., 2005; Willner, Brace, & Phillips, 2005; Lindsay et al., 2004). Lindsay and colleagues (2004) used a waiting list to develop the control group. The participants completed 40 sessions of anger management treatment. Self-report diaries of anger revealed a significant reduction in reported anger between the two groups at post-treatment. Additionally, there was a significant difference between the treatment and control groups for the percentage of post-treatment aggressive incidents. Those who received anger management treatment demonstrated improvements on all the measures, and the control participants did not show any improvements on the assessments. The number of re-offenses, significant aggressive incidents, and the research measures demonstrate the effectiveness of this anger management treatment (Lindsay et al., 2004).

Taylor and colleagues (2005) examined the use of a cognitive behavioral anger treatment for adults in institutional settings. The anger treatment group received 18 sessions of individual treatments. The routine care control group and the treatment group were assessed for a screener, pre and post treatment, and at a 4 month follow-up. The treatment group self-reported significantly lower anger scores compared to the control group and maintained these results at the 4-month follow up. Results also indicated that responsiveness to the anger treatment was not a result of higher IQ range. Staff ratings of anger did not produce significant results; however, the participants did reduce incidents of physical assault and aggression after treatment.

The previously discussed studies relied on a staff member or caregiver to assess anger in each participant. These measures focus on aggressive behavior and anger that the participants displayed. Willner, Brace, and Phillips (2005) used the Profile of Anger Coping Skills (PACS) to identify the anger coping skills that individuals with intellectual disabilities use. Seventeen adults attending a day service program participated in the study. The treatment and control groups were similar in ability and levels of anger. During treatment, the participants attended twelve, 2- hour sessions facilitated by two of the day-service staff members who were trained and supervised by a clinical psychologist. Some topics addressed during the sessions include triggers that initiate anger, physiological and behavioral components of anger, and behavioral and cognitive strategies to cope with anger-provoking situations (Willner et al.). Findings show that the ratings of anger significantly decreased for the treatment group and were maintained at a 6 month follow-up. Additionally, PACS data indicates a significant increase in anger coping skills for the treatment group. This controlled study demonstrates the effectiveness of cognitive-behavioral anger interventions.

Many other researchers examined the use of psychotherapy to produce a variety of outcomes, such as reductions in psychological distress, increases in knowledge about psychosis, improvement in self-esteem and interpersonal functioning, and decreases in levels of depression. In a naturalistic exploratory study of the effectiveness of individual psychodynamic psychotherapy for people with intellectual disabilities, results show that this method of therapy can significantly reduce psychological distress and improve interpersonal functioning (Beail et al., 2005). Further investigation with controlled studies is needed to determine the benefit of psychodynamic psychotherapy to people with intellectual disabilities. Beail and colleagues (2007) conducted another naturalistic study to examine and compare the outcomes of three groups of participants with intellectual disabilities and co-morbid psychological problems. Ultimately, the researchers were investigating whether the dose-effect relationship is evident in psychotherapy with people with intellectual disabilities. Eight participants had 8 sessions of treatment, 5 participants had 16 sessions, and 8 participants had a 24-plus session intervention. Both statistical significance and effect sizes indicate a positive effect of intervention across each of the treatment groups. Results also suggest that the participants made equally rapid gains in eight sessions, supporting the dose-effect relationship. This study is only preliminary evidence for a dose-effect relationship in psychodynamic psychotherapy for individuals with intellectual disabilities (Beail et al., 2007).

In a quantitative study, Newman and Beail (2005) examined whether clients with intellectual disabilities demonstrate changes in level of assimilation within and across sessions. Assimilation tracks changes in a client's understanding of their problematic experience during psychotherapy. The researchers trained a volunteer research team to rate eight transcripts of psychotherapy from sessions for adults with intellectual disabilities who were referred for treatment of psychological problems. Within session results indicate many of the participants exhibited lower levels of assimilation early in the sessions and higher levels later in the sessions. Across session data show that there was a statistically significant increase in assimilation levels across sessions. Results suggest that adults with intellectual disabilities do assimilate problematic experiences during psychotherapy (Newman & Beail, 2005).

Four researchers conducted studies examining the use of group psychotherapy sessions for adults with intellectual disabilities. Group settings can provide a safe environment for participants to explore their problems and practice new coping skills. In a pilot study of group therapy for women who have been sexually abused, the therapy was successful in improving sexual knowledge and in reducing trauma and depression (Peckham, Howlett, & Corbett, 2007). The treatment incorporated both a group for women who survived sexual abuse and an educational support group for the women's caregivers. Five of the 6 participants achieved reliable and clinically significant change in levels of trauma by the follow-up assessment (12-15 weeks after the group ended). Self-esteem did not significantly increase nor did the challenging behaviors significantly decrease, but this may have been because of the small sample size (Peckham et al.). Overall, the clients appeared to benefit from the group therapy by reducing levels of trauma and achieving group cohesiveness.

Another cognitive behavioral group intervention targeted adults with depression and a mild or moderate intellectual disability (McCabe, McGillivray, & Newton, 2006). Thirty four participants completed the intervention program and there was a control group of 15 participants. All of the adults had sufficient language skills for participation and were randomly assigned to the treatment or control group. There were no significant differences between the groups prior to treatment, but the post-test data indicates significantly lower levels of depression, higher social comparison scores, and significantly reduced frequency of negative automatic thoughts. Compared to the control group, the participants who received the group therapy intervention made significant progress in reducing depressive symptoms and evaluating themselves more positively when comparing themselves to others.

To evaluate group cognitive behavioral treatment (CBT) for men with intellectual disabilities and who engage in sexually abusive behavior, researchers interviewed 16 men who participated in this type of group treatment (Hays et al., 2007). A semi-structured interview was used to discover the participants' views and understanding after receiving group CBT. Most of the participants (75%) remembered that the group concerned sexual issues and admitted to having done something wrong or acknowledged having "sexual problems." Many of the men (69%) reported that they would like to attend another Men's Group. This study was helpful in exploring useful aspects of treatment from the participants' perspective; however, the measures did not assess the efficacy of the treatment.

The other group intervention focused on adults with intellectual disabilities who had convictions for arson (Taylor, Thorne, Robertson, & Avery, 2002). Fourteens adults (eight men and six women) participated in a cognitive behavioral treatment program for recidivistic arson. They received education concerning the dangers and costs associated with setting fires, analyzed their cognitions, emotions, and behavior they experienced when they started fires, and examined the positive/negative consequences of their fire-setting behavior. Results from pre- and post-treatment measures indicate significant improvements in attitudes and interests associated with fire-setting behavior. Additionally, the participants improved their anger disposition and self-esteem.

Summary

Overall, published studies on the effectiveness of psychotherapy for people with intellectual disabilities present positive results. It appears that children and adults can benefit from psychotherapy interventions to treat a variety of conditions. The literature has also shown that both individual and group interventions show benefits. Additionally, interventions that utilize ABA techniques in the psychotherapy context, cognitive, and more affectively oriented approaches have all shown some degree of effectiveness. The notion of "moderate" benefits of psychotherapy again appears supported.

DISSERTATIONS

Some have criticized meta-analyses and other reviews for an over-reliance on published studies. "Published" studies typically have been accepted for publication because they have demonstrated significant results. This may yield a bias resulting in higher effect sizes and overestimations of actual treatment effectiveness. This is sometimes referred to as the "file drawer" problem in which non-significant studies are "filed" away and do not get published, thus not receiving consideration in meta-analyses that use only published studies (Howell & Shields, 2008). McLeod and Weisz (2004) addressed this issue by analyzing the results of youth psychotherapy dissertation studies. They noted that dissertation studies are typically well-designed, include review (i.e., committees) at several steps, and are completed (i.e., published as a dissertation) regardless of the results. Dissertations may represent a more "objective" research base. Thus, we are reviewing the dissertations separately.

Children & Adolescents

Dissertation research on psychotherapy for children and adolescents with intellectual disabilities is quite limited. In one study, the investigator used participants with an age range of 6 to 46. The purpose was to examine the effects of sensory integrative therapy and functional communication training in reducing self-injurious and self-stimulatory behaviors (Hill, 1996). All of the 19 participants were in the profound range of intellectual disability. Seventeen of the 21 target behaviors reduced after the sensory stimulation therapy; however, only 8 of the behaviors decreased at a level of statistical significance. The sensory integrative therapy appears to be an effective intervention to reduce self-injurious and self-stimulatory behaviors in people with a profound intellectual disability.

In a single subject study, the researcher tested the efficacy of a social skills training procedure with an 8 year old girl with Down Syndrome and a moderate intellectual disability (Quintana, 2005). The social skills program targeted off-task inappropriate behaviors. Findings indicate a relationship between the implementation of the social skills program and a reduction in off-task inappropriate behaviors. The same program needs to be replicated with additional participants to illustrate overall effectiveness.

Adults

Several researchers examined the effectiveness of psychotherapy for adults with intellectual disabilities. In a study investigating group therapy to treat inappropriate sexual behavior in adults age 18 to 60 who have intellectual disabilities, the treatment group learned academic information about human sexuality (Daly, 1997). The 16-session group therapy program focused on social skills, sexuality, anger management, cognitive restructuring, and relapse prevention. Another group therapy intervention examined the effects of reality therapy on the self-determination of adults with developmental disabilities. The participants attended six group sessions, and both the treatment and control groups completed the pre- and post-test, a self-determination scale. The reality therapy had a statistically significant increase on the self-regulation, autonomy, and total self-determination variables from the pretest to posttest. The researcher concluded that group reality counseling can be helpful in increasing some factors associated with self-determination for adults with developmental disabilities (Lawrence, 2003). Another specific therapy that a researcher investigated is Acceptance and Commitment Therapy (ACT). Results indicate that the group intervention for adults with intellectual disabilities improved functioning, reduced psychopathology, increased psychological flexibility, and increased time spent focused on the importance of values. The principles included in ACT treatment may assist individuals with intellectual disabilities and mental health problems (Pankey, 2009).

A fourth dissertation discusses the issues of integration in group therapy (Blaine, 2003). Four adults with a developmental disability and five adults without a disability participated in group therapy together. The Brief Symptom Inventory and Target Goals are the outcome measures that obtained significant results; however, the differences were independent of the diagnosis of developmental disability. These findings indicate that adults with developmental disabilities can benefit from therapy, and it may be helpful to integrate people without developmental disabilities into group therapy. Another examination of the effects of group psychotherapy found that adults with dual diagnosis can benefit from group counseling (Oliver-Brannon, 2000). The group treatment included Rational Emotive Therapy and Person Centered Therapy. A single case analysis demonstrated that the treatment group displayed a reduction in target behaviors, learned problem-solving skills, and returned to the community to live and/or work. The other group of participants did not participate in group sessions and findings indicated the members of this group did not show a significant reduction in maladaptive target behaviors. The group setting appeared to be beneficial and produced an environment where participants could share experiences and knowledge with each other.

Other researchers examined approaches to teach relaxation skills to adults with intellectual disabilities. Goodrich (1993) assessed whether adults with all levels of intellectual disability can use relaxation as a coping skill to reduce maladaptive behaviors. Four participants, one from each diagnostic level of intellectual disability, received behavioral relaxation training sessions. Daily counts of maladaptive behavior reduced from baseline to follow-up. Methodological issues such as consistently in time of day sessions occurred, accuracy of maladaptive behavior counts throughout the study, and changes of the behavior management programs require this study to be replicated before generalizing results. Miller (2007) implemented an intervention to assess whether progressive muscle relaxation skills are effective in reducing anxiety. The participants, three adults with mild intellectual disability, learned progressive muscle relaxation skills during 30-45 minute sessions. Findings indicate a direct relationship between the acquisition of progressive muscle relaxation skill development and reduction in anxiety for all participants. A 1 month follow-up demonstrated maintenance of progressive muscle relaxation skills and continued reduction in anxiety.

In an examination of the effectiveness of poetry therapy with adults with intellectual disabilities, Campbell (2007) found that poetry therapy is an effective alternative therapy. Twenty-four participants were randomly assigned to two treatment groups that participated in poetry therapy and two control wait-list groups. Measures of psychopathology, self-esteem, and interpersonal problems were used to assess the effectiveness of the intervention. There was a significant decrease in distress associated with psychopathology and in interpersonal problems as well as a significant increase in self-esteem.

Another intervention for individuals with a dual diagnosis of an intellectual and psychiatric disability targeted improving quality of life. Sixty participants were assigned to either the treatment or control group (30 participants in each group). The treatment group received Interactive Behavior Therapy (IBT). Findings indicate that self-esteem and social skills building using IBT was effective at improving the quality of life for individuals with dual diagnosis. Some of the quality of life variables that increased include: social/belonging/community integration, empowerment/independence, competence/productivity, and overall perception of satisfaction with one's life (Sharp, 2005).

Summary

Dissertation research on psychotherapy for individuals with intellectual disabilities appears to lend further support of the benefits of psychotherapy for persons with intellectual disabilities. As noted, dissertations may represent a more "objective" research base. There has been more research with adults, and as such, more support of the benefits of psychotherapy with adults with intellectual disabilities.

IMPLICATIONS AND FUTURE DIRECTIONS

This review yields a number of conclusions and implications for future research:

- Research on psychotherapy with persons with intellectual disabilities continues to lack an adequate number of well-designed studies, particularly randomized controlled trials (RCT's) which represents the standard for establishing efficacy. Research can be improved with better specification of treatment (e.g., manualized treatments), better outcome measures, and clearer specification of diagnostic categories within the intellectual disability population. Obviously, more RCT's are needed.
- Despite the somewhat "less than rigorous" research base, an overall conclusion is that psychotherapy, as broadly defined, appears to be at least moderately beneficial. We offer that conclusion acknowledging that the interpretation of the literature remains somewhat subjective, and others could reach a different conclusion.
- As research evolves, more attention needs to be paid to the "ingredients" of effective and successful interventions. Better and clearer specification of adaptations to psychotherapy and to process variables (e.g., therapeutic alliance) that impact psychotherapy is needed.
- More research is needed specifically in the child and adolescent area. Given the number of children and adolescents served in the public schools, it appears that effectiveness studies done in that arena would be a welcome addition to the research base.

REFERENCES

Beail, N. (2005). Evidence base for behavioral interventions. *Mental Retardation, 43,* 442-445.

Beail, N., Kellett, S., Newman, D.W., & Warden, S. (2007). The dose-effect relationship in psychodynamic psychotherapy with people with intellectual disabilities. *Journal of Applied Research in Intellectual Disabilities, 20,* 448-454.

Beail, N., Warden, S., Morsley, K., & Newman, D. (2005). Naturalistic evaluation of the effectiveness of psychodynamic psychotherapy with adults with intellectual disabilities. *Journal of Applied Research in Intellectual Disabilities, 18,* 245-251.

Blaine, C. J. (1995). Interpersonal learning in short-term integrated group psychotherapy (Doctoral dissertation, University of Alberta, Canada, 1993). *Dissertation Abstracts International, 33,* 22.

Butz, M. R., Bowling, J. B., & Bliss, C. A. (2000). Psychotherapy with the mentally retarded: A review of the literature and the implications. *Professional Psychology: Research and Practice, 31,* 42-47

Campbell, L. (2007). Poetry therapy for adults with developmental disabilities (Doctoral dissertation, University of Rochester, 2007). *Dissertation Abstracts International, 67,* 7366.

Chambless, D. L. & Hollon, S. D. (1998). Defining empirically supported therapies. *Journal of Consulting and Clinical Psychology, 66,* 7-18.

Chorpita, B. F. The frontier of evidence-based practice. In A. E. Kazdin & J. R. Weisz, *Evidence-based psychotherapies for children and adolescents* (pp. 42-59). New York: Guilford Press.

Cohen, J. (1992). A power primer. *Psychological Bulletin, 112,* 155-159.

Crowley, V., Rose, J., Smith, J., Hobster, K., & Ansell, E. (2008). Psycho-educational groups for people with a dual diagnosis of psychosis and mild intellectual disability: A preliminarystudy. *Journal of Intellectual Disabilities, 12,* 25-39.

Daly, M. A. (1997). Group therapy to address inappropriate sexual behavior in a male population with developmental disabilities (Doctoral dissertation, Cleveland State University, 1997). *Dissertation Abstracts International, 58,* 2669.

Elvins, R., & Green, J. The conceptualization and measurement of therapeutic alliance: An empirical review. *Clinical Psychology Review, 28,* 1167-1187.

Eysenck, H. J. (1952). The effects of psychotherapy: An evaluation. *Journal of Consulting Psychology, 16,* 319-324.

Eysenck, H. J. (1952). The effects of psychotherapy. *Journal of Psychology, 1,* 97-118.

Fletcher, R. J., Loschen, E., Stavrakaki, C., & First, M. (Eds.) (2007). *Diagnostic Manual-Intellectual Disability: A textbook of diagnosis of mental disorders in persons with intellectual disability.* Kingston, NY: NADD Press.

Goodrich, D. M. (1993). Behavioral relaxation training with mentally retarded persons: Relaxation acquisition, relaxation as a coping skill, and generality and maintenance of effects (Doctoral dissertation, The University of Texas at Austin, 1992). *Dissertation Abstracts International, 53,* 3848.

Hays, S.J., Murphy, G.H., Langdon, P.E., Rose, D., & Reed, T. (2007). Group treatment for men with intellectual disability and sexually abusive behavior: Service user views. *Journal of Intellectual and Developmental Disability, 32*(2), 106-116.

Hill, C. (1996). Treating self-injurious and self-stimulatory behaviors with sensory integration: A comparison with communication training (Doctoral dissertation, California School of Professional Psychology Fresno, 1995). *Dissertation Abstracts International, 57,* 698..

Howell, R. T., & Shields, A. L. (2008). The file drawer problem in reliability generalization: A strategy to compute a fail-safe N with reliability coefficients. *Educational and Psychological Measurement, 68,* 120-128.

Hurley, A. D. (2005). Psychotherapy is an essential tool in the treatment of psychiatric disorders for people with mental retardation. *Mental Retardation, 43,* 445-448.

King, N., Lancaster, N., Wynne, G., Nettleton, N., & Davis, R. (1999). Cognitive-behavioral anger management training for adults with mild intellectual disability. *Scandinavian Journal of Behavior Therapy, 28,* 19-22.

King, R. (2005). Proceeding with compassion while awaiting the evidence: Psychotherapy and individuals with mental retardation. *Mental Retardation, 43,* 448-450.

Lawrence, D. H. (2003). The effects of reality therapy group counseling on the self determination of persons with developmental disabilities (Doctoral dissertation, Wayne State University, 2003). *Dissertation Abstracts International, 64,* 811.

Levitt, E. E. (1957). The results of psychotherapy with children: An evaluation. *Journal of Consulting Psychology, 21,* 186-189.

Levitt, E. E. (1963). The results of psychotherapy with children: A further evaluation. *Behavior Research and Therapy, 60,* 326-329.

Levitt, E. E. (1971). Research of psychotherapy with children. In A. E. Bergin & S. L. Garfield (Eds.), *Handbook of psychotherapy and behavior change* (pp. 474-493). New York: Wiley.

Lindsay, W. R., Allan, R., Parry, C., Macleod, F., Cottrell, J, Overend, H., & Smith, A. W. (2004). Anger and aggression in people with intellectual disabilities: Treatment and follow-up of consecutive referrals and a waiting list comparison. *Clinical Psychology and Psychotherapy, 11,* 255-264.

Lindsay, W. R., Olley, S., Baillie, N., & Smith, A. H. W. (1999). Treatment of adolescent sex offenders with intellectual disabilities. *Mental Retardation, 37*(3), 201-211.

Matson, J. L., Kazdin, A. E., & Senatore, V. (1984). Psychometric properties of the Psychopathology Instrument for Mentally Retarded Adults. *Applied Research in Mental Retardation, 5,* 81-89.

McCabe, M.P., McGillivray, J.A., & Newton, D.C. (2006). Effectiveness of treatment-programmes for depression among adults with mild/moderate intellectual disability. *Journal of Intellectual Disability Research, 50*(4), 239-247.

McLeod, B. D., & Weisz, J. R. (2004). Using dissertations to examine potential bias in child and adolescent clinical trials. *Journal of Consulting and Clinical Psychology, 72,* 235-251.

Metzloff, J. & Kornreich, M. (1970). *Research in psychotherapy.* New York: Atherton.

Miller, M. L. (2007). Teaching relaxation skills to adults with intellectual disability and generalized anxiety disorder (Doctoral dissertation, University of Wyoming, 2007). *Dissertation Abstracts International, 68,* 8405.

Murphy, G., Powell, S., Guzman, A.M., & Hays, S.J. (2007). Cognitive-behavioral treatment for men with intellectual disabilities and sexually abusive behavior: A pilot study. *Journal of Intellectual Disability Research, 51,* 902-912.

Newman, D.W., & Beail, N. (2005). Analysis of assimilation during psychotherapy with people who have mental retardation. *American Journal on Mental Retardation, 110*(5), 359-365.

Nezu, C. M., & Nezu, A. M. (1994). Outpatient psychotherapy for adults with mental retardation and concomitant psychopathology: Research and clinical imperatives. *Journal of Consulting and Clinical Psychology, 62,* 34-42.

Oliver-Brannon, G. (2000). Counseling and psychotherapy in group treatment with the dually diagnosed (mental retardation and mental illness) (Doctoral dissertation, The Union Institute, 1999). *Dissertation Abstracts International, 60,* 5230.

Pankey, J. (2009). Acceptance and commitment therapy with dually diagnosed individuals (Doctoral dissertation, University of Nevada, 2008). *Dissertation Abstracts International, 69,* 7922.

Peckham, N.G., Howlett, S., & Corbett, A. (2007). Evaluating a survivors group pilot for a women with significant intellectual disabilities who have been sexually abused. *Journal of Applied Research in Intellectual Disabilities, 20*(4), 308-322.

Peirce, J. T. (2006). Efficacy of imagery rehearsal treatment related to specialized populations: A case study and brief report. *Dreaming, 16*(4), 280-285.

Prout, H. T., Chard, K. M., Nowak-Drabik, K. M., & Johnson, D. M. (2000). Determining the effectiveness of psychotherapy with persons with mental retardation: The need to move toward empirically based treatment. *NADD Bulletin, 8,* 3-9.

Prout, H. T., & Nowak-Drabik, K. M. (2003). Psychotherapy with persons with mental retardation: An evaluation of effectiveness. *American Journal on Mental Retardation, 108,* 82-93.

Prout, H. T., & Strohmer, D. C. (1991). *The Emotional Problems Scales.* Lutz, FL: Psychological Assessment Resources.

Quintana, A. (2005). Efficacy of a social skills training procedure used on a child having moderate mental retardation (Doctoral dissertation, The University of Texas-PanAmerican, 2004). *Dissertation Abstracts International, 43,* 663.

Rachman, S. (1971). *The effects of psychotherapy.* Oxford: Pergamon Press.

Reiss, S. (1988.) *Reiss Screen for Maladaptive Behavior.* Columbus: IDS Publishing.

Sharp, D. L. (2005). The effect of self-esteem and social skills building on individuals with a dual diagnosis using interactive behavior therapy (Doctoral dissertation, Alliant International University Fresno, 2005). *Dissertation Abstracts International, 66,* 1736.

Smith, M. L., & Glass, G. V. (1977). Meta-analysis of psychotherapy outcome studies. *American Psychologist, 32,* 752-760.

Smith, M. L., & Glass, G. V. (1980) *The benefits of psychotherapy.* Baltimore: Johns Hopkins University Press.

Sterkenburg, P. S., Janssen, C. G. C., Schuengel, C. (2008) The effect of an attachment-based behavior therapy for children with visual and severe intellectual disabilities. *Journal of Applied Research in Intellectual Disabilities, 21*(2), 126-135.

Sturmey, P. (2004). Cognitive therapy with people with intellectual disabilities. *Clinical Psychology and Psychotherapy, 11,* 222-232.

Sturmey, P. (2005). Against psychotherapy with people who have mental retardation. *Mental Retardation, 43,* 55-57.

Sturmey, P. (2006a). Against psychotherapy with people who have mental retardation: In response to the responses. *Mental Retardation, 44,* 71-74.

Sturmey, P. (2006b). On some recent claims for the efficacy of cognitive therapy for people with intellectual disabilities. *Journal of Applied Research in Intellectual Disaiblities, 19,* 109-117.

Taylor, J. (2005). In support of psychotherapy for people who have mental retardation. *Mental Retardation, 43,* 450-453.

Taylor, J.L., Novaco, R.W., Gillmer, B.T., Robertson, A., & Thorne, I. (2005). Individual cognitive-behavioural anger treatment for people with mild-borderline intellectual disabilities and histories of aggression: A controlled trial. *British Journal of Clinical Psychology, 44,* 367-382.

Taylor, J.L., Thorne, I., Robertson, A., & Avery, G. (2002). Evaluation of a group intervention for convicted arsonists with mild and borderline intellectual disabilities. *Criminal Behaviour and Mental Health, 12,* 282-293.

Whitehouse, R. M., Tudway, J. A., Look, R., & Kroese, B. S. (2006). Adapting individual psychotherapy for adults with intellectual disabilities: A comparative review of cognitive-behavioural and psychodynamic literature. *Journal of Applied Research in Intellectual Disablities, 19,* 55-65.

Willner, P. (2005). The effectiveness of psychotherapeutic interventions for people with learning disabilities: A critical review. *Journal of Intellectual Disability Research, 49,* 73-85.

Willner, P., Brace, N., & Phillips, J. (2005). Assessment of anger coping skills in individuals with intellectual disabilities. *Journal of Intellectual Disability Research, 49*(5), 329-339..

CHAPTER 13

Ethical Issues in Counseling Clients with Disabilities

Dick Sobsey, Ed.D.

INTRODUCTION

This chapter presents general ethical principles as they pertain to counseling relationships, most specifically psychotherapy, and describes how they can be applied to the counseling of individuals with developmental disabilities. A great deal has been published about ethics in psychotherapy or in counseling in general, but very little has been published on the ethics in counseling clients with intellectual or developmental disabilities. While this gap in the literature is lamentable in many respects, it also raises a valuable question: Are there any differences between the ethics of counseling or carrying out psychotherapy with individuals with and without intellectual disabilities?

In writing this chapter, I begin from the assumption that there are no differences in principle, and only small and subtle differences in application. Therefore, the focus of this chapter is not the creation of a separate area of ethics discourse, but rather on how a unified concept of counseling ethics can be applied to working with clients with intellectual disabilities.

The terms *psychotherapy* and *counseling* have specific meanings as they are used in this chapter. As used here, *psychotherapy* refers to a wide range of psychological or behavioral techniques used to treat an identified psychological problem. As the suffix *therapy* implies, it is intended to heal or rehabilitate. As used here, the term *counseling* is broader. It may employ all of the same modalities and techniques as psychotherapy, but it may or may not be employed to treat a problem. Its goal is not always to *fix* something. It can also be employed simply to optimize adjustment or support the individual. For example, counseling may be used to assist an individual with an intellectual disability to make important decisions about where to live or what career to pursue in the absence of any pathology or need for healing. Therefore, in this chapter, I will use the term *counseling* to refer to the broader process and restrict the use of the term *psychotherapy* to instances when it specifically applies.

The remainder of this chapter is divided into three sections. The first of these briefly reviews the approaches to counseling ethics, the next applies these more specifically to counseling individuals with intellectual disabilities providing illustrative examples, and the final section briefly provides additional discussion.

COUNSELING ETHICS

The term *ethics* applies both to the values and principles that guide behavior based on what is considered to be morally right or acceptable and to the process by which we determine the morally preferred course of action. Values and principles provide a framework for making decisions. In many cases the "right" thing to do is obvious, and ethical decisions are easy. We know what is right and what is wrong and choose between them. In some cases, the "right" course of action is more difficult to determine, and in a few cases there is no "right" course of action, and we are forced to choose among what appear to be a variety of bad alternatives. While both the easy and difficult decisions may be guided by ethics, the role of ethics is often more obvious in making the difficult decisions because they often require us to consciously reflect on the ethical issues involved.

There are numerous approaches to counseling ethics. These approaches are not mutually exclusive and overlap considerably. A few prominent ones are described briefly here.

VIRTUE ETHICS

Virtue ethics are based on the attributes or qualities of the individual, in this case the counselor. This approach to ethics relies on the belief that a person's character is more vital to an ethical outcome than any external set of principles or rules. In this framework a counselor can be said to be ethical if he or she exhibits the ideal virtues of a counselor. These may include universal virtues, which apply to everyone, or specific, which apply only or primarily to counselors. Of course, universal virtues can have very specific applications to counselors.

Ideal virtues tend to be culturally determined, and different schools of counseling may have different sets of ideal virtues, but commonly identified virtues for counselors include prudence, integrity, respect, and benevolence (Altmaier, 2008). The prudent counselor exercises care in planning and delivering services by being thoughtful and practicing within the law and professional codes. The counselor who practices with integrity is honest and consistent. The respectful counselor recognizes the intrinsic dignity of all clients and treats them as valued individuals. The benevolent counselor consistently attempts to do good for clients and others.

UTILITARIAN ETHICS

Utilitarian ethics is based on the concept of the "greatest good for the greatest number." Utilitarianism focuses on consequences or outcomes rather than on the process or virtues of the individual (Truscott & Crook, 2004). The ethical counselor acts to reduce suffering in the world and to increase happiness. Psychotherapy attempts to reduce suffering for clients, and all counseling attempts to increase happiness for clients. While the pursuit of happiness may seem like a great fit for counselors and a simple approach, it may be critiqued as inadequate in some situations. For example, if lying to a client would make the client happier than telling the truth, would it, therefore, be more ethical? Also, the greatest good for the greatest number principle would mean that in some cases counselors should pay more attention to the welfare of others than what is best for their own clients. This might be justified in some extreme cases, but generally we would consider our first duty to be to our clients.

PRINCIPLE-BASED ETHICS

Probably the most commonly discussed approach to ethics is that of principle-based ethics. This approach identifies some basic rules or principles for ethical behavior. Typically these include nonmaleficence, beneficence, autonomy, justice, social responsibility, and integrity. Nonmaleficence means avoidance of doing harm. Beneficence is acting for the benefit of others. Autonomy requires counselors to allow and encourage clients to control their own lives and make their own decisions. Justice obliges counselors to act with fairness. Social responsibility demands that us to consider broader social consequences as well as the effect on our clients. Integrity requires truthfulness, internal consistency, and respect for cultural norms, professional practice standards, and the law. While the overlap between some of these principles and the attributes listed under virtue ethics is substantial, one important difference is that these principles are viewed more as external rules for everyone to follow than the virtues of individuals.

RELATIONAL ETHICS

Relational ethics derive moral behavior from reflecting on developing and maintaining respectful relationships between individuals in various roles (Bergum & Dossetor, 2009). These include relationships between counselors and their clients, clients and the significant others in their lives, theorists and clinicians, and other relevant relationships within the environment.

ECLECTIC CODES OF ETHICS

Each of the previously discussed approaches to ethics provides a useful framework for examining and understanding ethical behavior. In some cases, the approaches conflict with each other. For example, virtue ethics might dictate that the counselor is completely honest with the client, even if the client suffers as a result of the truth. Utilitarian ethics might dictate that the counselor prevents the client from suffering, even if honesty is compromised. In most cases, however, these varied approaches produce similar decisions based on overlapping premises. Furthermore, most actual codes of ethics employed by professional counselors, (e.g. American Psychological Association, 2002: National Association of Social Workers, 1999) do not fit neatly into any one of these approaches, but rather include some elements that can be traced to all of these approaches.

Professional codes of ethical behavior for counselors are extensive and have a long history. The American Psychological Association, for example, adopted its first code of ethics in 1952 and published nine major revisions by 2002 (Fisher, 2003). All of the provisions of these codes can be applied to working with clients with developmental disabilities. This chapter focuses on a relatively small number of elements of these codes and how they can be applied to work with individuals with developmental disabilities. Each of these discussions is introduced with a brief excerpt from one of the professional codes.

RESPECT FOR CLIENTS

Psychologists respect the dignity and worth of all people, and the rights of individuals to privacy, confidentiality, and self-determination. Psychologists are aware that special safeguards may be necessary to protect the rights and welfare of persons or communities whose vulnerabilities impair autonomous decision making. Psychologists are aware of and respect cultural, individual, and role differences, including those based on age, gender, gender identity, race, ethnicity, culture, national origin, religion, sexual orientation, disability, language, and socioeconomic status and consider these factors when working with members of such groups. Psychologists try to eliminate the effect on their work of biases based on those factors, and they do not knowingly participate in or condone activities of others based upon such prejudices. (American Psychological Association, 2002)

Social workers should not use derogatory language in their written or verbal communications to or about clients. Social workers should use accurate and respectful language in all communications to and about clients. (National Association of Social Workers, 1999)

Respect for clients is one of the most obvious ethical duties for counselors, but it is one of the most difficult to maintain, particularly for vulnerable clients with developmental disabilities. While we may all profess and strive for respect, it is important to recognize that attitudes are culturally transmitted and no one who is part of our culture can be entirely free of these culturally endemic biases. This includes people with disabilities and their advocates. Counselors need to think of respect for clients as a work in progress and repeatedly reflect on their own behavior and feelings.

The language that we use is often a good indicator of our underlying attitudes, and respectful use of language is important. Nevertheless, genuine respect can never be replaced with careful choice of words. In reality, it is easy to find examples of individuals who use all the correct terminology yet demonstrate an underlying lack of respect or to find other individuals who use dreadful terminology but demonstrate an attitude of genuine respect.

Person-first language is generally accepted as a standard for professional communication. This means we would typically say or write "person with an intellectual disability" rather than "intellectually disabled person." Of course, this linguistic convention has also been challenged as being euphemistic, indirect, and trivializing a disability. The intent of person-first language is to de-emphasize the individual's disability and emphasize other characteristics. Of course, this raises two questions: (1) Is a disability something that must always be de-emphasized, even when it is relevant, and (2) Can an individual actually choose to emphasize their disability as a part of his or her identity of which they are proud? These are important questions that do not have simple answers and have profound implications for counseling. Developmental disabilities have profoundly affected the lives of many individuals both directly and indirectly. While people are much more than just the product of their disabilities, their disabilities may be an important part of their lives and essential to their identities. Denial or trivialization of this aspect of their lives may make it very difficult for them to feel good about themselves. Nevertheless, for professional communication, person-first language is generally accepted as the respectful standard and should be used consistently.

For direct communication with clients and family members, terminology and usage should be individualized to reflect their own choices. For example, one might argue that there is nothing inherently wrong or stigmatizing about the term *retarded*. In some abstract sense this is true; however, this term has been associated with so many negative ideas and events that many individuals would be deeply hurt by its use. The fact that it would be hurtful to a client or to others is more than enough reason to avoid using this term, regardless of how well intended its use might be.

An additional issue in the use of disability terminology is relevance. Erving Goffman used the term master status to refer to traits that became the sole descriptor of an individual regardless of relevance. When an intellectual disability is relevant to the topic at hand, it should be mentioned. When it is irrelevant, it should be ignored. For example, if one says, "She was appointed guardian for her brother, who has an intellectual disability," we would assume that the intellectual disability is relevant to why a guardian was appointed. If one says, "she is two years older than her brother, who has an intellectual disability," it is unclear why her brother's disability is important.

Finally, non-stigmatizing language should avoid evaluative terms such as "suffers from autism" or "afflicted with a developmental disability." The exception would be when we are actually intending to point out suffering or affliction, for example, she suffers as a result of post-surgical chronic pain syndrome.

SOCIAL JUSTICE

Social workers challenge social injustice. Social workers pursue social change, particularly with and on behalf of vulnerable and oppressed individuals and groups of people. Social workers' social change efforts are focused primarily on issues of poverty, unemployment, discrimination, and other forms of social injustice. These activities seek to promote sensitivity to and knowledge about oppression and cultural and ethnic diversity. (National Association of Social Workers, 1999)

Psychologists exercise reasonable judgment and take precautions to ensure that their potential biases, the boundaries of their competence, and the limitations of their expertise do not lead to or condone unjust practices. (American Psychological Association, 2002)

Ethical counselors are committed to social justice, particularly when working with vulnerable individuals, such as clients with developmental disabilities. In some cases, this may require taking on a role of advocate or ensuring that the client has access to someone who can take on that role. For example, a counselor might be asked to provide trauma counseling to an individual who has been repeatedly assaulted by another client in his or her group home. This client might not have the option of moving to a safer environment and little or nothing has been done to ensure the clients' personal safety in the current residence. In such a case, it may be unethical to simply make the client feel better about a bad situation. Doing so may amount to implicit acceptance or endorsement of an unjust situation.

Of course, stepping into the role of advocate has the potential to affect the counseling relationship, especially if the target of the advocacy controls the client's access to counseling. In some cases, this dilemma can be avoided if the counselor can identify or recruit another source of advocacy for the client. With effective advocacy in place, the counselor can focus on therapy or counseling with a clear conscience. In the absence of another advocate, it may be necessary to assume this role.

COMMITMENT TO CLIENTS, CONFLICTS OF INTEREST & DUAL RELATIONSHIPS

Social workers' primary responsibility is to promote the wellbeing of clients. In general, clients' interests are primary. However, social workers' responsibility to the larger society or specific legal obligations may on limited occasions supersede the loyalty owed clients, and clients should be so advised. (National Association of Social Workers, 1999)

A psychologist refrains from entering into a multiple relationship if the multiple relationship could reasonably be expected to impair the psychologist's objectivity, competence, or effectiveness in performing his or her functions as a psychologist, or otherwise risks exploitation or harm to the person with whom the professional relationship exists. (American Psychological Association, 2002)

A counselor must reflect deeply on the central ethical question, "Who is my client?" The answer to this question may seem simple, but it is often complex in counseling the individual with a developmental disability. To answer the question, one may need to ask some other related questions. Who made the decision for the client to come to counseling? Who is paying the counselor? Who stated the problem that needs to be addressed or the goal of counseling? Whose interests may be served?

Third-Party Requests for Services When psychologists agree to provide services to a person or entity at the request of a third party, psychologists attempt to clarify at the outset of the service the nature of the relationship with all individuals or organizations involved. This clarification includes the role of the psychologist (e.g., therapist, consultant, diagnostician, or expert witness), an identification of who is the client, the probable uses of the services provided or the information obtained, and the fact that there may be limits to confidentiality. (American Psychological Association, 2002)

In many cases, individuals with developmental disabilities are referred for therapy or counseling by family members or service agencies. In some cases, the client with an intellectual disability may be passively cooperative or even be a reluctant participant in therapy. Very few individuals with severe intellectual disabilities identify the need for counseling or therapy independently. In addition the goals of counseling or problem requiring therapy is often identified by the person who requests the service and not by the service recipient. In a significant number of cases, the goal stated seems primarily to benefit someone other than the client. For example, counselors may be called upon to deal with "problem behaviors" of clients whose behavior disturbs other residents of a group home or disrupts the routine of an agency. Such circumstances raise serious ethical concerns.

While the interests of the client and family or agency making the referral may initially appear to be identical, this can change over time in the course of counseling. Koocher and Keith-Spiegel (2008) provide an interesting example of a psychologist employed by a school system to conduct assessments of student's needs. "When the special education budget began to show signs of strain, the superintendant instructed Dr. Rigor to administer shorter evaluations, produce briefer reports, and refrain from recommending additional services or evaluations..." (p. 502). Certainly, Dr. Rigor has a responsibility to his employer, and financial concerns can limit the availability of services. Nevertheless, the lack of service availability cannot ethically justify denial that a service is needed. Integrity and truthfulness require honest assessments, even when required services are unavailable. In addition, the pretense that a valid need does not exist may result in additional harm, since the documentation of unmet needs may be important for future expansion of services.

While the previous example refers to assessment, similar conflicts often exist in psychotherapy services contracted by a third party. The agency paying for a service may have a strong interest in brief, time-limited treatment, which may be very adequate in some cases but not in others. Counselors may be pressured to limit treatment, even when this limit is not in the client's best interest.

The ethical counselor also must determine that any psychotherapy or counseling has a significant benefit to the client, and that the client is a willing participant. In most cases, the benefits to a client should be direct. In some cases, indirect benefits may be justified, but such cases need to be scrutinized very carefully. An indirect benefit refers to a benefit to the client secondary to benefits to others. For example, a client might be referred to eliminate her behavior of yelling during church services. Typically, the client herself would not consider her yelling to be a problem that needs to be eliminated, and it is difficult to see how being quieter would directly improve her quality of life. However, there could be an indirect benefit. If the congregation finds her yelling so disruptive that they would ban her from their church and if she really enjoys church, then it could be argued that she benefits indirectly, since making things better for the congregation would lead to a better outcome for the client. Such indirect-benefit arguments can be made in many cases when behavior is considered in a social context, but they can be dangerous and difficult to evaluate.

The need for careful scrutiny of justifications based on indirect benefits is clear because they require balancing of a number of factors. Are the demands of others reasonable? In the previous example, we might want to know if the yelling is constant and very loud or infrequent and fairly quiet. Is the indirect benefit to the client large enough to justify altering the behavior? We might want to know if the client in our example would truly be devastated if banned from church or ready to move on to another activity with little annoyance. Finally, how intrusive would treatment need to be in order to alter the behavior? Is it possible that merely helping the client to understand that continuing her yelling behavior will mean being banned for church would result in a change of behavior or would some more intrusive treatment be required?

If clients do not initiate the counseling relationship, it is essential to determine their willingness to participate. Most clients with developmental disabilities will demonstrate an interest in the counseling or therapeutic relationship, provided that the nature of the treatment is not aversive or intrusive. Clients who exhibit a consistent pattern of escape or avoidance of counseling or therapy should not typically be required to continue. An obvious exception, might be court ordered treatment, but it is important to remember that even convicted offenders have a right to refuse treatment. Clients with intellectual disabilities should typically have the same right if they clearly express their refusal in some way.

An argument might be made that an individual with a significant intellectual disability is not competent to make his or her own decision regarding treatment, and therefore a guardian or substitute decision-maker should be appointed to make the decision on the individuals behalf. Such substitute consent decisions can be considered in three categories: (1) endorsement, (2) assent, and (3) conflict.

In endorsement, the client consents to treatment, but there is a question of the validity or adequacy of the consent. The guardian agrees with the appropriateness of the treatment and provides legal consent for the client to do what he or she would choose independently. Under normal conditions, this raises few ethical issues.

In assent, the client does not indicate either consent to or refusal of treatment. The guardian or substitute decision-maker provides consent and the client accepts treatment, even if the acceptance is passive, without evidence of objection. Under this circumstance, the counselor has a responsibility to try to determine what the client wants, but in some cases this will never be entirely clear. In this situation, assent of the client and consent of a guardian would typically be considered sufficient, unless the treatment posed a high degree of risk or there were a strong potential conflict of interest for the substitute decision maker.

In conflict, a client demonstrates the desire to refuse treatment in some way, but the substitute decision-maker consents to and requests treatment. This situation raises serious ethical issues that cannot be ignored or overridden by a simple determination that the client is incapable of making his or her own decision. In addition to the ethical issues, this circumstance raises legal issues that go beyond the scope of this chapter. Legal guidance or even court involvement may be necessary to resolve this issue. If a guardian previously has been appointed to make health care decisions, this does not automatically eliminate the client's right to refuse treatment in all cases.

From an ethical perspective, this conflict may be viewed as weighing the relative merits of ethical principles: Autonomy (the client's right to make her or his own decision), beneficence (the likelihood that the client's life will be made better by treatment), and nonmaleficence (the possibility that treating the unwilling client will do harm). In order to ethically justify involuntary treatment, there must be a compelling case that treatment is likely to produce very substantial benefits or prevent very serious harm in addition to reason to believe that the client lacks the capacity to make a reasonable decision.

Conflicts can also occur when counselors work with families or other groups.

> When psychologists agree to provide services to several persons who have a relationship (such as spouses, significant others, or parents and children), they take reasonable steps to clarify at the outset (1) which of the individuals are clients/patients and (2) the relationship the psychologist will have with each person. This clarification includes the psychologist's role and the probable uses of the services provided or the information obtained. (American Psychological Association, 2002)

> When social workers provide services to two or more people who have a relationship with each other (for example, couples, family members), social workers

should clarify with all parties which individuals will be considered clients (National Association of Social Workers, 1999)

When psychologists provide services to several persons in a group setting, they describe at the outset the roles and responsibilities of all parties and the limits of confidentiality. (American Psychological Association, 2002)

Family therapy including family members with developmental disabilities can be very effective and group therapy including one or more clients with a developmental disability has also been valuable in many cases. However, without a clear determination of who is and who is not a client, ethical issues are likely to arise. This determination is also essential to setting goals for psychotherapy or counseling. For example, if the entire family unit is the client, goals should be identified that affect the family as a whole.

While it may be useful in some cases to work with a group of clients that includes an offender and his or her victim, the potential for conflict of interest is great. Unless this potential can be addressed adequately, it may be impossible for one counselor to work ethically with both individuals.

TERMINATION OF SERVICES

(a) Social workers should terminate services to clients and professional relationships with them when such services and relationships are no longer required or no longer serve the clients' needs or interests.

(b) Social workers should take reasonable steps to avoid abandoning clients who are still in need of services. Social workers should withdraw services precipitously only under unusual circumstances, giving careful consideration to all factors in the situation and taking care to minimize possible adverse effects. (National Association of Social Workers, 1999)

(c) Except where precluded by the actions of clients/patients or third-party payors, prior to termination psychologists provide pretermination counseling and suggest alternative service providers as appropriate. (American Psychological Association, 2002)

The ending of a counseling relationship may be particularly challenging with many individuals with developmental disabilities (Mansell & Sobsey, 2001). This potential difficulty in terminating services can stem from a number of sources. The client may not understand the time-limited nature of the relationship. Many individuals with developmental disabilities lead isolated lives and may attempt to hang on desperately to any form of nurturing interaction. The client may not understand the difference between a counseling relationship and a friendship. These and other factors may lead to deep feelings of abandonment when services are terminated.

While it may be impossible to prevent problems with terminating services, the ethical counselor takes early steps to clarify the nature of the relationship to the client and remind the client periodically of the plan to terminate services. In some cases, a gradual increase in time between visits may be useful as preparation for termination. In other cases, helping the client make other nurturing connections can lessen over-reliance on the counseling relationship.

NORMALIZATION, DIGNITY OF RISK, AND AGE APPROPRIATE ACTIVITY

The professional codes of ethics published by the American Psychological Association and the National Association of Social Workers do not directly address the issues of intellectual or developmental disability. Several ethical principles have emerged directly from the field of developmental disability that are worthy of consideration.

Normalization, as used here, refers to making available normal activities, interactions, and patterns of life to people with developmental disabilities to the maximum extent practicable (e.g., Wolfensberger, 1972). It is often followed by a second part, which states that the normalization of the physical and social environment will result in normal behavior. While it is generally true that normal treatment contributes to normal behavior, it is not necessary to the ethical principle, which might be stated simply as the client with developmental disability should be treated like anyone else, unless there is a compelling reason for doing something differently. When there is a compelling reason for doing something differently, deviations from normal treatment should be as small as possible. The principle provides an important ethical foundation, but also has limitations. For example, the normalization principle should not be used as an excuse for neglecting legitimate needs or protections.

One specific application of the normalization principle is the ethical requirement for age-appropriate activities. Adults with developmental disabilities should not be required or encouraged to act like children and should be engaged in age-appropriate activities in normal environments (Brown et al, 1979). Again, this principle provides a valuable starting point for consideration of the client's best interest. This, too, however, has some limitations. One limitation is that adults without intellectual disabilities sometimes engage in childish activities. Well-educated physicians, engineers, and professors have often been known to wear ties or watches with cartoon characters, without major social consequences. Perhaps people with developmental disabilities should be allowed the same freedom. A second limitation is that the focus should be on developing adaptive age-appropriate behavior rather than on restricting age-inappropriate behavior. Using this principle to restrict the client's freedom of choice is difficult to defend ethically. Opening up new possibilities for more age-appropriate activities does not create the same ethical difficulty.

Dignity of risk is another valuable ethical principle. Families and agencies may be so focused on the safety of the client that they deny opportunities for a richer fuller life. The principle of dignity of risk says that individuals with intellectual disabilities must be allowed to take reasonable risks in order to achieve fuller, richer lives (Per-ske, 1972). It is important to note that this mandates *reasonable* risks, and it is a not intended to mandate a total abandonment of personal safety. Ethical counselors must reflect on the proper balance between risk and reward to assist the client and all others involved to respect the dignity of risk.

CONCLUSION

This chapter has provided a discussion of a variety of ethical issues in counseling and psychotherapy of clients with intellectual disabilities. It provides some general principles and identifies some, but by no means all, of the ethical issues. It raises ques-tions but provides few if any answers. The answers must be generated individually by finding a balance among principles based on the specific characteristics of the client and the circumstances.

Ethical decision-making is rarely simple. When the distinction between right and wrong is clear and absolute, there is little need for deliberation. It is a simple choice to do what is obviously right or not do what is obviously wrong. In the real world, however, the distinctions are rarely unambiguous. Sometimes, the decision appears to be between two actions that both appear to be in some way "wrong." The ethical counselor can only promise to reflect and deliberate honestly on the balance that best serves the needs of the client.

REFERENCES

American Psychological Association. (2002). Ethical Principles of Psychologists and Code of Conduct. Retreived from http://www.apa.org/ethics/code2002.html on 20 August 2009.

Altmaier, E.M. (2008). Virtue ethics. In F.T.L. Leong (Ed.), *Encyclopedia of counsel-ing* (vol.1, pp. 442-443). Thousand Oaks, CA: Sage.

Bergum, V., & Dossetor, J. (2005). *Relational ethics.* Hagerstown, MD: University Publishing Group.

Brown, L., Branston, M.B., Hamre-Nietupski, S. Pumpian, I., Certo, N., & Gruen-wald, L. (1979). A strategy for developing chronological-age-appropriate and functional curriculum content for severely handicapped adolescents and young adults. *Journal of Special Education 13,* 81-90.

Fisher, C.B. (2003). *Decoding the ethics code: A practical guide for psychologists.* Thousand Oaks, CA: Sage.

Koocher, G.P., & Keith-Speigel, P. (2008*). Ethics in psychology and mental health professions* (3rd Ed). New York: Oxford University Press.

Mansell, S., & Sobsey, D. (2001). *Counseling people with developmental disabilities who have been sexually abused.* Kingston, NY: NADD Press.

National Association of Social Workers. (1999). Code of Ethics. Retrieved from http://www.socialworkers.org/pubs/code/code.asp on 20 August 2009.

Perske, R. (1972). The dignity of risk. In W. Wolfensberger (Ed.), *Normalization: The principle of normalization in human services.* (pp. 194 – 200). Toronto, ON: National Institute on Mental Retardation.

Sobsey, D., & Truscott, D. (2008) Ethical considerations in the treatment of chronic pain. In S. Rashiq, D. Schopflocher, P. Taenzer & E. Jonsson (Eds.), *Chronic pain: A health policy perspective* (pp. 51-57). Weinheim, Germany: WILEY-VCH berlag GmbH & Co

Truscott, D., & Crook, K, (2004). *Ethics for the practice of psychology in Canada.* Edmonton: University of Alberta Press.

Wolfensberger, W. (1972). T*he normalization principle in human services.* Toronto: National Institute on Mental Retardation.

CHAPTER 14

Training Psychotherapy Interns to Work with People Who Have Intellectual Disabilities: Developing Generic Skills and a Multi-Theoretical Approach

Gerald M. Drucker, Ph.D.

INTRODUCTION

In this chapter I will describe the approach I have developed to training psychotherapy interns to work with individuals who have an Intellectual Disability in my community. This will, of course, reflect my own approach to psychotherapy with these individuals and others, drawing upon many sources and theories, guided by psychotherapy outcome research, and with the benefit of the fine tutelage I have received from my psychotherapists, supervisors, colleagues, interns and clients over the years.

In training interns to work with individuals who have intellectual disability, in addition to the educational responsibility, my goal has always been to expand the access and availability of quality psychotherapy and other mental health services to those with Intellectual Disability and other developmental disabilities, until they enjoy the same access that others in the community have. It is my hope to encourage others to do the same in their communities, as I believe it is beneficial on many levels: to the supervisor, to the intern, to the community, and, of course, most importantly, to those who have an Intellectual Disability, whose mental health problems and other problems in living have historically gone untreated in appropriate ways far too often.

BUILDING GENERIC SKILLS

In truth, once intellectual level is adjusted for, the process of psychotherapy with people who have an ID and supervising psychotherapy interns who work with them is not really that different. Intellectual capacity, educational level, and cognitive style of the client needs to be adjusted for and matched by the psychotherapist for all clients. After all, the Mild ID diagnostic cut-off of an I.Q. of 70 (plus or minus 5) is largely arbitrary and could have arguably been set as much as 10 points higher or lower (actually, I think it is about right in terms of functional capacity, but it is arbitrary). There is no empirical evidence that the process or outcome of psychotherapy differs by intellectual level (Prout and Newak-Drabik, 2003; and see Hurley, Pfadt, Tomasulo, & Gardiner, 1996, and Ryan, 2001), at least through the Mild ID range, who make up the great majority of individuals referred to psychotherapy from the DD population. (This is not to imply that those with lower intellectual skills or other disabilities cannot be helped by psychotherapy.) To the contrary, modern psychotherapy outcome research using meta-analysis suggests that while client variables and extra-therapeutic factors account for much of the variance in psychotherapy outcome (Asay & Lambert, 1999; Wampold, 2001), the single most important variable to psychotherapy outcome that the therapist can control, regardless of theoretical orientation, intervention utilized, or population treated, is the relationship the therapist can forge with the client: the working alliance. Norcross (2010) and others (see Duncan, Miller, Wampold & Hubble, 2010) consider this an empirically validated fact that has been replicated many, many times and the main thrust of many decades of psychotherapy outcome research. A positive working alliance is one of the best predictors of psychotherapy outcome (Horvath & Symonds, 1991; Martin, Garske & Davis, 2000; Shirk & Karver, 2003; Orlinski, Ronnestad & Willutzki, 2004; Norcross, 2010; and see Duncan, Miller & Sparks, 2004 and Duncan, Miller, Wampold & Hubble, 2010). The research verdict is clear: what works in psychotherapy is in the relationship. When one watches films or demonstrations of the masters of psychotherapy practicing their craft from various orientations (including behavioral, cognitive-behavioral, humanistic, existential, gestalt, psychodynamic, family systems, and others), what is striking in most is the quality of relationship and collaboration they have with their client(s) and the degree to which the client is willing to reveal what is going on in his or her life and to engage with the psychotherapist in an effort to improve it. So from my viewpoint, helping psychotherapy interns form a strong working alliance with their clients is the fundamental skill they need to develop and use if they are to be to be successful with their clients, regardless of what theories and interventions they and their supervisors choose to use or what populations they treat. The ability to form a positive working alliance is important and central to psychotherapy outcome and can be considered to be a generic skill that cuts across theoretical orientations and populations treated. For the psychotherapy intern working with those with an ID, as well as with others, it is the key to achieving competence.

A successful working alliance depends upon the ability of the therapist to meet the client where she or he is coming from. It requires the therapist to talk differently to an intellectually high powered professional than to an average working person or to a person with a mild level of ID. Forging a good working alliance requires that the therapist speak the client's language, adjusting the dialogue to the client's sensibilities including emotional state, intellectual capacity, age, socio-economic status, ethnicity, mood, energy level, language, and metaphors. In the attachment literature, this process is called attunement, and the caregiver is said to be attuned to the infant or toddler when their cues, moods, emotional states, and needs are recognized and dealt with effectively, helping the infant self-regulate both biologically and psychologically. It is a useful metaphor to apply to the concept of the working alliance in psychotherapy and has been used by Schore (1994, 2003, 2006), Siegel (1999), and others to explain how a working alliance is formed and why it is therapeutic. Schore argues that the empathically attuned psychotherapist acts as an "interactive regulator of the patient's dysregulated internal states" (Schore, 2006; p.8). This in turn, paves the way for the client (or patient) to learn to do this for him- or herself.

Of course, the first major task for the therapist is to open up the dialogue by encouraging clients to tell their story and then listening carefully to their narrative, concerns, reason for seeking treatment, their problems and strengths, and their goals and dreams. Listening actively and carefully is key. Norcross (2010) in his excellent review of the numerous studies showing that the therapeutic relationship is the most salient common factor in successful psychotherapy opens with a wonderful quote:

"Listening creates a holy silence. When you listen generously to people, they can hear the truth in themselves, often for the first time. And when you listen deeply, you can know yourself in everyone" (attributed to Rachel Remen, *Kitchen Table Wisdom*).

While doing this, the effective therapist stays alert for the emotions that are expressed, focusing on them and reflecting and clarifying the emotional content of the story. Educating clients to the process of psychotherapy, according them a great deal of dignity and space, respecting their need to open up in their own time and way, and communicating your belief in their ability to collaborate with you in an effort to improve their future, and encouraging their hope that they can achieve this is central to a good working alliance. Finding and commenting upon the observed strengths of the client is especially helpful and can help build upon the working alliance and the choice of intervention. Recent research suggests that understanding and respecting the client's beliefs and theory of change is important and helpful and needs to be incorporated into the therapy as well (see Duncan, Miller & Sparks, 2004), although from my perspective this may also include introducing clients to other theories of change and interventions that they may find helpful, utilizing the ones that they resonate with in a collaborative way. None of this is different in the psychotherapy of individuals who have ID once the therapist adjusts his or her language to the intellectual level of the client and accepts a slower pace of discussion. A client may need much encouragement and help to tell his or her story. Looking briefly at the literature on psychotherapy with other special populations serves as a good analogy. For example, papers and books on child psychotherapy suggest using language and metaphors that a child can relate to and understand and educating the child regarding the process of psychotherapy, while securing the child's motivation by making the therapeutic hour rewarding to the child. Often, at least initially, the psychotherapist must make the psychotherapeutic hour interesting and fun before it can become problem and solution focused. The literature on cross-cultural psychotherapy also emphasizes adjusting therapist language and demeanor to attune to cultural differences. The therapist's knowledge of the culture and/or the therapist's willingness to learn about it from the client promotes a collaborative relationship. What is required is achieving an understanding of the client's world and social context: the client's point of view. For those working with individuals with an intellectual disability this focus is the same. The first major task for the intern to master in psychotherapy with individuals at lower intellectual levels (or with any client) is using language that the client understands, in a way that helps the client fully articulate the client's reasons for coming to psychotherapy and the present circumstances of the client's life including his or her hopes, dreams, and fears. I try to encourage the intern to approach the client with a genuine curiosity about the client's life story. It may be necessary to give the client time to become comfortable with the therapist and the psychotherapeutic situation, and he or she may need help and explanation to do this. As is the case with all clients, especially with those whose motivation for therapy is questionable until they learn more about it, it really helps if the therapist can make the hour interesting, enjoyable and fun for the client. Because the vehicle for delivering the therapy to the client is the quality of the relationship, the focus must be on personally engaging the client. Following the client's lead on the client's topics of interest is always a good idea, but it is especially important initially. Finding out what they like, how they spend their time, and their special interests is part of this. I recall seeing a client early in my career whose major topic of interest was telling me, in great detail, about the football game he had watched the previous Sunday, and, at the time (as well as now) I was not convinced this was at all therapeutic. I was much more interested in, and asked questions about, who he watched it with, his relationship with that person, and so on. His focus however, was on just recounting the details of the game. I even asked him if that was what he really wanted to talk about with me, and he said it was. He did this a lot, and I was becoming convinced that therapy was going nowhere, until I talked to his social worker who told me that he seemed to be making much more eye contact with people at work and seemed happier and more responsive. His social worker encouraged me to continue seeing him. To this day, I am not sure what helped: listening to his infinite detail about the football game with interest, or the other, seemingly more relevant topics, that I managed to turn our discussion towards at times. But I am convinced that the apparent gains this young man made during the course of psychotherapy came, in part, from honoring the way he wanted to relate to his psychotherapist.

In all forms of psychotherapy with all populations, the therapist must reflect back what the therapist thinks the client is saying to make sure the therapist understands it correctly and to create the space that allows the client to correct or clarify as needed. With individuals with ID, as is the case when working with children or cross-culturally, it is especially important to keep checking in with the client to insure that the client understands what the therapist is communicating. Actually, this process of mutual reflection and clarification is basic to all good communication, but it is especially important to the psychotherapeutic process. When there are barriers to good communication, whether they be intellectual, linguistic, or cultural, it becomes exceptionally important to insure clear communication using reflection and clarification as well as specifically asking the client to explain his or her understanding of what the therapist is trying to communicate. For example, a middle aged, woman with mild ID referred because of mood swings and emotional lability, came to her appointment this morning expressing nervousness and apprehension about starting a vocational training program later this week. Her stated life goals are getting a job and her own apartment, both for the first time. The following dialogue ensued:

Client: I'm really worked up about this job thing on Thursday.

Therapist: What are you feeling?

Client: I'm really nervous

Therapist (normalizing then clarifying): It's pretty natural to feel nervous about starting something new. What are you scared will happen when you go?

Client (clarifying): I won't be able to do it, and they will fire me.

Therapist (reflecting): So you are telling yourself you won't do well?

Client: Yes.

Therapist (after direct reassurance that she is capable of doing anything requested in that particular program and reminding her of all her previous accomplishments, which include being a caregiver to an elderly family member and assisting in a care center kitchen, suggests a cognitive intervention for her anxiety): So next time you feel scared about how you will do, you need to remind yourself how well you did at the kitchen you worked at and how well you do at caregiving and tell yourself that you can do it. No job you get will be as hard as caring for an elderly person, and you do that really well.

Client: OK.

Therapist (checking to see if she understands the intervention): So next time you think you feel scared you won't do well, what do you need to do?

Client: I need to take a deep breath (she had been previously taught a relaxation technique to counter anxiety) and tell myself I can do it.

Therapist: That's it!

The psychotherapeutic intern working with an ID population is really building generic skills applicable in all settings while developing specific expertise and knowledge with the intellectually disabled. It is also an excellent place for the novice psychotherapist to start learning his/her craft.

ADVANTAGES TO TRAINING INTERNS TO WORK WITH PERSONS WHO HAVE INTELLECTUALLY DISABILITIES

Individuals with mild ID tend to present some unique advantages for the novice psychotherapist. Of course generalizations about any population can be wrong when applied to any given individual, and it is hoped that the reader keeps this in mind. It is dangerous to generalize when one serves unique individuals. While considering typical population characteristics, diagnoses, and personality traits can be useful tools to understanding and helping a given individual, these cannot be taken too dogmatically or applied too broadly; the particular individual or family in front of you always comes first. With this caveat in mind, the first advantage for training interns to work with individuals who have ID is that the course of psychotherapy tends to move slower. The euphemism "slow learner" is used for a reason, and psychotherapy is a learning process. The typically slower pace of therapy and the necessity of first focusing upon and developing the relationship with the client has a number of advantages for the novice psychotherapist and his or her supervisor. The interns do not have to think on their feet quite as fast, have more time to think about and understand what the client is saying, have more time to respond, have more time to gauge the client's reactions, and have more time to consult their supervisor and get input and guidance. There are other advantages as well.

Like any minority group that has experienced prejudice and discrimination, people with ID have all too often not been taken seriously and valued as people. They have often faced the same kind of discrimination and lack of opportunity that all people of difference face too often in our culture. In some ways the legal and human rights challenges people with ID face are perhaps more widespread, pernicious, and commonplace than those faced by people of color, simply because, as a culture, our widespread intellectual chauvinism and discrimination against people who are differently abled is still largely unrecognized. Many of the children and adults who have ID who are seen for psychotherapy have been traumatized or hurt by the segregation, discrimination, teasing, and social isolation they have experienced. As a result, they share many characteristics with other persecuted and oppressed minority groups. Issues around identity, distrust, fear, and low self-esteem, along with feelings of weakness, difference, disenfranchisement, hopelessness, persecution, and paranoia abound in these populations, along with many strengths that can be found when one is alert to them. One big difference is that those who have ID all too often do not have the benefits of a close-knit extended family and the unique cultural identity that are a source of strength to other minority groups. They have often not been listened to carefully, if at all, and have often not had their inner life, their thoughts, perceptions, and feelings respected and validated or their strengths recognized and appreciated. Almost all people appreciate and value it when someone does this, but for those who have often been devalued on every level, being treated as an important person is especially meaningful. For some, it is a novel experience. It forges the working alliance more than anything else and increases the motivation for continuing therapy and learning to improve their lives. For many, having the therapist do this teaches the person to start doing this for him- or herself, increasing the client's self-respect and helping the client become more aware and accepting of his or her own needs, feelings, perceptions, aspirations, and problems. Having their strengths recognized and encouraged helps with this a great deal (as is true for all clients). Intellectual Disability does not mean that the person is emotionally, morally, or spiritually disabled, and recognizing these strengths in this dimension of his/her life can be helpful to the client and sometimes inspiring to the therapist. For some, this kind of supportive psychotherapy can be the bulk of the therapeutic work, much as Carl Rogers exposited in his seminal work "Client Centered Psychotherapy" (1951), paving the way for symptom reduction, improved coping skills and self-regulation, as well as personal achievement.

Another characteristic of individuals with ID in general that can be advantageous for the intern is that they have typically been more dependent upon others, and many have experienced more enforced compliance in their lives than most. This can also present some obstacles. The novice psychotherapist typically feels unsure and somewhat inadequate as a therapist during the psychotherapeutic hour. (At least hopefully they feel this way, as too much confidence can be a dangerous thing for any psychotherapist, especially a novice.) However, the novice will generally feel less threatened and less challenged by an individual with an ID, who often also feels inadequate and unsure. Both the client and the novice therapist are moving carefully and slowly over new and challenging terrain. This is one example of parallel processes at work in both the supervision and the psychotherapy performed by the intern. Both the client and the intern are in a "one down" position in relation to the therapist and the supervisor respectively. The intern therapist's initial task is to create a safe enough interpersonal space for the client to disclose what is actually happening in the client's life, as well as the client's thoughts, feelings, and questions about therapy and the therapist. This task is mirrored in the supervisory relationship, as the supervisor must do this for the intern, finding a way to allow the intern to disclose the intern's real experience with the client, and his or her impressions, thoughts, feelings, doubts, and questions to the supervisor, much as the intern needs to help the client do this. Just as the therapist must facilitate ways for the client to overcome the problems and barriers to feeling relatively more comfortable in exploring and revealing the client's experience of his or her life to the intern, the supervisor must facilitate this for the intern in terms of his or her professional life. The supervisor and the intern must have a working alliance as well, and the supervisor, again in parallel process, models how this is accomplished within the supervisory relationship.

Typically it is easier for the supervisor to get the intern to disclose about the course of psychotherapy with the client and his or her experiences working with the client than it is for the intern to get the client to disclose. While both are in a one down position, the supervisor is dealing with a future colleague and apart from the supervisory responsibilities, which do include an evaluative element, can establish a collegial relationship as a teacher, mentor, and consultant with the intern, who usually is, and needs to be, relatively psychologically healthy. Because individuals with an ID have typically experienced more dependency, more enforced compliance, more prejudice, discrimination, disrespect, and outright trauma, they are usually more reluctant or fearful to disclose for many reasons, including feelings of shame, not wanting to displease the therapist, or for fear of being rejected, teased, or otherwise disrespected. They are more apt to agree with the therapist, to "yea-say" or fabricate answers so as to please the therapist, or simply just not disclose. These same kind of obstacles based upon feelings of incompetence can also be present in some interns in terms of how they relate to the supervisor, and the supervisor must be alert for them and help the intern overcome them to allow open, honest dialogue in the supervisory relationship. In this case as well, the supervisor is modeling for the intern how this can be accomplished, in a process similar and parallel to what occurs in psychotherapy. However, it is much more difficult to overcome the pervasive feelings of being "one down" that cause these behaviors in the process of therapy with people who have ID, and they seem to re-occur more frequently. Phrases I have found helpful in the psychotherapeutic process to overcome these kinds of feelings include "I am working for you," "you are the boss in here," "I want to make sure I understand what you are telling me," and "you need to tell me if I make a mistake or get it wrong." When working with those who feel one down it helps to be less of an authority figure, to level the playing field and help the client be more in charge and more responsible for his/her own therapy by indicating that you are willing to follow the client's lead. This process of empowerment is also mirrored in the later stages of the supervisory relationship, as the intern becomes more competent and experienced and earns the supervisors trust. People with ID are also typically less informed about the psychotherapeutic process than referrals from the general population. Like clients who are young, culturally different, or uneducated, they need far more education about what psychotherapy is, how it works, and what the rules are in terms of boundaries, limits, what to expect, and how it differs from a social relationship. While this educational task needs to be accomplished with all clients in all populations, more time needs to be spent with those with an ID, and it needs to be more carefully explained and re-explained much more with them. This is true for a number of reasons. Firstly, people with an ID require simpler language to understand the concepts, requiring interns to really know and have internalized the concepts they are explaining, rather than repeating the language they learned in their training. People with an ID also require more repetition and re-explanations in different ways, using concrete examples, and need to be checked in with in different ways, such as being asked to re-explain or given a concrete example, to insure they really understand rather than feign understanding. Of course, all this needs to be done without being pedantic and irrelevant to the clients. Their needs come first, but they will present opportunities where communicating this information will be appropriate.

While interns are always encouraged to find their own style and use their own words, the supervisor shares phrases, techniques, interventions, theoretical points of view, and other ways of thinking about and relating to the client that the supervisor has found useful in similar situations. The intern is often free to use the ones the intern resonates with and feels comfortable using. This does not mean that the intern has complete autonomy. Because the supervisor is legally and ethically responsible for the intern's actions and the course of therapy, the supervisor must insure that certain boundaries, rules, and standards of practice are met. The intern must practice not only within the client's level of comfort and tolerance, but within the supervisor's as well. In this respect individuals with ID offer a number of additional advantages for the intern and his or her supervisor. While this may not be true in all settings or for all clients, most clients with ID who are referred for psychotherapy typically have a "safety net" in place. They usually have a social worker or service coordinator who can share background information and facilitate adjunctive referrals. Many persons with ID live within a setting that provides ongoing support and supervision offering an additional level of safety, although this can sometimes be problematic in itself, as the process of psychotherapy should always facilitate choice, self-determination, and thinking for oneself, qualities still not universally appreciated in the supervised settings in which these clients live. While this can be challenging for both the intern and the supervisor, it does give the intern an opportunity to learn about and work with other agencies and the system of resources in place within the community.

Clients who have ID who are referred with a major mental illness will often have a psychiatrist and a call system for emergencies in place. If not, these can often be arranged by the social worker, offering an increased level of safety and information. Thankfully for the process of training interns, many clients who have ID are referred for uncomplicated depression and/or anxiety, often secondary to a life transition. Also, because the incidence of mental health problems is far greater in people who have ID than in the general population, there is a high need for services, allowing the supervisor to attempt to select referrals that are within the novice psychotherapist's ability level. All these factors allow the supervisor and the intern to practice within their comfort level most of the time, allowing the intern "to learn to walk before they run."

Finally, internships that focus upon or include experience with individuals with ID help not only to meet a need that often goes unfilled, but also to increase the number of therapists available within the community who have the skills, knowledge, familiarity, and willingness needed to serve people with an ID, as well as build bridges between the mental health and ID service communities in productive ways.

BUILDING A SUPERVISORY RELATIONSHIP AND INTERN SELECTION

There is a large literature on supervision as well as a fair number of experimental studies regarding supervisor and supervisee characteristics, the latter thoroughly reviewed by Leddick & Dye (1987). It is beyond the scope of this chapter to thoroughly review the supervision literature, but key points will be noted and references given. A good reference work to start with for additional reading would be Watkins' *Handbook of Psychotherapy Supervision* (1997). Forms of mentorship and supervision exist in most fields and professions and have been around for a very long time. For example, joining a medieval guild required a long period of apprenticeship, and many trades unions still require this (e.g. plumbing; electrician), while almost all health care professionals must initially practice as an intern or trainee. Internship and supervision in psychology and psychotherapy, as in other professions and trades, serves several purposes. In addition to providing the intern with hands-on education and training that will better prepare the intern to be an autonomous professional, it serves as a clinical container that limits risk for the client and increases comfort and confidence for the intern during this learning period. Supervisors also serve as an important gatekeeper to the profession, and all supervision has an evaluative element. Because of this and because there is an inherent power differential in this relationship, expectations, structure, process, and limits of the relationship need to be clearly understood and spelled out in a written contract (sample contracts can be found at http://www.cfalender.com/super.pdf and http://www.psychboard.ca.gov/applicants/sup-agreement.pdf among other places).

Psychotherapy supervision initially emerged from the psychoanalytic movement and the work of Sigmund Freud. There are many models of supervision that, not surprisingly, mirror the theory of psychotherapy used by those writing it. For example, one of the most influential psychodynamic models of supervision is that of Ekstein and Wallerstein (1972). In their model, one of the goals of supervision was to increase feelings of empowerment, competence, and autonomy in the intern so as to reduce the intern's understandable anxiety. Ekstein and Wallerstein first elucidated the concept of parallel process where the supervision process is not only didactic and educational for the supervisee, but also therapeutic, mirroring in many ways the therapeutic relationship. The supervisor, while primarily an educator, must create a collaborative working alliance, some have called this a "learning alliance", with the supervisee, as discussed above, where the supervisor actively uses many of the same techniques and skills used to create and maintain a working alliance in therapy, modeling for the intern this therapeutic stance. Since many of the same dynamics present in therapy are also present in the supervisory relationship, the supervisor, in identifying and working through any obstacles to open and honest dialogue about the intern's actual experience of doing psychotherapy, is again modeling the same kind of therapeutic process and stance the intern will need to learn to use in psychotherapy. In this process, personal issues for resolution by the supervisee to deal with in his/her own psychotherapy are identified for the intern. However, just as the client in psychotherapy is not the only source of obstacles to a successful relationship, neither is the supervisee. As a culture, we place a high value on self-reliance and independence, and, partly as a result, we tend to look down upon those who need help. Neither interns nor clients are self-reliant or independent, and as therapists and supervisors we need to be alert for such disrespectful attitudes in ourselves and in others. For example, a supervisor who disrespects an intern may be caught up in the community's disrespect for an unlicensed individual, similar to the community's disrespect for the differently abled, acting out the idea that "I am smart, you are not" or "I am licensed, you are not." Similarly, a supervisor who feels inadequate or challenged by an intern may compensate with an "expert" stance, which does not model a working alliance or help create a "learning alliance" and reduces the intern's sense of curiosity and ability to be honest and genuine.

The competent psychotherapist is always dealing with many unknowns, especially with a new client. Identifying these unknowns, struggling with finding tentative answers, hypothesis testing, and staying open to new information that may be elicited and disclosed, and modifying one's opinion and ideas based upon that new information is basic to the process of psychotherapy; it is also one of the greatest sources of stress for the psychotherapist. The supervisor needs to respect this process, discuss dealing with it with the intern and actively model how to work with it in the supervisory relationship. All involved have to disclose and discuss what they don't know and ask honest questions that may lead to important, but always tentative, answers.

The client-centered model of supervision is based on the work of Carl Rogers and stresses that the supervisor act very much like the client-centered therapist during the therapeutic hour, with genuineness, empathy, and warmth, simply reflecting back what the intern would say with much acceptance. However, as educationally lacking as this may sound to some and out of touch with what trainees prefer now that this has been surveyed (discussed below), the client-centered school did insist on a major innovation, in addition to stressing that interns need a high degree of acceptance and support. Interns were required to provide the supervisor with audio- and videotaped treatment sessions, which they then viewed together. This technology was also adopted in Family Systems schools of supervision, along with live, interactive supervision, and remains today an invaluable tool for the supervision process. The intern gets direct objective feedback on his or her own behavior as a therapist with his/her clients, observing both mistakes and missed opportunities, as well as strengths and skills, that the intern never would have recalled and discussed without such objective feedback. I found this invaluable in my own supervision many years ago, as I would clearly recognize and be confronted with my own initial ineptness. When I remarked upon this, my supervisor would give me the backhanded reassurance that "in 20 years it will come automatic." (He was right, but it motivated me to do better immediately.) Audio- and videotaped sessions remain a powerful learning tool for the supervisory experience, as it helps promote self-reflection (which also can often be a psychotherapeutic goal). Client selection and consent needs to be handled carefully in order to use recordings of psychotherapy sessions. One needs to get written permission from the client, who needs to be carefully selected so as not to adversely impact the therapy. With clients who have ID you need to make especially sure they are comfortable with it and don't feel coerced.

The Cognitive Behavioral model of supervision as espoused Albert Ellis, Donald Meichenbaum, and others is as direct and logical as its therapeutic interventions: the supervisor is a directive expert, therapy skills are behaviorally defined, the supervisor is responsible for defining and teaching them, and the intern is responsible for practicing them until competent, with the supervisor evaluating the skills of the intern and giving direct feedback (Ellis, 1991).

Family systems models of supervision, in addition to using videotape and/or live active supervision during the therapy hour, as well as conjoint sessions where the intern and supervisor are co-therapists, focuses upon how the family interacts as a living system in terms of boundaries, alliances, sub-systems, and dynamics, and upon the impact of the family of origin. The focus in supervision is upon how the family therapist joins, interacts, and intervenes with the family to produce change.

There are developmental models of supervision which focus on the individual growth process of the intern, with the supervisor gradually encouraging and allowing more autonomy as the intern shows greater competence (Loganbill, Hardy, & Delworth, 1982; Stoltenberg & Delworth, 1988). Role perspective models (Bernard, 1997; Stenack & Dye, 1982) emphasize the different roles a supervisor can take (teacher, counselor, or consultant), depending upon what the intern needs to learn or deal with at a particular time in the intern's development as a competent professional.

Neufeldt, et al. (1997) surveyed trainees to determine what they valued in a supervisor as well as reviewed previous research and opinion, most notably a critical review of the literature on trainee expectations and preferences done by Leddick and Dye (1987). The sum of these findings seems to be common sense and from my experience, both as a supervisee and later as a supervisor, seems to have much face validity. Trainees appreciate more structure, direct supervision, didactic teaching, and the provision of handouts early in the supervision, with a shift to collaborative guidance later in supervision as the competence and confidence of the intern increases. They prefer supervisors who are empathic, warm, genuine, congenial and flexible and who give direct feedback on their clinical interventions, model clinical techniques during supervision, and use self-disclosure about clinical challenges and solutions. If one assumes that trainees know what is good for them, they seem to be pointing to qualities that would make for a good working or learning alliance and supervisors who are attuned to their needs at any point in time. I would even go further and suggest that similar to psychotherapy outcome research, in supervision the quality of the working alliance determines to a great extent the success of the relationship. All of the above mentioned models of supervision can be useful when used at the right time and/or incorporated in to the supervisor's style.

There are a number of qualities to look for in an intern applicant, whether or not the intern is serving individuals with ID (and their families). Again there is a large literature on this subject. The Association of Psychology Postdoctoral and Internship Centers (APPIC) cites a list of foundational competencies, basic clinical and personal skills, and personal dynamics that can be trained and shaped. They also provide one of the most comprehensive and standardized evaluative tools, The Psychology Trainee Competency Assessment Form, as well as many other evaluative tools, forms, and resources available online at their web site (http://www.appic.org/training/7_1_training_subject_rev_1_08.htm#Supervision). Frame and Stevens-Smith (1995) elucidate a number of intern qualities to look for, including openness, flexibility, positive attitude, cooperation, willingness to accept feedback, awareness of impact on others, ability to deal with conflict, acceptance of personal responsibility, and appropriate and effective expression of own feelings. The way I would phrase what I look for in an intern includes good social skills and judgment, the ability to accept and connect with a wide variety of people, genuine curiosity, interest in and appreciation of others, and good listening and observational skills. Especially important is the ability to be accepting, empathic, nurturant, and compassionate in a genuine way, along with the capacity to be attentive and emotionally attuned to another by reading facial expression, body language, and other non-verbal cues and communications. Also important for the intern is the ability to be self-observant and in touch with one's own reactions and issues as they pertain to the psychotherapeutic process. In this respect, it is important for the intern to be relatively psychologically healthy. It is extremely helpful if the intern has had his or her own psychotherapy as well, and, if not, it should be encouraged. Not only will it give the intern a better knowledge of him- or herself and his/her own trouble areas and issues, but it will, just as importantly, give the intern the experience of what it is like in the "other chair" during the psychotherapeutic hour. If it were up to me, all psychotherapists would be required to have this experience. I personally think one of the best ways to learn the art of psychotherapy is by experiencing it firsthand. This gives the developing psychotherapist lessons that neither training nor supervision can convey fully, although in some ways a competent supervisor, as discussed earlier, is mirroring the psychotherapeutic process in helping his or her intern to develop.

Carl Rogers, in *Client Centered Psychotherapy* (1951) and subsequent writings, posited 3 qualities essential for successful psychotherapy. He called them unconditional positive regard, accurate empathy, and congruence. By unconditional positive regard he meant that the dignity and worth of the individual is respected and honored in ways that communicate to the client that the therapist considers the individual's being and becoming to be inherently worthwhile, regardless of what problems the individual may reveal or mistakes he or she might make. Accurate empathy Rogers defined as being able "To perceive the internal frame of reference of another with accuracy and with the emotional components and meanings which pertain thereto as if one were the person, but without ever losing the 'as if' condition" (1959, pp. 210-211). I would phrase this as imagining what it might be like for you if you were in the client's shoes, while taking into account how the client might be different from you based upon your knowledge of the client and what he or she tells you. By congruence, Rogers meant that the therapist's genuine attitudes and feelings accurately mirror what the therapist expresses to the client; in other words, the therapist is genuine. Rogers of course elaborated much more on these qualities, and the reader is referred to his books. Rogers believed these qualities alone were enough to produce therapeutic change. My own feeling is that these qualities are foundational skills for the intern psychotherapist to develop. In films of various master therapists using different psychotherapy approaches, as noted earlier, these qualities seem to cross theoretical boundaries and form the foundation of the working alliance, which much psychotherapy research shows as so essential to positive outcome. It is essential for an intern to have this ability. Although the ability can be developed, many of the prerequisite skills and attitudes must already be present in the intern. Fortunately, there seems to be a self-selection process at work here and many interns come with the foundational interpersonal skills and qualities needed. I can assess an intern's knowledge base and training regarding the wide range of theoretical approaches and interventions, the DSM-IV/DM-ID and the diagnostic process in general, APA ethics, child abuse/dependent adult reporting requirements, confidentiality and other legal issues, practice standards, and other issues that form part of an intern's required knowledge base. Any educational deficits in this regard left by their training program can be addressed by tutorial, assigning a program of individual study, and continuing education classes. But I can't build the social skills and social judgment needed to accurately assess and read another individual and connect with that individual on his/her level in the one or two years I might have with an intern. While I think this ability grows throughout one's professional career, one must come with a prerequisite amount of this set of abilities, just as one must come with a prerequisite level of training. I am not suggesting that the psychotherapy intern be given a full battery of personality tests (although some have done this). I have supervised interns with a number of different personality styles, both introverts and extraverts to name one dimension, and it is my impression and belief that no one personality style is best suited. Kitzrow (2001) utilized the Myer Briggs Type Indicator (which looks at personality type on a 4 dimensional scale: introversion vs. extroversion; sensing vs. intuiting; feeling vs. thinking;

judging vs.perceiving) to analyze the interactional and learning styles of supervisors, identifying benefits and deficits to each style. Just as supervisors have different styles based upon personality type, so do interns. Watkins (1997) applied attachment theory/attachment style of the intern, along with other dimensions, to understanding the supervisory relationship. Each intern must develop his/her own style of being a therapist based upon who the intern is and what works best for him or her, just as each supervisor-intern dyad must find a supervisory style of interaction that fits for them. The formation of the supervisory "learning alliance" mirrors what goes on in the therapeutic working alliance because in each of these dyads, the leader, either the supervisor or the therapist, must take responsibility for tailoring his/her style and approach to the personality of the intern or client. Psychotherapy approach and style must be congruent with who the intern is as well as who the client is, and each intern will hopefully find ways, in collaboration with the client and in consultation with the supervisor, to form a working alliance and utilize a range of theoretical approaches and interventions that the intern finds he or she can use effectively. Psychotherapy interns are attracted, based upon who they are and their academic training program, to different theoretical approaches to psychotherapy. (Of course the supervisor can only supervise approaches that the supervisor is competent in, and this needs to be taken into account during intern selection.)

Outcome research (discussed below) that has compared one psychotherapy approach to another has shown over and over that no one approach is superior. My own experience is that interventions drawn from any number of approaches can be useful to a given client when selected to match that client and the client's presenting problem(s). What is important is to elicit client feedback regarding how the client feels about trying and using a given approach and its effectiveness and to stay with approaches that match the client's sensibilities, comfort level, and degree of success experienced. It behooves the therapist to have a "large tool belt" in addition to the skills needed to form good working alliances. Similarly, this therapeutic process is mirrored in supervision. Based upon feedback elicited from the intern about the intern's training, about each of the client's presenting problems, and about the intern's experiences working with the client, the supervisor can suggest that the intern broaden his/her theoretical approach and consider different types of interventions. These may be taught by the supervisor or learned in continuing education workshops. Just as the intern must check in with his or her client regarding the course of psychotherapy and be guided by the client's feedback, the supervisor needs to elicit the intern's ideas and feelings about trying and using a given intervention. Supervision is a collaborative process focused upon helping a given intern find ways to help a given client. At each level, both the supervisory and the therapeutic, it is important to cultivate the art of the practical, eliciting feedback about what seems to be helpful and what gets in the way. The most important allegiance is not to a given supervisory or therapeutic approach, but to being helpful to a given intern or a given client, based upon the feedback that person gives on how things are working. Duncan, Miller and Sparks (2007), reviewing the large amount of outcome research that calls into question the much touted superiority of "evidence based practice" and manualized interventions, have argued instead, in this and other publications, for the use of "practice based evidence," i.e. utilizing client feedback to guide the therapy. While they argue for written feedback, and cite evidence of its effectiveness, my experience is that good psychotherapists and supervisors are constantly being guided by the feedback they elicit and receive. This requires both flexibility and a broad knowledge base.

Just as it is essential to recognize and comment on the client's strengths and find ways to use them to help overcome the client's difficulties, it is important to do this for the intern as well. The supervisor is not only responsible for the client's well being as related to the course of psychotherapy conducted by the intern, but for broadening and deepening the education and competence of the intern.

The mechanics of the intern's placement need to be specifically addressed. I have had intern's in both my private practice, where by California law they must be my employee, and at the agencies I work at where they are either an employee of the agency or on a field or voluntary placement, for their own training and to meet the supervision requirement for licensure. I greatly prefer supervision in an agency setting because it is less of a dual relationship (without the business of running a business with the intern as an employee). However, many competent psychotherapists can make this work to their satisfaction. In either case, I ask the intern for at least a one year commitment, primarily for client welfare but also because the process of supervision takes at least this kind of time. It helps to have a written contractual document with a clear explanation of duties, responsibilities, and expectations, as well as the understanding that the first two or three months is a built in probationary period where either supervisor or intern can exit the relationship if things don't seem to be working or the fit is not right. This underscores the need for careful intern selection because this can be difficult for the clients referred (as well as for the intern and supervisor) and needs to be avoided. It is important for both the intern and the supervisor to be clear on state law regarding the kind of license the intern is seeking (in California this may be either for Psychologist, Marriage and Family Therapist, or Licensed Clinical Social Worker (LCSW)) as well as academic and licensure requirements for supervised hours. They should also be clear about the ethics code regarding supervision of the APA or other relevant professional organizations (such as AAMFT or NASW). Supervision in many ways is guided by the same considerations and boundaries as psychotherapy, as it is an equally important professional responsibility and should not be entered into or taken lightly. In California, the law for interns calls for a minimum of one hour of direct face-to-face supervision weekly, or 10% of total hours worked, whichever is greater. This is a very minimal requirement, and usually more time is needed, especially in the first few months of the internship. Thankfully, interns in a community practice don't walk into a full caseload but accrue clients one at a time, allowing each to be discussed fully with the supervisor.

RATIONALE FOR A MULTI-THEORETICAL APPROACH AND DEVELOPING A TREATMENT PLAN

My academic training, of course, exposed me to most major theoretical points of view. In graduate school I taught the Theories of Personality course for a number of years which helped me understand and internalize multiple theoretical points of view. Looking at the development of psychology as a science and comparing it to other scientific disciplines convinced me that utilizing multiple theoretical points of view is one hallmark of a mature science. Historically, psychology in general, and psychotherapy in particular, has wasted much time on theoretical wrangles and debating seemingly conflictual points of view that have often generated more heat than light. However, this divisiveness seems to be giving way to a more collaborative synthesis as new information from research in neuroscience, child development, attachment, psychotherapy outcome, and other areas are integrated into our theoretical systems. Psychotherapeutic theories and approaches are, after all, models or metaphors that often describe similar things in different languages with different metaphors. Meanwhile, psychotherapy outcome research, especially meta-analytic studies and studies that pit one type of psychotherapy versus another, find little in the way of differences in efficacy based upon differing theoretical approaches. The sum of these many studies is that psychotherapy works regardless of which theoretical approach is utilized. This is a very robust finding that has been replicated numerous times with different populations and diagnoses over many years (Asay & Lambert 1999; Wampold, 2001, 2010; Brown Dreis, & Nace, 1999; Elkin et al., 1989; Godley, Jones Funk, Ives & Passetti, 2004; Luborsky, Singer & Luborsky, 1975; Rosensweig, 1936; Shadish & Baldwin, 2002; Wampold et al., 1997; and see Duncan, Miller & Sparks, 2007 for a recent and brief review and Hubble, Duncan & Miller, 1999, Duncan, Miller & Sparks, 2004, and Duncan, Miller, Wampold, & Hubble (2010) for more lengthy reviews.). Client and therapeutic relationship variables seem to account for much of the variance and seem to be more predictive of therapeutic success as noted earlier. At the same time, there seems to be an emerging logic in the psychotherapeutic community of a structured eclectic approach based upon who the client is and what the client's presenting problem(s) and life situation are, utilizing different theoretical approaches and interventions as tools that may prove effective as first or second choice interventions and mixing and matching based upon client feedback and response. Psychotherapy always draws upon personality theory, if not explicitly then certainly implicitly, because any psychotherapeutic intervention implies a theory of behavior, whether it be biological, environmental (e.g. behavioral, family systems), cognitive, psychodynamic, attachment theory, or based upon individual differences and symptom presentation. Harry Stack Sullivan, founder of the interpersonal theory of psychiatry (Sullivan, 1953) which focused upon people as social beings and personality as something observed in the social world (back when most psychiatrists did more than prescribe medication) once said, "We are all simply more human than otherwise." The clients who get referred for psychotherapy are "people first," whether they have ID or not, and clearly function on many levels – biological, behavioral, cognitive, emotional, and social, to name a few. They need to be treated as people who function on each of these levels, in other words, they need to be treated as whole persons first. Arnold Lazurus' Multi-Modal Therapy (1989) has developed a systematic approach to psychotherapy that attempts to do just that. It has been my experience that many psychotherapists use a structured eclectic approach and seem to outnumber the theoretical purists. Outcome research seems to show that all get equal results as noted above, but from my perspective, similar to Lazurus's, every level of functioning and approach to therapy needs to be considered and anything that may help discussed.

Background information and social history must be understood, psychotherapy explained, symptoms known, goals agreed upon, and working alliance established and constantly maintained as a primary consideration (and as elaborated above all this can and should be therapeutic and sometimes is the bulk of the therapeutic work). Once this is accomplished, a treatment plan – a road map for psychotherapy – needs to be considered.

VIEWING THE CLIENT THROUGH DIFFERENT THEORETICAL AND DIAGNOSTIC "LENSES"

Because psychotherapy is an art, an art based upon theory and science to be sure, the psychotherapist (and the intern's supervisor) is often struggling with many unknowns. Where does this client fit into the DSM (DSM IV/DM-ID) if at all? Does a clear diagnosis present itself? (Many clients seem to be atypical and are not best described by one or several diagnostic categories.) What might precipitate the greatest symptom reduction in the shortest possible time? Are any specific interventions strongly suggested by the client's presentation? What is the client capable of and willing to do? For example, psychoses, depression, anxiety, and ADHD are often greatly alleviated by psychiatric medication, especially when severe, and this option needs to be discussed with the client and his or her caregivers. Sometimes this needs to be very strongly encouraged and supported, as is the case for psychoses and suicidal depression. Everyone involved, client, intern, and supervisor, is on firmer ground when a clear diagnosis can be made and a psychotherapeutic approach that has strong empirical support for treating that diagnosis utilized, as long as it does not jeopardize the working alliance, which outcome research makes clear is the primary consideration. Behavioral and cognitive behavioral interventions for depression and anxiety can often be helpful if the client is willing to utilize them. Posttraumatic Stress Disorder (PTSD), another common problem, can often be helped using Eye Movement Desensitization and Reprocessing Therapy (EMDR) or other cognitive behavioral approaches. Should the client be experiencing a great deal of conflict with his/her family or spouse and this seems to play a major role in the client's distress, family or couples therapy is often a good option to pursue. This can give an opportunity for the intern and the supervisor to see a family or couple conjointly, either as an adjunct to the individual therapy or as the treatment of choice. This can be a great learning experience for all concerned and can address these kinds of presenting problems most efficiently. It all depends upon the client, the client's strengths, goals and beliefs about how to reach those goals, the client's presenting problem and symptoms, and the quality of relationship that the client and psychotherapist can make and maintain.

Developing a treatment plan is a collaborative effort between the client and the intern, and the intern and the supervisor. In discussing a particular client to develop a possible treatment plan with an intern, I initially ask the intern to formulate what makes sense to the intern, both diagnostically and therapeutically, given the intern's sensibilities, training, and experience with the client. I may share how I would approach this issue and what I have felt has been helpful in similar situations. The primary concern is client welfare, and, depending upon the competence of the intern and the severity of the client's situation, this may include the supervisor becoming quite directive at times. The supervisor is responsible for both the client and the intern. Whatever diagnostic formulation and treatment plan is arrived at, the supervisor has an educational responsibility to also share where in the theoretical or diagnostic spectrum a given formulation and intervention fits. Controversies, opposing points of view, and empirical evidence in this regard should be discussed, as well as how other psychotherapists might think about and approach this particular client. I want the intern to develop into a knowledgeable professional who develops his or her own style of doing psychotherapy, utilizing many sources of evidence, information, ideas and "tools." Whatever formulation and plan is arrived at in this collaboration, the intern is actively encouraged to hypothesis test its appropriateness using client feedback regarding comfort level and effectiveness. Maintaining the working alliance comes first, but finding something that the client and those involved with the client find helpful is key. Is this way of thinking about the client helpful to the course of therapy? How are the client and the intern feeling about the course of therapy? Is there any symptom relief or behavioral change? As new information becomes revealed in the course of therapy does it challenge any existing formulations or interventions? When a given approach is rejected by the client or seems to be ineffective or causing additional problems, it is time to try something else. It is helpful to think about diagnostic formulation and theoretical approaches as different "lenses" with which to view and understand the client, the life the client leads, and the life the client wants to lead. A diagnostic or theoretical "lens" is only as good as it is useful in helping the client. Multiple lenses can help us get a better picture of the whole person together with the person's aspirations and goals. Considering the individual's learning and trauma history, relationships, social supports, sources of strength, sources of stress, behavioral patterns as seen and reported by others (think twice about these), likes and dislikes, loves and hates, living arrangements, and daily patterns are all important to consider. Especially important, as noted earlier, is understanding the client's theory of change and how life would be for the client when this change occurs. A key consideration for all clients, but especially those with ID, are their hopes and dreams for a better future (eyes on the prize!). Many individuals who have an intellectual disability have not articulated their hopes and dreams or had their dreams encouraged. Many do not know the options available to them, and need to be educated about these possibilities. Their feelings about themselves and their disability come into play strongly here. Many have been told, implicitly or explicitly, that they cannot do things, such as live independently, date, have a job, or exercise choice. Thankfully this is becoming much less frequent, but it is still common, especially in older clients who have lived with their family for many years. In these situations the family needs to be educated and helped to change as well, so they are not working at cross-purposes with the therapist and client. Clients, especially clients with ID, need to feel that they are working on a better future for themselves and that their symptoms and problems are merely barriers to this, rather than defining who they are. All diagnoses, theoretical formulations, and interventions considered and utilized need to be in the service of this overriding goal, as defined and perceived by the client. For this reason, it is important to look for interns who are flexible and open to learning and trying different approaches to psychotherapy.

GAUGING SUCCESS AND ENDING THERAPY

Getting client feedback on progress in reaching the client's goals is important, and I encourage interns, as I do myself, to keep getting client feedback on that as therapy progresses. Start getting feedback after the first few sessions, as some report help and change quite early. As the presenting problem gets resolved and the client's goals are reached, it is time to discuss ending therapy. Also, this needs to be discussed when no progress is being made, when the client seems to have lost interest, or when there are many missed appointments. Many clients with ID are exquisitely sensitive to rejection, and ending therapy is best made as mutual decision between therapist and client. Some like to taper down and feel most comfortable with that, with appointments gradually going down to every 2 weeks and then every month. Some are most comfortable with ending therapy rapidly, knowing they can come back if they so desire. Some clients strongly desire to keep coming in even when it seems like no progress is being made. While alternative strategies of intervention need to be discussed, such as medication or trying another approach or another therapist, in this case, I encourage interns to listen to their client and what the client wants rather than insist that the intern knows best. People change on their own timetable, and it has been my experience that more errors occur in the direction of too early a termination than with continuing with therapy too long. Many people, but especially people with ID, tend to progress slowly. Usually, if someone has the genuine motivation to come in – and the therapist needs to insure this is the client's own desire – the person is getting something important from therapy, even if the therapist does not fully understand it. Sometimes, the psychotherapy is helping the client maintain his or her current level of functioning, and some deterioration will occur if the therapy is terminated too early. Sometimes there is no observable change or very subtle change occurring for quite awhile, and then progress is made rapidly. My tendency, and I encourage the intern to do this as well, is to trust the client and the feedback the client gives to insure there is a high degree of mutuality and respect for the client's desires in any decision made. For many, knowing that the door is open and the client can return to therapy if he or she so desires helps the client make the decision to stop coming. Being in the same community for many years, I have been honored to know some clients who have come in episodically, years apart, whenever they have faced major stressors or losses, a big decision, a life transition, or have had a reoccurrence of their mental illness. A number of the interns I have supervised have gone on to licensure and private or agency practice in this community, and some have been able to take their existing clients from their internship with them when they go. This is a "win-win" as it maintains client welfare and continuity, while helping the intern jump start his or her practice. Some of the intern's clients and their families have, over the years, also used the intern episodically as a needed resource.

CONCLUSION

Like other writers on supervision, I too have found it impossible to discuss the subject of supervision apart from my own approach to psychotherapy. Psychotherapy is an extremely diverse field, and I realize that there are many psychotherapists out there who practice extremely differently than I do. That is just fine, as I think we all need to embrace diversity even in therapeutic approaches, and the outcome research comparing these approaches seems to say that they all work as long as the client is honored and respected, without which there can be no working alliance. I would encourage all experienced psychotherapists who work with people with ID to consider taking on an intern. I have found it extremely rewarding on many levels, and I think most would. In addition to helping a colleague in your community learn the basics of professional practice and develop into an autonomous professional with hopefully some feeling for, experience with, and commitment to the mental health of people with ID, I think it will be rewarding on other levels both personal and professional. I think that in the process of supervision, the supervisor may discover just how much he or she has learned and perhaps not had the opportunity to articulate, until the supervisor attempts to teach it to someone else. It will also reveal what you don't know or are unsure of, and discussing these points honestly with the intern can be a learning experience for both. Often, especially if you are lucky enough to have a talented intern, you may just learn a great deal from him or her. Certainly the need for more mental health professionals, especially psychotherapists, serving those with ID is there, because if the epidemiologists are even close to ballpark there are too many individuals with intellectual disabilities going untreated, not to mention the family members and others who support them and need all the help they can get. It would also be my hope that larger structured intern training programs would accept referrals from the ID community as a matter of routine, if they are not already doing so, as I think that in addition to benefiting the ID community, serving these individuals would help the training programs and the learning curve of the interns and trainees in them.

REFERENCES

Asay, T.P., & Lambert, M.J. (1999). The empirical case for the common factors in therapy: Quantitative findings. In M.A. Hubble, B.L. Duncan, & S.D. Miller (Eds.), *The heart and soul of change: What works in therapy* (pp. 33–56). Washington, DC: American Psychological Association.

Bernard, J.M. (1997). The discrimination model. In C.E. Watkins, Jr. (Ed.), *Handbook of psychotherapy supervision*, (pp. 310-327). New York: John Wiley.

Brown, J., Dreis, S., & Nace, D.K. (1999). What really makes a difference in psychotherapy outcome? Why does managed care want to know? In M.A. Hubble, B.L. Duncan, & S.D. Miller (Eds.), *The heart and soul of change: What works in therapy* (pp. 389–406). Washington, DC: American Psychological Association.

Duncan, B.L., Miller, S.D. & Sparks, J. (2004). *The heroic client: A revolutionary way to improve effectiveness through client-directed, outcome-informed therapy.* San Francisco: Jossey-Bass.

Duncan, B.L, Miller, S.D. & Sparks, J. (2007). Common factors and the uncommon heroism of youth. *Psychotherapy in Australia, 13,* 2, 34-43.

Duncan, B.L., Miller, S.D., Wampold, B.E., & Hubble, M.A. (Eds.) (2010), *The heart and soul of change* (2nd ed.). Washington, D.C.: The American Psychological Association.

Ekstein, R. & Wallerstein, R. (1972). *The teaching and learning of psychotherapy.* New York: Basic Books.

Elkin, I., Shea, T., Watkins, J.T., Imber, S.D., Sotsky, S.M., Collins, J.F., et al. (1989). National Institute of Mental Health Treatment of Depression Collaborative Research Program: General effectiveness of treatments. *Archives of General Psychiatry, 46,* 971–982.

Ellis, M. (1991). Critical incidents in clinical supervision and in supervisor supervision assessing supervisory issues. *Journal of Counseling Psychology, 38*, 342–349.

Frame, M.W. and Stevens-Smith, P. (1995). Out of harms way: Enhancing monitoring and dismissal processes in counselor education programs. *Counseling Education and Supervision*, 35, 118-129.

Godley, S.H., Jones, N., Funk, R., Ives, M. & Passetti, L. (2004). Comparing outcomes of best-practice and research based outpatient treatment protocols for adolescents. *Journal of Psychoactive Drugs, 36*(1), 35–48.

Horvath, A.O., & Symonds, B.D. (1991). Relation between working alliance and outcome in psychotherapy: A meta-analysis. *Journal of Counseling Psychology, 38,* 139-149.

Hubble, M.A., Duncan, B.L., & Miller, S.D. (Eds.). (1999). *The heart and soul of change: What works in therapy.* Washington, DC: American Psychological Association.

Hurley, A.D., Pfadt, A. Tomasulo, D. & Gardiner, W. I. (1996). Counseling and psychotherapy. In J.W. Jacobson, & J.A. Mulick (Eds.), *Manual of diagnosis and professional practice in mental retardation* (pp. 371-378). Washington, D.C.: American Psychological Association.

Kitzrow, M.A. (2001). Application of psychological type in clinical supervision. *Clinical Supervisor, 20,* 133-146.

Lazurus, A. (1989). *The practice of multimodal therapy: systematic, comprehensive- and effective psychotherapy.* Baltimore: John Hopkins University Press.

Leddick, G.R., & Dye, H.A. (1987, December). Effective supervision as portrayed by trainee expectations and preferences. *Counselor Education and Supervision,* 139-154.

Loganbill, C., Hardy, E. & Delworth, U. (1982). Supervision: A conceptual model. *The Counseling Psychologist, 10*, 3-42.

Luborsky, L., Singer, B., & Luborsky, L. (1975). Comparative studies of psychotherapies: Is it true that 'everyone has won and all must have prizes'? *Archives of General Psychiatry, 32*, 995–1008.

Martin, D.J., Garske, J.P., & Davis, M.K. (2000) Relation of the therapeutic alliance with outcome and other variables: A meta-analytic review. *Journal of Consulting and Clinical Psychology, 68,* 438-450.

Neufeldt, S.A (1999). *Supervision strategies for the first practicum* (2nd ed.). Alexandra, VA: American Counseling Association.

Neufedt, S.A., Beutler, L.E., & Banchero, R. (1997). Research on supervisor variables in psychotherapy supervision. In C.E. Watkins, Jr. (Ed.), *Handbook of psychotherapy supervision* (pp. 508-524). New York: John Wiley.

Norcross, J.C. (2010): The therapeutic relationship. In B.L Duncan., S.D. Miller, B.E. Wampold, & Hubble, M.A. (Ed.), *The heart and soul of change* (2nd ed.) (pp. 113-141). Washington, D.C. The American Psychological Association.

Orlinski, D.E., Ronnestad, M.H. & Wiillutzki, U. (2004). Fiftey years of process-outcome research: Continuity and change. In M.J. Lambert (Ed.), Bergin and Garfield's *Handbook of psychotherapy and behavior change* (5th ed.) (pp. 307-390). New York, John Wiley.

Prout, H.T. & Newak-Drabik, K.M. (2003). Psychotherapy with persons who have mental retardation: An evaluation of effectiveness. *American Journal of Mental Retardation, 108(2),* 82-93

Rogers, C. R. (1951). *Client-centered psychotherapy; Its current practice, implications and theory.* Boston: Houghton-Mifflin.

Rogers, C. R. (1959). A theory of therapy, personality and interpersonal relationships, as developed in the client-centered framework. In S. Koch (Ed.), *Psychology: A study of science (Vol. 3)* (pp. 184-256). New York: Mc Graw Hill.

Rosenzweig, S. (1936). Some implicit common factors in diverse methods of psychotherapy. *American Journal of Orthopsychiatry, 6,* 412–415.

Ryan, R. (2001). *Handbook of mental health care for persons with developmental disabilities.* Canada: Diverse City Press.

Schore, A.N. (1994). *Affect regulation and the origin of the self.* Mahweh NJ: Erlbaum.

Schore, A.N. (2003). *Affect regulation and the repair of the self.* New York: WW Norton.

Schore, A.N. (2006). Right brain attachment dynamics: An essential mechanism of psychotherapy. *California Psychologist, 39 (3),* 6-8.

Shadish, W. R., & Baldwin, S. A. (2002). Meta-analysis of MFT interventions. In D. H. Sprenkle (Ed.), *Effectiveness research in marriage and family therapy* (pp. 339–370). Alexandria, VA: American Association for Marriage and Family Therapy.

Shirk, S.R. & Karver, M. (2003) Prediction of treatment outcome from relationship variables in child and adolescent therapy: A meta-analytic review. *Journal of Consulting and Clinical Psychology, 71*(3), 452-464.

Siegel, D.J. (1999) *The developing mind.* New York: The Guilford Press.

Stenack, R.J. and Dye, H.A. (1982). Behavioral descriptions of counseling supervision roles. *Counselor Education and Supervision, 22,* 295-304.

Stoltenberg, C.D. & Delworth, U. (1988). Developmental models of supervision. Its development. Response to Holloway. Professional Psychology: *Research and Practice, 19,* 134-137.

Sullivan, H.S. (1953). *The interpersonal theory of psychiatry.* New York: Norton.

Wampold, B.E. (2001). The great psychotherapy debate: Models, methods, and findings. Hillsdale, NJ: Lawrence Erlbaum.

Wampold, B.E. (2010). The research evidence for the common factors models: A historically situated perspective. In B.L. Duncan, S.D. Miller, B.E. Wampold, & M.A. Hubble(Eds.), *The heart and soul of change* (2nd ed.) (pp. 49-81). Washington, D.C. The American Psychological Association.

Wampold, B. E., Mondin, G. W., Moody, M., Stich, F., Benson, K., & Ahn, H. (1997). A meta-analysis of outcome studies comparing bona fide psychotherapies: Empirically, 'All must have prizes.' *Psychological Bulletin, 122*, 203–215.

Watkins, C.E., Jr. (Ed.) (1997) *Handbook of psychotherapy supervision.* New York: John Wiley.

Authors

Daniel J. Baker, PhD
Associate Professor of Pediatrics
Elizabeth M. Boggs Center on Developmental Disabilities
Robert Wood Johnson Medical School, UMDNJ
New Brunswick, NJ

E. Richard Blumberg, PhD
Associate Professor
Department of Special Education, Language & Literacy
The College of New Jersey
Ewing, NJ

Brooke K. Browning, MS
Doctoral Student, School Psychology
Department of Educational, School, and Counseling Psychology
University of Kentucky
Lexington, KY

Margaret Charlton, PhD, ABPP
Clinical Psychologist
Aurora Mental Health Center
Aurora, CO

Gerald M. Drucker, PhD
Psychologist
Private Practice
Eureka, CA

Eric J. Dykstra, PsyD
Licensed Psychologist
Developmental Enhancement, PLC
Jenison, MI

Valerie L. Gaus, PhD
Clinical Psychologist
Private Practice
Cold Spring Hills, NY

Judith L. Hill-Weld, MS, LMFT
Licensed Marriage & Family Therapist
Private Practice
Nevada City, CA

Jeffrey Kauffman, MA, LCSW
Psychotherapist
Jeffrey Kauffman Psychotherapy
Chester Springs & Ardmore, PA

Marvin B. Lew, PhD, ABPP
Adjunct Professor
Center for Psychological Studies
Nova Southeastern University
Fort Lauderdale, FL

J. Dale Munro, MSW, RSW, FAAIDD
Clinical Supervisor
Regional Support Associates
London, Ontario, Canada

Theodosia R. Paclawskyj, PhD, BCBA
Assostant Professor
Department of Psychiatry and Behavioral Sciences
The Johns Hopkins University School of Medicine
Faculty, Behavioral Psychology
Kennedy Krieger Institute
Baltimore, MD

H. Thompson Prout, PhD
Professor
Department of Educational, School, and Counseling Psychology
Director of Research, Human Development Institute
College of Education
University of Kentucky
Lexington, KY

Nancy J. Razza, PhD
Adjunct Assistant Professor of Pediatrics
The Elizabeth M. Boggs Center on Developmental Disabilities
UMDNJ – Robert Wood Johnson Medical School
New Brunswick, NJ 08903

Bronwyn L. Robertson, MSEd, LPC
Psychotherapist
Rock Landing Psychological Group
Newport News, VA

Dick Sobsey, EdD
Professor Emeritus
University of Alberta
Edmonton, Alberta, Canada

Daniel J. Tomasulo, PhD, TEP, MFA
Faculty
New Jersey City University
Jersey City, NJ

Index

DATE DUE

DEC 05 2011		
JAN 1 7 2013		